THE GREAT INGRATITUDE-
BOMBER COMMAND IN WORLD WAR II

JAMES FYFE

'The day might not be far off when aerial operations, with their devastation of enemy lands and destruction of industrial and populous centres on a vast scale, may become the principal operations of war'.

Field Marshal Jan Smuts, 1918.

Copyright 1993

James Fyfe

ISBN 1 872350 75 5

Published by

G.C. BOOK PUBLISHERS LTD

WIGTOWN

SCOTLAND   DG8 9HL

Printed by

CROMWELL PRESS

MELKSHAM

WILTS

This book is dedicated to

The Aircrews of Bomber Command 1939 - 1945

THE GREAT INGRATITUDE

FOREWORD

In the Second World War no other organisation within the British Armed Forces was surrounded by such controversy as Royal Air Force Bomber Command; indeed its strategy, its aims and its achievements have been regularly and heatedly discussed for half-a-century and have come in for their due share of criticism, much of it adverse.

The divergences of opinion show no sign of abating, and in fact the Gulf War, then the Harris statue, gave the controversy a new lease of life. This book endeavours to suggest that Bomber Command, far from being guilty of a dubious policy and of the moral transgressions of which it has so often been accused, was a potent, decisive and necessary force in hastening the eclipse of the Nazi régime, not only through its carpet bombing of German cities, but by virtue of other crucial accomplishments which seem to be only too readily belittled or even forgotten.

The aircrews themselves have had to bear much of this criticism; yet no other fighting men were engaged, over a long, continuous period, in such a unique and traumatic experience; an experience in which the chances of survival were lower than they were in any other sphere of combat, because every operation flown over Germany was essentially a battle between each individual aircraft and the defensive might of the Reich. Nor was any other wartime leader called upon to shoulder such an awesome burden of responsibility as their Chief, Sir Arthur Harris, who planned and laid on a major battle almost every night from February 1942 until early May, 1945.

The Air Offensive was a new concept in warfare and one which will never again be repeated on such a vast scale. In the space of just over three years, the Command had grown, thanks largely to Churchill and Harris, from an impotent dwarf into an omnipotent giant, capable of sowing unprecedented havoc in practically every corner of Europe, although it was the Nazi homeland which received its main attentions. The cost, in terms of intelligent young men, in machines, in general tears and sweat, was horrific.

I have put much emphasis on the crews themselves - and on one representative crew in particular who, like their aircraft, have been given fictitious names - how they were trained, how they lived and how they died; on their fears and how they tried to cope with them; what they went through over hell-holes such as Berlin and the Ruhr; how they fared as prisoners of war and as members of the occupying forces in Germany; what was done about the thousands who lay in unknown graves all over Europe and especially in Germany itself; and the incomprehensible treatment they and their leader received when post-war honours were being handed out.

If the American Army Air Forces operating from UK bases are mentioned only in connection with Bomber Command's activities, this should in no way be interpreted as a dismissal of their enormous contribution to the Air Offensive, in which they too suffered grievous losses. But their tactics were different and it was mainly the Lancasters and the Halifaxes which flattened the Third Reich into an urban desert. This is a book on Bomber Command.

When the reader has digested the many diverse and major roles it played, as recounted in the following pages, he might come round to the view that not only did Bomber Command bring the Second World War to an earlier conclusion than would otherwise have been the case, but even question whether the Allies could ever have gained victory without it.

I am indebted to all those ex-operational aircrew who so willingly offered me their support and who checked the manuscript; in particular I would like to mention former Lancaster pilots Andy McLean of Dumfries and Jack Lett of Hornchurch, also the latter's rear gunner, Donald Irving of Annan; Angus Malcolm of Kirkbean, who spent two years as a prisoner in a Stalagluft; ex-Luftwaffe jet pilot Hans Gösewinkel; Norbert Burger, mayor of Cologne, and all those other Germans who experienced saturation raids and supplied me with much pertinent information; and, finally, my friend Tony Wickson of Telford, my former wife Kathleen and my son Cameron for their continual help and encouragement.

James Fyfe.

The Great Ingratitude

CONTENTS

The Great Ingratitude

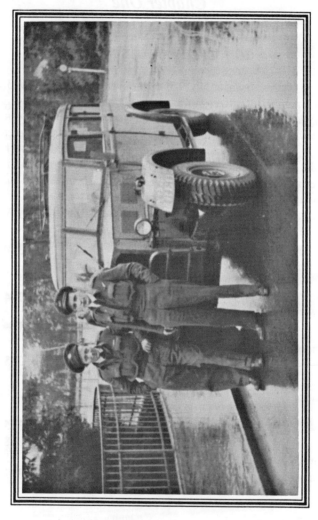

An MRES unit in Germany, 1946.

RAF Missing, Research & Enquiry Service

Chapter One

GOMORRAH - AND ITS AFTERMATH

It was around 9.30 on the evening of July 27, 1943, a date which a number of citizens of a certain German city, still alive half-a-century later, have never forgotten and never will forget, not even in the dotage which many of them are fast approaching or have even reached.

Flight Lieutenant Iain Candlish eased himself down from the crew bus and momentarily paused to glance up at the monster outlined against the darkening Lincolnshire sky. It was at such moments that his apprehension about what lay ahead was to some extent assuaged by its aura of sinister and lethal power. Enlarged and modified by A V Roe from the unsuccessful twin-engined Manchester, this was the superb weapon which was beginning to perform its allotted task with such deadly efficiency. This was the machine which, night after night and on an ever-increasing scale, was battering the Third Reich to its very foundations, thereby effecting the plan to erase from the map its great cities - of which there were many - by fire and blast, and, by so doing, ensuring that its life-span would fall somewhat short of the one thousand years predicted by its Leader. This was the sophisticated tool which Sir Arthur Harris, appointed Chief of Bomber Command some eighteen months before, sincerely believed would, if despatched regularly and in sufficient numbers, reduce Germany's military potential to such a state of impotence and create in the populace such a degree of terror, that the Nazis would be forced to beg for peace.

This was the Lancaster.

While viewing the Luftwaffe blitz on London from the Air Ministry roof when he was in charge of 5 Group, Harris had remarked: "They are sowing the wind." Now they had the man, they had the instrument, and Warsaw, Rotterdam, Coventry, London itself and all the others were being, or were about to be, avenged; and at a horrendous rate of interest.

On the night in question, the operation was code-named *Gomorrah*; the victim-to-be: Hamburg.

The Great Ingratitude

Germany's second largest city and greatest seaport, with a population of nearly two millions and a centre of heavy industry, almost all of it war-orientated, had already received the close attentions of Bomber Command on the night of July 24/25 and of the American Eighth Air Force during daylight on July 25 and 26. The RAF force of almost 800 aircraft had caused widespread structural damage, much dislocation of public services, and claimed many lives. The success of the raid was due largely to the fact that *Window* (strips of metallised paper to confuse the enemy radar by giving false echoes and thus rendering attacks by night-fighters less formidable) had been dropped for the first time and the bombing device known as *H2S* (which showed up the outlines of the target area on a screen) had also played its part. The American attacks, though less heavy than those of their British colleagues, had added to the conflagrations below and helped to guide the next night's bombers to the target.

It was as if these onslaughts had been made to prepare Hamburg for its greatest ordeal of all, for worse, much worse, was yet to come.

***

Candlish had not taken part in the Bomber Command raid of July 24/25. He had been on leave. So for him it was a quick transition from the peace of rural Perthshire, isolated by geography from most of the realities of war, to the drama in which he was once again about to participate. Only a day or two before, and sometime around midnight, he had paused during his sea-trout fishing on the River Dochart near Crianlarich to stare up at the great star-studded canopy of the Scottish sky. Soon, he reflected, it would be the other side of the North Sea and the German sky, and anything but empty, and where the stars would pale into insignificance in the presence of even brighter lights which would be much, much nearer and anything but friendly. Worlds apart. Heaven and Hell separated by only a few hours flying time.

But at least he was glad to be out of the truck. The journey out to the aircraft was the period when the butterflies, which had been increasing in number all day from the moment his and his crew's names had appeared on the operations board and especially during briefing, started to flutter uncontrollably and weak jokes were forced in voices an octave higher than usual, reminiscent of the timbre characteristic of choir boys.

Bomber Command in World War II

After a few words with 'Happy Hannah's' ground staff, who were there for take-off procedures and always waited for her to be airborne - and usually returned the following morning hoping to welcome her back - the crew climbed aboard and each of its members settled down to his various tasks. Candlish opened his window and shouted "Contact!". On receiving acknowledgement of the order, he pressed the starter button of the port inner engine - always the first to be started (by using a mobile accumulator on the ground, already connected to the engine by the ground crew). It began to turn slowly and then once its revs had increased, Candlish throttled back until the engine was just ticking over. The other three were then set in motion, one at a time, and warmed up. During this period of waiting, the pilot and the flight-engineer made several instrument checks. The four Merlin engines were performing perfectly. After what seemed an inordinate length of time - in fact it was only about six minutes - Candlish signalled the men on the ground to remove the chocks and started to taxi out. The butterflies, which had been less active while they had all been attending to their different jobs, gained a new lease of life, spurred on by the quivering earth as other Merlins were revved up in readiness for take-off.

Candlish cautiously steered 'Happy Hannah' along the perimeter track, gunning first one outer engine, then the other, to keep her within the confines of the narrow tarmac. The two port motors roared as he swung her round into wind with the runway stretching ahead. His eyes swept over the appropriate instruments as he made one final check.

Then the order from Flying Control: the order to go.

With the brakes on, Candlish pushed forward the four throttle levers controlling five thousand horse-power and 'Happy Hannah' vibrated in her every bolt and screw. She was like a powerful dog straining at the leash and Candlish, satisfied that all four engines were functioning with maximum efficiency, eased the throttles back to reduce the revs, released the brakes and re-opened the throttles gently and smoothly. The Lanc, given her head, moved forward in the gathering dusk with a shudder and a thunderous roar, as if overjoyed to be freed of her fetters, then, slowly at first but with the tremendous thrust gradually getting the better of her heavy load, she picked up speed. Like all of her breed, she displayed an innate tendency to swing to port. This Candlish corrected by slightly increasing the revs of the port engines. The navigator kept on calling out

The Great Ingratitude

the airspeed and when they were about one-third of the way along the runway and it was a matter of getting the Lanc off the ground as soon as possible, Candlish pushed forward on the stick so that her nose dropped and her tail lifted. This meant she could now be steered by using the rudders rather than the engines, at which point the throttles were advanced to the maximum (with the assistance of the engineer) to obtain full power. She was now 'beyond the point of no return' but at around 100 mph her wheels began to bounce and at 105 mph she was airborne, albeit with not too much runway to spare, and each member of her crew heaved a sigh of relief: no loss of engine-power at the vital moment to send them and their bomb-load into the ground, which would have been enough to blow half the airfield, let alone themselves, to oblivion. 'Happy Hannah' climbed sweetly, apparently pleased to be clear of mother earth and once again in the element to which she rightfully belonged. The first hurdle was over.

She was on her way, she and 786 others - 352 Lancasters, 244 Halifaxes, 116 Stirlings and 74 Wellingtons - from the vast patchwork of bomber stations which straddled the flat farmlands of Suffolk and Norfolk, of Lincolnshire and South Yorkshire. Almost five and a half thousand highly trained pilots, navigators, bomb-aimers, wireless-operators, flight-engineers and air-gunners, many of them still a year or two short of twenty-one and officially not yet men, braced themselves for the task ahead.

They were on their way; not only to Hamburg, but on a course which would confirm with frightening indubitability - if there had been any doubt in German minds before - the clear-cut policy of Bomber Command from now on; and, perhaps even more alarming, the Command's ability to implement it with ever-growing frequency and an ever-growing maelstrom of ever-bigger bombs.

Hamburg had been chosen to lead the way.

***

Candlish pointed 'Happy Hannah' towards the Midlands in order to gain some height. The target was to be bombed from 18,000 feet and a fully laden Lanc took a long time to struggle up to that altitude. Moreover, the higher you were, the safer it was, so that operational height had to be attained with minimum delay.

Candlish's navigator gave him a course of 078° and they headed for the North Sea to join the main stream at a given latitude and longitude - a miraculous feat of faultless navigation in a densely-packed sky - so that the whole force could advance in a loose 'gaggle', keeping together for maximum protection and, in order to saturate the defences, drop the entire bomb-load in as short a period of time as possible. Down below Fenland villagers wending their way homewards from the local pubs halted and peered upwards on hearing the mighty droning that seemed to go on without end, and made mental notes not to miss the radio news in the morning. These were, perhaps, the only occasions during the Second World War when a significant proportion of the civilian population knew regularly of a large-scale military operation an hour or two before it actually took place.

At just over 9,000 feet, Candlish gave his crew the order to don oxygen masks. This was strictly enforced from an altitude of 10,000 feet because above that height and especially from 14,000 feet, mental capacity decreased rapidly; this was especially dangerous since someone not using oxygen was quite convinced his faculties were functioning normally - hence the practice of putting young trainees in a sealed chamber and telling them to keep on writing their names on a sheet of paper. As the chamber was gradually deoxygenised and their writing ultimately became the most illegible squiggle - with the clarity of which they were quite satisfied - the lesson was well and truly rammed home.

'Happy Hannah' broke through the cloud barrier, three thousand feet thick, about a couple of miles up. The contrast to the murky conditions which had prevailed on the ground back at base and the zero visibility of the climb was immediate, and it was total; above them, the crystal-clear heavens with every star in every galaxy trying to outdo its neighbour in luminosity, beneath them an apparently solid layer of the whitest cotton wool. It was an experience which, long before the days of large-scale air travel, was denied to nearly all but them, and one which never failed to impress even the longest-serving crews. It was as if they had suddenly entered another world of which they were the sole inhabitants; it made them feel they had a clearer conception of the meaning of eternity and it was a feeling made more intense by the special circumstances of their situation. This was particularly true in the case of the rear-gunner, all on his own right in the tail of the aircraft, sitting almost in space itself, surveying the endless vault of the heavens and its twinkling myriads of lights set at a distance so great as to be incomprehensible to human understanding, and often wondering how long it would be before he was welcomed into its bosom.

The Great Ingratitude

Climbing steadily towards operational height, Candlish searched the sky for colleagues and, in spite of the good visibility, saw none.

Later, when they were well on their way across the North Sea, his mid-upper gunner did spot a Lanc flying a little higher to starboard. Crews never ceased to wonder, especially in fine weather, at the rareness of such a sighting when so many aircraft were heading for the same destination. But, at the same time, they well knew the reason - the sky is a very big place and, at night in particular, a fast-flying aircraft needed to be only seconds ahead of a companion, or not far above or below him, to remain unobserved; and they were continually reminded of having company not too far away when they felt the slipstream of other aircraft.

All sorts of ruses, mainly dog-legs and diversionary attacks on other German cities, called 'spoof raids', were used to confuse the enemy and prevent him from concentrating his fighter force on the approach to the main target or over the target itself. The night in question was no exception, with a few Mosquitoes being sent to Duisburg and Wellingtons to other cities, while Operational Training Units also sent out aircraft. Further, the main bomber stream, instead of turning south-east at a point on the coast in the vicinity of Cuxhaven - which would have clearly revealed its objective - carried straight on due east and right across the south of Denmark to give the impression it was bound for either Berlin or one of the Baltic ports such as Lübeck or Rostock. Having reached Lübeck Bay around midnight, it swung round to the south-west and on a direct course for the city which was still nursing the wounds inflicted on it in the three previous raids starting on the night of July 24/25. The fire services were still engaged in extinguishing the remains of the conflagration created by the earlier attacks, while other units were still busy trying to carve a way through thoroughfares blocked by rubble. Hamburg was in no state to withstand yet another paralysing assault by Bomber Command.

The enemy fighters were again largely, but not entirely, thwarted by *Window,* and Pathfinder aircraft had marked the target area with yellow, red and finally green indicators. But with the absence of the usual numbers of Messerschmitt 110s and Junkers 88s the anti-aircraft gunners were letting fly with everything they had, which was more than a little. It was the task of the first waves of the force to let loose their high explosive bombs in order to expose as much combustible material as possible, into which those following would pour their thousands of incendiaries.

Bomber Command in World War II

Still some miles to the north, Candlish and his bomb-aimer could already see the markers and the nascent fires. 'Happy Hannah' began to shudder as a torrent of shells exploded around her. The curtain was going up.

"Skipper to crew. We're nearly there. Keep a look-out for fighters, especially if the ack-ack suddenly stops. All right back there, Benny?"

"Nae worse than usual, Skipper. Maybe a bit better even - I'm only half-frozen. But better that than roastin' doon there in that bloody lot. Christ, it's bright. I'm fair dazzled. It's like ..."

"All right, Benny, quell it!"

"Yes, Skipper, I'll be a good boy!"

"Bomb-aimer to pilot. Southern end of the Aussenalter Lake coming up. TIs visible just beyond it. Bomb doors open. Alter course five degrees to starboard." (TIs was short for 'Target Indicators').

"Roger."

A minute or so later: "Left...left. Right a little. That's it. Hold it. Steady, steady. Hold it there! Bombs gone!"

'Happy Hannah' lunged forward and upwards as if to express her delight at being relieved of the great load in her belly. Candlish kept her straight and steady for about 30 long seconds to get the photograph which would show where the bombs had dropped. Then:

"Bomb doors closed!"

"OK, let's go, I can smell breakfast."

***

Four miles below the departing Lancaster, in a small house in a side-street a few minutes walk from the Elbe, lived Herr and Frau Kirschner. They had had two sons, one of whom, a lieutenant in a Panzer

The Great Ingratitude

division, had died at the hands of partisans on the Russian front and the other, a submariner, had been posted missing on an Atlantic foray after his boat had been ripped open by a Catalina of Coastal Command. Since then, they had merely carried on from day to day, sadly resigned, finding some solace only in each other's company and perpetually terrified at the thought of the day when one of them would be left entirely alone. Like the majority of their compatriots, they too had grave doubts about the outcome of the war and 'went along' with Hitler mainly because they were powerless to do anything else. Inwardly they cursed him for all he had brought upon them. The jubilation and pride they had experienced when Werner was awarded the Iron Cross in the days of glorious conquest had long since been dissipated. They knew now how much such things were worth.

For the fourth time in as many days, they sat in their cellar, hugging each other tightly, wincing at the massive explosions and the trembling of the earth and aware of an ever-growing heat. They did not even hear the 4,000 pound bomb as it hurtled down to land on the road outside and cause a detonation so loud that it numbed the brain rather than the ears. They were blown out of each other's arms and as their bodies flew apart, a falling beam practically severed Frau Kirschner's head from her shoulders. Her husband pulled out his torch and for a second gawped through the dust at the grotesqueness of her anatomy and at the blood which gushed out as if from a pipe in full flow.

Oblivious to the pain of his own injuries, he ran round the cellar, alternately screaming and choking. He never fully recovered his reason.

All in the space of an hour, the trauma and the fate of the Kirschners befell thousands upon thousands of their fellow citizens, creating a seemingly endless catalogue of incinerations, asphyxiations, mutilations, mumifications, or simply death through plain shock; and all this from one end to the other of the stricken city, in the basements of the theatres and cinemas, in the bars and flesh-pots of the Reeperbahn, in the factories and the tenements of Hammerbrook and Altona, of Harburg and Borgfeld. And this was just one large single raid, on one single night. Multiply it several times over - because this was the plan - and the sum of awesome destruction and human suffering about to be inflicted on the Fatherland would reach levels hitherto quite impossible to imagine or comprehend.

Heil Hitler!

Bomber Command in World War II

A huge orange ball of fire erupted just ahead and to starboard of 'Happy Hannah'.

"We can have their breakfasts too," muttered the bomb-aimer.

As an innocent pyrotechnic display, it would have beaten anything seen by anyone up till then. But this was a deadly stream of multicoloured tracers and exploding shells, exploding aircraft and burning wings and engines, with searchlights contributing with everything else to light up a sky that was of an eerie bluish-white and brighter than day. Candlish had all four throttles almost fully open. They had felt one or two heavy bumps, but so far so good.

On the north-west outskirts of the city, where the ack-ack batteries had not been pulverized in the attack and the searchlights were even more numerous, heavy flak became more intense, more accurate. 'Happy Hannah' seemed to be doing her best to emulate a frisky young stallion. Candlish held on to the control column, his knuckles bared white inside his gloves. Then they were coned.

Candlish threw the Lanc violently to port and dived. The glare became less intense. Then they were out. The amount of flak lessened, then dwindled to almost nothing. The minutes ticked away.

"Navigator here, Skipper. North Sea ahead. Alter course to 250 on hitting coast."

"Roger."

Then, a sudden cry from Benny in his outpost in the tail:

"110 comin' in from starboard. Corkscrew! Corkscrew!"

Candlish's reaction was immediate and he threw the aircraft down and from side-to-side, then started to climb using the same tactics. But the Me 110, not to be shaken off, managed to find them again. He came in fast, straight towards Benny, who opened up at the same moment as the German. 'Happy Hannah' shook and quivered as shells from the fighter's 30mm cannon raked her fuselage just ahead of the rear turret and tore into her starboard wing. She began to swerve and rock and Candlish had again to struggle hard to keep her on a more or less even keel.

The Great Ingratitude

He was about to address the crew but was stopped from doing so by a shout from the flight-engineer:

"Fire in starboard wing, close to outer engine."

Candlish glanced out and backwards. "Right, we'll dive. Hope there's no one beneath us!" That was one of the things the crew liked about their skipper: seldom "I", nearly always "we".

He pushed the Lanc down steeply through three thousand feet and the fire dimmed and went out. Then he pulled back hard on the stick, intending to regain the height they had lost, but the fire, brief as it had been, or perhaps something else, had damaged the starboard-outer, which was coughing and spluttering and had shed its cowling. The propeller was immediately feathered (which entailed switching off the engine and altering the angle of the blades of the propeller so that the latter would not 'windmill'). Being the aircraft it was, the Lancaster would get them home very comfortably on three engines, a little less comfortably on two, and sometimes, under favourable conditions, even on a single.

"Skipper to crew. Everyone all right?"

They all answered except the mid-upper gunner.

"Skipper to mid-upper. Are you OK, Musty?"

"OK Skipper, but my left leg feels a bit wet and sticky. And I don't think I've peed myself."

"See to him, Marc." 'Marconi' was 'Happy Hannah's' wireless-operator.

"Roger."

After a short pause: "He has a leg wound, Skipper. Bleeding a little, but not too bad. Superficial, I think. He says there's not much pain. I'll bandage it up."

"Good lad. New course, Navigator?"

"256 for the moment, Skipper. I'll give you a correction once I'm organised.''

The starboard aileron had been damaged by the Messerschmitt's shells or the ensuing fire and the Lanc turned more sluggishly than usual. But once she was on a straight course, this did not cause too great a problem.

Dark sea below. No fighters. No flak from German ships. No conversation. Just the sweet purring of three Merlin engines. In spite of the damage they had sustained and the knowledge that as a result of it, something else might well start to go wrong, the whole crew, including Musty with his wounded leg, felt the worst was over and were more relaxed. Even with reduced power and at reduced height, they were consoled by the thought that with every passing minute 'Happy Hannah' was taking them almost three miles nearer home.

But Benny wasn't so sure of the exact situation after something like half-an-hour had elapsed:

''Skipper, rear-gunner here. Have we slowed doon a lot on the three engines? We're no' hoverin' like a seagull in a strong head-wind, are we?''

''No, airspeed 200 mph and not much of a wind. Why d'you ask that, Benny?''

''Well, Hamburg back there doesnae seem to be gettin' much further into the distance.''

''Benny, we're nearly one hundred miles from Hamburg. D'you not hear the bacon sizzling?''

The rear-gunner checked his oxygen mask. No, he wasn't light-headed. He shut his eyes for a few seconds and looked again and the sensation was the very same. ''Time I had a wee rest from this game,'' he muttered to himself. But inwardly he was aware of the only possible reason - an ever-increasing conflagration visible from an ever-increasing distance. God, had they done that? Had Hamburg been made from tinder? He had seen his share of fires, but, Jesus, this!

Other viewers, about the same distance from the city as the crew of 'Happy Hannah', in large centres like Bremen, Hanover and even Magdeburg, gazed out at the same time from upstairs windows and attics, thinking some large fire had broken out a few miles away. When they learned the truth, which was not long in coming, a dreadful feeling of foreboding descended upon them.

***

Back at base, priority had to be given to captains with more serious landing problems than Candlish, and with banking capability reduced because of the impaired aileron (the trouble, he found, had worsened) he had to coax the Lanc somewhat erratically round a wide circuit three times before finally receiving permission to come in. In spite of loss of pressure in a front tyre, of which he had known nothing, and hence a fair amount of skewing around, he managed to keep her on the runway. As she gradually slowed, she became easier to control, and finally came to a stop. Their troubles were over. At least for the moment. Yes, for the moment. For they were all acutely aware that on a job like theirs, annihilation could come at any time, often in a flash. Yet they always tried their damnedest to dismiss the thought that a safe return was likely to be nothing more than a postponement of the inevitable.

"Marvellous landing, Skipper. I've only lost two teeth this time. No, seriously Skipper, you put her doon like a wee feather!" The voice was Benny's.

"I take it you're angling for my egg again, Sergeant?" Candlish didn't care for fried eggs and invariably sent his over to the Sergeants' Mess for his irrepressible little rear-gunner.

'Happy Hannah's' crew, apart from Musty Coleman who was taken direct to the station hospital, had to report for immediate debriefing and answer an Intelligence Officer's probing and seemingly interminable questions about the accuracy of the bombing, fighter activity before the target, over it and on the way home, the weight of ack-ack fire and the location of the batteries, any bombers or fighters they saw destroyed or in trouble and anything at all that might be helpful in assessing the success of the raid or useful for future tactics. Weary, and therefore economical with their words as Candlish's men were, their interrogator was nevertheless left in no doubt about what had apparently happened to Hamburg - and that was even before the fires had reached their zenith and embraced each other in one all-consuming mass of flame. When he was satisfied he had wormed out of them all he could, he allowed them to escape to breakfast. Thereafter they fell thankfully into bed. Reports from crews

Bomber Command in World War II

arriving later served to confirm the overwhelming success of the operation. Despite their exhaustion 'Happy Hannah's' crew slept only fitfully. But in this respect they were more fortunate than Hamburg's surviving citizens, even than those - of whom there were not many - who remained unscathed by the night's events. No sleep at all for any of them, only a living nightmare which would return to haunt them for weeks, for months, for years. Some 40,000 others were already asleep, however, and in their case it was the deep, untroubled sleep of eternity.

***

Those living in the most easterly counties of England had not forgotten the great swelling roar of the night before. Hence all ears were glued to their wireless sets to hear the morning news bulletins:
"This is London........."
The news rocketed round the world. It went out in a multitude of languages, on a multitude of frequencies, to all the dark corners of all the subjugated lands of Europe and to more distant continents:
"Last night a large force of aircraft of Bomber Command, mainly Lancasters and Halifaxes, again attacked Hamburg. Crews taking part report a massive conflagration such as they have never before witnessed. This is confirmed by the pilot of a recently returned reconnaissance aircraft who said the entire city appeared to be engulfed in a raging inferno with flames rising hundreds of feet into the sky. Twelve of our bombers are missing. We hope to be able to give further information in a later bulletin.
On the Russian front...."

***

That same evening, another voice was heard when a navigator switched on the radio in the Sergeants' Mess. All ears pricked up as the familiar nasal tones, pregnant with hate, filled the room:

"Jairmany calling ... Jairmany calling ... Last night your bombers wrote a further chapter in the criminal history of the RAF. Your maniacal terror fliers came in large numbers to Hamburg and caused great fires which destroyed nearly all the hospitals, schools and churches in the city.

The Great Ingratitude

Hundreds and hundreds of helpless patients were burned alive in their beds and thousands and thousands of ordinary citizens in their homes. Some superficial damage was done to industrial plant but it was the residential areas which bore the brunt of this fiendish and pointless attack. Is this how the British wage war? Against defenceless women and children and the elderly and the bed-ridden? Is it not time you realised what a bunch of gangsters Churchill and his cronies are? Is it not time you realised that your wonderful Bomber Command heroes are the filthy instruments used by international Jewry to perpetuate crimes of which the Devil himself would be ashamed? But at least some revenge was wreaked on your murderous airmen because large numbers of your planes were blasted out of the German skies and many of their occupants died in just retribution for the many innocent Germans they had slaughtered in such a horrendous fashion..."

"Switch that bloody thing off, for Christ's sake!" shouted someone. "Haw-Haw's going too far this time. He must be a right bloody idiot- how the hell can we flatten every hospital and school and church and house in Hamburg without hitting anything else? He's not even funny tonight."

'Lord Haw-Haw', as the British public called William Joyce, who was to be hanged as a traitor in London in 1946 for his regular anti-British broadcasts from Germany during the war, possessed the most vituperative voice ever heard on radio before or since. The bigger the lies and the more venomous the tones, the clearer it was to his listeners that the Nazis had just suffered a major reversal and Bomber Command was always pleased to hear him at his scathing best after a big operation; and in wartime Britain, where public entertainment was severely curtailed (in any case many people were reluctant to venture forth in a black-out in which the intensity of the darkness had to be experienced to be believed), Haw-Haw was regarded by the populace at large as an evening entertainer of no mean ability, if unwittingly so.

Benny had come into the Mess just in time to catch the last few words before the broadcaster was cut off:

"Switch the bloody thing on again! It's the only decent entertainment we get aroond here." Someone who knew about the fire that existed in the rear-gunner's belly and enjoyed his repartee, hastily obliged.

"... and when Jairmany's new secret weapon is ready - and I assure you, my friends, that this will be in the not too distant future - you will get a taste, multiplied one thousand fold, of the suffering you are causing the innocent citizens of the Reich. Hamburg will be nothing compared to what is already planned for London, Birmingham, Manchester, Newcastle, Glasgow, Edinburgh ..."

"Whit about Auchenshoggle?" roared Benny, "Ye cannae leave it oot!"

Once the laughter had subsided, the rear-gunner was at it again:

"The next time I go tae `Jairmany' I'm goin' tae drop a cookie right doon that bastard's fuckin' throat. An' a delayed action one at that, so that he can sit there retchin' for a bit, tryin' tae spew it up before it goes off." (A cookie' was a 4,000 pound high explosive bomb).

"... So the RAF terror fliers are warned. If they continue their bloodthirsty flights over Jairmany, it simply means that their own mothers and fathers and sisters and brothers will be mercilessly annihilated in a horrible manner - when the weapon is ready, my friends, when the weapon is ready. Good-night. Be with you again soon."

"Bollocks!" roared Benny, "secret weapon my arse! I'm tellin' ye, Haw-Haw, I'll keep a wee squib 'specially for you the next time I come tae see ye. Just for you, son. It'll be aboot 12 feet long an' filled wi' aboot five tons o' TNT. Good fuckin' night tae you tae!"

***

Although the raid had obviously been highly successful, Bomber Command was still not fully aware, in its immediate aftermath, of the colossal destruction it had wrought. But, from various sources, the news soon filtered through. Colonel Galland, the brilliant fighter ace who had participated in the Battle of Britain and had long been advocating a substantial increase in the Luftwaffe's night fighter force to cope with what he rightly suspected was about to come, spoke of the Hamburg catastrophe and of its effect on its citizens, the population in general and the Nazi hierarchy:

"A surge of abject terror emanated from the agonised city and spread to all corners of the Reich. Horrendous details of the massive conflagration which could be seen from a distance of 120 miles were soon known to everyone. An endless procession of woebegone refugees, struck

The Great Ingratitude

dumb by their horrendous experience, made for the surrounding provinces and the inhabitants of every large town or city could be heard to say: `What Hamburg got yesterday, we can get tomorrow.' Berliners, seized with panic, were evacuated. The frightening story of Hamburg spread rapidly to the most far-flung villages of the land.

As far as the progress of the war was concerned, this was a critical psychological point. All of Germany had reeled on learning about Stalingrad, but Hamburg was here, right in the heart of the Reich. Both in the government and the High Command, one could now hear the words: 'The war is lost'.''

A secret German report which fell into British hands at the war's end described what actually happened in the city at the height of the fire storm:

''Trees three metres thick were sheared off or torn from the ground, men, women and children were hurled into the flames by a hurricane which exceeded 150 mph. Everyone was stricken with terror and didn't know what to do. If they tried to escape from the flames engulfing the air-raid shelters by running out into the open, they were forced to rush back into them on exposing themselves to high-explosive bombs. They were then suffocated by carbon-monoxide fumes and their bodies reduced to ashes - each shelter had in fact become a crematorium. The fortunate ones were those who stood up to their necks in canals and other waterways until the heat had considerably lessened.''

Albert Speer, Hitler's Minister of Armaments, said later: ''Hamburg put the fear of God into me. If another six major cities were devastated in such a manner, Germany's armaments production would be brought to a complete halt.''

Speer's apprehension was well-founded. One of the country's largest and most important industrial centres had suffered a calamity never before experienced anywhere on the face of the earth. With the massive incendiary attack heating the air to a temperature of around 1000°C, fire-laden air rushed through the streets, carrying with it joists and beams and doors and miscellaneous pieces of furniture, and anything not yet ablaze did not remain so for long. Human beings were sucked into the typhoon and were later found shrunken to less than half their living size. Uninflammable objects, misshapen to the point of being unidentifiable, were propelled hundreds of feet into the sky and often came to rest in places far beyond the confines of the Nazi homeland.

What Bomber Command had in fact created, though not

Bomber Command in World War II

deliberately (which does not mean to say it wasn't welcomed by the Air Chiefs) on the night of July 27/28, was the first great fire storm in military history. It was the result of the successful use of *Window*, accurate target marking, and a heavy HE attack followed by the raining-down of thick cluster upon cluster of incendiaries (a single Lanc could carry hundreds of them) as seeds might be sown in a field, on to a densely built-up area with narrow side-streets, in an age when wood served more purposes than it does now. Add to that the fact that everything was bone-dry after a long spell of hot, sunny weather and you had all the essential ingredients for the holocaust which ensued. But the overriding factor was Bomber Command's increasing ability to accurately swamp a chosen area with a huge tonnage of HE and incendiary bombs, thereby creating fires of such magnitude and intensity that they joined together and spread rapidly to engulf the greater part of an entire city - in the case of Hamburg somewhere in the region of 575 of the 787 participating aircraft dropped their loads in an area only two miles long and one mile wide. Hamburg was the writing on the wall, in large red letters, for places like Darmstadt and Dresden and Pforzheim; and perhaps in slightly smaller letters, but still very red, for every important town in the Reich.

A respite for the torn city? Far from it. Two nights later (July 29/30) 777 bombers set off - 340 Lancasters, 244 Halifaxes, 119 Stirlings, 70 Wellingtons and 4 Mosquitoes - and 700 crews claimed to have hit the target. But the use of *Window* was now less effective as the Luftwaffe had already adopted counter measures. There was also a greater concentration of fighters, which patrolled at high altitude and found their constant dream realised when they looked down and saw enemy planes clearly outlined against the fires which were still fierce and widespread and now being stoked afresh. A number of the attacking aircraft became victims of their own success and 11 Lancasters, 11 Halifaxes, 4 Stirlings and 2 Wellingtons were shot down and a total of over 40 damaged.

On this occasion, the plan was to destroy the northern districts which so far had escaped with only minor damage. Although the Pathfinders had made a rare error by marking an area just to the south of that part of the city already devastated on July 27/28, where some bomb-loads fell and were thus wasted, huge fires were created in residential Barmbek and Wandsbek in particular (which put great pressure on the depleted and exhausted fire services) and heavy damage was caused although there was no repeat of the fire storm. It was during this raid that nearly 400 people died from carbon monoxide poisoning when a big

The Great Ingratitude

department store in Wandsbek collapsed in one mighty heap and blocked all exits from its underground shelter.

On the night of August 2/3, a further 740 aircraft took off with the purpose of erasing from the map of Germany whatever was left of Hamburg. The composition of the force was similar to that of the nights of July 24/25 and 27/28 - 329 Lancasters, 235 Halifaxes, 105 Stirlings, 66 Wellingtons and 5 Mosquitoes. Unfortunately, the attack was fated to be more or less a complete failure from the start and perhaps its greatest value was a psychological one - bringing home the point that Bomber Command was now in a position to lay on a huge operation night after night and would not be satisfied until every large city in the land was totally destroyed.

This time the weather was the culprit. Over North Germany it was atrocious, with dense cloud filling the sky up to 15,000 feet and some of it reaching up to 30,000 feet. There were violent thunderstorms with very turbulent air and torrential rain, causing aircraft to crash when the controls became iced-up. The Pathfinders found target marking to be quite impossible and a large percentage of the bombers turned back. Others let loose their loads, their argument being that it was Germany which was beneath them and it was infinitely better to let them fall on Nazi soil than take them back home. After all, it meant a safer and speedier return to base and a landing less fraught with danger.

So the inhabitants of small towns in the North German countryside, on both sides of the Elbe, and from Hamburg itself right up as far as Cuxhaven, who by now were accustomed to hearing and seeing heavy raids being made on the big sea port, got a taste of what it was like to come under attack by Bomber Command. One of those to suffer was a small place called Elmshorn, situated about eighteen miles downstream from the city centre and about six miles east of the river. Here some crews spotted a burning building through gaps in the cloud and, thinking it must be a worthwhile target (in fact lightning was probably the cause of the fire) they released their bombs, wrecking over 250 houses and killing nearly 60 people, some of whom were refugees from Hamburg. Considering the small amount of worthwhile damage done by such a large force of bombers, the raid was a costly one: 13 Lancasters, 10 Halifaxes, 4 Wellingtons and 3 Stirlings were lost.

In a matter of ten days, the so-called 'Battle of Hamburg' was over. As with another 'Battle' - that of the Ruhr (Chapter 10) the city would continue to be bombed regularly, if not on such a massive and concentrated scale, until the final weeks of the war. Yet there were four

Bomber Command in World War II

further large incursions, all of which took place in 1945, which deserve mention.

On March 8/9, 312 four-engined bombers, mostly Halifaxes, set out with the aim of demolishing the shipyards where the new and fast type XXI U-boats were being assembled. Ten tenths cloud, however, meant inaccurate bombing and little real damage was caused (the liner *Robert Ley* was destroyed); on March 21/22, 151 Lancasters and 8 Mosquitoes attacked and put entirely out of commission the Deutsche Erdölwerke oil refinery without loss to themselves; on March 31, a strong force of 361 Lancs, 100 Halifaxes and 8 Mosquitoes made a further attempt, this time in daylight, to make sure the new U-boats would never put to sea, but were again hampered by thick cloud. However the German records state that considerable damage was done to industrial plant and communications in a large area in the southern part of the city, and also in Harburg (the smaller part of Hamburg south of the Elbe). The bombers were unexpectedly set upon by a surprisingly large number of fighters - Luftwaffe squadrons were by now believed to be practically non-existent - and 11 were destroyed; on April 4/5, Harburg was paid a visit by 327 aircraft, all Halifaxes apart from 36 Lancasters and 14 Mosquitoes, and this time the target was the Rhenania oil refinery. Weather conditions were favourable and the raid was a huge success, the plant being almost totally razed. Two of the Lancs and one Halifax failed to return to base.

On the night of April 8/9, Bomber Command went to Hamburg in strength for the very last time: 423 heavies (263 Halifaxes and 160 Lancs) and 17 Mosquitoes tried to blast the shipyards once again, and once again they were largely thwarted by the presence of too much cloud. The intended target did not escape entirely, however, and the Altona district of the city also took a hammering; then on April 9, in daylight, a much more moderately sized force of 57 Lancasters caused mayhem in the hitherto indestructible submarine pens when these were subjected to the devastating power of Grand Slam and Tallboys (see Chapter 19).

During the one year and nine months which elapsed between the Battle of Hamburg and the raids just recounted, the city was disrupted on umpteen occasions by Mosquitoes, sometimes by a lone machine but usually by between 12 and 50. In the main, these raids took the form of 'siren tours' and were designed to keep already overwrought and jaded citizens out of their beds and so render them unfit for the toils of the morrow; and it was perhaps fitting that the curtain finally came down on Hamburg on the night of April 13/14 - a mere three weeks before the

The Great Ingratitude

end of hostilities - when an abnormally large force of 87 'Mossies' bade a sort of farewell to a city which was never to forget the special treatment it had received at the hands of RAF Bomber Command.

But Hamburg will be remembered primarily for the cataclysmic attacks of late July and early August, 1943. In those four operations Harris had despatched 3,000 bombers and had dropped 9,000 tons of high-explosives and incendiaries. The cost had been 86 planes and over 500 airmen. The other side of the balance sheet showed that some 50,000 Hamburgers had been killed, many thousands injured, that some 15 square miles of the city had been either gutted or completely demolished by the raids which began on July 24 and especially by the fire storm on July 27/28 (the most rewarding night of the lot for Bomber Command in terms of acres laid waste). Buildings destroyed included well over 300,000 dwellings, nearly 3,000 shops and 600 factories. A large number of public buildings, schools, churches and hospitals had been reduced to piles of rubble. To cause further difficulties for the emergency services, twelve bridges over the Elbe had disappeared into the river. Small wonder that Goebbels described the bombing of the city as "a calamity so great as to stagger the imagination." Small wonder, too, that two-thirds of its population fled to seek succour in other parts of the Reich.

So the damage wrought went far beyond the physical. It was assumed, and rightly so, that every Germany city was on Harris's hit list and each and every citizen wondered when their turn would come. Hamburg became a word synonymous with mass destruction and death in its most gruesome forms, and people throughout the length and breadth of Germany paled at the very sound of its name.

Hamburg also confirmed what Bomber Command had suspected ever since the highly successful (incendiary for the most part) raid by 234 aircraft on the Baltic port of Lübeck on March 28/29 1942, which had destroyed 62% of the town's buildings, mainly due to the narrowness of the streets and their old timbered houses - that if you were out to destroy a city, it was often much casier to burn it down than to blow it up. Obviously, much depended on the building materials used and the lay-out of the town, but there were many urban centres in Germany where these two essential factors combined to provide ideal conditions for Bomber Command to show its tremendous potential as a fire-raising force..........

***

Bomber Command in World War II

It was a trying time both for the military forces and the political leadership, because for the first time victories were being replaced by defeats. El Alamein, Stalingrad, and now Hamburg. Hitler and Goering and all their sub-lieutenants knew that Bomber Command's great victory was an ominous sign. They were not thoroughly convinced that Harris's sworn threat to devastate their towns and cities from end to end, and from one end of the Reich to the other, was merely propaganda to frighten both the populace and themselves out of their skins, but was exactly what the Bomber Chief intended to do. They must have had cause to regret London and Coventry, realising that Britain had taken the stick out of their hands and would use it to beat them with Hamburg-like blows which they could not long endure unless wholesale counter measures were immediately implemented. But, fortunately for Bomber Command, although competent Luftwaffe leaders such as Milch and Galland pressed continually for a strong night-fighter force as by far the most effective means of dealing with the big bomber formations, it was believed by those at the top of the political tree, and, more importantly, by the king-pin himself, that large and numerous batteries of anti-aircraft guns and searchlights provided the best defence against them. They did not seem to have learned from the fact that during the Battle of Britain, Fighter Command, with meagre resources which had been whittled down to its last reserves of Spitfires and Hurricanes, had still managed to inflict unacceptable losses on a massive Luftwaffe (1733 bombers and fighters destroyed) and to compel it to bring its campaign to a halt. Probably Hitler thought that his night-fighter force was strong enough, if its potential was bolstered by thousands of ack-ack guns, to turn the tables on Bomber Command and convince it that its strategy of area bombing was much too costly to be viable.

In typical fashion, he also spurned the council of knowledgeable men such as General Kammhuber who, with others, and as early as 1941, had advocated that a large part of the Luftwaffe night-fighter force should be based in Northern France; from there, they could soon fly to the eastern areas of England at the propitious moment and wreak havoc amongst the British bombers as they returned to base, when they were often badly damaged, the crews tired or wounded, or both, and when the aircraft were at their most vulnerable while coming in to land. In fact this was a possible ploy on the part of the enemy which caused Harris and his subordinates much concern and will be fully dealt with in Chapter 16. Suffice to say for the moment that the Führer made it clear that he preferred

The Great Ingratitude

the citizens of badly-bombed towns to see, with their own eyes, Lancasters and Halifaxes and their 'murderous' crews plunging on to German soil rather than hear about them being destroyed in England. But, as we shall find, he did sometimes relent just a little ...

One thing was certain, however; the battle now being fought and about to be fought with ever-increasing ferocity, was to be the second leg, the first one having been the Battle of Britain, of a home-and-home tie. The RAF held a lead from the first encounter, but it was a lead which the Germans were determined to nullify - and then, literally, to grind Bomber command into the ground.

Following Hamburg, Hitler's first step was an unequivocable order to Speer to pull out all the stops, and the Armaments Minister, using his undeniable gifts of ingenuity and diligence, did not dilly-dally; by the early autumn of 1943, the main towns of the Reich were ringed by some 33,000 ack-ack guns - manned by the most élite regiments of the Luftwaffe - and by huge concentrations of searchlights, while large sections of the German electronic and optical industries were engaged in producing more and more equipment for air defence. The output of fighters, though falling far short of what it might have been, began to expand considerably, because Speer, who agreed with Galland and company that a strong night-fighter force was by far the best means of combatting the bomber threat, was not afraid to ignore, at least partly, his Führer's orders when he thought it was vital to do so and he could get away with it - as, for instance, when the end of the war was only days away and he refused to carry out Hitler's command to destroy what remained of Germany's industry. Figures went on rising each month throughout the rest of 1943, and in 1944 his factories turned out no fewer than 8,500 single and 2,700 twin-engined aircraft (a 300% increase on 1943 production figures), all of the former and the great majority of the latter being fighters (the offensive-minded Führer had in fact given orders that the industry should concentrate on bomber production). It was a performance which was to have much significance for Bomber Command and its crews, especially since 75% of the fighter force was earmarked for home defence, and it was Harris's undoubted misfortune that in Albert Speer he had an adversary endowed with a spirit as resolute as his own.

The scene was set for a heavyweight contest destined to top the bill as far as aerial warfare was concerned. Speer would pull no punches in an effort to produce the weapons needed to destroy Bomber Command, and Harris intended to deal a knock-out blow by destroying

Bomber Command in World War II

everything Speer built and manufactured. If rebuilt, it would be destroyed again, and again, *ad infinitum.*

It might well be asked where Goering, as head of the Air Force, stood in the planning of the defensive operations against Bomber Command. He had been at the peak of his power and greatly admired in 1939 after the Luftwaffe's eminently successful role in the blitzkriegs in Poland and in 1940 in the West; but he had begun to fall out of favour when his fighter and bomber squadrons did not prevent the evacuation (as he had assured Hitler they would) of the 338,200 troops massed on the beaches at Dunkirk, something which the Wehrmacht's tanks could have easily achieved; the Battle of Britain was a further set-back; then the crux had come at Stalingrad when he promised - and failed miserably - to provide Field Marshal Paulus's beleaguered Sixth Army with essential supplies in January 1943. Thereafter, he seemed to more or less withdraw from the scene to languish on his estate at Karinhall, often dressed in exotic clothes and hopelessly drugged out of his mind as he drooled over the art treasures he had plundered from almost every nation in Europe. He continually censured his underlings Milch and Jeschonnek for the Luftwaffe's gross deficiencies, but it was he himself who had been to blame for his lack of foresight in conceiving an air force only as a means of aiding advancing infantry (a concept which British army chiefs had also shared) and in neglecting the development of the long-range heavy bomber. Hitler appeared to be quite content to let him stew in his own juice and, when the Reichsmarshall did make his presence felt once again, it wasn't until the last days of the war, when he foolishly telegrammed the Führer, requesting confirmation that he should fill the latter's shoes on his demise - and was promptly arrested.

But the die was cast and the stage was set for the bloodiest and most prolonged air battle in history. In the wake of Hamburg, in early August 1943, Bomber Command was riding high. It was perhaps, in one sense, at its zenith. This was the force which, right from the earliest days of hostilities, when Britain was, at best, impotent everywhere and, at worst, suffering a string of defeats, had carried the war on to German soil and had sent over one thousand bombers - the greatest armada that had ever taken to the air and a magical figure which had captured the imagination - to attack Cologne on 30th May 1942; time and time again it had plastered the vast and heavily defended industrial conurbation of the Ruhr, which produced a large proportion of the enemy's weaponry; it had penetrated to more distant cities like Berlin and Munich, Stuttgart and Nuremberg;

The Great Ingratitude

to the Baltic ports of Lübeck and Rostock; even across the Alps to Turin and Milan to remind Mussolini that he was not forgotten; there was hardly a German town of any consequence which had not already felt its growing weight; its audacious 617 Squadron had burst the formidable Ruhr dams in May 1943, thereby creating a legend; and now, just two months later, it had gained its most impressive victory of all - the virtual destruction of Hamburg - and with it almost universal respect and admiration.   The British and American publics, the United States Army Air Force and even the normally ungrateful Russians had saluted its crews and their Chief. Bomber Command was a force to be reckoned with, a new and mighty weapon in waging modern war, perhaps even a means of bringing the present one to an early conclusion.

From now on, gigantic steps would be made in that direction.   They would be largely successful, but the cost to the Command in men and machines would be horrific;   and so it was the height of irony that the triumph of Hamburg, which brought about a huge increase in the German air defence system, all but caused the downfall of Bomber Command.   Consequently, there would be much whispering in certain circles about the military justification for the Air Offensive and the morality of it all;   and questions would be asked in high places.

Things would start to get just that little bit sour ....

Chapter 2

A DRIVER AND HIS TEAM

Iain Candlish was the product of a middle-class Scottish home, the second son of a Lowland family in which the values placed on education were traditionally Scottish and, therefore, of paramount importance. As a boy of 12 at his local primary school he had won a bursary to one of the country's most prestigious secondaries, where he more than held his own in classes where the academic standard was as high as in any similar institution. When he obtained a very commendable batch of passes in the Senior Leaving Certificate Examination, which was the nomenclature in those days, his parents were advised that he was definitely university material and they decided there and then that that was where he would go. But like so many fated to be of his generation, his well laid schemes and vocational aspirations were rudely turned upside down by the more grandiose aims of the moustached gentleman from Linz.

Having completed his first two sessions studying for an Honours Degree in German Language and Literature at St. Andrews, he was actually spending his third university year (1938-39) at Nuremberg when the lighted fuse began to sizzle more rapidly towards the waiting keg and he came home in July 1939, intending, if by some miracle war was averted, to start off on the last lap of his studies in the old North Sea town the following October. But from what he had witnessed in Germany, he had good reason to believe that there was little chance of redonning the famous red gown for any length of time. Indeed, from his observations of the power of the German war machine, and of the arrogance and euphoria that seemed to grip the Wehrmacht, he was sometimes tempted to the sombre thought that he might not wear that garment again for a long time to come, if ever.

With the commencement of hostilities on September 3, Candlish was aware that very soon he would be called to the colours, most probably to those of the Army, but he had an intense dislike of military discipline (to which he had been introduced as a cadet in his school's Officers' Training Corps), which seemed to assume that young men should be mere automatons and forced to carry out distasteful and meaningless

The Great Ingratitude

tasks to satisfy the sadistic tendencies of some loud-mouthed NCO. Flying, however, had always interested him since the day, some years before, when his father had treated him to a five-shilling trip at Renfrew Airport. His own flights of imagination told him that he would much prefer the freedom of the skies to the harsh and stifling atmosphere of the army parade-ground.

So he offered his services as aircrew, was accepted for training as a pilot, and the scarlet of St. Andrews was replaced by the blue of the Royal Air Force Volunteer Reserve. After passing through the different grades of Flying Schools, he gained his wings towards the end of the following year at the height of the Luftwaffe blitz on London. Steady, reliable and always flying by the book, he was considered to be bomber rather than fighter material, and by the summer of 1941 he had mastered twin-engined trainers. The next step was learning how to handle a Wellington and after an intensive course which involved long, cross-country flights in all kinds of weather, he and his crew were deemed to be ready for the real thing, and were posted to an operational squadron in Norfolk.

On their third operation, an attack on Kiel (which they didn't even see because of the prevailing weather conditions) they were nevertheless met with a terrific barrage of ack-ack fire sent up by gunners who were obviously determined to defend the naval base at all costs. A shell tore into the fuselage near the cockpit and Candlish suffered shrapnel injuries to his left leg and arm. With help from other members of the crew, he managed to steer the 'Wimpey' back to base, but his injuries turned out to be more complicated and difficult to heal than expected, and it was only after the best part of a year had passed that he was again considered fit for operational flying. This meant an extensive refresher course, an introduction to the first of the four-engined bombers and a new crew, all of whom were to stay together, more or less, until fate stepped in once more.

It was a crew which was typical of many in Bomber Command. They settled to become an efficient team, each dependent on the others, each bothering little about difference in rank in a situation where it mattered not one damn whether you were a Squadron Leader or a Pilot Officer or a Sergeant, whether you had a row of gongs on your tunic or merely beer stains. Death, after all, was a great leveller and in a Stirling, which they were flying, it was never very far away. The great, slow, lumbering brute, an easy target for both fighters and ack-ack with its low speed and poor ceiling, had in addition a tendency to ice-up easily and to

Bomber Command in World War II

display nasty little habits while taking off and landing.   Scathingly denounced as a death-trap by Harris himself, it had entered service in 1941 and was a major weapon in Bomber Command's armament until 1943, after which it was used mainly as a transport aircraft, towing gliders during the Invasion and to Arnhem. But Candlish and his crew survived, although not without incident, eight trips in an aircraft which they never liked, including attacks on such hot spots as Essen, Gelsenkirchen, Stuttgart and one of the most trying of all - Berlin.

The various members of a bomber's crew en route to a target said little to each other, speaking only when it was really necessary. A sudden warning might come from one of the gunners that a fighter was approaching from a certain direction, a less hurried remark from the flight-engineer that one of the engines was overheating slightly, or a change of course might be given by the navigator.   Each man was absorbed for the most part in the task which he had to perform, even if, as in the case of the gunners, it was no more than eternal vigilance.

That does not mean to say that during those short periods when they were as relatively safe from attack as they ever would be - for instance when they had just left the English coast behind and they were on their way out over the North Sea - their thoughts did not sometimes stray to personal matters.   It might be their family at home, the girl they had recently met in the town or village near their base, or perhaps how many times they had yet to undergo this nightmare before completing their first tour of thirty operations before "enjoying a rest" as an instructor at a Heavy Conversion or Operational Training Unit.   On the way back, they were usually too tired and drained to think about anything.   But if their aircraft and they themselves were undamaged and everything was functioning well, the steady, powerful drone of the engines could be a comforting sound.

It was during the moments which were almost devoid of tension that Candlish would sometimes think of the fishing holidays he had spent in Perthshire, of peaceful pre-war days at St. Andrews, or of his year in the enemy's homeland.   Not only was he well-versed in the German language, which he spoke fluently after his sojourn in Nuremberg, and wrote with an educated style, but he possessed a broad knowledge of the entire history of the country from Attila onwards and had made a specialised study both of the classical period of its literature and of its history from Bismarck to Hitler's appointment as Chancellor. He had had direct experience of the Nazi régime and often wondered how a nation of

The Great Ingratitude

80 million human beings, which had produced colossi like Goethe and Schiller, Beethoven and Einstein, which excelled in all fields of art and science, had allowed itself to become governed by a band of power-mad psychopaths and sadists who practised the politics of the sewers. He often saw in his mind's eye the great fanatical parades of Nuremberg and Munich and could still hear the thunderous cries of "Sieg Heil!" and "Heil Hitler!".

But Candlish's case was exceptional. The great majority of aircrew knew little about Germany or its history. They had been brought up between the wars in the general belief that all Germans were bastards and that this fellow Hitler and his side-kicks were the biggest German bastards that had ever been. They had heard of Goering and Goebbels and Himmler, but certainly not of Heydrich or Eichmann, of Frank or Kaltenbrunner. They had, on the whole, little idea until enlightened when it was all over, or almost all over, of the extent of the evil code on which the Third Reich was based, and their hatred of Germany stemmed rather from the slaughter of the First World War and the manner in which the Luftwaffe had devastated British cities at the beginning of the Second. The Holocaust was as yet largely hearsay and its magnitude unknown. When he had the time and the inclination, and his colleagues were willing to listen, Candlish filled them in; and they ended up by possibly being the best informed crew in Bomber Command on things German.

For one reason or another, but mainly because of death, injuries or sickness, there were periodic changes in the composition of Bomber Command crews. Candlish was fortunate in having a regular team for some time before the Battle of Hamburg and for quite a spell after it. His navigator was Flying Officer Bob Ainsworth, from Knaresborough in Yorkshire, who had been accepted for a Maths. degree at a northern university but had decided to become an airman for the time being at least. He was a meticulous, quietish and rather serious-minded young Englishman who had lost an elder brother in the retreat to Dunkirk. An expert in dead-reckoning navigation, which was an invaluable asset to have when electronic aids were faulty or had packed up, he worked hard and unceasingly in his 'office' behind Candlish and, even on nights of ever-changing winds and poor visibility, the accuracy of his navigation was often quite remarkable.

Flying Officer Tom Courtney, who had worked in his father's building business in Salford, was the bomb-aimer. The oldest member of the crew at 26, he was married with an infant son. A devoted family man, he would   often worry about air raids on Manchester when he himself was in far greater danger.   Endowed with a high sense of responsibility and absolutely dependable, he had been taught by Candlish to fly 'Happy Hannah' in straight and level flight when out on training exercises (which operational crews were regularly required to do), just in case such a skill might sometime become useful.

The flight-engineer was Flight Sergeant Peter Whyte, an Australian from Queensland.   A former garage mechanic in Brisbane, he was mad about engines of any description and the four Merlins were his pride and joy.   He invariably attended servicing by the ground crew, some of whom reckoned that his sensitive ear could detect faults before they were recorded on his instruments.

Pilot Officer 'Marc' Robertson was the wireless-operator. A huge man of well over six feet and as broad as they come, he hailed from Bristol.   Although nearly always of cheerful disposition, he had a perpetual worry about having to bale out.   He was always saying that if he didn't get stuck in a hatch or a door, his enormous bulk would take him down far too fast and he would hit mother earth much harder than any creature of more normal dimensions, and maintained that there should have been especially large parachutes for men of his size.   The others would gibe him about reducing 'Happy Hannah's' cruising speed and bomb load.

The mid-upper gunner was a Londoner, Sergeant 'Musty' (short for 'Mustard') Coleman.   He had just won his place as a centre-forward with a Third Division football club when the outbreak of war put paid to such frivolous pursuits and after some time on ground duties, Musty 'remustered' to a job where his shooting had to be of a different kind and for much higher stakes.   He had been the type of player who made up for any lack of subtleties in his play by barn-storming tactics and he knew only one way to goal - straight ahead.   His attitude as a crew member was much the same, and the mere glimpse of an enemy fighter was enough to have his Brownings sending hundreds of rounds towards it.   He epitomised the Air-gunners' motto - ''We aim not to please''.

The rear-gunner, 'Tail-end Charlie' or, more commonly, 'Arse-end Charlie', we have already met.   Sergeant Benny Ramage came from one of the less affluent quarters of Glasgow - which, in the context of the thirties and forties, is saying something.   He had left school at the then statutory age of 14 and had been working as a riveter in a Clydebank shipyard when he got the urge to fly - from watching seagulls, he said.   Surrounded by them as he often was while perched somewhere on the great ship that he was helping to build, he envied their freedom to soar away into the skies whenever they liked, which suggested to him a way of escape from what was a hard life in an unsympathetic environment. His lack of inches (he was not much over five feet) was well compensated for by his quite disproportionate breadth, which seemed to be about the same as his height. Although rough-tongued and quick to anger if he judged that he or his were being unjustly treated, he was kindly, nearly always in high spirits and with a bigger than average share of that bawdy, spontaneous wit which is the hallmark of so many of the natives of Scotland's greatest city. In those days, when wildlife was not accorded the consideration it enjoys now and when, in any case, minds were hardened by the circumstances of war, Benny used to delay testing his guns on training exercises over the North Sea or the Atlantic until he came across a flock of gulls. Following the staccato-like rattle of his four Brownings the crew would see hundreds of white feathers drifting down towards the water like large snowflakes. When mildly chastised by his colleagues, he would tell them that he had had it in for the cheeky, squawky buggers ever since one of them had stolen his midday 'piece' as he sat astride a girder in Clydebank. He said it had contained the only piece of cheese they had had in the house and that there would be no more until the next pay-day. Uncomplaining except in jest, as alert as a weasel and blessed with the night vision of an owl, he too embodied all the qualities required of an air-gunner.

In a heavy operational bomber the stress and strain on every crew member was tremendous, but it was men like Benny who, by common consent, had the worst job of all. 'Tail-end Charlie' was marooned right at the extremity of the aircraft, isolated from all his companions, who were, apart from the mid-upper gunner, in close proximity up front. Usually the first target of attacking fighters, who knew that with the rear-gunner out of action they practically had the aircraft at their mercy and could rake it from tail to nose almost with impunity, it meant that his chances of survival were somewhat smaller than those of other members of the crew - and these were small enough. It was therefore perhaps anomalous that, although each gunner was at least a sergeant, he had much less chance of aspiring to commissioned rank than a pilot or navigator; in fact the latters' hopes of doing so were realised three times more often than his.

Virtually sitting out in space, in the middle of a hostile sky, cramped in the confines of his tiny turret, he was far from any heating that was available, usually frozen to the marrow and sometimes hardly capable of pressing his gun-buttons when the moment came. There was no room for his parachute beside him, and even if uninjured, he had great difficulty in getting out quickly to put it on (often his turret doors were buckled by the extreme heat) when the order was given to bale out - if he heard it, because his intercom was in many cases severed after an attack and he could be completely out of touch with what was happening. Surrounded by thousands of rounds of ammunition, he was in constant danger of being fried alive, for even if the fire was well up front the phenomenon known as 'Venturi effect' soon drove the flames back along the fuselage towards him and his clothing, designed solely to keep out the cold as much as possible, was in no way fire-resistant or bullet-proof; he might even be catapulted into space, still inside his turret, after scything cannon fire from a fighter had shorn it from the rest of the fuselage. In fact more than one heavy bomber staggered back to base with both turret and its occupant missing; while the uninjured members of the crew were falling into bed, he could still be entombed in his metal capsule, lying broken amongst his Brownings, in some German field or wood or city street.

In a Command in which all flying personnel were venturesome young men, Candlish's crew was typical of the efficiency and courage which had to be displayed night after night, week after week, even month after month for those who lasted that long. All were aware of the ordeals they were expected to endure. A heavy bomber, they well knew, with its volatile load of over two thousand gallons of high octane petrol, of at least four to six tons of high explosive and incendiary bombs, of 14,000 rounds of ammunition, with its endless pipelines of hydraulic oil and all its electrics, was nothing less than a flying death-trap which in a mere matter of seconds could become a flying coffin.

It wasn't the easiest way of going to war.

Chapter 3

PER ARDUA AD ASTRA

If the RAF motto - 'Through Hardships to the Stars' - was a singularly appropriate one for its aircrew as a whole, it was perhaps even more so for those who flew with Bomber Command.

The great majority of them came from 'middle-class' homes and had been educated in the grammar schools of England, Ireland and Wales, in the academies of Scotland and in similar institutions throughout the Empire.   (Some, like Candlish, but not many, were university undergraduates or even graduates).   All had to pass a rigorous medical examination, with special attention to heart, eyes, ears and teeth - the tiniest hole in one of the latter caused intense pain after a rapid change of air pressure.   Night vision too, especially in the case of the gunners, had to be of a very high standard.

As the RAF, and Bomber Command in particular, began to expand rapidly fairly early in the war, it became obvious that the UK, with its combination of crowded skies, generally foul flying weather and insufficiency of airfields - many as there were - was no place to train a massive bomber force.   This could normally be done in this country as far as the flight-engineers, wireless-operators and air-gunners were concerned, whose courses were shorter, if no less demanding; but it was the training of the pilots, navigators and bomb-aimers which presented the main problem because it was both long and arduous, and much of it had to take place in the air.

Hence the creation, in 1940, of the Empire Air Training Scheme.   By the summer of 1943, about the time of Hamburg, it had reached its peak with over 330 flying schools.   Apart from those in the UK itself, most of the others were in Canada, but there were significant numbers in South Africa and Rhodesia, and many pilots were trained by American instructors on United States airfields.   Impatient youngsters of 18-19 years of age (and some in their early twenties) were kitted out, inoculated and vaccinated during a three-week spell in places like the Air Crew Reception Centre in St. John's Wood in north-west London; this was followed by a three-month ground course at an Initial Training Wing, where they were given a good grounding in subjects such as Principles of

Bomber Command in World War II

Flight, Navigation and Meteorology; then, for budding PNB (Pilot/ Navigator/Bomb-aimer) cadets, the next stop was Elementary Flying Training School, where they were instructed for three weeks on the much-loved Tiger Moth biplane, at the end of which many of them made their first solo flight. They were then classified for Pilot, Navigator or Bomb-aimer training and some of them went off to centres such as Stratford-on-Avon for a toughening up course, conducted by the RAF Regiment. Thereafter, they received about a week's embarkation leave, then reported to the huge overseas dispersal camp at Heaton Park in Manchester, which, for many, meant a long spell of absolute boredom as they waited - and waited. The bottle-neck which developed fairly early, and worsened in 1943 and 1944, did little for the restless spirit of these youngsters, and the RAF started to send them for a few weeks to busy Heavy Conversion Units and Operational Training Units, partly to relieve their boredom and partly to let them see what went on in such places. If they were lucky, they would get the odd trip in a four-engined bomber going out on a long daytime training flight, if not so lucky in one which was scheduled to practise circuits and bumps - take-offs and landings - all night long, usually in an ambling Stirling. Then back to Heaton Park, another extended wait and eventually the great day when their name was called out at the parade in front of the famous bandstand -they were off! Two mornings or so later, having spent some eight hours in a dismal, blacked-out train, sometimes without a corridor, they stepped out on to a quay, often at Greenock, and were hustled into a rat-ridden warehouse for a make-shift breakfast. Then on to a tender and out into the estuary of the Clyde where these young men, most of whom had hardly been out of their own backyards until they had volunteered for aircrew, excitedly climbed aboard massive liners such as the *Queen Elizabeth, Queen Mary, Mauritania* and *Aquitania* at the Tail o' the Bank, and sailed across the North Atlantic, whiling away the hours playing cards or seeing if they could break the time record in quoting the names of all the 49 States which then made up the USA. Many thrilled at the great distant glow in the night sky that heralded their imminent arrival in New York, marvelled at the Statue of Liberty as they sailed up the Hudson and into the heart of the city itself, a city with no blackout, to be greeted on disembarkation by motherly Red Cross ladies handing out candy and peaches and delicious drinks in unimaginable profusion. Then the long train journey up through Massachusetts and New Hampshire and Maine, and finally into the province of New Brunswick in Canada, to the reception camp at Moncton, where they remained for about a fortnight before entraining once more,

The Great Ingratitude

this time for flying schools in Ontario and Manitoba, in Texas and Arizona, for a gruelling course which lasted for about a year. But there were spells of leave, during which most of them took off for places like Chicago, St. Louis or Vancouver, depending on where they were stationed and on the time they could spare for travel.

If not rejected at some stage and they won their wings, sergeant's stripes were immediately sewn on their tunic sleeves. Some of them who had been products of University Air Squadrons (where they had completed an Arts course in conjunction with RAF training) tore the same stripes off a day or two later and replaced them with a broad, white armband to indicate they had been commissioned with the rank of Pilot Officer. Their new uniforms were not usually purchased until they arrived back in the UK.

Then (unless, like a few, they were posted to Coastal Command stations such as Comox on Vancouver Island for further training), they went back to New York or Halifax for the return trip across the 'Pond'. However, if they were stationed in Ontario and were lucky in the draw, they went as passengers in one of the new Lancasters built next door to the Air Observers' School at Malton (later to become Toronto Airport) and had their first taste of the aircraft they were likely to get to know a lot better in the not too distant future, landing at Gander in Newfoundland to refuel and then again at Shannon on the west coast of Ireland. Those who returned by sea found it was altogether a different experience from the outward journey, when they had been practically the sole passengers. This time the huge ships were packed to the gunwales with American soldiers and airmen, and they were reminded that they were going back to where a war was going on. A dozen or so of the new 'sprog' officers shared a cabin intended for two, while sergeants slept just about everywhere, even on the open decks during the summer months. The liners crossed the Atlantic alone, relying on their speed to protect them from submarines. During the hours of daylight they altered course every few minutes but at night they ploughed on in a straight line. Compared to the three-week long voyage of the slow-moving convoys, they covered the three thousand miles in a matter of four or five days.

After disembarkation leave, the young airmen usually completed a short 'familiarisation course', during which two-seater Tiger Moths were used to get the pilots and navigators accustomed to the very different flying conditions which prevailed in British and European skies. Pilots found themselves taking off in weather so wretched that all flying would have been judged to be entirely out of the question at their recent Empire fields, and navigators had a particularly rough time of it. After the almost perfect visibility they had enjoyed and the ease of map-reading in countries where rail and road junctions were infallible pin-points by virtue of their rarity, they now found these to be virtually useless because of their superabundance. Thick cloud, fog and ever-changing winds did nothing to help matters and when, at Advanced Flying Training School, they 'graduated' to Avro Ansons and had to undertake much longer flights, many of them at night, they often became completely lost and crashed into Welsh and Scottish mountains; or ran out of fuel, necessitating recourse to parachutes. It was not only operational flying which had its perils.

The next stage was Heavy Conversion Unit (twin-engined to four-engined aircraft), then Operational Training Unit, entailing long, testing flights, mainly nocturnal, in rain and snow and electric storms up as far as the north of Scotland and the Outer Hebrides, or across to Cornwall and out over the Atlantic. And also over the North Sea, sometimes to deceive the Germans about the destination of the main stream operation. After all, that's the way they would be going. Finally, the climax to the whole long, complicated process - a posting to an operational bomber squadron. The end of the road. Often in more senses than one.

Chapter 4

THE BIG CITY

It was, many claimed, inappropriate and even strategically unsound, that the decision to throw at least half the entire strength of Bomber Command against the German capital came at a time when the Allied Air Forces were committed to *Pointblank*, the huge softening-up operation which was essential as a prelude to the invasion of the Continent (Operation *Overlord*). British and American military and political leaders had no illusions about the hazards involved in landing large armies on a coastline defended by a formidable Atlantic Wall and, if and when a foothold was established, about facing up to some of the most élite and fanatical divisions of the Wehrmacht and the Waffen-SS. Therefore it was imperative that the opposition offered by the Luftwaffe in particular - the possible existence of hundreds of fighters on airfields in Northern France haunted the planners of Overlord day and night - and by all forms of defence in general, including large gun emplacements, should be reduced to an insignificant minimum.   The second aim, to prevent reinforcements being brought up, was the destruction of all important centres and lines of communication from the Reich to the Atlantic and North Sea and, if rebuilt, their repeated destruction until they fell into Allied hands; the commanders' nightmarish fear that the great armies might be driven back into the sea, resulting in the most disastrous military catastrophe in history, would thus be largely removed.   The only way of achieving this was by the deployment of overwhelming air power, mainly in attacks on aircraft factories and synthetic oil plants in the months prior to the Invasion and as long after it as was necessary.

There were high-ranking experts, both British and American, who thought it nothing short of enigmatic that the Chief of Air Staff, Sir Charles Portal, upon whose shoulders lay the responsibility for seeing that the RAF's contribution to *Pointblank* was implemented to the hilt, did not put Air Chief Marshall Harris firmly in his place and tell him categorically to forget, for the time being at any rate, his obsession with German cities, including Berlin, and to co-operate fully with the United States Army Air Force in selecting key targets, such as oil.   But for some obscure reasons - amongst them what many critics ascribe to weakness on his part - this Portal failed to do, and his wilful Commander defied his general orders by ignoring *Pointblank* policy as far as he could and carrying on in his own old, sweet way. The most uncharitable of the historians say that Portal should have shown Harris the door (see Chapter 6), but both he and Churchill had a lot of sympathy for the Bomber Chief's views as they had fallen victim to the euphoria created by Hamburg; and at that time they were not convinced that he was wrong in claiming that Bomber Command could now deal what might prove to be a mortal blow to the enemy, as it now seemed capable of obliterating any city, no matter how big; yes, even the German capital itself. In any case it was highly unlikely that the Prime Minister would have agreed to the sacking. Apart from being held in high esteem by his own aircrews (in spite of all they said about him) Harris was far too popular with the British public, and his departure from the scene would have been a severe blow to national morale. In fact, the situation was somewhat analogous, if less sinister, to that of Hitler and Rommel when the Führer considered it would be most unwise to execute his much-loved Field Marshal for his part in the assassination attempt, and concocted a more expedient means of seeing him on his way.

And so the man who was leading Bomber Command, eternal thorn in the flesh of Eisenhower, and at times of Portal and of Churchill himself, not to mention a host of lesser men, remained at his post, determined to co-operate as little as possible with the "panacea merchants" as he called them - those who firmly advocated the bombing of specific targets rather than the saturation of whole urban areas - and to give Germany's cities no time to get their breath back. He believed that a break in momentum would not only allow them to go unmolested but would tend to nullify much of the terror and the feeling of hopelessness that he was convinced his bombers were creating in the Third Reich, and which would hasten its collapse. To Harris a night without a raid on a German town was a night lost to Bomber Command and a further extension to the duration of the war, and he kept on offering all kinds of plausible reasons for sending his crews to saturate Munich or Frankfurt-am-Main or Duisburg - or Berlin - instead of concentrating on specific industrial installations. Either the weather or the instruments were not good enough for the accurate bombing that was necessary, or the target was too difficult to identify. After all, he said, the Command had become what it was, a carpet-bombing night force, because of the great problems involved in finding and hitting single

The Great Ingratitude

buildings, no matter how large, or small groups of buildings, even in daylight. Damn it, his crews were taking a big enough battering as it was, and he had no intention of having more of them slaughtered with much less to show for it. Whole cities, on the other hand, did not present the same difficulties. You knew when they lay beneath you, and when they did, you drenched them. You completely flattened whole areas and, therefore, all the factories they contained. If you clobbered the lot, you hit something. In other words, statistical probability was far more effective than selectivity.

Argument closed. Berlin was next.

***

Shortly after Hamburg, Harris had said: "I feel certain that Germany must collapse before the programme, which is more than half completed already, has proceeded much further. We have not far to go. We must get the United States Army Air Force to wade in in greater force and if so, we can get through it very quickly. We can wreck Berlin from end to end if the Americans will come in on it. It will cost between us 400-500 aircraft. It will cost Germany the war."

Unfortunately, the Americans, who had chosen to ignore the devastating losses - and the advice - of Bomber Command when the latter had tried long-range and unescorted penetration into Germany in daylight, had attacked the ball-bearing plants at Schweinfurt and Regensburg on August 17, 1943, when they lost 51 aircraft, one-fifth of their total force, and at Schweinfurt again on October 14, when 60 out of 291 Fortresses fell from the skies and 140 were damaged. Such losses were clearly unsustainable and they had immediately discontinued unescorted daylight missions over Germany, not being in any mood to be massacred yet again, not for Harris or anyone else. Consequently it would not be until the advent of the long-range Mustang P-51B in December, 1943, a revolutionary machine which defied all the established laws of aeronautical engineering and proved that you could in fact produce a fast and highly manoeuvrable fighter which had the range to accompany bombers all the way to and from a distant target in the Reich, that General Ira Eaker, Commander of the Eighth Army Air Force, would even contemplate taking on a target as daunting as Berlin. (When the Mustangs, at least 50mph faster than either the Me 109G or the Fw 190, and more manoeuvrable, did arrive to fuss around the cumbersome bombers over long distances, the Americans still suffered fairly high, if smaller, losses). So Eaker could hardly be blamed, in the late autumn of 1943, for declining Harris's invitation, and Berlin was destined to be primarily a job for Bomber Command.

***

An Intelligence Report dated November 4, 1943 stated: "The maintenance of morale is the gravest single problem confronting the home (German) authorities. The full effects of an air attack since the devastation of Hamburg have become known in all parts of the country. The increasing death toll is an important factor and coupled with military failures, the general attitude is approaching one of peace at any price, and the avoidance of wholesale destruction of further cities in Germany."

The authors of the Report were to learn later that this assessment of the situation, if a reasonable one at the time, was quite erroneous. They seemed to be largely unaware of the well-disciplined and totally subservient nature of the German civilian population which, sleep or no sleep, terror or no terror, assiduously carried out its everyday tasks under a harsh totalitarian régime, controlled by the icy grip of a Gestapo which rooted out any waverers, showed them no mercy, and made an example of them for all to see. Nor did they appear to realise at that moment that Hitler was using Germany and its people merely as a vehicle for his own megalomaniac ambitions and that, if the worst came to the worst, he would not care one iota about their ultimate fate. Further, the Allied policy of 'Unconditional Surrender' was exploited by the Führer to demonstrate to his subjects that he and they had no alternative but to soldier on to the bitter end as their country would be reduced to a sea of ashes in any case. Those who survived would be left to crawl like savages amidst the ruins of their homeland, living like starving rats, subjected to the utmost depths of depravity and humiliation.

An accurate prediction.

***

Apart from its prestigious position as the chief and largest city of the Third Reich and the seat of Nazi government, Berlin was also the site of innumerable factories, producing a considerable proportion of the nation's war requirements. It accounted for no less than one-half of the total output of heavy guns and one-quarter of the tanks, one-tenth

The Great Ingratitude

of all aero-engines and precision instruments, and at the same time, boasted a huge electrical engineering industry. It had been a regular target for Bomber Command right from the earliest days of the war, when poorly-equipped Blenheims and Hampdens and Whitleys, (the Wellingtons were somewhat better), quite unfit for the task allotted them, were sent on a hopefully round but all too often single trip of some 1150 miles with a puny bomb load and little idea of where to drop it - when or if they ever got there. Contrary to optimistic meteorological forecasts, the weather, so often Bomber Command's worst enemy, could be so bad that crews were blown miles off track or were immersed in cloud and couldn't even find the city. In fact they were usually so disorientated that locating the target became a matter of secondary importance and their first priority a safe return to base. In such circumstances they would set a course more or less due west, and, if unable to pin-point their position somewhere en route, just hoped they would hit the English coast somewhere.   Some of the more determined would search around for a gap in the clouds, through which they might spot something that looked as if it was worth bombing, eventually run into fighters or out of fuel, and pay the penalty.   When, in clearer skies and with kinder winds the target, normally a large factory, was correctly identified, the bombs which were intended to raze it invariably missed by anything between three and five miles.   In fact the early raids on Berlin, by small formations of 10 to 60 aircraft, took the form rather of a gesture of defiance to the enemy (Goering had arrogantly told the Berliners that no RAF bomber would ever reach the capital, otherwise they were at liberty to call him Herr Schmidt - or Herr Meier - or a fat Dutchman, whichever version is preferred) - and as a sort of morale-booster to the British public, who so far in the war had had little to crow about and were more than gratified to learn that the Germans were being paid back in their own coin for the raids on London and elsewhere. Little was it known that the vaunted attacks on Berlin were largely ineffective and that the negligible amount of damage done in no way justified the relatively high cost in men and machines.

It might not be out of place to mention at this juncture that the first ever raid on Berlin had taken place on August 25/26, 1940, when approximately 40 Hampdens and Wellingtons found the city enveloped in cloud, and the sum total of success was the destruction of a wooden summer-house in the suburb of Rosenthal.   Two people were slightly injured and the majority of the bombs fell on farmland in the surrounding country areas - which gave rise to the joke among Berliners that the British were trying to starve them out. But this smug attitude was destined to be of short duration and they were to find that the RAF would soon have the means to destroy more than the occasional summer-house ...

By late 1942, thanks mainly to Harris's determined efforts, Bomber Command was steadily growing in strength, and by the late summer of 1943, the impotent daytime dwarf of 1940 and 1941 had become a nocturnal giant - and one which would rarely go to sleep.

***

Apart from its increasing numbers, the Lancaster had undergone improvements to make it an even more efficient machine. The Stirling, on the other hand, because of its heavy losses, was withdrawn from all operations over Germany after the attack on Berlin on November 22/23, when the Battle was still in its infancy. In Harris's opinion, it constituted a dire threat not only to the crews who had to fly it, but to the Lancs and Halifaxes which, because of the Stirling's poor ceiling, had to operate at a much lower altitude than they might have done in order to accommodate it in the main stream - thus increasing the risks to themselves; also, for such a large machine, its bomb-carrying capability was small and when the Germans dismissed it as a 'tired crow' they were not too wide of the mark. The Halifax, too, had its faults, and suffered losses of 15% in the winter of 1943/1944 when some squadrons were depleted by a demoralising 20-25%. So it too was withdrawn after a particularly disastrous raid on distant Leipzig on February 19/20, when 34 of the 255 taking part were destroyed (Lancaster losses for the same attack amounted to 44 out of 561). Only the more efficient Halifax Mark III proved to be fit for the task and to lend its weight to main stream attacks on the Reich.

Obviously, the demise of the Stirling and of earlier marks of the Halifax meant a temporary diminution of the heavy bomber force and, therefore, a decrease in tonnage dropped - about one-fifth. But it also meant that Bomber Command was now almost exclusively a Lancaster force as far as heavies were concerned. The elusive and ubiquitous Mosquito, of course, would go on stabbing and jabbing and causing general disruption until the very end of the war. Like the Lanc it was a winner all the way.

Crews who had had the good fortune to survive trips both to Berlin and elsewhere were now far more experienced, but on the other hand losses increased as the Battle became more ferocious and replacement crews, often straight from OTUs, had a harrowing baptism when their very first 'op.' was to the capital. However, more skilled Pathfinders were available to mark the target with flares and, as they circled it, to give any necessary instructions to main stream captains. More advanced electronic navigational and bombing aids were also becoming available.

The Battle of Berlin began on the night of November 18/19, 1943, and ended (with the sixteenth major attack) on March 24/25, 1944. Apart from these large raids by 600-900 aircraft, the city was thrown into disorder almost nightly by small to moderate formations of Mosquitoes for the express purpose of giving its already hard-pressed citizens no peace by sending them into cold 'bunkers' and at the same time calling out all the emergency services and forcing the authorities to take a host of other precautionary measures. No one could be sure that the attack would not develop into something big.

But it was not only the Berliners who had to undergo such a spate of traumas: there was no other sustained attack carried out during the entire campaign which the crews of Bomber Command found so demanding, so demoralising, so terrifying; and which took such a monstrous toll of its resources. If 'Kanalkrankheit' ('English Channel sickness') was an appropriate term conjured up by the Luftwaffe bomber crews in 1940 to describe their feelings of foreboding as they left the shores of France and headed towards the waiting Spitfires and Hurricanes, then 'Berlinitis' was a correspondingly suitable term for the trepidation of Bomber Command crews en route for the Nazi capital; except that, of the two, Berlinitis was a more debilitating disease - and, thanks to Berlin's savage defences, to the much longer duration of each operation and of the Battle itself, it was much more likely to be terminal. Berlin generated its own special brand of fear.

The reasons were not far to seek. Berlin lay some 575 statute miles from the centre of Lincolnshire as the crow flies - the bombers normally took a more devious route - and the trip there and back lasted between eight and nine hours, most of it more often than not over heavily-defended enemy territory. The great distance they had penetrated into Germany was one factor which had an adverse psychological effect on the crews, similar to the feeling of foreboding experienced by many soldiers of the Wehrmacht when they found themselves harried far inside Russia - it was a long way back. Once they were beyond Hamburg to the north, and Hanover to the south, Harris's airmen knew the Germans knew that they could have only one possible destination; and the further they flew to the east, the less effective became their radar and electronic aids, the majority of which depended on signals from transmitters in the UK. In fact Berlin was far beyond *Gee* range (positional fix obtained by navigator from wireless signals) and from that of *Oboe* (a radar pulse which the pilot heard and which kept him on course, and also told the bomb-aimer the exact moment when he should release his load). *H2S* (outline of the target, something like a film negative on a small screen) also gave a poor and often useless picture of the ground below. These aids, and others, are more fully described in Chapter 12.

All these factors were in themselves bad enough, but there emerged a further grave threat to the aspirations of Bomber Command: the considerable strengthening of the ground defences apart (Chapter 1), the Luftwaffe night force changed over to much more effective tactics. The fighters, instead of being confined to 'boxes' along the route it was anticipated the bombers would follow, now patrolled the area in which they were known to be and used all their individual skills to find them. These fighters, mostly single-engined, were given the name 'Wilde Sau' ('Wild Boar'), and it was ironic that Bomber Command's hitherto eminently successful use of Window had compelled the Luftwaffe to adopt this new and rewarding strategy because the clouds of metallised strips had rendered the box system of defence useless. But now the *Window* was plotted by radar, permitting the Germans to ascertain the position and progress of the main stream and to guide the 'Wild Boar' machines on to it.

The latter reaped a rich harvest amongst the out-going and homeward-bound bombers, but because of bad winter weather and their lack of navigational aids, they regularly got lost in the dark, ran out of fuel and crashed. So they, too, suffered heavy losses and a slight variation in the method of tackling the stream was introduced: 'Zahme Sau' ('Tame Boar') fighters (twin-engined Me 110s and Ju 88s), equipped with good navigational devices and a radar set which was eventually capable of cancelling out the effect of *Window*, were kept informed of the exact whereabouts of the bombers, no matter how often they swung off on dog-legs, and were then left to attack them using their own tactics. As the skill of the German airmen increased with practice, they took a correspondingly greater toll of the heavies, and more than a little of their success could be ascribed to a further innovation - the installation of upward-pointing twin cannon in the Me 110, called *Schräge Musik* ("Jazz Music"). The fighter would creep up unobserved beneath the bomber and let loose a shattering burst, which was normally lethal. In fact many of the crews attacked in this way did not even know what had hit them: their machine was either blown to bits or suddenly sent spiralling down to earth. Initially, some of the German crews also perished when their shells penetrated their victim's bomb-bay, but their colleagues soon learned there were safer aiming-points, such as the wing areas between the engines. Many of these pilots became much-lauded 'Experte', with the resultant honours and hero-worship that has always been the lot of the fighter pilot. Perhaps the most famous amongst them was Major Prinz zu Sayn-Wittgenstein, Commander of No. 2 *Nachtjagdgeschwader*, who accounted for four Lancs in quick succession during the raid on Magdeburg on January 21/22, when over 40 of the bombers shot down were claimed by night-fighters. Altogether, this pilot was credited with 83 victories before being shot down by a Mosquito.

The very effective 'Tame Boar' system went into operation when the bombers' radio sets were being tested on the ground at their bases in England. These were monitored by the Luftwaffe to ascertain the approximate size of the attacking force, whose progress across the North Sea was then followed, thanks to the *Window* released by their crews (one of the frequent examples of a revolutionary device introduced by one side being turned to advantage by the other once it had got hold of it). On several occasions one or two fighters, having found the bomber stream, adopted a rather sinister ploy by flying along with it, as if keeping it company, and while so doing would send back to the German controllers vital information about its course, height and speed. Others would drop flares into the heart of the stream as a guide to the fighters which were in the vicinity.

There were other influences which all combined to cause Bomber Command much angst and to reduce the effectiveness of its aim to annihilate Berlin: the "sprog" crews which had to replace those the city (or other cities) had already claimed and who, due to their lack of experience, were to suffer the highest casualties and cause losses to snowball, leading to the need for even more replacements, a situation which was aggravated when veterans completed their tour and went off for a rest; the long, roundabout routes which increased flying time, thus putting extra strain on already tired crews, and also meant that bomb loads had to be partly sacrificed for the extra petrol required; the high winds which prevailed throughout most of the winter and caused havoc with target indicators and resulted in the main stream becoming scattered and, therefore, less effective and more vulnerable; and the generally bad atmospheric conditions which could result in the icing-up of control surfaces and sub-zero temperatures for the crews, besetting them with the problem of keeping mind and eyes alert; in fact, frostbite was a real hazard and could have fatal consequences.

The four-and-a-half month long Battle of Berlin was a highly complicated game of cat and mouse between the Luftwaffe on the one hand and Bomber Command on the other. The latter did everything in its power to counteract every spanner that the enemy threw in its path and due credit must be given to the boffins of TRE (Telecommunications Research Establishment) at Great Malvern in Worcestershire, who produced a whole series of new technical aids; the Command made full use of the Pathfinder squadrons, upon whose skill and resoluteness the success or failure of each attack largely depended, for apart from accurate marking of the target area, they largely nullified the effects of decoy fires by using inimitable combinations of coloured indicators (see Chapter 12); it organised "spoof" raids by Mosquitoes on other cities, in which they frequently dropped a 4,000 pound "cookie" or marker flares to simulate the beginning of a large-scale raid; fighter versions of the same aircraft flew all over North Germany to confuse the defences and strafed enemy airfields, not only those lying on the main stream's route but many which were some distance from it; crews learning their trade at Operational Training Units flew in large formations almost as far as the German coastline before turning back; the Halifaxes and Stirlings which were no longer involved in penetrations into the Reich were sent out on *Window* dropping exercises and on big mine-laying operations in the North Sea and the Baltic; more dog-legs than normal were flown by the main force and unusual routes were followed - even neutral Sweden was overflown if the occasion demanded. FIDO (Fog Investigation Dispersal Operation), consisting of a series of flame-spouting pipes (using petrol) was installed along many runways to clear the hazard long enough to allow a bomber to land safely; every effort was made to jam the flood of instructions relayed by the Luftwaffe controllers to its fighters and native German speakers, (with women standing by to step in if necessary), were employed to broadcast erroneous information to the enemy pilots, telling them, for instance, that they must come in and land as their airfield was becoming shrouded in fog, and generally creating such confusion between those on the ground and those in the air that tempers were lost and efficiency greatly impaired; the bomber stream of some 800 aircraft was telescoped into a length of only 60-70 miles and the bombing run was so concentrated that

The Great Ingratitude

this mighty force could release its entire load in just over 15 minutes; in short, Bomber Command left no stone unturned as it endeavoured to cut down losses and to achieve maximum success. To what extent all its ruses succeeded will never be known, but it is quite certain that, without the measures taken, the level of achievement would have been much less and the price paid considerably higher. And the price was high enough.

Berlin was a huge, sprawling city, quite unlike other towns in Germany with their dense concentration of factories and compact residential areas. Its industry was scattered all over the place, covering some 20 square miles, and its thoroughfares were wide and flanked by parks and open spaces (such as the Tiergarten - the Zoo - which, on the night of November 26/27, received a large number of bombs, resulting in the death of most of the animals and the escape of the survivors into the neighbouring streets, where panthers, leopards and jaguars had to be shot). Such large 'empty' areas meant that the chances of creating a fire storm on Hamburg lines were very much reduced. Of this Harris was well aware, but still believed that Bomber Command, now being provided with the means necessary to maintain a prolonged onslaught by hundreds and hundreds of Lancasters, would eventually pulverize the German capital and break the spirit of the nation.

It had to be a winter campaign, when the force would be protected to some extent by the long hours of European darkness and the city's dehoused citizens would suffer additional misery. Winter also entailed the atrocious flying conditions already described but there were always disadvantages, no matter when you went.

Harris decided that B-Day would be November 18.

That very night, 440 Lancasters and 4 Mosquitoes took off for the capital and some time later close on 400 aircraft, mostly Halifaxes, headed for the much bombed twin towns of Mannheim and Ludwigshafen - a large diversionary attack to put the defences in turmoil and to lure the fighters away to the south-west. The ruse at least partly succeeded since the "spoof" raid cost 23 machines, while only 9 failed to return from the primary target. Unfortunately Berlin was blotted out by ten-tenths cloud and both markers and bombs had to be dropped blindly. Consequently no particular area received saturation treatment but a number of factories were demolished, in addition to the inevitable destruction of dwelling-houses. Four nights later, 764 aircraft, the majority of them Lancasters, paid the city a further visit (the last operation in which the condemned Stirlings took part) and delivered 2,300 tons of bombs for the loss of 26 bombers. This was the biggest raid of the war on the capital so far and in spite of the solid cloud base, which had persisted from November 18, it was also the most devastating attack of the whole Battle. There were mini-fire storms in the central and western districts of Tiergarten, Charlottenburg and also out at Spandau, with smoke billowing up to a height of over 18,000 feet. About 2,000 Berliners died and roughly 175,000 were dehoused; but there was also total destruction of 23 large industrial plants, including a tank factory and premises belonging to Siemens (electrics).

Two more raids took place before November was out, and the average loss rate so far was just over 4%, a figure which was regarded as encouraging. It was also ominous, however, that as German opposition stiffened and the new techniques adopted by the Luftwaffe night-fighters were improved with practice, the rate began to rise as the New Year approached.

This was hardly surprising because the capital's already awesome defences, which were now being strengthened even further, made it the most heavily defended city on the entire continent of Europe. It was surrounded by a tight ring of ack-ack batteries which sent aloft what was at times an almost solid and seemingly impenetrable barrage of shells, and in addition had large Luftwaffe night fighter groups *(Nachtkampfgeschwader)* at its disposal. And now that the Germans rightly suspected that the early destruction of Berlin was the primary aim of Bomber Command, its defences were made even more formidable by the transfer, no doubt to Stalin's delight, of large numbers of guns and fighters from the Russian front. As things hotted up during that long, dark winter of 1943/1944, life became a nightmare for both Berliners and Bomber Command crews. While the former were forced to spend night after night in cold, damp shelters or cellars, their senses paralysed by the hellish noise and by the earth heaving and shuddering all around them, to come out in the light of morning to gaze upon the smoking ruins of their own homes or their entire street, or even quarter, the airmen suffered no less 20,000 feet above, because they felt they had flown into a flaming madhouse from which no escape seemed possible. This was the beginning of the period when they feared that every trip would be their last, when their chances of survival were lower than they had ever been, or perhaps would ever be. Few crews got through ten operations and many failed even to approach that figure.

It was on the western approaches to the capital that there was a growing tendency for crews to become less resolute and to drop their bombs before being engulfed in the heat of the inferno. Refusing to fly over the centre of the city - it was no mean feat to have reached its outer perimeter - they unleashed their loads short of the target area, often causing "creep-back" as aircraft following them reckoned the edge of the fires was far enough. These "fringe merchants", as they were dubbed, later tried to console themselves with the thought that they had at least released their bombs on the Nazi capital, even if only on its peripheries, and perhaps hit something. Their attitude was: "That's Berlin down there, isn't it? Well, drop the bloody things and let's go!"

This laxity on the part of some crews, which became evident sometime before the end of 1943, was a sure sign that morale was falling, and that Berlin was largely responsible. To add to their anxieties, some enemy fighter squadrons had begun to come out half-way across the North Sea to meet them, so that the bombers were under almost constant attack on the outward journey and, if they survived the time spent over the city itself, on the homeward leg as well, when the aircraft were frequently damaged and the exhausted men inside them, some perhaps wounded, were less able to cope with any further emergency.

As morale continued to fall it was time for those in the upper echelons of the Command to feel apprehensive about the immediate future, and Harris himself grew more and more concerned as Group Commanders reported that an increasing number of crews were aborting with little apparent justification for doing so. There were even stories of undamaged aircraft landing in non-belligerent countries such as Sweden and Switzerland, or of crews baling out over these safe havens (post-war investigations however, revealed that in the case of the RAF airmen, this rarely, if ever happened, unless their machine was in no fit state to get them back to base. The Americans did find, on the other hand, that a number of their Fortresses and Liberators did put down, for only one obvious reason, in these countries). Senior officers throughout Bomber Command were tortured by the thought there might just be a possibility that, if the present tempo was maintained, crews might collectively say "No more". It was clear for all to see that even back in the temporary safety of their bases, there was little to raise their flagging spirits: there were too many empty beds in which friends had slept, too many empty places at breakfast table, too many extra eggs available which no one wanted. But the bed and the breakfast places were soon filled with newcomers from Operational Training Units. The conveyor belt that produced new recruits kept rolling relentlessly on, in the same mechanical way as the one which brought new Lancs rolling out of the factories. It was a process that appeared to the crews as if it might go on for ever. They had been assured time and time again that what they were doing would make Berlin, and hence, Germany, crack. But Berlin did not crack. Germany did not crack; and they knew only too well where the cracks were appearing.

***

By the turn of the year, 'Happy Hannah' had already been twice to the capital and, miraculously, had returned with no more damage than a few holes in the fuselage and wings, a partly-shot off elevator, and a slightly wounded mid-upper gunner. Amongst other towns, Frankfurt, Stettin, Brunswick and Magdeburg, and targets in France, had also received her attentions without mishap to herself or her crews, who were beginning to wonder how long their luck would hold. They were becoming obsessed by the number of operations they still had to complete before reaching the magical thirty and gaining a respite as instructors at Operational Training Units before embarking on the final tour of twenty - by which time, perhaps, Harris's prediction would have been proved correct. It said a lot for Candlish - nearly everyone on the Squadron thought he was out of his mind - that although he had already attained the first obligatory figure, he had decided to carry on so that he and his crew could remain together in a situation which was not unlike that of being afflicted with something akin to a terminal disease. The figure '30' was the life-prolonging pill which gave you a remission (before you were chucked into the cauldron for a second time) and completion of the next 20, the wonder drug which meant a complete and quite unexpected cure. But a remission was not easy to come by in 1943 and 1944, especially if you were a regular visitor to Berlin. The total cure was then something of a rarity, and the longer you survived, the stronger became your conviction that you were living on borrowed time and your number must be nearly up. Every extra day was a bonus, but a bonus of doubtful worth when taut nerves became ever tauter and were being stretched to breaking-point.

***

The Great Ingratitude

   Candlish and his crew reported for briefing in the late afternoon of February 15, 1944. NCOs of the RAF Police stood at the door scrutinising everyone and on entering the room the sight of the large veiled map of Europe was, as usual, a traumatic moment for the airmen - they knew not what lay beneath. Once they were all seated, the Station Commander himself, amid a subdued hush, stepped on to the platform while fingers twiddled with mascots such as rabbits' feet or inscribed nutshells, or whatever. The silence was audible as a hundred young men asked themselves: Where will it be? The Ruhr, not termed 'Happy Valley' for nothing, wasn't far, but by God you knew when you got there, even long before that. They prayed that it wasn't one of the distant cities of the south-east either, but most of all, they prayed that it wasn't that unmentionable hell-house ... A nice short dawdle to a target in Northern France or Belgium would be much better. In and out and home again in no time.

   The curtain swished. The red ribbon stretched away to the east, almost to the end of the Reich. A communal sigh of foreboding filled the room. Then,

"Christ, the Big City!"

"See Berlin and die!"

"All aboard for the Hades Express!"

"That's us, the Battered Bastards of Berlin."

"Anybody want a single ticket, going cheap?"

"A free trip to the Berlin illuminations! Very generous to us is old Uncle Butch!"

"Berlin? Great! Mind if I take my granny along for the ride, Skipper? She just adores bright lights and crackers!"

From Benny Ramage, just a simple: "Fuckin' Berlin!"

   The forced humour displayed might have tended to be schoolboyish in character, but that was understandable as most of them had been schoolboys not so long before. And, after all, they didn't have much chance of remaining boys for long.

The Commanding Officer spoke generally about what they were doing to Berlin and about what they intended to do to it that very night, for this was to be the heaviest raid on the capital so far, with 891 aircraft - 561 Lancs, 314 Halifaxes and 16 Mosquitoes taking part. There would be support and diversionary operations by a further 179 Lancasters, Stirlings, Halifaxes and Mosquitoes - 47 Stirlings and Halifaxes would be 'gardening' (sowing mines) off Kiel, 24 Lancs would bomb Frankfurt-on-Oder, 23 Mosquitoes would shoot up night-fighter stations in Holland, while a few others were detailed to attack Aachen and 48 aircraft were engaged on Resistance operations. It was to be a typically busy night for the Command. The Station Commander was followed by the Intelligence Officer, who outlined details about the route. At a given position, they were to suddenly swing well to port and overfly the north of Denmark; then a further big course change would take them down towards Lübeck and Rostock, to deceive the Germans into thinking one or other of these Baltic ports was probably the target. He also talked about flak batteries, expected fighter opposition, bomb and petrol loads; it was then the turn of the Met. Officer with his usual over-optimistic forecast, which was greeted with the customary expressions of derision; then the Navigation Leader, pointer in hand, gave full particulars about each leg to be flown; the Gunnery Leader repeated his regular spiel about constant vigilance and a reminder that the gunner's job was to help to get the aircraft there and back again, not to indulge in any stupid games which might only attract the enemy towards them and to attack only when attacked themselves; the Signals Leader talked about the transmitting of messages and about Group broadcasts, while the Station Flying Control Officer gave details of take-off times and landing procedures. Finally, the Station Commander asked if there were any questions, which there weren't, so they were told that there was transport waiting outside to take them to the mess for their meal. They were then issued with escape-kits containing items such as a handkerchief map of Western Europe, small compass, glucose, and before departing from the room they handed to a couple of WAAFs any personal items which might be of value to the enemy should they be shot down. A comforting thought!

After eating (with little relish), donning the various items of flying clothing - polo-necked jerseys, inner and outer suits and flying boots, and collecting parachutes and Mae Wests, crews would normally sit silently, most of them smoking, as they were transported out

The Great Ingratitude

to the waiting bombers in noisy unsprung Bedford trucks (driven by WAAFs) which did nothing for queasy stomachs. Their subdued mood was in stark contrast to that of the night before when, in an inebriated or semi-inebriated state in the local pub or on the way back from it, they had bawled out inelegant lyrics, if that is the right term, as a means of allaying the fear that never deserted them.

> *Goering said we couldn't*
> *Ever bomb Berlin,*
> *Well my friend we're on our way,*
> *To hit you on the chin.*
> *A fuckin' great blockbuster*
> *Right in your ugly mug,*
> *Exit Marshal Goering*
> *In pieces on the rug.*

> *And when we get back again*
> *Old Butcher he will say:*
> *No rest for you tonight, my lads,*
> *No screwin' in the hay,*
> *A pleasure trip to Stuttgart*
> *Is what is on the cards,*
> *Fireworks and lights and rat-a-tat,*
> *What fun you lads do have!*

Bravado? Arrogance? Certainly not. These songs served the same purpose as the fiendish banshee of the bagpipes and the blood-curdling cries of the kilted Jocks as they 'went over the top' - because that is exactly what the crews were doing - in the preceding war. They acted as a rudimentary defence mechanism, born out of fear, the overwhelming nature of which it was fortunately given to few others to experience. It was fear, simple unadulterated fear of the hellish reception they knew always awaited them, fear of the inferno that could engulf them if they were hit; fear of collision with another aircraft, either one of their own or an enemy fighter; fear of receiving a 'friendly' bomb from above; fear of being trapped in a blinding cone of searchlights and waiting for annihilation; fear of the nauseating grip of air sickness and of the paralysing cold, both of which could fatally reduce their ability to carry out their duties; fear of iced-up ailerons and elevators which would render their plane unmanoeuvrable and send them diving earthwards in an uncontrollable spin; fear in such circumstances of being unable to bale out. Paradoxically, fear of parachuting into the midst of a mad circus of bombers and fighters, of falling bombs and ascending shells, fear of descending into a city aflame; fear of being captured by the SS or hate-filled civilians; fear of having to struggle home in a crippled aircraft and of the possibility of having to ditch in the uninviting waters of the North Sea (the Lanc in particular was a notoriously bad 'floater'); fear of returning to a fog-bound England; fear of a crash-landing, especially if the bomb doors had jammed and they were still carrying their lethal load; fear that this night might be their last on earth; even fear of being afraid and fear of being incapacitated by it; fear of fear itself. Fear ... all consuming fear.

***

'Happy Hannah' had risen into the air at 21.35 hours and less than half-an-hour later was sitting in the main stream some eighty miles out from the coast, when the rear-gunner suddenly shouted through his intercom:

"Big explosion away below and behind us, Skipper. Kite must have gone into the drink. Good God, there's anither yin! What the hell's goin' on? Nae fighters already, surely? Or is it what I think it is?"

"OK Benny, not to worry if you see more. Skipper to crew: Ignore any explosions you see at water level for the next half-hour or so. You've all a good idea of what's happening. But note them in your log, navigator."

Candlish and Benny were right in their interpretation of the huge detonations beneath. Some time before, a directive had demanded an increase of well over one ton in bomb load for raids on Berlin, which meant that an already heavily-taxed bomber was being taxed even more. Extra weight reduced speed, height and manoeuvrability, and so this unwelcome innovation produced exactly the opposite effect to the one intended, as the reaction of a considerable number of crews was to jettison the most effective bomb in their bay - the 4000 pound high explosive 'cookie', as soon as they were some distance over the sea. In view of the special circumstances which characterised attacks on the capital, it was undoubtedly an ill-conceived move by the Air Ministry in the first place and merely resulted in many crews having to cope with a greater load during a precarious take-off and climb, only to get rid of a substantial part of it once it was thought safe to do so. Air Vice-Marshal Donald Bennett, the Pathfinder leader, reported that his own crews saw such explosions regularly, when the offensive was at its height, so the addition to the bomb load turned out to be counter-productive. But this practice came more or less to an end in late 1944, when a photoflash operated with the dropping of the 'cookie'. This measure, however, was not taken until long after the main Battle was over, and if things had been left as they were while it was in progress, a heavier concentration of high explosives would have fallen on the capital.

On the night in question, Candlish experienced a feeling of guilt when he felt tempted to do the same as some of the other captains but, like most of them, he rejected it for several reasons: he considered it would be a blatant admission of the extent of his own apprehension and, therefore, detrimental to crew morale; it entailed collusion between himself and them - and that was distasteful to him. And what if some of them objected? What would he do then? And how would he feel? It would also be an act of insubordination, justified as it may have seemed; and last of all, he wanted to drop his full load, and not just part of it, on to German slates and tiles rather than on to salt water. In any case, if their number was up, it was up, extra bomb load or not. Or so he tried to tell himself.

They still glimpsed, through gaps in the thickening cloud, the occasional 'cookie' as it erupted far below, but that was all. Then at 22.45 came a call to Candlish from Ainsworth:

"Time to turn north, Skipper. New course 061. Now!"

"Thank you Bob. It's not often we awaken the Danes - I think the last time was Hamburg. Tom, Musty, Benny - keep your eyes peeled for fighters. Shouldn't be many up this way, but best to be sure. Still awake back there, rear-gunner?"

"Oh what a wonderful dream you've just spoiled, Skipper. There I was, wi' ma hand on the knee o' this lush bit o' skirt - a right toff from Kelvinside - an' I was just ..."

"OK Benny, save it for the real thing."

Bomber Command in World War II

Unknown to them, the bombers' track had been plotted by the Luftwaffe as soon as they had left England's shores behind, but the unexpected alteration of course to the north had put the majority of the German fighters outwith their range - for the time being at any rate.

Another forty minutes went by.

"Navigator to Skipper. Danish coast should be just ahead."

"Yes, Bob, I think I can see it."

Then after a further twenty minutes:

"Navigator to Skipper. Change course now. 172."

"172 it is. Thank you."

'Happy Hannah' flew smoothly on.

"Just crossing Baltic coast now, Skipper, between Lübeck and Rostock. 125 miles to go. Change now to 112."

The Lanc's nose now pointed straight towards Berlin, straight at the heart of Hitler's Germany, at the heart they were pounding so much it would soon cease to beat. At least that's what Harris had told them.

"Skipper to gunners. Anything to be seen? Tom?"

"Nothing Skipper. But the cloud's thickening."

"Yes. Musty - what about you?"

"Can't see anything."

"Benny?"

"Not a damned thing, Skipper. Jerry must be havin' a night off. Aboot time, too, the buggers are ... Correction - ack-ack gunners doon there startin' a shootin' party.   Feel that wee shudder?''

      'Happy Hannah' had reacted a little, but only a little. Perhaps a timely warning, for further bumps and judders followed.

''Havnae got oor height right, Skipper.   Here's hopin' they're a' drunk.''

      Benny had just finished speaking when a solitary searchlight, away ahead of them, pierced a gap in the clouds.

''Ho, ho, they've put the front door light on to welcome us.'' The voice was that of Musty Coleman.

      Just as if the first searchlight had been a pre-arranged signal, dozens of others were immediately switched on, their long, probing fingers cutting almost vertically upwards through the cloud gap.

''They've got all the lights in the house on now,'' whispered Tom Courtney.

      As expected, these were the harbinger of a shower of flak.   Although Candlish had swung 'Happy Hannah' hard to starboard and missed any shells aimed in their direction, it seemed to her crew that she was trying to shake herself to bits.

''Bloody awful petrol they must have put in, Skipper.''

      Following a tremendous explosion ahead of them and to port, a huge orange ball of fire plummeted earthwards.

''Skipper to crew: That could have been a scarecrow. Won't harm anyone, we hope.''

      'Scarecrow' was the name given to the type of German shell which, rumour had it, was propelled into the main stream and exploded by a time-fuse, its purpose being to simulate the disintegration and blazing death throes of a British bomber, and give new and inexperienced crews the jitters.   But it was never actually proved that such a device existed.   In any case it was difficult to see why they should be required over

Bomber Command in World War II

places like Berlin. The real thing was there aplenty.

Candlish's ears were suddenly pierced by a yell from Musty Coleman:

"Fighter from starboard!"

His last two words were drowned out as he gave it a three-second burst. "Christ, Skipper, it's collided with something." Pieces of flaming metal cascaded all over the sky and there were tell-tale "pings" as fragments found a target in 'Happy Hannah's' fuselage.

"Party's getting into full swing. Early, too. Still fifteen minutes to go." The voice was Bob Ainsworth's.

In fact the navigator was proved to be wrong because the next ten minutes passed with nothing to worry them but the odd searchlight battery and sporadic ack-ack, but you never knew what the enemy's tactics would be on any given night. Perhaps the fighters were piling themselves up in a massive block over the capital, allowing the bombers to get as far as possible from home before pouncing in anger and then harrying them for miles when they left the city. In fact the German pilots had been instructed to keep clear of Berlin so that the ack-ack guns would be free to send up a more pulverizing barrage than ever; however, German military discipline was not always as perfect as we are led to believe and flak or no flak, the fighters aimed to single out their victims as they overflew the city, with the inevitable consequences for Bomber Command.

"Navigator to Skipper. Target straight ahead. Five minutes."

"Bomb-aimer to pilot. I can see glow through cloud. Sky markers visible. Bomb doors open."

"Roger."

Some distance in front of them, an aircraft blew up and Candlish reckoned it must have been a Pathfinder. Its load of multi-coloured flares shot all over the place and there were vivid splashes of red and green and yellow which temporarily blinded him. Indeed, every passing second took them into an ever brighter sky and by the time they were approaching Siemensstadt, one of Berlin's western suburbs and for them the target area, acre upon acre of the city was fast becoming engulfed by what would ultimately be 700 large and 600 medium-sized fires, their combined glare so intense that it punctuated the cloud barrier to form around them that eerie bluish-white glow, with its dazzling luminosity, which crews particularly associated with Berlin. Exploding shells and burning wings and fuselages served to add further to what was nothing but a madhouse in the air. For the first time since they had left base, 'Happy Hannah's' crew could see bombers everywhere, most of them with bomb doors gaping open, others with them already closed as they sheered off to starboard to make their escape. Some trailed fire and smoke as they plunged down upon the capital. As a last unwitting gesture, they would add fuel to the flames. A few parachutes could be seen, one of them going down far too fast as it was well alight.

Such sights made them all the more impatient to get rid of their load. Yawning 33-feet-long bomb doors always seemed to offer an open invitation to some devil-may-care Me 110 pilot armed with *Schräge Musik* to crawl up underneath them and pump in a few of his shells to blast them to kingdom come. They knew they would never know it had happened, but that was small comfort while they were still alive and kicking.

"Sky marker coming up, Skipper. Keep her steady. Left ... Too much - right, just a little. Hold her there, hold it ... Bombs gone!"

Their load went hurtling down towards the big industrial complex.

"Bomb doors closed!"

On being shorn of her bombs, 'Happy Hannah' jumped her usual one hundred feet and increased her speed, which was further raised when Candlish pushed all throttles fully open and threw her round in a tight turn to starboard. He was just levelling her out when there was an abrupt cry from Coleman:

"Fighter from starboard!"

Bomber Command in World War II

The mid-upper got in a rapid burst just as Candlish was throwing 'Happy Hannah' round again, but so too did the fighter. Whyte shouted that a fire had broken out by his instrument panel. Smoke began to drift along the fuselage and he doused the blaze with a fire-extinguisher. It died down in seconds and the smoke began to clear, thanks to a strong current of air sweeping in through a jagged six-inch hole where a couple of his gauges had been. Sometimes structural damage could actually be beneficial. It was no time to be choked by poisonous fumes.

The fighter, a Ju 88, did not come back. Either Coleman had got him or he had gone off to find an unsuspecting and easier victim.

Still using full revs on all four Merlins, Candlish set a provisional 275° on the compass and they headed out of Berlin, barely avoiding a vertically-plunging colleague who had appeared from above, streaming fire from wing to wing. No hope of any of them getting out. Candlish was reminded of the "See Berlin and die!" remark in the Briefing Room. Many a word was said in jest - or semi-jest, as was more likely to be the case prior to a visit to this place, even for those going to it for the first time, because they knew all about its reputation.

"Corkscrew starboard! Corkscrew!" It was Benny this time.

Candlish complied by sending 'Happy Hannah' weaving, first down to starboard, then down to port, then up to starboard and up to port, only for her to be straddled by a fighter, an Me 110 this time, just when he was straightening her out again. Shells raked the fuselage and the awful din rose above the noise of the engines. Peter Whyte went over backwards into the gangway and rolled on to his stomach. As soon as they were back on an even keel, Ainsworth turned him over. His oxygen mask and his helmet had been torn away and the navigator stared aghast at what was left of his face and neck. He tried to swallow back his sickness, unsuccessfully, struggled against his nausea and grabbed a chart which he threw over Whyte's head. Hardly able to speak, he staggered up to Candlish, tapped him on the shoulder and indicated by sign language and his own distraught features that they no longer had a flight-engineer. Peter Whyte had dropped his last load on Germany.

Candlish involuntarily tightened his grip on the stick and stared straight ahead. Then shook himself and turned his gaze to right and left. Ainsworth went back to his table - and took longer than usual to give the new heading:

The Great Ingratitude

"Stay on present course for the moment, Skipper. New one coming up pronto."

A Lanc flying above them and a short distance ahead suddenly transformed itself into a huge ball of fire. The brightness of the sky was still intense but less so and Candlish thought he glimpsed a dark shape slip beneath another bomber over to port. This was more or less confirmed when this aircraft also disintegrated in a great shower of flame. Must have been one of the jazz boys. The poor bastards could so easily have been them.

"Tegel Lake right beneath us, Skipper. Can see a fair bit of it. That's why there are no flames." Marc Robertson, who was now watching the dead engineer's instrument panel, shouted:

"Oil pressure in port outer very low, Skipper."

He had hardly finished his sentence when the engine in question appeared to run amok and began to emit a horrendous, high-pitched whine. Candlish slammed the requisite throttle fully shut.

"Feather it, Marc" It could be a life-saver if individual members could carry out duties normally the lot of someone else.

"Port outer feathered."

As the glow from Berlin paled in the distance, fighter opposition had apparently disappeared. But perhaps it was only an interlude while the machines returned to their bases to refuel and reload. 110s and 88s and 190s could soon catch up.

Soon, however, it became quite obvious why there were none. The cloud had thinned and miles of sky were abruptly illuminated by dozens and dozens of searchlights. Candlish swung 'Happy Hannah' round to starboard and increased speed on all three good engines.

"Expect some rocking now. They don't put on a display like that to show us the way home."

Ack-ack shells came flying up in massive salvoes, and the Lanc lurched violently and continually in the turbulent air. It didn't seem possible to get through such a barrage without feeling its brunt, and it wasn't. She lunged when a shell blew a hole between the starboard engines and sprayed metal far and wide, some of which penetrated the fuselage but miraculously injured no one. Candlish managed to heave 'Hannah' up again and fought to keep her level. Another shell hit the fuselage a few feet in front of Benny who, surrounded by his ammo belts, was out of his turret as quickly as the confined space allowed, and succeeded in extinguishing the resultant fire. More hits were registered on wings and body, control cables were damaged, and the Lanc was bucked about like a buoy in a storm-tossed sea. She became a handful to hold straight and level, and base was a long way off; and, like each of the other heavies in the vicinity, she was on her own. The close proximity of friends meant nothing, as they were powerless to help and knew that every passing second could put them in an identical situation. Friends just watched and hoped.

But the amount of flak diminished, then petered out altogether. Just as well, as another telling hit might well have been the coup de grâce. But, as someone once said, when the going gets tough, the tough get going. 'Happy Hannah' was tough, and she kept going, even if she was more or less just hanging together.

"Navigator to Skipper: Difficult to say exactly where we are. My air speed indicator and altimeter are both u/s. Will try to get a pin-point."

"Skipper here, Bob. Sizeable stretch of water coming up - Lake Gulper?"

"Give me a second, Skipper. ... Yes, its Gulper all right. We're going too far north. Hold on ... New course 270. Will try to get a wind and give you an alteration. Your air speed indicator OK Skipper?"

"Impossible to say. Inclined to go mad at times. Would judge air speed to be around 180."

The starboard-inner spluttered, then picked up again. Then came another splutter, followed by a sort of wail. Then it stopped.

"Feather that one too, Marc."

"Starboard-inner feathered. Are you managing, Skipper?"

The Great Ingratitude

"Just about. How far to the coast, navigator?"

"I reckon just over 200 to the Zuider Zee."

"Right, if we're attacked again we won't have much chance. We're going down into that cloud."

As 'Happy Hannah' put mile after mile behind her, everyone's confidence grew. But then Candlish found he was getting reduced power on the starboard-outer, although it seemed to be turning over smoothly enough. He judged that their air speed must now be a good way below the 180 mark. That starboard-outer had to keep going. And the port-inner. They both did.

"Skipper to navigator. I just glimpsed water below. Dutch coast?"

"I reckon it's the inner shore of the Zuider Zee. North Sea in a few minutes."

That was good. It meant that the Continental land mass was behind them and, hostile as the North Sea could be, there was something almost neutral about it by comparison; and at least if they were forced to ditch, there was, with every passing minute, as good a chance, and eventually a better one, of being picked up out of the drink by RAF Air Sea Rescue, with their fast motor launches, as by the Germans. Each half-minute brought them more than a mile nearer home, even at this speed.

"Skipper to crew: We're losing height. Chuck out everything we're not likely to need. And that includes your sextant Bob. You always say it's no bloody use anyway. Any idea of a more accurate course?"

"Sorry, Skipper. We should be within Gee range by now but it must be u/s. Difficult to work out a wind when I don't know the airspeed. But if you steer 260 we shouldn't be far out; somewhere around 150 miles to base; little idea of ETA, if that matters."

"It doesn't. It's getting old Happy down that counts. They can keep our breakfasts hot."

Bomber Command in World War II

They began to wonder if that would be necessary some 100 miles and 40 minutes later when the starboard-outer, which had continued to run satisfactorily if not perfectly, started to cough and then to sound as if something large and heavy had gone berserk inside it. It too, was feathered. They began to lose height much faster.

"How far d'you reckon now, Bob?"

"Maybe 40 miles to the coast, but anywhere between 20 and 60."

"Right. Skipper to crew: We're down to something like 6,000 feet and losing height pretty fast. But we should soon be crossing the English coast. So no need to worry about swimming. If any of you want to jump, better start getting yourselves ready."

"But what about you, Skipper? Does that mean you're going to jump after us?"

"No, I'm going to attempt a landing. But all of you bale out if you want to. It's likely to be safer."

"Count me out, Skipper. We've survived your bloody landings so far."

"Me too, Skipper, I'll choose the lesser of the two evils!"

"Aye, you've gradually knocked oot most o' ma teeth, anyway. I've no' that many left."

"Nice lot, aren't you? We're all staying together, then?"

"You bet."

"Sure are."

"We always have, and we're still here."

"We're no' leavin' ye now, Skipper. We're a' goin' to walk oot o' this auld lass in one bunch!"

The Great Ingratitude

"God," thought Candlish, "it's all up to me," and set his teeth for the last hurdle. The `auld lass', as Benny had called her, was in a bad way, but he was determined he would hold her straight to the bitter end and put her down, somehow, and bring her to a halt in as large a piece as possible. He kept telling himself she was a Lanc, that she would make it.

"Light's a lot better. What's that village down there, Bob?"

"Hitcham."

"How far to base?"

"About 60."

"Much too far. We can't be far from Stradishall, can we?"

"No, just hold on ... yes, alter course five degrees to port. 16 miles."

"Right. See to it, Marc. Tell them we need to get down as soon as possible - just airborne and no more, instruments u/s, aircraft hardly controllable. That should be enough."

"Roger."

Fortunately, Stradishall's Stirlings were still out on a long night training flight and not due back for some time. Permission to land was granted and all airfield emergency services alerted to prepare for a crash-landing by an operational Lancaster. A searchlight pierced the sky as a guide and the runway lights were switched on, even although by now it was almost fully day. Ambulances and fire-tenders stood ready, their engines running, to tear along the perimeter.

"Right, everyone, I can't promise this will be like dropping on to a feather bed. You might be about to lose those remaining teeth, Benny. Come up here beside us. Everyone to observe emergency landing procedures."

The runway came into view, the lights faint but still visible.

Bomber Command in World War II

"Runway about 3 miles ahead. I'm having a job keeping her straight, so hold tight. Little idea of air speed. Having to judge it by the ground. Hydraulics possibly gone and can't risk just one wheel coming down, so it has to be a belly-landing. As soon as we come to a stop, get out as soon as you can. Leave Peter where he is - doesn't matter about him for the time being. Just get out. Right, here goes. If you haven't prayed before, this might be a good time to start."

They were flying at just over 90 mph and very close to stalling speed. Then the port-inner rattled and banged and gave up. With all thrust gone, 'Happy Hannah' dropped towards the tarmac, hitting it seconds later amid a horrendous noise of tearing metal as bits of her flew off in all directions. She, or what was left of her, slewed round and crunched to a stop.

The crew, all bashed and bruised but, incredibly, with nothing more serious than a twisted ankle suffered by Tom Courtney and facial lacerations by Candlish (the latter not nearly as bad as they looked) were helped out of the aircraft by brave and willing hands - no one was overfond of going anywhere near a bomber which had just crash-landed - and led quickly away to a safe distance. But there was no fire. It was as if 'Happy Hannah' had looked after them until the very last moment. Well, nearly all of them. Peter Whyte was placed in an ambulance as the rest watched.

They were ushered into a second 'blood wagon' and driven to the camp hospital to have their various injuries examined and treated. An hour after landing, they were still deaf after nearly nine hours of engine noise, still unsteady on their feet after the continual vibration. Their own base was immediately informed of their whereabouts and their condition and they were told that transport would come for them by 9 o'clock. They would be debriefed as soon as they got back. Then some sleep, if they were lucky.

They were to learn later that the operation, which had dropped over 2,600 tons of bombs on the city (then a record for one night) and which was to be 'Happy Hannah's' last, had cost 43 heavy bombers, excluding their own (26 of them of the same breed and the rest Halifaxes), two of them from their own squadron; that two of its aircrew (Peter and a young bomb-aimer) had been brought back dead; that four others who, if they did recover, would never be any use for anything, and were already on their way to places where such obscenities were treated. So there would

The Great Ingratitude

be a further twenty empty beds in their billet that night. But not as bad as in the raid against Leipzig four nights later, when 78 out of a force of 823 was the cost and the Halifax IIs made their last operational trip to Germany; not as bad, either, as the final major attack on Berlin on March 24/25, when 72 out of 811 were lost. Not to mention the Nuremberg affair six nights after that (Chapter 13), when 96 out of 795 failed to return and many more were destroyed or severely damaged on getting back to England. It was hardly surprising that during the Gulf War, former Bomber Command aircrew couldn't help but ponder over reports that a single Tornado and its two crew members were missing.

After some breakfast, Candlish asked to be driven out with his crew to have what they knew would be a last look at 'Happy Hannah'. They stood in a silent group beside her, each with his own thoughts, but which weren't really his own at all, as they were common to each and every one of them; broken and useless she now was, but she had seen them back even when she was in her death throes and deposited them, if none too gently, on safe home soil. She had taken them to the Reich a score of times, to the industrial towns of the Ruhr in the west to Berlin and Magdeburg in the east, from Bremen and Hamburg in the north to Munich and Stuttgart in the south and left her mark in the form of some 140 tons of high explosives and incendiaries. With all her electronic equipment, she had cost an enormous sum of money, £35,000 - at a time when a workman's average wage was £3 per week. She had also cost a friend's life. But what had she cost the enemy? How much material destruction had she caused? How much terror had she created? How many Germans had she killed or maimed? How did you assess such things? You couldn't, because you would never know. Perhaps just as well.

How long would things go on like this? Apparently inexhaustible supplies would ensure that the shelves were restocked. Candlish's crew would get a new Lanc and they would get a new engineer. That was the order of things. You just soldiered on.

For Candlish and his team, it was hardly an appropriate moment to hear, just two days later when 'Happy Hannah' was being towed away in pieces for salvage and scrap, a certain announcement from higher authority. This stated that a Lanc had to go to a German city only once to wipe off its own capital cost, and that the results of all subsequent sorties were clear profit. So after Berlin and Hamburg and all the others, 'Happy Hannah' must have repaid herself several times over. Good for her! According to these economy-minded bloody civil servant idiots, few of whom had ever seen a bomber station, another 20 or so 'Happy Hannahs' could be produced at no real extra cost. At no real extra cost? And what about Peter Whyte? Had he cancelled out the cost of his training, estimated by Harris even in those days at £10,000, after completing three or four of his ops.?

The crew couldn't have been due their six days' leave at a better moment. Six long weeks had passed since their last one, and these had been the most hectic they had ever known. They felt like old men, exhausted in mind and body.

After penning a letter to Australia, Candlish went to his beloved Perthshire, where the spring salmon would be running. Courtney took himself off to bleak and dismal Salford, but heaven to him because that's where his wife and little boy were; Robertson to Bristol and a few quiet trips into the Somerset countryside; Coleman back to London's Camden Town and perhaps the odd game of football; Ainsworth to picturesque Knaresborough to spend most of his time with a mother who was still heart-broken over the loss of an older son; Ramage to the rough and tumble of Clydebank, to the noise of the shipyards and the noise of the pubs; and Whyte to a village cemetery in Suffolk, on the other side of the world from his Queensland home. By the time Candlish's letter arrived there, the flowers they had placed beside him would be well and truly withered.

***

Berlin. A short word. Just two syllables. Pronounced in the batting of an eye. But perhaps the most emotive word ever uttered by thousands of aircrew on a hundred bomber stations, because Berlin was the most harrowing experience in the brief but tumultuous history of RAF Bomber Command. Nuremberg, as we shall see, was bad. The Ruhr was bad. There were others that were bad. But for sheer sustained ferocity and stress and strain the Battle of Berlin eclipsed everything else. Two decades later, one 5 Group navigator, who had survived half-a-dozen operations to the Nazi capital, summed up his experiences graphically and succinctly: "You felt you had been to Hell and back, and each trip seemed to be worse than the last; Berlin tore at your guts and at times you thought you had been thrown into a cement-mixer. Quite frankly, I don't think I was ever the same man again; even after twenty years, I can relive it just as if it happened last night. Berlin will be with me for ever."

The Great Ingratitude

The Battle lasted four and a half months, until the night of March 24/25 1944 when, as a sort of farewell gesture from the heavy bomber squadrons, 811 aircraft, 577 of them Lancasters, set off. In order to offset the dangers of collision and to paralyse the defences, they went in at heights varying between 19,000 and 23,000 feet in five two-minute waves of up to 180 and in the space of only eight minutes, they rained down 6,000 tons of bombs. It was an operation which bore a strong resemblance to the Nuremberg tragedy six nights later (Chapter 13), in so far as a north wind, not forecast and of unprecedented force, carried many aircraft miles off course, especially on the return flight, when some of the bombers which overflew the Ruhr paid the penalty. The markers dropped over Berlin were blown away to the south-western suburbs and it was there that a large number of dwelling houses were destroyed and 20,000 people dehoused; however, big industrial plants were also hit and the raid could not have done much for the morale of the Führer's personal SS unit, the élite Leibstandarte Adolf Hitler, whose depot was left in a shambolic state. But once again, Berlin showed itself to be capable of absorbing no end of punishment - the Berlin Philharmonic continued to perform, in spite of numerous Mosquito attacks, until March 1945 - and of handing it out as well. This last major raid, in which the German defences accounted for 72 bombers, revealed without a shadow of doubt the growing strength of the opposition. Harris was pounding Berlin, as he said he would, but by God, at what a price. During that winter period alone, Bomber Command flew 9,111 sorties against the capital, including 1,647 within ten days. It lost 587 aircraft, mostly Lancasters, in the process, and a further 859 suffered varying degrees of damage. It also lost some 4,000 airmen. When peace came, it was found that almost 6,500 acres (33%) of the city had been destroyed, some of it on other RAF raids and some during Mustang-escorted daylight attacks by the Americans, but by far the most of it during Harris's winter campaign. Altogether, Berlin had to cope with a massive 50,000 tons of high explosives and incendiaries; and again a high proportion of that load fell during the so-called 'Battle'.

After Hamburg, Harris had said that the destruction of Berlin would cost 400-500 bombers but that it would cost Germany the war. It had cost Bomber Command alone nearly 600 aircraft, and Germany still showed no sign of capitulation.

In order to appreciate Bomber Command's overall effort during that hectic winter, it should be borne in mind that while the focal point of attack was Berlin, no fewer than 11,113 sorties were flown against other targets, notably Mannheim, Frankfurt-on-Main, Nuremberg, Leipzig, Brunswick and Schweinfurt, which brought the total tally of aircraft lost to 1,047, with 1,682 damaged or written off in England. January was the blackest month of the whole year, claiming 352 bombers missing and 416 damaged, with well over 2,000 aircrew dead or taken prisoner. It was during this period that Harris calculated a man's chances of completing a first tour of operations as less than one in three.

Although the Battle of Berlin was fought mainly by Lancasters (7,249 sorties compared with 1,644 by Halifaxes and 50 by Stirlings), the vital part played by the twin-engined de Havilland Mosquito as a Pathfinder was out of all proportion to the number sent (156). This beautifully sleek and remarkable machine - of which 7,781 were built - was away ahead of its time and was much admired and envied by the Luftwaffe, including Goering himself. It was built largely of wood (by redundant furniture-makers!) hence often referred to as the 'Wooden Wonder', had a ceiling of 36,000 feet (yet often got up to almost 40,000) and a maximum speed in level flight of 425 mph. Despite its apparent frail method of construction, it could take quite a hammering from ack-ack and cannon shells, was easy to repair and could be employed in any capacity. In its many different versions, it was fighter, bomber, fighter-bomber, intruder, reconnaissance aircraft, Pathfinder, ship destroyer, minelayer, courier and 'weather-eye', and so fast that when engaged on certain duties it carried no armament - which enhanced both its speed and performance considerably. It was much employed by the Pathfinder squadrons (Chapter 12) and could carry a 4000 pound HE all the way to the German capital - a superior load to that of the American B-17 (Flying Fortress). So elusive and troublesome did the tough little 'Mossie' become to the German defences that any Luftwaffe pilot who shot one down was credited with the destruction of two aircraft.

The Mosquito had both astounded and fascinated an audience of senior RAF officers when its designer and test pilot, Geoffrey de Havilland, had thrown the prototype all over the sky as early as November, 1940. But the four-engined bomber (the first of them, the Stirling, made its maiden flight in May, 1939) was the new Air Staff concept in an Air Offensive which would carry the war on to enemy territory and the twin-engined machine was on its way out; consequently, the Mosquito, despite its scintillating performance, was looked upon by many as a retrograde step and it was only thanks to the foresight of others that it was eventually put into production and issued to squadrons in

The Great Ingratitude

November 1941.   The only regret was the delay that could have been avoided.

Bomber Command Mosquitoes alone flew 39,795 sorties and dropped 26,867 tons of bombs (including 10,000 'cookies'), a tonnage which exceeded the total delivered by all of the Command's earlier aircraft right from the Fairey Battles and Blenheims to the Manchesters and Fortresses, and second only to that of the four-engined heavies - and all for the loss of only 389 machines.

But the Mosquito's main role, as far as Bomber Command was concerned, was as a target-marking aircraft, and this function it performed superbly throughout the entire Battle of Berlin and on most large-scale attacks on the Reich.   But it did much more: it flew all over Germany almost every night, usually in small formations but visiting enough cities to keep the air defences and emergency services on their toes, having them all guessing as to the real destination of the main stream, disrupting the much-needed sleep of millions of military personnel and war workers and invariably leaving evidence of its visit in the shape of a 4,000-pounder.   During daylight, the Mosquito was an indefatigable will-o-the wisp which appeared from nowhere, darted here, there and everywhere, a hornet which went in fast, came out fast (in low-level attacks it was invariably on the distant horizon before the defences got their act together) and rarely failed to leave its sting behind.   So apart from being a nocturnal nuisance, it was also a daytime destroyer, in which capacity it attacked, unarmed, hundreds of small and difficult precision targets at zero feet (it could hardly miss) all over Europe, dropping delayed action bombs on factories and fuel dumps and bridges and railway junctions and scaring the living daylights out of German soldiers and civilians of all nationalities as it thundered just over their heads at fantastic speed.   Each sortie flown deep into enemy territory at 20-50 feet was an arduous if exhilarating business, and the ultimate test of skill on the part of both pilot and navigator, the former having to climb or bank steeply to avoid obstacles such as church steeples and high tension cables, and the latter to identify pin-points - an exceedingly difficult task when streaking along just above the ground. High-flying if need be, and practically impossible to catch at any altitude, the Mosquito ruled the roost in German skies until the appearance of the Luftwaffe's jets, but which (as we shall see in Chapter 17), came too late to be of any real significance.   By then the Mossie had played its part.

And it was a part it played right till the moment when Berlin was squirming in its final agonies: like a terrier, the Mossie would not let go. Raids on the capital by groups of 6-80 Mosquitoes went on continually until April 20/21, only hours before Marshal Zhukov's leading tank units entered the eastern suburbs, and while Hitler, limping around in the strange atmosphere of his bunker beneath the Chancellery, apparently impervious to the stark reality of the situation, insisted that the few remaining members of the Reichstag staff inspected, for the umpteenth time, the model for the rebuilding of his home town of Linz. Starting at nightfall, attacks had been made at intervals by a total of 76 aircraft and it is quite possible that the Führer of the rapidly disintegrating Third Reich, due to die by his own hand only nine days later, heard the thump of the last bombs to be dropped by the RAF on his shambles of a capital. These were the four 500-pound HE which fell from a Mossie, piloted by Flying Officer A C Austin and navigated by Flying Officer P Moorhead, at exactly 03.14 hours German time. It was perhaps fitting that the aircraft which had plagued Berlin almost nightly for years should have made its presence felt almost at the very end...

The Mosquito was, in fact, such an efficient example of aeronautical engineering that, at one point, well on in the war, an intriguing theory started to go the rounds of the bomber stations: one Mossie was worth seven Lancs! This astounding assertion was reached on the grounds that the smaller machine carried at least half the bomb load of the Lanc on deep penetration flights into Germany; it cost £12,000, about one-third the price of the Lanc; it suffered only one-tenth of the Lancaster's casualties and required a crew of only two (pilot and navigator) compared to the heavy's seven. Therefore, as far as dropping bombs was concerned, two Mossies and four airmen could do the same job as one Lanc with seven crew members aboard. That meant about £10,000 was saved on production costs and £30,000 on aircrew training - but on the latter outlay much more in fact because losses of Mosquito personnel were relatively very small, and accordingly fewer men required to be trained. Some mathematical genius had taken all these factors into account and arrived at the formula: one Mosquito = seven Lancasters!

All this may have sounded like a very convincing argument, but the Mossie could not carry a Tallboy or a Grand Slam, and a number of important precision targets were destroyed by these huge weapons; more importantly, however, Mosquito losses were so much smaller because many of their operations were surprise low-level attacks or high-speed reconnaissance, with only a single or a few aircraft involved. Had they appeared over strongly defended cities in Lancaster-size

The Great Ingratitude

formations, they would then have been more vulnerable to both anti-aircraft fire and fighters. Nevertheless, it was an interesting hypothesis, with perhaps more than a grain of truth in it, and it certainly bore testimony to the many admirable qualities of a machine which proved its worth and versatility over and over again.

The degree to which the Mosquito tormented the Luftwaffe was illustrated in comic manner in one of Lord Haw-Haw's broadcasts when he told his listeners that because the U-boats were sending so much of Britain's raw materials to the bottom of the Atlantic, she was being forced to make her aeroplanes out of wood. He must have been ignorant of the fact that the balsa used in the Mossie's construction came from the forests of Ecuador, the birch from Canada and the spruce from Alaska. Or if he did know, he conveniently omitted to mention it...

***

Some senior officers who were involved in the planning and execution of the Battle maintained that Berlin was more than a failure, that it was no less than a defeat. Air Vice Marshall Ralph Cochrane, Commander of 5 Group, said: "Berlin won. It was just too tough a nut to crack." Air Commodore Bufton, Chief of Bomber Operations, described Harris's determination to destroy the city as "that of a gambler doubling up on each losing throw." Harris himself, being the man he was, did not openly admit that Berlin had been too much for Bomber Command, but the emphasis he put on the difficulties it had presented as a target suggested that he had found the results disappointing; and it was obvious even to him that it was no second Hamburg, where much the same acreage had been laid waste with far fewer sorties and only one-tenth of the casualties. Other critics, trying to balance the undeniable vastness of the devastation caused against the heavy cost, opted for a good draw. That was probably being over-generous towards Bomber Command in view of the fact that the city continued to function and to produce right until the end of the war, even if on a much reduced scale, but, irrespective of who was right, Berlin was destined to be one of the most controversial actions in a campaign which itself was highly controversial.

But at least one definite fact emerged from the Battle: Bomber Command had learned in its formative years that deep daytime penetration into Germany was nothing short of suicide. Now it had also learned that, faced with an even stronger and better equipped fighter force, determined to defend not only the capital, but all major towns at all costs, it was becoming much too costly at night as well.

That was the crux of the matter. Berlin was just too redoubtable a proposition to be dealt a knock-out blow. Forgetting the inevitable comparison with Hamburg, enormous havoc had nevertheless been wrought on factories, dwelling-houses and apartment blocks (one-third of all homes were rendered uninhabitable by March 1944), on gas and electrical supplies, on public buildings and on communications; thousands of soldiers and civilians, who could have been more profitably employed elsewhere, had been drafted into the city in ever-increasing numbers both for its defence and the maintenance of essential services. And, although its morale did not crack, it must have been sorely tried. No human being can put up with continual heavy aerial bombardment and remain unaffected. But was the price, as many claimed, too high? Because the price was hundreds and hundreds of British heavy bombers which lay in pieces in and around the city, all over Brandenburg and Lower Saxony, and in the icy waters of the North Sea. The price was the thousands of young men who lay, often coffinless and nameless, in cemeteries large and small, in communal graves and even in back gardens, all over the Third Reich.

Should Harris, in the November-March period, have concentrated solely on Berlin and also poured down into it the massive tonnage he had despatched during that time to Mannheim and Leverkusen and Frankfurt and Augsburg and all the others? Had he fallen victim to his own determination to give Germany's largest towns no rest? Should he have put all his bombs in one basket as he had done at Cologne in May 1942? In that case he might, as he had hoped, have "wrecked Berlin from end to end." Perhaps. But he had mistakenly believed that, with the considerable forces then at his disposal, he could annihilate Berlin without giving any respite to other cities. The Second World War had its share of `ifs' and `buts' and even with that blessed faculty called hindsight, it is impossible to know the answer. And even if Harris had succeeded in wiping the Nazi capital from the map, it is highly debatable whether this alone would have brought Germany to her knees.

Mind you, it would have helped.

Chapter 5

THE MORALITY OF ALTITUDE

One of the most controversial issues raised by saturation bombing was that of civilian casualties (which again loomed large in the Gulf War). As far as the Second World War is concerned, it remains a question to which neither time nor hindsight has brought an acceptable answer and there are many who, after all these years, still point an accusing finger at an unrepentant Bomber Command for what they term a display of acute moral insensitivity.

Dr Noble Frankland, addressing the Royal United Services Institution in 1961, expressed his own view in unambiguous terms:

"The great immorality open to us in 1940 and 1941 was to lose the war against Hitler's Germany. To have abandoned the only means of direct attack which we had at our disposal would have been a long step in that direction."

On November 26, 1943, the Marquis of Salisbury wrote to Sir Archibald Sinclair (Secretary of State for Air):

"Sir Arthur Harris really gives one a shake. These attacks are to go on 'until the heart of Nazi Germany ceases to beat'. This would seem to bring us up short against the repeated Government declarations that we are bombing only military and industrial targets... there is a great deal of evidence that makes some of us afraid that we are losing moral superiority to the Germans."

Sinclair replied:"There has been no change in the Government's bombing policy. Our aim is the progressive dislocation and destruction of the German military, industrial and economic system. I have never pretended that it is possible to pursue this aim without inflicting terrible casualties on the civilian population of Germany. But neither I, nor any responsible leader on behalf of the Government, has ever gloated over the destruction of German homes... You told me that it is Sir Arthur Harris's answer to my message which has shaken you; and, in particular, his reference to the heart of Germany ceasing to beat and you interpret that as meaning that the `residential heart of Berlin is to cease to beat'. But

Bomber Command in World War II

Harris is an airman, and thinks of Germany in terms of war. He thinks of Berlin as the heart of the German war organism.''

There were certainly elements in nearly all walks of British life who raised horror-stricken voices over the nightly occurrence during which men, women and children were blown to bits or roasted alive. This view was particularly prevalent as the campaign intensified from the beginning of 1944 onwards (85% of the total tonnage of bombs were delivered during the final 16 months of the war). Some objectors even went so far as to claim that Bomber Command crews were committing, on a scale ten, nay, twenty fold as great, the very acts of terror and indiscriminate slaughter that the Luftwaffe had visited on umpteen towns and cities and to which the SS and the Gestapo were subjecting the enslaved peoples of Europe. Deep concern was also expressed in some quarters about the destruction of historic buildings and beautiful monuments, and to those critics it was pointed out that in the carpet bombing of huge areas, which was Bomber Command's policy, it was strategically impossible to show consideration for such treasures. (When the Vatican asked the Allies not to bomb the Eternal City, the reply it received was in the same vein: if the destruction of a target was considered to be militarily desirable, then that target would be destroyed, irrespective of its proximity to no matter what; that was perhaps sad, but as far as they were concerned, was of little consequence. Nothing was to delay progress towards victory).

It is true that in the early days of Bomber Command, crews were not allowed to drop their loads where they would be a threat to civilians - even docks were avoided and ships could be attacked only at sea. But as total war developed and with it the Command's potential, it became clear that the launching of an aerial bombardment of the magnitude envisaged could not preclude human death and suffering on an unprecedented scale. Destruction of property and destruction of life were indiscerptible; it was quite impossible to have the one without the other, and what had to be avoided at all costs was a repeat of the out-pouring of British blood in 1914-18. If the struggle against the Third Reich could be switched from a war of attrition on the ground to a war in the air, in which Germany would take the brunt, so be it; no more Passchendaeles, no more Ypres; and the desert would be in Germany this time.

***

The Great Ingratitude

Candlish and his crew returned from leave and arranged to meet that same night in the Sickle and Scythe, not far from the airfield. An hour or two together in the pub was the best way of settling in again.

They sat down at a table in a corner of the lounge and some of them spoke briefly about how they had spent their time. On the whole there was little of interest to report.

"And what about you Benny? Did you manage to behave yourself up there in Glasgow?" The question came from Marc Robertson.

"Ach, nothin' much tae tell ye. You know very well the Skipper here keeps tellin' me tae keep ma nose clean an' that's what I always try tae dae. Mind you, there was one nicht I nearly forgot an' I could easily have broken somebody else's. There I was, standin' peacefully havin' a quiet think tae maself at the bar in the Puffer doon beside the water when this joker I ken came staggerin' up tae me an' said:

"Brylcream boys! Fuckin' RAF! Fuckin' RIFF-RAFF! think y'er great, eh? think y'er the bees knees, don't ye?"

"And what happened, Benny?"

"I tried tae keep ma temper an' just told him that if he didnae get oot o' ma sight in a couple o' seconds I would knock his teeth so far doon his throat that he would have tae eat through his arse."

"My God. And then?"

"Ach, he knew better. He disappeared oot the door in a shower o' sawdust."

For those unaware of the amenities offered by the less salubrious Glasgow hostelries of those bygone days, spitoons were placed at convenient intervals on the floor and surrounded by a liberal layer of sawdust. If the spitoon was missed, which it usually was, the sawdust served to absorb the heavy bronchial phlegm frequently ejected by those who over-indulged in full-strength Capstan or Woodbines or rolled their own, the latter often made from the contents of fag-ends picked up from the gutters.

Bomber Command in World War II

After a short period during which they all seemed content just to sip their beer quietly, Tom Courtney mentioned that on the Sunday before his return he had accompanied his mother to church in Salford at her request. In his sermon the vicar had gone on at some length about British bombers killing innocent German civilians. It was something, Courtney said, that he himself had had on his mind for some time and what he had heard from the mouth of an eloquent speaker had not made him feel any better.

"I can't help it. I just don't feel happy about it."

"I'm glad you've said that, Tom. I've been having similar thoughts myself for some time now. I don't think of it when we're on an op., just sometimes when I'm shaving or something." It was Bob Ainsworth who spoke.

"Yes, bombing factories is one thing, even if we kill war workers. That, I suppose, is fair enough as they are helping Hitler's war effort. But we are going far beyond that. We must be. Housing estates, big tenement blocks, hospitals, old folks' homes, the lot. We're slaughtering women and children who have nothing to do with Hitler."

Musty Coleman chipped in:

"But they killed ours in the Blitz. They kill everywhere. Look at Poland and Russia and ..."

"Two wrongs don't make a right."

Benny detested clichés:

"In this case they bloody do. I heard aboot some minister shoutin' the odds just like that from his pulpit up on Loch Lomondside somewhere. What do the likes o' them know aboot it? I wish we could have taken them tae Berlin the last time. Look, Tom, I can only speak for maself, but I sit up there aboot half a fuckin' mile frae the rest o' ye, wi' only the angels, or, more likely the Devil for company, night after night, in that bloody refrigerator they ca' a gun-turret, trussed up like a Christmas turkey wi' its days numbered, a' ready tae be roasted, an' you're sayin' we should feel guilty. I've had enough o' this fuckin' war an' if bombin' Germany, civilians an' all, is goin' tae shorten it, as Butch says, an' gets me back tae Clydeside an' pumpin' in rivets, that's fine. I used tae think it was a helluva life, but it was a picnic compared tae this. At least ye knew ye were goin' home every night, no' tae much maybe, but ye didnae get buggers tryin' tae blow ye tae simithereens two or three times a week. Maybe some bastard would have a swipe at ye in the pub noo an' again wi' a bottle, but that was all. An' dinnae forget this - I saw them pilin' up the coffins in the street - big ones an' a lot o' wee ones as well - at the time o' the Clydebank blitz, so I dinnae see why we should bother too much. An' dinnae forget that these bloody Germans could be puttin' us in a wooden box any day - or just throwin' what's left of us intae a bloody hole in the ground, more likely.''

It was true that ministers of religion stood up, usually in rural pulpits, throughout the land and condemned Bomber Command for the 'crimes against humanity' already mentioned. Usually these opinions were expressed in places like Mallaig or Aboyne, in St Ives or Ambleside, in Trawsfyndd or Cwmduad, where the inhabitants had probably never heard the ominous wailing of an air-raid siren. Many aircrew reacted to these tirades with feelings which ranged from mild irritation to anger; and Benny's reaction was as vehement as any:

''They're a shower o' sanct...sanctimonious - is that the right word? - auld goats. They stand up there in their pulpits lookin' an' soundin' like craws in the moult as they croak awa' or bleet like a sheep lost oot on the heather. I would like tae take the auld buggers wi' us on oor next trip, an' then on the next one, and then next, an' if they hadnae died o' the jitters by then, I would chuck them oot wi' the bomb-load. Stupid bastards.''

Tom Courtney couldn't suppress a smile:

''You're a hard wee man, Benny!''

''I was brought up in a hard world, an' it'll be a lot harder if these bastards beat us."

''We're also destroying a lot of beautiful and famous buildings which will be gone for ever. We're bombing history.''

Bomber Command in World War II

"We're bombin' fuckin' Germany. We're making history."

"What do you think, Skipper, you haven't said anything?"

"I know a lot of the crews are aware of what is being said, often by prominent people, and are hurt by the fact that there is seldom any mention of the risks we ourselves run, as if the Germans were the only ones who were suffering. And remember, it was these same Germans who put Hitler into power. Now, I'm afraid, they're having to pay for it."

"Yes, but would you walk into German homes armed with a flame-thrower and incinerate a mother and her children as they lay in their beds? Let's face it, that's exactly what we're doing - burning and choking and battering them to death. Look what we did to Hamburg. Look at Berlin. The fact that we don't see the results from 20,000 feet up is why we keep on doing it. And we're too much concerned with our own survival even to think about it. But we're doing it just the same. We would refuse to do it at ground level."

With these words, Courtney anticipated a phrase which was to come into vogue some time later - 'the morality of altitude'.

"Yes, you have a point, and perhaps a good one. But, brutal as it may sound, killing civilians is coincidental. We are not trying to kill them. As Benny says, Butch believes he'll win us the war by turning entire German cities into rubble. That way we hit all the factories and lessen the effort against us. It is an unfortunate facet of war, and of this one in particular, that whole populations are involved. Civilians are the victims of circumstance. If Hitler had a bomber force comparable to ours, he would be doing exactly the same thing. He's already done it, hasn't he? It's war which is all wrong, Tom. It brings out the worst in everybody. I understand your feelings, but try to think of it this way: we are killing thousands of ordinary Germans, but it is up to us to bring this war to an end as soon as possible, otherwise many more people will die - our own, Germans, and those who live in the occupied countries. It would be a great mistake to allow this to happen, and the greatest mistake of all would be for us to lose this war. God knows what would become of us then. I think I've already told you all enough about the Nazis for you to know what I'm talking about."

The Great Ingratitude

Courtney appreciated the raw logic of his Skipper's argument, but knew that what he was doing would go on disturbing him. Indeed, long after hostilities had ceased it began to haunt him. But he was one of the unfortunates. Most of the airmen of Bomber Command were concerned primarily with self-preservation. They had quite enough to contend with as it was, and if any of them were permanently affected by their experiences in the years that followed, and many of them were, it was mainly due to their long period of fear-laden existence or to physical injury, rather than to any feeling of guilt.

Little of worth can be added to what Candlish said. War brutalises human beings irrespective of race, irrespective of background. In fact if this were not so, they would not be able to participate in it efficiently and that is one of the unpalatable factors that are part and parcel of the whole evil process. Hitler's Reich had to be defeated. There was no room for half measures, which meant that the kid gloves had to be removed and all the stops pulled out.

Bomber Command complied to the letter: there was no other way.

Chapter 6

BUTCH

Air Chief Marshal (later to become Marshal of the Royal Air Force) Sir Arthur Harris, KCB; OBE; AFC; succeeded Air Chief Marshal Sir Richard Peirse as Commander in Chief of Bomber Command on February 23, 1942. His appointment came at a moment when the Command, which had achieved little up till then (apart from its role in helping to dissuade Hitler from invading Britain for the time being at any rate by destroying large numbers of barges in the Channel ports, and several small and generally abortive attacks on targets in Germany) was gaining gradually, if still slowly, in strength and purpose. By the end of the Harris era, and the war itself, it had grown, thanks largely to him, into a force of hitherto unimagined power. The Americans were to have more planes, but a smaller destructive capability.

In fact when Harris took over, Bomber Command was still struggling to gain the recognition its new leader firmly believed it richly deserved. He was quite clear in his mind as to its requirements; brought up in the Trenchardian school of the thirties, which maintained that the only way in which Great Britain could defend herself in any forthcoming struggle - and no one had any doubts as to the identity of the potential foe - was by such a sustained and apocalyptic attack on the enemy homeland that it would be something 'no country in the world could endure'. It was calculated that an overall strength of 4000 heavy bombers would be necessary. In February, 1942, Bomber Command had just over 400 aircraft, of which nearly half were Wellingtons. Five of the others were Lancasters.

In the early years of the war, if not in the closing stages, this policy had Churchill's whole-hearted support: ''There is one thing that will bring the enemy down and that is an absolutely devastating attack by very heavy bombers from this country on the enemy homeland. We must be able to overwhelm them by this means, without which I do not see a way through.'' But few men anywhere, with the exception of some far-seeing airmen who had flown with the Royal Observer Corps in World War 1, envisaged the potentiality of a large bomber force and the important role

The Great Ingratitude

it could play in a European or world struggle. Only a handful -including Harris - realised that they could have at their disposal a weapon that could change the whole conception of modern warfare, if given the chance. In simple terms, to the two spheres of battle which had existed for centuries - the land and the sea - was to be added a third - the endless tracts of the sky. They were to be proved right.

A Chief of Staff memorandum dated July 31, 1941, was in similar vein: "We must first destroy the foundations on which the German war machine rests - the economy that feeds it, the morale which sustains it, the supplies which nourish it and the hopes of victory which inspire it. Then only shall we be able to return to the Continent and control portions of his territory and impose our will upon the enemy... It is in bombing, on a scale undreamt of in the last war, that we find the new weapon on which we must principally depend for the destruction of German economic life and morale."

Harris went even further. He was unshakeable in his belief that, if he was given a bombing force of sufficient magnitude - he did not quarrel with the proposed figure of 4000 planes but insisted that they must be equipped with the most sophisticated navigational aids - he could win the war outright. Soldiers would be superfluous as fighting men and would merely fill the role of policemen in an already vanquished land, while the seamen's task would be limited to the transportation of the occupying troops and their food and equipment.

Not unnaturally, all this was much derided by the Army and the Navy, the former still seeing bombers, as late as 1942, only as a kind of aerial artillery which might help somewhat to soften up enemy ground forces prior to an advance by tanks and infantry, while the Navy contemptuously pooh-poohed the idea of a bomber getting anywhere near a warship without being blown to pieces. No doubt the Army revised its opinion during the Invasion, if not before in North Africa, and the Navy was obliged to admit its debt to the Sunderlands and Catalinas of Coastal Command during the Battle of the Atlantic, not to mention Bomber Command for its sinking of the Tirpitz and other formidable units of the German High Seas Fleet. In fact the RAF sank more enemy capital ships than the Navy did and the bomber was instrumental in rendering battleships obsolete as instruments of war. The Pacific theatre was to prove that the aircraft-carrier was a far better proposition.

Harris was a born battler; no dilly-dallying with him, no shilly-shallying - as his crews sometimes put it: "He doesn't piss about."

Bomber Command in World War II

And they, of all people, should have known. Once he had made up his mind, he pursued his aims with complete and unswerving single-mindedness, and God help anyone who got in his way. Those of his subordinates who had the temerity to question any of his decisions, even if their challenge was in the nature of a respectful suggestion, were seen to wither under the onslaught of a tongue which could drip with sarcasm; and so strong was his personality and the esteem in which he was held (despite his shortcomings), that even orders from above often appeared to be couched in the form of polite requests rather than peremptory commands. But no matter how they were worded, he was apt to ignore them completely if they met with his disapproval. And he usually got away with it. He was at times almost a law unto himself, of which no further proof is required than his frequent excuses for not carrying out orders with regard to *Pointblank* and *Overlord*.

It almost goes without saying that Harris did not suffer fools at all, and he was known to place in that category men of proven wisdom if their views were at loggerheads with his own. For red tape and for those who were slaves to it, he had absolutely no time whatsoever, and as he entered Air Ministry his normal greeting to top civil servants, as he bored into them with those penetrating blue eyes, was a: "Good morning! And how do you plan to thwart our war effort today?" Or something worse. Small wonder he had few friends - and many enemies.

Churchill once said that everyone had a cross to bear, and that his was the Cross of Lorraine, a reference to his constant problems with the prestige-seeking and ever-demanding Charles de Gaulle. Harris, in his dealings with the 'pen-pushers' at Air Ministry, with whom, as a man of action, he had little affinity, must have felt he too had a weighty cross to bear. Senior officers of the Army and Navy were also a constant source of irritation; Harris was convinced that their main concern was not to have their thunder stolen by this new upstart of a Service (the RAF) and its Bomber Command, whose leader thought little of their own efforts and their needs and egotistically believed he could win the war on his own. On more than one occasion his answer to their disparaging remarks about the bomber's capabilities took the form of a verbal hand-grenade which shattered both their ill-conceived suppositions and their equanimity.

Harris exasperated even those in his own camp, such as Air Commodore Sidney Bufton, the Director of Bomber Operations, by his successful defiance of Air Ministry instructions, especially during the period when *Pointblank* should have been implemented in full. Yet he

The Great Ingratitude

was wise enough to relent at times, perhaps sending a huge force of his bombers to liquidate an oil plant. But such operations seemed to be no more than expediency on his part, designed to show that he was willing to co-operate now and again, but still insisted that the war would be won sooner if he kept on with his carpet bombing of the cities. In his memoirs he wrote with true Harrisian bumptiousness: "Naturally I did not quarrel with the decision to put the bomber force at the disposal of the invading army once the die had been cast. I knew the armies could not succeed without it." He was indeed fortunate that for a time *Pointblank* provided him with the opportunity to divert his main strength to specific targets: it partly veiled the fact that, in spite of the devastated state of a growing number of German towns, there was still no sign of capitulation by the enemy. When, in December, 1943, during the Battle of Berlin, it became crystal-clear to all that Bomber Command was up against it, he made the rather outrageous statement that he could bring about Germany's collapse by a definite date - April 1, 1944 - if he could launch 1500 sorties every night against her main industrial centres. In the then prevailing climate such claims were viewed by many as ill-considered assertions by a man desperate to prove that he was right and everyone else was wrong, because he had at last realised that his much vaunted campaign was not bringing the results he had expected; and when April came along and the Nazis still looked far from being defeated, this provided the non-believers with even more reason to denigrate him further. But it did no good: Harris remained as stubborn as ever, and the formula too remained the same.

Although outspoken, abrasive and prone to a vitriolic which cut like a scythe, he had a way with words in general and displayed a sense of humour which was as sharp as it was original (for example, on being informed one day by one of his more audacious assistants that the crews were getting fed up going to Essen, his immediate reply was a succinct: "So is Essen."). He was also far from being insensitive or unimaginative and felt deeply for the aircrews who served him with such devotion. If, unlike Churchill, he paid few visits to the places where the war was being fought - in his case the bomber stations - it was because he had his nose to the grindstone 12 hours a day and seven days a week and in all his time at Bomber Command Headquarters, he never took leave and had only two weekends off. As he said himself: "As Commander in Chief I had to lay on every day in ever changing weather conditions a major battle whether this happened or not. There came a point every day when as C-in-C I had to say `yes' or `no', subject to various conditions including

Bomber Command in World War II

the Met. Report. I could not jaunt around the country and keep everything in mind.'' In other words he spent long hours each day weighing up the odds, choosing the night's target, reading intelligence and weather reports, deciding on the number of aircraft to be involved, tactics and diversionary raids, all this in readiness to put dozens of bomber stations into a frenzy of activity and show that Bomber Command was pitting its strength regularly and inexorably against the enemy.

Yet his aircrews, to whom he was a remote figure they rarely, if ever, saw, felt close to him nevertheless and were even affectionate, if reluctantly so, towards him. It cannot be denied that some of them judged him to be aloof and apparently uncaring, but there was not a single one in their ranks who did not appreciate the crushing load of responsibility their leader had to shoulder day and night throughout the period of his command, not the least of which was his self-imposed obligation to prove that what he was making them do was right. The critical decisions which he had to take on many occasions, usually compelled to hold them back till the very last moment and more often than not involving the deployment of hundreds of big bombers and the lives of thousands of his airmen, would have broken many strong men in mind and body; that he did not flinch or weaken was a tribute to his indomitable character, his resolve to see the whole damned thing through to the best of his ability right to the very end. It is not an opinion, but a fact, that Arthur Harris held the most exacting Command of the entire Second World War; no other leader was constantly faced with a situation such as his. As he himself pointed out, whereas an Army or Navy Commander might fight three or four major battles in the course of a long war, Bomber Command did this practically every night, and usually with grievous losses. No other Commander had to cope with such an awesome programme.

The British public called him 'Bomber' or 'Butcher' Harris - the second appellation because he was the man who was destroying Germany and killing Germans. But when his crews used it - shortened to 'Butch' - it was usually because he was killing them. Yet there was no intended malice on their part. It was typical of the sense of humour which helped to support them through their own ordeal. He was one of them, an airman, and they were grateful for his awareness of the gulf that existed between earth-bound civil servants at Air Ministry who were completely ignorant of what went on in the air, and themselves, who knew only fighters and flak, atrocious weather and physical discomfort, and the fear which continually gnawed at their entrails. Never were the twain to meet. And

The Great Ingratitude

Harris knew it. He also made sure his crews knew he knew it.

They, therefore, appreciated his condemnation of policies which put them at greater risk with little to gain - a good example was the extra bomb-load to Berlin (Chapter 4) - and were right behind him in the fierce arguments he had with the bowler-hatted decision-makers when he was ordered, on his appointment as Commander in Chief, to continue with the dropping of propaganda leaflets over German cities. As might be expected, he made it quite clear that he was not going to have ack-ack guns and fighters hurl shells at his crews while they bombarded the enemy with bits of paper. He attacked this utter waste of men, machines and endeavour in his usual scathing way: as far as he was concerned bombers were made for delivering bombs and he was not having their role relegated to that of vans carrying news sheets, or that of his crews to newspaper boys; further, he had not become Chief of Bomber Command to provide the citizens of the Third Reich with regular supplies of toilet paper. Allied - and German-leaflets are dealt with in detail in Chapter 21.

No one was more cognizant of the fact than Harris that his airmen were continually subjected to a multitude of dangers, and he did everything in his power to increase their chances of survival. He vociferously condemned any type of aircraft which he judged to be a hazard, with or without enemy intervention, to the men who flew in it; the Stirling and the Manchester he branded as little better than flying coffins and the Halifax too, although a useful workhorse, was unsuitable for deep penetration raids into Germany. It was his doing and his alone that all heavy bombers except the Lancaster - his 'shining sword' - were phased out from the most demanding operations. It was thanks to him too that so much time and money was spent on the best navigational and bomb-aiming aids that the scientists could produce. Yet he was forced to fight tooth and nail for everything he got and had to endure a vehement torrent of objections from those who were appalled that such a high proportion of the war budget was being drained off to satisfy his 'whims'; and the verbal battles he fought on the ground were often as ferocious, if less dangerous to his person, as those which his crews fought in the air.

Such goings-on were not unknown to the men who manned the bombers, and their faith in him was unshakeable, which was just as well during the grim nights of 1943-44 when they were taking an awful pasting and were resigned to the fact that death would very probably come on the next trip or the one after; yet they believed in him totally and found him an honest if a hard taskmaster. Between him and them there existed a very special and indefinable rapport which can be appreciated only by men who have waged war in the air. As to what Harris thought of his crews and their precarious existence, we can do no better than quote from his 'Bomber Offensive', published in 1947:

"There are no words with which I can do justice to the aircrew under my command. There is no parallel in warfare to such courage and determination in the face of danger over so long a period... It was, moreover, a clear and highly conscious courage; the risk was taken with calm forethought, for aircrew were all highly skilled men, much above average in education, who had to understand every aspect and detail of their task. It was, furthermore, the courage of the small hours, of men virtually alone, for at his battle station the airman is virtually alone. It was the courage of men with long-drawn apprehensions of daily `going over the top'. They were without exception volunteers, for no man was trained for aircrew who did not volunteer for this. Such devotion must never be forgotten. It is unforgettable by any whose contact gave them knowledge and understanding of what these men experienced and faced.''

To the man in the street Harris embodied many of the sterling qualities which had endeared Churchill to the nation as its war leader. The attitudes of the two men towards the jobs they held were basically similar - get on with it and hit the enemy hard and where it hurts most. They were seen as two of a kind, both epitomising the spirit that was needed to fight back and the determination that was necessary to eventually overcome a powerful and relentless adversary. Harris's field was by definition a narrower one, but the reverence in which he was held by the nation and his charismatic appeal were probably equalled only by that accorded to Montgomery.

It seemed to be the lot of senior commanders, both Axis and Allied, however, that many of their problems arose from friction amongst themselves; we can think of the disputes Hitler had with most of his generals, the antagonism that existed between Rundstedt and Rommel, between Eisenhower and Montgomery, between Eisenhower and Patton, between Patton and Montgomery; and, in the RAF, between Portal and Harris.

We have already seen (Chapter 4) that if someone else and not Portal, had been Chief of Air Staff, Harris could well have been dismissed, but dismissed he was not, and this in spite of Portal's assurance to the Combined Chiefs of Staff at the 'Octagon' Conference in Quebec in September, 1944, that even with Bomber Command no longer under

The Great Ingratitude

the jurisdiction of SHAEF (Supreme Headquarters Allied Expeditionary Force) and granted its previous autonomy, it would wade in with the American Army Air Force and concentrate on oil targets in order to starve German industry and the German Navy, Army and Air Force, of their very life-blood. Portal now saw the dissolution of the enemy's oil supplies as the No. 1 priority in bringing the country to its knees, and he trusted that he would have Harris's complete co-operation. Otherwise Bomber Command would go down in history for its controversial policy of razing vast urban areas and the US Air Force would steal all the thunder by severing Germany's jugular vein and bringing about her collapse. It is interesting to note (Chapter 14) that General Spaatz feared the opposite - that Harris, by his saturation bombing, would attain this end before he did himself by his attacks on the German oil and aircraft industries.

In a letter to Portal in November, Harris had complained indignantly about Bomber Command being regarded by some as a dog's body to be put at their disposal whenever the fancy took them. There were "too many cooks engaged in stirring the broth". They were all after him, including the Admiralty (Lancasters sank the Tirpitz on November 12) and "even the defunct SOE (Special Operations Executive, which had supplied Europe with agents and weapons for years) has raised its bloody head and produced what I hope is now its final death rattle. In the last 18 months Bomber Command has virtually destroyed 45 out of the leading 60 German cities. In spite of Invasion diversions, we have so far managed to keep up and even to exceed our average of two-and-a-half cities devastated a month ... there are not many industrial centres of population left intact. Are we going to abandon this vast task, which the Germans themselves have long admitted to be their worst headache, just as it nears completion?" In other words, only a few surviving towns, and part of Berlin, had yet to be given the treatment.

Portal said in his reply:

"At the risk of your dubbing me "another panacea merchant", I believe the air offensive against oil gives us by far the best hope of complete victory in the next few months."

Harris continued to repeat his belief that the destruction of German cities was the quickest way to finish the war. Then Portal sent a further letter:

Bomber Command in World War II

"You refer to a plan for the destruction of the 60 leading German cities, and to your efforts to keep up with, and even to exceed, your average of two-and-a-half cities devastated each month; I know that you have long felt such a plan to be the most effective way of bringing about the collapse of Germany. Knowing this, I have, I must confess, at times wondered whether the magnetism of the remaining German cities has not in the past tended as much to deflect our bombers from their primary objective as the tactical and weather difficulties which you described so fully in your letter. I would like you to reassure me that this is not so. If I knew you to be as whole-hearted in the attack on oil as in the past you have been in the matter of attacking cities, I would have little to worry about."

By early December, however, Harris was again showing signs of giving practically all of his attention to the cities and he was told by Portal that he was not "putting his heart into it". The situation worsened when the Chief of Air Staff suggested that had it not been for the American onslaught against the Luftwaffe (in the air and on the ground) Harris might well have found that his losses over the Reich were unsustainable. To a man with the fighting qualities of Harris this was fighting talk of a high order: "I will not willingly lay myself open again to the charge that the lack of success of a policy which I have declared at the outset ... not to contain the seeds of success is, after the event, due to my not having tried. That situation is simply one of heads I lose, tails you win, and it is an intolerable situation ... I therefore ask you to consider whether it is best for the prosecution of the war and the success of our arms, which alone matters, that I should remain in this situation." In other words, if his campaign against the cities was to be given up and 'panacea targets' substituted, he would go.

Portal was in a quandary, and his letter of reply was more or less a *carte blanche* to his Bomber Chief:

"I am very sorry that you do not believe in the Oil Plan, but it is no use my craving for what is evidently unobtainable. We must wait until after the end of the war before we can know for certain who was right, and I sincerely hope that until then you will continue in command of the force which has done so much towards defeating the enemy, and has brought such credit and renown to yourself and to the Royal Air Force."

The Great Ingratitude

No doubt Harris smacked his lips in anticipation. God help the remaining towns of Germany...

It is always difficult for posterity to know the complete truth about the conflicting views of senior officers and their personal relationships, but those who censure Portal for not adopting a harder line with his intransigent Bomber Chief are perhaps guilty of an over-simplification of what was undoubtedly a trying situation for both men.

Portal was well aware of Harris's dynamic qualities and his complete devotion to his task; he knew of no one who could have more forcefully filled the post of Head of Bomber Command; nor did anyone have to tell him that, as we have pointed out, Harris held what was undisputedly the most continually onerous and exhausting Command of the war. In fact each man respected and admired the other. Portal's fine analytical mind, and his ability to see things from another's point of view, told him how best to handle Harris and he recognised that by reasoned argument he was far more likely to get him on his side than by issuing unequivocal orders; and if Harris sometimes appeared to treat such orders in a manner which in the other Services would have been interpreted as insubordination, this was because his intimate liaison with the Chief of Air Staff allowed for a certain amount of latitude in their interpretation. Harris's own attitude to Portal is obvious from his own words: "Portal had great strength ... his intellectual powers were outstanding; nobody could be more lucid. And he was a fighting man through and through, in spite of his quiet and modest manner." It is hard to imagine such an assessment coming from a man reputed to be continually at loggerheads with his superior; certainly not from someone as forthright as Bert Harris. (It was as "Bert" he was known to those closest to him).

There are facts which suggest that, as World War 2 reached its climax, Harris's continued policy of area bombing did not meet with Churchill's full approval. The Prime Minister could easily have taken the necessary steps to ensure that his Chief of Bomber Command was honoured in the way of all those high-ranking commanders (see Chapter 20) who had made outstanding contributions to final victory, but didn't. Accordingly, one cannot help but ponder how much the letter written to him by Churchill, just a few days after the European struggle ended, was lacking in sincerity:

"Now that Nazi Germany is defeated, I wish to express to you on behalf of his Majesty's Government, the deep sense of gratitude which is felt by all the nation for the glorious part which has been played by Bomber Command in forging the victory. For over two years Bomber Command alone carried the war to the heart of Germany, bringing hope to the peoples of Occupied Europe and to the enemy a foretaste of the mighty power which was rising against him. As the Command expanded, in partnership with the Air Forces of our American Allies, the weight of the attack was increased, leaving destruction on an unparalleled scale to the German military, industrial and economic system. Your Command also gave powerful support to the Allied armies in Europe and made a vital contribution to the war at sea. You destroyed or damaged many of the enemy's ships of war and much of his U-boat organisation. By a prolonged series of mining operations, you sank or damaged large quantities of his merchant shipping. All your operations were planned with great care and skill; they were executed in the face of desperate opposition and appalling hazards. They made a decisive contribution to Germany's defeat. The conduct of these operations demonstrated the fiery, gallant spirit which animated your aircrews and the high sense of duty of all ranks under your command. I believe that the massive achievement of Bomber Command will long be remembered as an example of duty nobly done.''

Fine words indeed, all true, and richly deserved. A pity that Churchill did not provide more convincing proof of his professed beliefs. An outstanding airman might then have graced the Royal Air Force for a while longer, serving it under a distinguished title which would have befitted both the man and what he had accomplished.

Chapter 7

THE BOILER HOUSE AND THE BEAST IT FED

The operational station was the aircrews' home, if that is the right word, for the foreseeable future. It was the home of many thousands of young fliers on airfields so numerous that when plotted on a blank map of England they made those counties from South Yorkshire to Suffolk look like a plan of the London underground. It was also the home of the heavy bomber.

The majority of the stations were situated in open country, usually miles from any sizeable town, and for that reason, and others, each had to be a self-sufficient entity able to provide all the amenities any town could offer (it was said that the only thing lacking was a 'red light' district).   But, unlike a town, and in consequence of the particular way in which Bomber Command operated, it throbbed with life as much by night as it did by day. Few individuals felt any desperate need to leave it in order to indulge in their favourite pursuits. There were dances, cinema shows, sports facilities - and usually plenty of attractive young WAAFs around, including a number who felt great sympathy for the aircrews and were not averse to their amorous advances. Each station was in the front line of battle with its own well-equipped hospital, and surgeons who attended to all injuries apart from those requiring highly specialised treatment. Victims of severe facial burns - and there were plenty of those - were transferred to East Grinstead and treated by the eminent New Zealand plastic surgeon, Archibald McIndoe.

Any visitor arriving at the main gate and its adjacent guard-room immediately entered a vast area of administration blocks, billets, messes, briefing rooms, lecture rooms, parachute rooms, hangars and aircraft repair workshops, garages for trucks and vans, armouries with their massive stocks of bombs and ammunition, huge stores of petrol and oil, and a host of other equally vital services. A large bomber station had a complement of up to 2500 personnel, of whom about one in ten were aircrew, and roughly 100 people were required to keep one heavy bomber serviceable and to send it off against the enemy. This was a never-ending task as the four-engined machine was a complicated and demanding brute.

Bomber Command in World War II

There were also bruised and battered aircraft that had weathered the storm the previous night and had to be towed away and repaired. The roar of aircraft engines, either being tested or warmed up for take-off, went on continuously, as did the strident noises of machinery in the workshops. Trucks and vans and bicycles and personnel ran about all over the place, attending to the thousand and one duties that had to be performed. It was ding-dong stuff 24 hours a day and the tempo never halted for a moment. But during their off-duty hours, aircrews (and ground staff) did venture out to the nearest village or town, using 'station buses' or their own cycles or motor bikes. The pub provided a welcome change from the familiar faces in the mess, and friendships were often struck up with the locals who found their quiet, rustic way of life shattered by crowds of youngsters who were living on a razor edge, and showed it.

The amount of organisation required to prepare each squadron for a big raid was complex in the extreme. On an average-sized station, something approaching 175 tons of bombs, 400,000 rounds of ammunition, 65,000 gallons of high octane petrol (Lancasters alone consumed almost 230 million gallons during the war), 2000 gallons of oil, 6250 litres of oxygen, 30 gallons of coffee and 200 pounds of sandwiches, glucose sweets and chocolate had all to be handled and put into the aircraft. Up to 130 bomb trolleys were used and, in addition, dozens of other transport vehicles such as petrol bowsers (it took all the contents of one to fill a single Lanc). Intelligence Officers were required to have ready everything required for briefing - maps, photographs, and all the detailed information crews needed to know about the route, the target and its defences, while the weathermen's job was to inform them of the latest known winds, cloud formation and height, chances of icing and anything at all relevant to atmospheric conditions. Each aircraft had to be checked minutely - and double-checked. Engines, guns, bomb-doors, everything was subjected to the closest scrutiny and, if a fault was found, mechanics got to work on it immediately and kept at it until it was rectified. This often involved a pre-op. test flight by its crew. Towing vehicles stood prepared to remove any unserviceable aircraft out of the way and ambulances and fire-tenders positioned themselves on the perimeter at the ready when the squadron was about to take off.

Apart from the occasional test flight which had to be made, sometimes at the last minute, crews took no part in all this, only in the briefing. All they could do was wait. Their turn would come soon enough.

The Great Ingratitude

Ground staff and crews were often on very friendly terms with each other, with little of the cold, rigid discipline and the superior attitude of officers towards other ranks that was often characteristic of the Army and Navy. This was partly due to the dependence of the airmen on 'erks' who were perhaps no more than Leading Aircraftmen or Corporals; and this resulted in a quiet, easy relationship which stemmed mainly from an acute awareness of one another's responsibilities, and mutual respect. The aircrews knew only too well how much a safe return could be attributed to the conscientious spirit and competence of their mechanics, and the latter in turn saw with their own eyes what the airmen were going through. They would invariably see them off on each operation and would wait up, or rise early, to greet them when they landed. They felt immensely proud of the aircraft with whose maintenance they were entrusted and did not mind working on her out in the open in all weathers - a heavy bomber rarely saw the inside of a hangar except when undergoing two-week long overhauls after 500 and 1000 flying hours - and they even kept the interiors of the aircraft clean and tidy.

It is not considered necessary to describe in detail the earlier machines available to Bomber Command, the most important of which were the Wellington (as good as anything in its day and better than most), the Hampden, the Whitley, the Manchester (unpopular and a failure, but from which emerged the Lancaster), and the Stirling, the first of the four-engined bombers. Although all of these achieved as much as their limitations allowed and were crewed by 'pioneers' who, by virtue of the experience they had gained, contributed much to those who were to follow in their wake when the offensive gathered momentum, it was the Halifax and in particular the Lancaster which made Bomber Command the force it was (the unique position of the Mosquito has already been dealt with in Chapter 4).

This is shown by the number of operations carried out by each type: out of the total number completed by Bomber Command (389,000), the Lancaster could claim 156,192, the Halifax 82,773, the Wellington 47,409, the Mosquito 39,795, the Stirling 18,440, the Hampden 16,541, the Blenheim 12,214, the Whitley 9,858, the Boston 1,609, the Fortress 1,340, the Manchester 1,269, the Ventura 997, the Liberator 662, and others 710. Between them the Lancaster and the Halifax carried out 61% of all sorties - the Lanc 40% and the Halifax 21%. 3,431 Lancs and 1,884 Halifaxes were lost.

Bomber Command in World War II

The Handley Page Halifax Mark 1 began its operational career in 1941 and with a range of 1860 miles, a 5800 lb bomb-load and maximum speed of 265 mph, it promised to be capable of doing the job demanded by Bomber Command. Its first operation (six aircraft) took place against Le Havre on March 11/12 and the only aircraft lost was one which was attacked and shot down by a 'friendly' fighter while on its way back to base. The Mark II (Rolls-Royce Merlin 20 engines instead of the Vultures fitted to the Mark I) was manufactured in large numbers in 1942 and, although it did a worthwhile job, it suffered from a lack of power which restricted both ceiling and range; consequently it was decided that the Mark II was no longer suitable for attacks against strongly defended targets well inside the Reich and took no further part in such operations after September, 1943. But the Mark III appeared in February, 1944 with four 1650 hp Bristol Hercules engines and proved itself to be a much better proposition, able to carry a full bomb load at a height of 24,000 feet and to cover almost 1300 miles. It was a reasonably efficient machine and played its part in large scale night attacks, sometimes outnumbering the Lancs present.

But it was undoubtedly the Lancaster which could claim to be the flagship of Bomber Command from the end of 1943 until Germany's surrender in May, 1945. In 1944 Harris said: ''We have reached the extraordinary situation in which the labour devoted to the production of Lancasters alone is believed to be equal to that allotted to the production of the whole equipment of the Army.'' He must have allowed himself a little smile of satisfaction.

The Lancaster was 70 feet long and $19^1/_2$ feet high, with a wing span of 102 feet. It cruised at 216 mph and could attain 266 mph. Fuel consumption was in the region of 1.5 gallons for every mile covered and 10 gallons during take-off. Its ceiling was about 23,000 feet, but this varied according to the amount of fuel and the weight of bombs carried. Its normal bomb load (Mark I) was 14,000 lb. but later versions (Marks II and III) were slightly modified and could lift off with the colossal 'Grand Slam', which, like the famous 'bouncing bomb' used to breach the Ruhr Dams (Chapter 19), was the brain-child of Barnes Wallis. Armament consisted of four .303 Browning machine-guns in the rear-turret - which could pump out 1200 rounds a minute - and twins in the front and mid-upper turrets. The amount of ammunition carried was 14,000 rounds. The Lanc had room for some 2200 gallons of petrol and this capacity was utilised on many occasions when the target was well inside Germany or

The Great Ingratitude

Northern Italy, or when the aircraft flew on to North Africa from Southern Europe. Lancasters delivered 608,612 tons of bombs all over the Continent, representing 64% of the total dropped by Bomber Command during the entire war. The number of incendiaries which were released from their bomb-bays came to no fewer than 51½ million.

The Lanc was a tough and reliable machine and often made it back to base in such a pitiful state that it was a miracle that it had remained airborne over hundreds of miles. Its durability was further illustrated by the fact that some 28 machines completed 100 or more operations. Yet the infernal nature of the campaign can be judged from Lancaster losses alone - almost half of the 7366 built were destroyed in action. Ten Victoria Crosses were awarded to members of Lancaster crews.

There was no other heavy bomber produced during the Second World War, either Allied or Axis, which approached the Lancaster in all-round efficiency. That is one reason why *pro rata*, it suffered fewer losses, great as these were, than any other type. That is why Harris called it his 'shining sword', and from his stronghold at High Wycombe, King Arthur wielded his Excalibur with ever mightier blows. As could be expected of one so prone to hyperbole in most things relating to Bomber Command, he claimed that no other single weapon in the Allied armoury contributed so much to the winning of the Second World War as his beloved Lancaster. Perhaps those who flew Spitfires or sailed the Atlantic in submarine-hunting corvettes or drove Churchill tanks might not have been entirely in agreement with him, yet it remains an indisputable fact hat had the Lanc not been available in large numbers when it mattered most, and if Britain had only had the other heavies at her disposal, Bomber Command might well have been obliged - some would even say would have been obliged - to call a halt to the whole campaign; after all, there were those who considered such a step desirable when losses reached worrying proportions; and, as is clearly shown by the figures quoted above, even the Lancasters were far from being immune ...

***

By virtue of its reputation as the machine which more than any other was breaking the back of Germany's industry and reducing its towns to endless acres of ashes, the Avro Lancaster was regarded by the RAF in particular and by the British public in general with a mixture of admiration, awe and pride. It had become a name as well known and esteemed as the Spitfire and the Hurricane. But whereas the famous fighters had played a role which was primarily defensive and had saved the nation from possible or even probable defeat, the Lancaster was a weapon of attack, and the means to attack had been lacking for far too long; and so the concept of hundreds of Lancasters paying regular visits to German cities was one which fired the imagination and the bomber's very name became synonymous with revenge, justifiable destruction of the Fatherland and better prospects of an earlier victory.

Describing the Lanc in such glowing terms is unfortunately tempered with a feeling of guilt on my part; this is because I am acutely conscious of the fact that there were, and still are, crews, especially those who flew Halifaxes, who resented the publicity accorded the Lancaster. That is clearly understandable. But surely, if the latter was a superior aircraft to the Halifax, which it definitely was, then Halifax crews deserve all the more credit for their achievements in what was a more vulnerable machine. It was Bomber Command which wrecked Germany, and if it was the Lanc which wrecked it more than anything else this detracts in no way from the substantial and invaluable part played by other types. Pray let the matter rest there.

Chapter 8

MUSSOLINI GETS A TASTE

The question has often been asked why Bomber Command gave Italy only a relatively tiny taste of the medicine it rammed continually down Germany's throat; why her northern industrial centres did not come in for the same treatment as their German counterparts.

There seemed to be reason enough to do so: apart from the importance of such targets to the Italian, and therefore to the Axis war effort, Britain must surely have wanted to reap revenge for the contemptible 'stab in the back' on June 10, 1940, which Mussolini had delivered only when he became certain that France's collapse was assured; the poor quality of the opposition expected from the Italian defences (Italy was the only major combatant to use biplane fighters throughout her active part in the war); and perhaps the best reason of all - the generally unwarlike nature of the Italians themselves, altogether different from that of the stoic and well-disciplined Germans. It was firmly believed that the Italians never had much stomach for a fight when the odds were not too good; and certainly they would have found that the things thrown at them by Bomber Command were somewhat more lethal than the Abyssinian stones and spears which, a few years before, they had heroically faced with tanks and aircraft; it would therefore seem reasonable to conclude that regular onslaughts by Bomber Command would have had an immediate and profound effect on the Italian people, that it could even have brought about their insurrection and the early downfall of the Duce. It is true that the route across the Alps entailed a long and challenging flight, yet on most occasions this presented no overwhelming problems for even the Whitleys and Wellingtons, and certainly less so for the four-engined heavies which succeeded them; and the duration of the operation was little longer than that to Berlin.

Why then did Bomber Command not unleash much more of its fury on Hitler's partner? There were sound reasons for not doing so: firstly, it goes almost without saying that the British rightly regarded Germany as being by far the main enemy, and the early demise of Italy, however welcome, would have had no effect whatsoever in bringing the

Bomber Command in World War II

Nazis to heel. The reverse was certainly not the case. Subsequent events proved these predictions to be correct when Italy threw in the towel in September, 1943. The British were also aware that Italy had never fought a war without changing sides at some stage - in fact she had once done so twice. Again they were proved right when she joined the Allied cause shortly afterwards. Churchill and his cabinet knew from the start that if they could turn the tide Italy would be a fickle and unreliable ally of the Germans, prone to political and military collapse, bombing or no bombing, and events were to prove in the long run that Hitler would have fared far better without his partner Mussolini who, thanks to his obsession to capture a share of the Axis thunder, got himself into all sorts of embarrassing military situations (in Greece, for example) which required the timeous intervention of the Führer to extricate him and wipe his bloodied nose. There was rather more than a glimmer of truth in the remark that it was much more preferable to have the Italian army against you than with you. Rommel for one would no doubt have agreed.

While Italy was still in the war Bomber Command had not yet attained the strength it was to possess from the second half of 1943 onwards; hence its resources had to be used where results would be most effective in the long term, and the long-term foe was Nazi Germany. It was of greater tactical importance to wreck a Messerschmitt factory in Regensburg than a Fiat plant in Turin. At the same time many thought it incomprehensible that at least one or two heavy 'token' attacks were not launched against large Italian urban areas during the Battle of the Ruhr, if for no other reason than to indicate to Hitler's ally that her arsenals were ear-marked for the same treatment as Essen or Dortmund - and to make them ask themselves if they were about to be the victims of a similar holocaust. In circumstances where Italian ack-ack gunners were so jittery and inept as to blow the roofs off their own buildings when half-a-dozen Whitleys were overhead, how would they have reacted to an overpowering attack by a force of 700-800 Stirlings, Halifaxes and Lancasters? If general panic invariably developed amongst a city's inhabitants when a bomb landed half-a-mile away how could they ever have coped with a raid on such a scale?

Even à few very heavy bombardments in 1942 or early 1943 would arguably have had a devastating effect on the morale of the already war-weary Italians, who had known little else but a string of humiliating failures in North Africa and Greece, and the entire liquidation of some of their divisions in Russia; to all of which could be added their

The Great Ingratitude

growing dislike of the superior and domineering Germans ...

It has been suggested that the abundance of priceless art treasures and monuments, even in industrial areas, acted as a deterrent to major attacks by Bomber Command. But that had nothing to do with it - the USAAF, for instance, sent 700 aircraft to drop 1100 tons of bombs on Rome on July 19, 1943, and visited the city at other times as well. As we have already seen, the Allies did not intend that consideration for the finest examples of art or culture, or anything else, should slow their progress along the hard road to victory.

Although Allied aircraft based in the Mediterranean made several attacks against targets in Sardinia, Sicily and southern Italy, mainly in support of invasion forces, it was the cities of the industrial North with which Bomber Command was principally concerned. Yet only three of these were to experience incursions of any consequence - Turin, Milan and Genoa. The others, which received only a few minor calls, can be dealt with briefly:

A few Wellingtons and Whitleys went to San Giovanni on September 1-2, 1940; on October 23/24 the destination for 53 Halifaxes, 51 Stirlings and 18 Wellingtons was Genoa, but the area was shrouded in ten-tenths cloud and Savona, 30 miles distant, was mistakenly bombed instead; on February 4/5, 1943, four Lancasters of the Pathfinder Force tried out a new type of bomb on La Spezia, a 'proximity fused' 4000 lb HE which was detonated 300 or 400 feet above the ground, the idea being that the blast effects would cause more damage than in the case of the conventional bomb which exploded on contact (whether results were satisfactory or not remains unclear, but probably not as this type of weapon was not manufactured in quantity); four more Pathfinder Lancs attacked La Spezia's docks on February 14/15; but the port was to experience something rather different on April 13/14, when 208 Lancs and three Halifaxes caused extensive damage. Four Lancasters were lost and this was probably the first occasion on which damaged Bomber Command aircraft flew on to land in North Africa - the three that did so were repaired and returned to their English bases; less than a week later, on April 18/19, a slightly smaller force of 173 Lancasters and five Halifaxes arrived over the harbour installations, while eight Lancs did a bit of 'gardening' ('sowing' mines) off the coast. The bombing by the main stream was slightly off target, but a lot of damage was done to public buildings and to the main railway station; on June 20/21, the 60 Lancasters which had attacked (without loss) the Zeppelin works at Friedrichshafen on Lake

Bomber Command in World War II

Constance (where Würzburg radar sets were produced for German night fighters) caused some bewilderment amongst the Luftwaffe defences operating in France when they did not encounter the Lancs on their return journey. They had in fact flown from Friedrichshafen to North Africa, and on their way back to England on the night of 23/24 June, 52 of them bombed La Spezia, creating further havoc in the docks and also hitting an oil depot and an armaments store.

On July 15/16, 1943, an electrical-transformer station near Bologna was attacked (as was another near Genoa) by 12 Lancs of 617 Squadron in an effort to deprive the railway system of its power and therefore to halt the movement of German troops and supplies to Sicily, but little success was achieved (the aircraft flew on to North Africa). The following night seven Lancasters bombed the Cislago transformer station accurately; then, on July 24/25, while the first raid of the Battle of Hamburg was taking place, 33 Lancasters returning from North Africa dropped their loads on Leghorn docks but the target could not be seen for mist and the amount of damage could not be assessed.

It was the city of Turin which could claim the doubtful privilege of playing host to Bomber Command more often than any other in Italy. The day following Mussolini's entry into the war, on June 11/12, 1940, its citizens were led to wonder, when death and destruction came to their very doorstep, whether the Duce, by triumphantly marching across the border into South-east France, had perhaps acted rather rashly in his bid to share the spoils of Nazi victory. 36 Whitleys (which had to refuel en route in the Channel Islands) had set off to bomb some of the town's factories, but because of atrocious weather in the area of the Alps more than half the force failed to reach Italy. However the nine which made it to Turin found the city lit up like a fairground - perhaps those manning the defences thought that in far-off Italy they were immune to RAF attack. The lights went out as soon as it was realised what was happening and the aircraft dropped their bombs on railway yards instead of the prescribed industrial installations. The two Whitleys which were lost both crashed in France, and these were Bomber Command's first Italian casualties. Seventeen of Turin's inhabitants were killed and 40 injured, and although the operation was little more than a pin-prick it was not seen as such by the Italians, however, who, wondering if such an experience was to be a regular occurrence, raised their arms to heaven and expressed their horror at the very thought. Yet they had a couple of months in which to calm themselves before the RAF came once more on the night of August 13/14, when 35

The Great Ingratitude

Whitleys divided their attentions between Turin and Milan; a fortnight later Turin's sirens wailed ominously once again when half-a-dozen Whitleys arrived over the city; a few more went to the same target on September 1/2, on September 5/6, on December 4/5 and 11 Wellingtons on January 11/12, 1941; then came a long pause until September 10/11 of the same year, when 76 aircraft -56 Wellingtons, 13 Stirlings and seven Halifaxes - plastered the city centre and the Fiat steelworks. The next raid did not take place until November 18/19, 1942; on that night 77 bombers recorded hits on the Fiat factory and further damage was caused in the city centre. (It was on this operation that Squadron Leader B V Robinson brought his Halifax back to England all on his own; after he had ordered the crew to bale out, a rush of in-coming air had extinguished the fire). Renewed fears amongst the inhabitants of Turin that Bomber Command were again interested in their city were confirmed two nights later when the strongest force yet to cross the Alps (86 Lancasters, 54 Wellingtons, 47 Halifaxes and 45 Stirlings) started many large fires and caused the death of 117 people (120 suffered injury). The Italians knew all about what had happened to Cologne the previous May and a raid even on the scale they had just experienced was to them irrefutable confirmation of Bomber Command's growing potential and a harbinger of what might lie in store. The situation became even worse on November 28/29 when 228 aircraft, just over half of them Lancasters, accurately bombed the Royal Arsenal and introduced Italy to the power of the 8000 lb bomb. (It was during this raid that Australian Flight Sergeant R H Middleton descended to 2000 feet and made three approach runs in an attempt to correctly identify the target; an ack-ack shell exploded in the cockpit and both pilots and the wireless operator sustained serious injuries. The co-pilot, Flight Sergeant Hyder, took over the controls [the captain was unconscious] and the bombs were released; but the Stirling was hit again over the city and over France as well. Flight Sergeant Middleton, conscious once more but grievously wounded, very weak, with blurred vision and almost incapable of speech, realised a safe landing was out of the question and ordered his crew to bale out. Five of them got down safely but the captain and two of his colleagues died when the Stirling crashed into the sea. Flight Sergeant Middleton received a posthumous Victoria Cross and his co-pilot the DFM. Middleton's body was later recovered and he was buried at Mildenhall).

The following night (November 29/30), 29 Stirlings and seven Lancasters attempted to bomb the Fiat works but weather conditions were deplorable and only 18 of the aircraft crossed the Alpine barrier and dropped their loads. Results were never clearly established.

A week later, on December 8/9, 108 Lancs, nine Halifaxes, nine Wellingtons and seven Stirlings returned to Turin; the target was well illuminated by the Pathfinders and accurate bombing was achieved, both industrial and residential areas being severely damaged; fires burned for a long time and 212 citizens were killed and 111 injured. The next night a larger force of 227 bombers (115 Lancs, 47 Halifaxes, 40 Wellingtons and 25 Stirlings) droned over the city but the target area was partly obscured by smoke from the previous fires and results were less good; a further 73 people lost their lives and almost 100 were injured. Twenty-four hours later (three raids in a row) 82 aircraft, mostly Halifaxes, set off from base, but many of them were beset with icing problems and the larger part of the force was compelled to turn back before the Alps were reached; only 28 of the aircraft dropped their bombs and the amount of success achieved was never ascertained.

Turin enjoyed a respite until February 4/5, 1943, a night on which 77 Lancasters, 55 Halifaxes, 50 Stirlings and six Wellingtons - 188 aircraft in all - left plenty of material evidence of their visit, and 29 civilians were killed and 53 injured; five months were to elapse before the next raid on July 12/13, when conditions were wellnigh perfect for the 295 Lancasters - the largest force Italy had yet known - which released their loads on the city centre and in the area just to the north of it, causing immense damage and the death of 792 of the city's inhabitants. (It was on this raid that Wing Commander J D Nettleton of 44 Squadron, who had won the Victoria Cross for his part in leading the low-level attack on Augsburg in April, 1942, (see Chapter 19) was shot down by a German fighter while crossing the English Channel on the way home. His entire crew perished with him).

Exactly one month later 152 aircraft, most of which were Stirlings, carried out a concentrated raid on the city, although the Italian authorities reported only about 100 casualties and very few mortalities. Perhaps no RAF Victoria Cross was more richly deserved than that awarded to Flight Sergeant A L Aaron, a 21-year old from Leeds, whose Stirling was raked and badly damaged on the approach to the target. The navigator died instantly and other members of the crew were injured. Flight Sergeant Aaron himself was severely wounded in the chest and the right arm, which was rendered useless, and, as if that was not enough, he had taken a bullet in the jaw and lost part of his face; seeing their skipper was in a dreadful state and obviously quite incapable of flying the aircraft,

The Great Ingratitude

the bomb aimer and flight engineer pulled him from his seat, dosed him with morphia and, taking over the controls, headed for North Africa with one engine out of commission; on reaching the coast Flight Sergeant Aaron came round and twice tried to take over the controls to attempt a landing; however he was too weak and wracked with pain to cope and, unable to speak, he used his left hand to write out instructions on how to get the aircraft down - which caused him even more pain and sapped his remaining strength. The airfield had to be circuited four times and the Stirling landed at the fifth attempt. Tragically Flight Sergeant Aaron died a few hours later, an event rendered even more tragic when medical opinion stated that he would probably have survived had he not taken so much out of himself by trying to return to his seat to take over when the aircraft reached North Africa; and the episode took on an even sadder aspect when it was learned that the machine-gun fire which had crippled the Stirling on the run-in to the target had come from the rear-gun turret of a 'friendly' bomber.

On August 16/17, 1943, the night before the big attack on Peenemünde (see Chapter 11), Turin was the chosen target for Bomber Command's final raid on Italian cities; 154 aircraft, the majority of them Stirlings, inflicted a lot of damage on the Fiat motor works and the immediate vicinity.

Milan was attacked only half as often as Turin, the first time by 10 Whitleys on August 24/25, 1940; other small raids followed on August 26/27, on September 1/2, and on October 24 (in daylight). The city was not troubled again until October 24, 1942, when, also in daylight, each of 88 Lancasters made its own way across France and got into formation over Lake Annecy. The Italians were shocked when exploding bombs - 135 tons fell in 18 minutes - and not sirens were the first indication that Bomber Command had arrived; many large fires developed and, apart from the destruction of about 400 houses, hits were scored on the Caproni aircraft factory, Fascist Party Headquarters, the University and the prison; about 180 people died. Four Lancasters were lost.

The very same night Bomber Command returned, this time with a slightly less formidable force of 25 Halifaxes, 23 Stirlings and 23 Wellingtons, of which four Wellingtons and two Stirlings failed to return. Bad weather en route to the target scattered the formation and those aircraft which overflew neutral Switzerland were greeted with ack-ack fire, obviously intended to warn them that they had no right to be where they were. Only just over half the bombers dropped their loads and it was suspected that results were poor. Milan was not attacked again until

Bomber Command in World War II

February 14/15, 1943, on this occasion by an all-Lancaster force of 142; although results were uncertain the raid seemed to have been successful due to concentrated bombing and crews could still see the glow of the fires when they had completed 100 miles of the return journey. Only two Lancs were lost.

Then, on August 12/13, Milan experienced a bombardment by the largest formation of Bomber Command aircraft ever sent against an Italian city; while Turin was being visited by 152, Milan was called upon to cope with no fewer than 504 - 321 Lancasters and 183 Halifaxes. The Milanese were given an idea of what it was like to be subjected to a moderately-sized attack and of what their northern allies had been putting up with regularly. About 1000 citizens died, and apart from other extensive damage, the main railway station, the Alfa-Romeo motor works, and three other major factories were devastated; nor did the La Scala opera house come off lightly. Two nights later 140 Lancasters (only one was lost) disrupted Milan once more and nothing short of panic gripped the city when this raid was followed the next night by a visit from 199 Lancasters. Seven aircraft, most of which crashed in France while on their way back to England, was the cost of this final raid on Milan.

The first 'raid' carried out against the ancient city of Genoa, Italy's main port and a great centre of shipbuilding and engineering, was effected by a couple of Whitleys on June 11/12, 1940; the second took place on June 15/16, when eight Wellingtons attacked it from a French airfield near Toulon, about 200 miles to the south-west; a few more Wellingtons visited it the next night. No aircraft were lost in these small and tentative operations to Genoa and more than a year and three months were to pass before the crews of 39 Wellingtons and two Stirlings reported accurate bombing on September 28/29, 1941 (three Wellingtons were lost).

On October 22/23, 1942, Genoa was chosen for the restart of the bombing of Italy just at the moment when the Eighth Army was beginning its offensive at El Alamein: 112 Lancasters, assisted by Pathfinders, released their loads accurately in ideal conditions, and none were lost. Bomber Command intended to add to the destruction the following night but, as already mentioned, the 122 aircraft taking part erroneously bombed the coastal town of Savona. The results were never assessed.

On November 6/7, 1942, a concentrated attack was made by 72 Pathfinder Force Lancasters, of which two were shot down; most of the bombs fell on residential areas.

The Great Ingratitude

The next night 175 aircraft - 85 Lancs, 45 Halifaxes, 39 Stirlings and six Wellingtons wrought further havoc, and photographs confirmed the crews' claims that bombing had been most effective; on November 15/16, successful results were again obtained by a force of 78 - 40 Halifaxes, 27 Lancasters and 11 Stirlings; Genoa was then spared till July 15/16, 1943, when 617 Squadron tried to destroy an electrical transformer station near the city, but the target was concealed by mist.

A few weeks later Italy had become very unstable politically (she surrendered to the Allies on September 9, 1943) and it was to help hasten her collapse that Genoa underwent its last raid on August 7/8. On that same night Turin and Milan were attacked as well, the combined force totalling 197 aircraft, all of which were Lancs.

The RAF bombardment of Italian cities hardly deserved to be termed an "Air Offensive"; in comparison with the effort against Germany it was no more than a side-show, and a small one at that, amounting to about 60 raids in all and costing no more than 76 aircraft (most of them claimed by the Luftwaffe over France). The defence of Italy's cities was found by Bomber Command crews to be pop-gun stuff compared to the vicious and deadly cannonades with which they were greeted over the Reich - and alert and lethal fighters hardly ever entered the fray. The Italians were perhaps fortunate that their country surrendered when it did: if it had continued hostilities until 1944 or, even worse, 1945, by which time a huge and hungry Bomber Command was combing Europe for targets, they might well have had to endure what for them would have been quite unendurable.

Chapter 9

LMF

At the end of the war Air Marshal Sir John Slessor, who had been in command of 5 Group, Bomber Command, then became Assistant Chief of the Air Staff and finally Head of Coastal Command, (in which capacity he played a brilliant role in defeating the U-boats in the Battle of the Atlantic), said: "The compulsions of 1915 and 1940 produced two of the most unbelievable manifestations of human courage and endurance in the history of war - the infantry of 1914-1918 and the bomber crews of 1939-1945."

Modern psychologists tend to make great play of telling us things our grandmothers knew, for example that fear is one of the strongest instincts in all living creatures and is the direct result of the strongest instinct of all - self-preservation; hence the degree of fear experienced is in proportion to the extent of the threat, real or imagined, to that self-preservation. Paradoxically, the most frightened man may be the most courageous one of all if he keeps his fear concealed from others and does not allow it to affect his judgement or his actions.

The aircrews' way of waging war was a very special one, hitherto unknown. The fact that their battles virtually started in their own quarters and ended there - if they were lucky -created a situation also hitherto unknown. Deep over enemy territory one night, where they were surrounded by a powerful enemy bent on their destruction, and at home the next evening with their friends in the cosy atmosphere of the mess or village pub, where the bartender and the locals, unlike them, could almost guarantee they would be there for some time to come, the airmen could not be sure whether they would ever be there again. These were circumstances which were *sui generis* in the history of warfare, and distinctly different from the role played by other combatants. The aircrews' position bore no resemblance to that of the soldiers who might be on the battlefield for weeks on end, or to that of the sailors in a slow-moving Atlantic convoy, far removed from regular evenings of social contact with ordinary human beings in a familiar milieu, and in the front line for an uninterrupted period which was long enough for them to adjust. The airmen never had this advantage, if it can be termed thus, since their thoughts were ever on the morrow and on where they might then be. Their bizarre situation - completely safe one night and in extreme jeopardy the next -and the fact that they had always to start fighting from cold, did a lot to increase tension and the awareness of the unpredictability of what the fates held in store for them. A brief escape was possible only during the leaves which they were granted every six to nine weeks. At the height of the Offensive in particular they regarded such a break as a stay of execution and spent it quietly at home or, for those who couldn't stand trying to act normally in the bosom of their families, it took the form of days of alcoholic oblivion in London or some other city.

Although they suspected, but didn't know it for certain then, they topped the casualty league by a substantial margin (almost 60% of Bomber Command aircrew were killed or wounded). No other fighting man, be he commando or submariner, had less chance of survival. This is vividly borne out by the fact that the average life of a Lancaster in 1943-44 was 14 operations - and many of those which did return carried dead men aboard.

It is not therefore surprising that one of the principal problems confronting Bomber Command was the maintenance of morale, especially in the 'hot period' (1943-44) when the strain on crews became all too evident and losses were so heavy that it was being asked in places that mattered whether the moment had not come for the brakes to be applied. Although it was true that their spirits had fallen to a worrying extent, the great majority of operational airmen kept plodding on with that amazing resilience which appeared to be part of their make-up. For one thing they believed, or tried to believe - in spite of evidence to the contrary all around them - as people in general are wont to do, such as the 60 cigarettes a day smoker or the excessive drinker, that it would never happen to them. Unlike the front-line soldier they saw few dead or wounded or the wreckage of war strewn all around them, only now and again the body of one of their own crew or severely damaged bombers that had struggled back to base. Even of the presence of the enemy they witnessed little at first hand, perhaps only the momentary glimpse of an attacking fighter, and they were miles above the men operating anti-aircraft guns and searchlights.

The nature of their task, which entailed, for most of them, concentration on instruments even when over the target area, was such that they could never work themselves into a fighting frenzy, which is one way of overcoming, or at least reducing, fear. They were fighting what was in fact an unseen enemy. They could look down on the large fires they had lit but the human and material devastation they had caused lay hidden from their eyes. The fear-allaying thrill and morale-giving boost accorded the soldiers or sailors who saw their fire destroy an enemy tank or sink an enemy ship, in other words of being able to observe the immediate effects of their efforts, was an experience largely denied to them. There were exceptions, such as the exhilarating sight of the Möhne Dam collapsing or the sinking of the Tirpitz, but these were rare opportunities indeed. They seldom, if ever, knew on any particular night if they had won or lost, and it was not until many months or even years later, after it was all over, when many of the survivors flew over the worst-bombed areas, that they gained any real notion of what they had achieved. But by then it was a little late for cheers or euphoria. If these were their victory fruits they were never seen or savoured at the time it mattered most, when they were in the thick of it and destined to go somewhere else and do the same thing the next night or a night or two later. Had they witnessed the havoc they were creating when they were actually doing it they might have been spurred on and felt somewhat less the clammy grip of fear.

The 19 or 20-year old, up till then often cloistered in the secure bosom of a middle-class family and rather naïve in the ways of the world, had to cope, in the course of a few weeks - or perhaps just a few days - with indescribably horrendous experiences and sights which would have appalled the most hardened surgeon; for a large number of thinking and sensitive youngsters this meant an abrupt and savage transition from life as they had known it, to an experience of far too much far too soon. They seldom saw their comrades - some of them close friends - in accompanying aircraft which simply disappeared from the skies in one explosion amongst many. They never knew just when or where or how they had 'bought it'. It didn't help, either, when their own impending end was hinted at in brutal fashion when they came upon an orderly collecting together their friends' personal effects to have them sent off to their next of kin. These things cut deep and gave rise to thoughts which were hard to put into words. Thus was conceived the spawn which would gradually mature to become what Bomber Command, somewhat euphemistically, yet revealing welcome sensitivity, termed LMF - 'Lack of Moral Fibre'.

Early on in the war, towards the end of 1940, it had become blatantly obvious that crews could not go on for ever, that there must be come criteria established as to how much they could reasonably be expected to endure.

A committee of officers, varying in rank from the higher echelons down to Squadron Leader, and wisely including a majority of operational flyers, deliberated long and hard; and it was they who decided, after taking a number of factors into consideration - an eight or nine hour flight, for example, to a distant target in the Reich was clearly a much more demanding task than the same time spent in a flying-boat patrolling the waters of the Atlantic - that a first tour should amount to no more than 30 operations, which would then be followed by about nine months as an instructor at an HCU or OTU before the commencement of a second batch of 20 trips; and that thereafter the airman would not be asked to participate further. It was reckoned that such an arrangement offered him a 50-50 chance of survival. Not very good odds. If he was still *mens sana in corpore sano* after 50 ops. (and it did sometimes happen), it was up to him entirely whether he embarked on a third tour. One cannot help but reflect that had the committee met again three or four years later, as perhaps it should have done, it might have been just a little more generous with its requirements.

The magic goal of 30 was the longed-for target of all first tour crews and they regarded every extra entry in their log-books as a further step towards that milestone and at least temporary salvation. They knew that once that figure was attained they were due a lengthy respite and cherished the hope that by then the war might be over. Most airmen experienced mixed feelings when for some reason the bomber stream was recalled after they had gone through all the traumatic preparations and were over the North Sea or had just reached occupied territory. Such aborted sorties did not count and they felt that on such occasions they had been shabbily treated. As the life-prolonging goal of 30 approached, each operation became akin to a game of Russian roulette and nerves more taut than ever.

Up until about mid-1943 Station Commanders varied in their attitudes towards cases of aircrew who reported sick - with fear. Some treated the matter rather after the manner of the First World War, as unpardonable, ignored psychiatric reports and brought the hapless man before a court martial: from the second half of 1943 onwards, as the pressure mounted, few resorted to such extreme measures. It was realised that a man smitten with LMF deserved to be treated with understanding, even with sympathy. After all, like all aircrew, he was a volunteer, and as he had made the grade and put a number of ops. behind him he could hardly be classed as a namby-pamby. In most cases a few weeks' rest on a non-operational station restored the airman's equilibrium. But problems arose with those who did not admit their fear and regularly reported sick with minor ailments that could not be dismissed as non-existent.

Another cause for concern was the rumoured defections to the neutral countries of Sweden and Switzerland - yet not one single definite case of such desertion by a British bomber crew was ever proven (apparently it did occur on occasion in the USAAF). Although a number of RAF personnel baled out over these countries or landed their aircraft on their soil, this occurred only in emergency, when the chances of a safe return to base were either impossible or highly unlikely. A total of 13 bombers (eight Lancasters, four Mosquitoes and one Wellington), landed or crashed in Switzerland; of the airmen involved 36 were killed (the bodies of the others were never found) and 33 were interned for the duration of the war. Sweden offered safety to aircraft crippled over Norway, Berlin and the Baltic ports and no fewer than 64 of them sought asylum there - mainly Lancasters (30), all of which were wrecked. Some of their crews landed by parachute.

"Fringe merchants" there certainly were, especially on operations to Berlin, who did drop their loads prematurely so as to avoid the dangerous target area and be on their way home again as soon as they could. This, however, was very difficult to prove in the case of any particular aircraft and very little could be done about it. It often meant that certain attacks did not succeed as they might have done, because once bombs started to land short of the target a snowballing effect developed as later arrivals released their loads just before they reached the outermost fires, resulting in the phenomenon known as "creep-back", which could extend for miles. Bennett's Pathfinder crews (Chapter 12) were particularly critical of 'fringe merchants' and they could hardly be blamed for being so; after all, they had run the gauntlet of the defences to ensure accurate marking only to find their efforts partly nullified by the action of some main stream crews obviously more concerned about their own safety than anything else.

Medical officers and aircrew were quick to note the symptoms of LMF in a colleague, usually in the mess. Gruffness, bad temper, unsociability, quarrelsomeness and even bellicosity, excessive drinking, trembling hands or a facial twitch, either singly or in combination, provided unmistakeable signs. In the case of pilots the first indication could be regular early returns to base, for which 'engine trouble' formed

The Great Ingratitude

the main excuse.

But Bomber Command appreciated the admission of fear by a man who was genuinely incapacitated by it. If he remained silent and carried on he was likely to make gross errors of judgement which might have dire consequences for the entire crew, especially if he was a pilot or navigator; and, further, panic-stricken voices at the height of an attack did nothing to keep others cool and self-possessed. In fact it was believed that aircraft were lost because certain aircrew members had kept their secrets to themselves, petrified at the thought of the ignominy which would be their lot if they made their problems known. They knew that they were likely to lose both brevet and rank and be remustered to ground duties, a situation that many thought would be as hard to bear as their state of permanent fear; there was just no way in which they could win.

LMF presented the greatest headaches for the bomber chiefs when Germany's defences reached their most formidable and losses mounted to their highest level of the war and only 10% of crews were managing to complete a first tour. But with the gradual demise of the enemy night fighters force - thanks in large part to the USAAF - the situation eased and finally all but disappeared. But not before it had left a mark on many, a mark which was to stay with them in the years ahead; and if Allied combatants suffered from 'post-combat stress disorders' after the brief and almost casualty-free Gulf War in early 1991, one can imagine how poignant the stress must have been in the case of those who survived regular operations with Bomber Command, particularly around the time of the Battle of Berlin, and who found that they simply could not take any more. Surely we can forgive them - if in fact there is anything to forgive.

Chapter 10

HAPPY VALLEY

The Ruhr, a conurbation roughly 50 miles long and 15 miles wide, and one of the major manufacturing regions of the entire world, was the power-house of German heavy industry and consequently earmarked from the very beginning of the war for the continual attentions of Bomber Command. No other part of the Reich underwent such heavy and regular attacks from the bombers.

Apart from its obvious attractions as a most worthwhile target, one of its advantages was its relative proximity to the English bases. Bomber Command had learned early in its career that the longer a bomber had to stay in the air the more vulnerable it became. A 1000-mile trip meant a full load of high octane fuel, more prolonged exposure to fighters, flak and bad weather, more miles to cover in a possibly crippled aircraft, and, in may cases, exhausted crews faced with a tricky landing. The Ruhr meant a flight of only half that distance. Further, as electronic navigational and bombing aids were developed, it was (unlike Berlin, for example) well within their effective range.

But the attractions ended there. This great arsenal's defences were, as might be expected, of an order calculated to give any marauding aircraft the hottest of receptions and to demonstrate that any attack made on it would be a most unviable proposition. Further, it was constantly veiled in a thick industrial haze which, prior to the advent of aids such as *Gee, Oboe* and *H2S* (Chapter 12), made the finding and identification of individual towns, not to mention individual targets such as large factories, a matter of extreme difficulty, whether by day or by night. Bombing was erratic to say the least, loads were often released on the wrong town or even in open country, although there was always the consolation that, provided you were in fact somewhere over the area, you did have a chance of hitting something of importance, so great was the acreage taken up by industrial complexes contributing to the war effort.

Although the Ruhr Valley should be exactly what it says - a region comprising the towns lying along the Rhine's tributary the Ruhr - which enters the parent river at Duisburg - in other words Dortmund,

The Great Ingratitude

Bochum, Essen, Bottrop, Gelsenkirchen, Oberhausen, Duisburg and a host of smaller towns such as Castrop-Rauxel, Watten, Gladbeck and Homberg, Bomber Command used it in rather a loose sense to include the whole industrial area of Rhineland-Westphalia on the Rhine and the River Lippe as well, and therefore embracing Hagen, Wuppertal, Remscheid, Solingen, Düsseldorf, Mönchen-Gladbach, Krefeld, Neuss, Hamm, and even Cologne, which after all was only 17 miles distant from Düsseldorf. Again there were several lesser known centres lying in their midst. The Ruhr provided by far the greater part of Germany's coal supplies and almost half of its electricity. Iron, steel and chemical products predominated.

The crews feared its dense concentration of ack-ack batteries, equipped mostly with the excellent 88-millimetre dual purpose guns, and the many fighter squadrons based on its western approaches. Another worry was the possibility of having to bale out over an area where you were just as likely to clatter down on to roof-tops or electric cables or into waterways as on to open ground. From 1943 onwards the fear of reprisals from bomb-crazed civilians - rough handling or even worse - became a further source of anxiety to those forced to abandon their aircraft over much-bombed cities, and especially those of the Ruhr. Goebbels had written magazine articles in which he had stated that RAF airmen should be treated like wild dogs - the German civilian population was not slow to react to such remarks from above - and Hitler himself was known to rant and rave at them regularly and to threaten them with all sorts of retaliatory measures. A typical outburst erupted after a raid on Munich in the summer of 1944, in which Heins Handschuhmacher, an actor and close friend of Hitler's mistress, Eva Braun, was killed. Eva had been quite upset and had launched into a vehement diatribe in which she cursed the RAF and the USAAF for all the terror and wretchedness they were causing. The Führer, apparently quite affected by her words, promised he would repay the Allies one hundredfold ... and woe betide the *Terrorflieger* who now fell into German hands ...

We know that members of aircrew did arrive in prison camps with rope marks around their necks after being rescued from irate civilians in the nick of time by the German Police or Luftwaffe, and who reported that some of their comrades had not been so lucky. Like the little Minister of Propaganda, the inhabitants of many towns wanted airmen to be put to death as soon as they landed. On one occasion a group of people in Essen, the city which was to head the league for the record number of heavy attacks by Bomber Command, had their emotions whipped up into a frenzy by an army captain called Hayer, with the result that three members of a crew were literally kicked to death. Another soldier by the name of Arberger shot and killed four baled-out airmen in March, 1945. Both men were eventually executed by the British authorities. One Flight Lieutenant, liberated from a Stalag Luft camp at the end of the war, reported that when he and his six crew members landed by parachute they were immediately seized by maddened civilians. He himself had been 'strung up last and cut down first' and so rescued within seconds of expiring - incredibly by the Gestapo.

By the early spring of 1945 Hitler had become thoroughly disgruntled with the performance of the Luftwaffe in general and with its miserable attempts to stem the bomb flood in particular, and commanded that it should hand over all captured Allied airmen to the SD (*Sicherheitsdienst* or 'Security Police') for summary execution. This order, drafted in the presence of Koller (Chief of German Air Staff), Keitel and Kaltenbrunner, was received by them with icy stares and a stunned silence; after which they suggested that such a step would only encourage similar treatment of German prisoners in enemy hands. Once out of the Führer's presence the three officers agreed that the order should be ignored, and in a further interview with Hitler a week or two later, Koller made it known to him in no uncertain terms that there was no possibility of either the Luftwaffe or the SD complying with such instructions. Such an act of insubordination earlier in the war would have brought instant dismissal from office and, more than likely, something far worse, but by now the writing was plain for all to see and Hitler's absolute and unquestionable authority was showing definite signs of cracking.

But even without the implementation of the Führer's wishes there were many who seized the opportunity to wreak their wrath on the men who descended into the towns they had agonized for years, and it is known for certain that many crew members received brutal treatment from frenzied mobs; what will never be known is the number - and it could be substantial - who lost their lives in such a ghastly manner, as all knowledge of the true fate of dead or missing aircrew could be so easily denied, and it was suspected that bodies were burned or disposed of in places where they would not be sought; and in the chaos and the turmoil that characterised post-war Germany the odds were all against successful investigation. Although specific incidents were not obviously known to operational aircrew, they had heard disquieting rumours - and these added yet another hazard to all those they were already called upon to face. As might be expected, it was seldom that the SS or the SD or the Gestapo intervened to dissuade would-be assassins. Their young, fanatical members in particular were more likely to offer the civilians encouragement or perform the act themselves. So when an airman had to resort to his parachute his chances of being molested or not often depended on who got to him first; if it was the Police or the Luftwaffe he was usually all right; if not he could be in dire straits. As we shall gather from the following pages, it is not surprising that airmen forced to abandon their aircraft were at greatest risk in the Ruhr.

Up until the spring of 1943 the 'Valley' had been visited many times by the old Hampdens and Whitleys, Wellingtons and Stirlings, which created a certain amount of damage here and there, but in reality such raids were little more than pin-pricks and caused no serious loss of production. But the scene was soon to change and the 4-month 'Battle of the Ruhr' was heralded by the curtain going up on Essen, the heart town of the region and the home of the gigantic Krupp works since 1811. Between the opening raid on March 5/6, when 442 aircraft attacked the city, and July 25, when, perhaps appropriately, the curtain went down on the same target (immediately after which Dr Gustav Krupp suffered a stroke from which he never recovered) with the visit of 705 aircraft, 43 major assaults were made on the Ruhr area. It was one of the trio of battles which included Hamburg and Berlin, but in this case the dates are somewhat misleading, since Germany's industrial heartland was regularly attacked throughout the war - the March-July period of 1943 being simply a massive concentration of heavy raids to be followed by what is sometimes referred to as the 'Second Battle of the Ruhr' between October 1944 and April 1945.

During the March-July period in 1943, the attack on Essen on March 5/6 was followed by a spate of bombardments intended to reduce the Ruhr's manufacturing capacity to a state of impotence. Not a single Ruhr town escaped, and Essen (2775 sorties), Duisburg (1980), and Cologne (1755 and 1543 of them in the space of 10 days) were the worst to suffer. Enormous damage was done but the cost to Bomber Command was 1000 aircraft and over 6000 airmen killed or taken prisoner. That was a horrendous price to pay and it was typical of the crews that they dubbed the area 'Happy Valley', when 'Death Valley' might have been a much more appropriate description. There was as little happiness for them as there was for its inhabitants. They regarded the Ruhr in much the same way as they did Berlin - it was one of the places where they were likely to 'get the chop', to 'go for a Burton' or to 'buy it'. They therefore relished the reduction in such operations when Harris, as he himself put it, was compelled to use the bomber force mainly to "pave the way for the Allies advance into Germany". But, like MacArthur in the Philippines, he swore he "would be back".

It is not difficult to understand why the crews welcomed the cessation of large saturation raids, even though they suspected it was no more than a temporary one: by the time the Battle of the Ruhr ended the strength of the German air defences was increasing at an alarming rate. It was calculated that Luftwaffe fighter disposition had been reapportioned to 16% in the Mediterranean, 27% in Russia and an ominous 57% on the Western Front; and that by the second half of 1943, after Hamburg, these figures became even more significant for Bomber Command: 14%, 20% and 66% respectively - and rendered even more disturbing by the expansion in production of fighter aircraft. By then too the number of anti-aircraft guns in the Reich had reached the 40,000 mark and more than one million personnel, either full-time or part-time, were engaged in air raid defence.

But Harris kept his word. By the autumn of 1944, by which time the armies were firmly established on the Continent, Harris was able, in spite of his disagreements with Portal, (Chapter 6), to turn most of his attentions once more to his first and permanent love - or hate - Germany's cities, which signalled the opening of the second 'Battle'. Thanks to the Allied presence in France, operating conditions were now much more favourable for his Lancasters and Halifaxes and Mosquitoes with the positioning of radar stations nearer the Reich, and in addition he could rely on fighter support from captured airfields. There was also improved equipment in the bombers and more of it, and, as the campaign progressed, the only problem was an unexpected one - a shortage of bombs. As fast as the factories made them his greedy bomb-bays sucked them in, spewed them out and cried for more. Indeed with 1500 serviceable bombers ready for action and with plenty of crews to man them, Harris found himself compelled for a period to live almost hand-to-mouth because his bomb cupboard was nearly bare. The Bomber Chief had all but got himself into the same predicament as US General 'Blood and Guts' Patton, who had swept across France at such speed that he had outpaced his supply lines, for Harris was threatening to use up his bombs faster than the factories could produce them. Had he had time, some of those engaged in this work might well have been honoured by a visit from a certain very high-ranking

The Great Ingratitude

RAF officer. They wouldn't have considered it an honour for long when suddenly subjected to the vocal explosion which would no doubt have been their lot.

And so it transpired that in the last quarter of 1944 the whole considerable weight of Bomber Command was being hurled once again, but this time in a manner which transcended anything which had gone before, against the boiler-house of German industry, and against other cities where everything was not yet flattened. Harris was now in a position to send an apparently endless stream of bombers, both by day and by night, in a frenetic effort to deal the final blow. Every town, from the largest like Essen and Duisburg and Cologne, down to the smallest, such as Neuss and Homberg, experienced a bomb-delivering shuttle service which must have been the nearest thing to hell on earth for their millions of inhabitants. During daylight on October 14, for example, the hapless city of Duisburg was visited by 1013 fighter-escorted bombers which released 3574 tons of high explosives and 820 tons of incendiaries, then the same night was called upon to face up to a further 1005 (half of them Lancasters) and to absorb another 4040 tons of high explosive and 500 tons of incendiaries, after which it looked as if the city had been hit by a major earthquake, while at the same time 233 Lancasters and seven Mosquitoes were dehousing 80,000 people in more distant Brunswick. Then it was residential Bonn - the future Federal Capital - and trips well outside the Ruhr to Stuttgart and Hanover. On October 25 Essen received 4538 tons from 1055 planes (900 high explosives, including 509 'cookies', because it was reckoned there was little left to burn), and the following day the same place had to cope with a further 771 aircraft. Small wonder that German reports stated Krupps to be ''completely paralysed''. Yet although Essen could no longer be classified as one of the country's major industrial cities, it was to undergo two other big attacks (316 and 540 bombers) in the following weeks. The list went on and on: 243 to Homberg (mostly Halifaxes), on October 25, 733 to Cologne on October 28, 905 on October 30/31 and 493 on October 31/November 1. 922 went to Düsseldorf the next night; Bochum (749 on November 4/5, Solingen (173 on November 5), Gelsenkirchen (738 on November 6), Neuss, Dortmund, Oberhausen, Mönchen-Gladbach ... Duisburg had to endure further agonies on November 30 (576) and on December 17/18 (523); Cologne (351 on November 27 and 470 on December 30/31); Hagen (504 on December 2/3); and away from the Ruhr the story was the same: Koblenz, Freiburg, Karlsruhe, Heilbronn, Soest, Osnabrück, Giessen, Ludwigshafen, Ulm, Munich, Gydnia, Trier and others ... and others. The avalanche went on and on till the end of the year - the same policy - the same results - the same vast areas of destruction. It is also worth noting that the enormous consumption of shells by the German air defences resulted in a serious shortage of ammunition on both the Western and Eastern Fronts.

As we know (Chapter 6) Harris was, during this period, supposed to be using his force mainly to deprive Germany of her remaining oil supplies. So what happened? Apart from some plants which no doubt suffered damage in the aforementioned saturation raids, Harris did lay on some 13 operations in November and December, 1944 (when the weather was suitable) against specific targets. These were in Wanne-Eickel (near Bochum), to which he despatched 277 aircraft on November 9 and 309 on November 18/19; in Castrop-Rauxel (near Dortmund), which he attacked with 122 Lancasters on November 11 and with 273 on November 21/22; he sent 183 to Homberg (near Duisburg) on November 20, 160 to the same plant the following day, and similar-sized forces on two other occasions; the huge installation at Leuna, near Leipzig, which was defended by 460 heavy anti-aircraft guns, entailed a one thousand mile round trip and was severely damaged by 475 Lancasters and 12 Mosquitoes on December 6/7. Other oil plants were bombed at Harburg, Duisburg, Dortmund and Bottrop. To Portal it did seem a rather puny effort since only just over 2000 oil sorties had been flown in November and December, whereas his Bomber Chief had seen fit to launch around 10,000 on area raids; even so Harris had rained down 10,000 tons on oil targets, which he no doubt considered to be a magnanimous gesture on his part, and it was certainly no mean figure even if dwarfed by the weight of the saturation attacks; in fact the tonnage he had dropped on such installations in November exceeded that released by the Americans.

1945 and the beginning of the last few months of the war brought no change of heart on Harris's part, although operations were somewhat curtailed by unfavourable weather conditions in January. It appeared that the Commander in Chief was more determined than ever to realise his prophesy of compelling Germany to lay down her arms before the Allied armies put a foot on her soil. In that 4-month period Bomber Command flew 44,289 night and 18,545 day sorties, a total of 62,834, during which it dropped 181,740 tons of bombs and lost 711 aircraft. March, with 67,637 tons, could lay claim to the highest monthly total of the entire war - in fact as much as what all enemy targets received during the first two years and ten months of hostilities. Thousands upon

The Great Ingratitude

thousands of bombs shattered Nuremberg (521 aircraft), Hanover (664), Hanau (482), Munich (654), Stuttgart (602), Ludwigshafen (396), Wiesbaden (495), Goch (464), Chemnitz (717), Dresden (805, please see Chapter 18), Wesel (different raids, totalling well over 600 bombers), Dortmund (514 Lancasters and 14 Mosquitoes), Essen (342 aircraft, and 300 HE and 11,000 incendiaries fell on Krupps alone, many of the former just turning over the rubble), Pforzheim (399, which caused a fire storm and the deaths of 17,600 people (see Chapter 19), a figure exceeded only in Hamburg and Dresden), Mainz (458), Mannheim (478), Cologne (858, its last raid of the war and the results of which were succinctly put by a German expert on bombing - "Das war das Ende von Köln"). By that time the city's pre-war population of 650,000 had fallen to 300,000, most citizens having fled; all production came to a halt in Dortmund on March 12, when 1108 aircraft, mostly Lancasters, released a record tonnage of 4851; Wuppertal-Barmen (354 aircraft), Nuremberg (293), Würzburg (236), Witten (324), Paderborn (286), Kiel (599 and four days later 482), Potsdam (512 -which was the last major raid by Bomber Command on a large German city), Bremen (767). In addition there were many smaller operations by up to 220 bombers against towns all over Germany. Nor were the Mosquitoes ever idle.

Yet while all that was going on Harris did step up his attacks on oil, amounting to about 60. The biggest was to Leuna on January 14/15 (573 Lancasters and 14 Mosquitoes). On February 8/9, 475 Lancasters and seven Mosquitoes went to Pölitz, where not a further drop of oil was produced. (Speer later described the loss of this plant as a huge setback to the German war effort). Plants at Dulmen, Castrop-Rauxel, Recklinghausen, Bochum, Zeitz, Brux, Wanne-Eickel, Ruthen, Sterkrade, Rositz, Kamen and Farge were all destroyed or severely damaged, if not on the first visit then certainly on a second. (The raid on Farge, a small port on the Weser north of Bremen, was particularly interesting; apart from the attack on its oil-storage depot, a U-boat shelter was also hit and its 23-foot thick concrete roof penetrated by two Grand Slams, leaving behind a mountain of rubble). Although the tonnage dropped still amounted to only a small proportion of the total which pulverised cities, it was considerable even so, and Harris must have felt he had been even more generous than in the previous autumn by diverting even a greater part of his force from his first priority.

In accordance with the Harrisian principles of saturation bombing, the towns of the Ruhr, like all the others, had received bomb

Bomber Command in World War II

loads commensurate with their size; it might therefore be apposite at this juncture to summarise briefly exactly what happened to the main centres chosen for annihilation:

Although one main stream attack with 1979 tons was enough to knock out 94% of Wuppertal-Elberfeld, (and to kill 2000 of its inhabitants in half-an-hour), it required 28 main force attacks and 39,907 tons to flatten 50% of the much larger city of Essen, and 22 to wreck 1994 acres (61%) of Cologne with 28,699 tons; Dortmund, population 650,000, a great steel town specialising in constructional and railway material, endured nine large-scale raids, 18,295 tons and had 923 acres laid waste (54%); Duisburg, the home of half-a-million people and the greatest river port in Europe with its 120 miles of frontage, was the outlet for goods manufactured in the Ruhr. It sustained 18 large attacks and received 29,010 tons with 1424 acres destroyed, amounting to 48% of its total area; the 700,000 citizens of Düsseldorf, the capital of North Rhineland-Westphalia with heavy engineering and chemical industries, and the commercial and financial headquarters of the Ruhr, had 64% of their city destroyed (2003 acres) by 18,099 tons of bombs; Krefeld, on the western bank of the Rhine and situated midway between Duisburg and Düsseldorf, had a population of 125,000. It received only two heavy bombardments but these wiped out 714 acres, amounting to 47% of the target area; Witten (37,000 inhabitants), was accorded only one large raid during which 1081 tons fell on it and completely wrecked 129 acres, 62% of the town; Wuppertal-Barmen was blitzed on two occasions with 3448 tons, which razed 655 acres (58%); Hamm, whose marshalling yards had been pounded by Bomber Command on various occasions since the summer of 1940, had 39% of its built-up area (140 acres) destroyed by 94 Lancasters in a single attack.

I apologise if much of the foregoing appears to the reader to be a rather boring batch of statistics, but I shall have achieved my purpose if he is left in no doubt as to the utter inexorability of the aerial onslaught against the industrial might of the Fatherland and the scale of the German torment which was appurtenant to it.

When units of the American Ninth Army penetrated into the Ruhr in early April, 1945, they found square mile after square mile of nothing but rubble. In Essen they gazed with awe upon the Krupp factories, upon the endless acres of piled masonry, the huge twisted girders which protruded from it, and the tons and tons of broken machinery - irrefutable proof of the power of the heavy bomber used en masse. Alfred Krupp

The Great Ingratitude

himself, who had been awarded the Nazi Cross for his enormous contribution to German armaments production, was later to be tried at Nuremberg as a war criminal for his use of slave labour and sentenced to 12 years imprisonment.

It is worth noting that during those hectic final months of the Bomber Offensive Harris was far from being alone in his convictions as to how large bomber fleets could best be employed. Contrary to American military policy, General Carl 'Tooey' Spaatz, who had taken over in January, 1944, as Commanding General of the Strategic Air Force, and Eisenhower himself, gradually came round to the view that the limitless destruction made possible by overwhelming air power could result in a much earlier Nazi defeat, and this, as we shall see (Chapter 18), was the exact policy adopted with regard to Japan.

During the final months of 1944, and especially during the first four of 1945, Bomber Command found itself capable of launching two main force attacks on the same night, and was like a dog freed of a restraining leash. No longer was it compelled to contend with the ferocious skies over Germany through which it had had to battle its way not so long before, and which had exacted such a monstrous toll of its bombers and of the blood of its highly trained young men. On the contrary it flew with gusto and went exactly where and when it chose, even into the remotest corners of the Reich - even to Königsberg, for instance, as early as August 20, 1944, a town now Russian and called Kalingrad, and which had had no previous experience of the things done by Bomber Command; this was an operation which had entailed a round trip of over 1600 miles and left homeless 134,000 of the city's inhabitants, who had considered themselves completely secure on their distant bay in the Baltic; and the cost was only four aircraft.

Throughout these later stages of the campaign the Command carried out a significant proportion of its operations during daylight - and in this connection it should be emphasised that its ability to do so was in fairly large measure thanks to the annihilation of the Luftwaffe's fighting force by the United States Army Air Force; but at the same time it must also be remembered that Bomber Command had continued to operate on full throttle when the enemy night force was at its most powerful; it had not waited till it possessed some strong counter-measure such as the Mustang long-range fighter or until opposition from the German Air Force had almost ceased to exist. It had soldiered on, and had paid the price.

Bomber Command in World War II

It was quite ironic that by the autumn of 1944 Bomber Command had at its disposal the electronic wizardry which made bombing by night as accurate as bombing by day, yet was no longer obliged to operate during the hours of darkness simply because the Luftwaffe was but a shadow of its former self. The peoples of the occupied countries, the millions of Allied PoWs, foreign slave-workers and inmates of concentration camps, had for a long time stared skywards, with thanks in their hearts, at the vast formations of Fortresses which had penetrated far into the Reich in daytime once fighter protection became available; now they had further reason to rejoice as they beheld the equally unforgettable sight of hundreds of Lancasters criss-crossing the whole country in the same way; at last those below actually glimpsed the bombers which, heard but unseen , had for years rained down a special kind of terror in the dead of night; and now, although RAF raids still took place on a large scale between dusk and dawn, many Germans too gazed for the first time upon the famous and feared Lancasters; the terrors of the night had now become the terrors of the day as well. There was no respite, none.

The crews, especially those who had somehow survived 1943 and early 1944 and were still operating, were quite elated at the turn of events and climbed into their aircraft in a far different frame of mind than was the case before; gone was the stomach-retching fear, the sweating and the nightmares, the twitches and the truculence; and if the former fear was not altogether replaced by a feeling of gay abandon, it was by one rather of mild apprehension as they set out on an incursion which still promised enough danger to render it exciting. But as the German defences offered less and less opposition this attitude too, began to wear off, and was replaced in turn in some cases by a growing feeling of guilt, and even shame. Bomber Command crews had been used to fighting their way there and back and the instinct of self-preservation had rarely permitted thoughts of what was going on beneath; for many of them that was no longer the case; they began to feel they were taking unfair advantage of a hopelessly weakened enemy obviously in no state to hit back. They hadn't been accustomed to this sort of thing and it bothered them. It bothered some of them even more when they read in the newspapers or heard on the radio opinions which suggested that by early 1945 Bomber Command was no longer conducting a strategically justified bombardment of Germany, but rather was punishing the whole nation, innocent and guilty alike, but mostly innocent. But these sentiments, it must be said, were largely expelled, for a time at any rate, when the full horror of the extermination camps was brought to light.

During that final phase of Bomber Command's offensive it would perhaps not be out of place to spare a thought for the few pilots the Luftewaffe could send into action; if operations over enemy territory had become something akin to shelling peas as far as the bomber crews were concerned, for those manning the German fighters it must have been like having teeth drawn: lack of airfields, lack of instructors, lack of time and a chronic lack of fuel had cut their length of training to a dangerously low level; in fact it would be no exaggeration to say that most of them (often little more than boys) had to learn the finer points of flying as they fought - needless to say with predictable results. Some youngsters, after a few lessons on gliders (no fuel required) found themselves, incredibly, in the cockpit of the fast and whimsical Me 262 jet (Chapter 17). The situation was as desperate as that.

So throughout the final eight months of the war the great manufacturing centres of the Ruhr and the other cities of Germany, which had suffered indescribable agonies for a period of years, were regularly and relentlessly battered; it was a matter of bombs, bombs and more bombs, released at such a tempo and in such profusion (up to 5000 tons on a single urban target in 15-20 minutes was the usual formula) that Butcher himself must have felt something akin to complete satisfaction as the last buildings were hammered into smoking rubble, and the rubble into dust which hung thick in the atmosphere on windless days and imparted an even ghostlier aspect to the towns and cities that had died. The term 'coventriering' of a city had, when applied to the towns of the Reich, become the greatest descriptive understatement of the war. British opponents of Harris's policy did not hesitate to make the cruel jibe that he was laying a country in ruins to prove what was now a useless point, and purely for self-glorification. Such an accusation must have sickened him because whatever undesirable character traits he might have had, neither deviousness nor self-aggrandizement figured amongst them.

Yet as Germany, virtually defenceless, went down for the final count and lay prostrate, it was demonstrated beyond all measure of doubt that the collapse of civilian morale, so confidently predicted by the exponents of saturation bombing, had been a gross miscalculation. The subjects of the Reich had continued - admittedly only God knows how - to go about such daily tasks as were still demanded of them in a vast no-man's land where life seemed hardly worth the bother of living. There is little doubt, bearing in mind the huge reverses on both the Eastern and Western

Bomber Command in World War II

Fronts, combined with the bombing, that had they been the subjects of a more benevolent régime, they would have been relieved of their sufferings by the late autumn of 1944 at the very latest. The effects of the aerial onslaught should have been the last nail in the German coffin, but the citizens of the Reich were more terrified of their own authorities than they were of the ordeal that came from the skies - which is saying more than a little. Hitler and his henchmen had subjugated them to their own indomitable will, and it was only when peace came that the Allies realised how little the Nazi hierarchy, and the Führer in particular, had concerned themselves with the fate of the German people, and had merely used them as a vehicle for the fulfilment of their own political aims.

So the obedient, well-disciplined Germans, with their traditional respect for - and fear of - their lords and masters, had gone on climbing about over the heaps of debris that had been their houses and factories, their offices and public buildings, their cinemas and theatres, their hospitals and churches, denied the basic necessities of life and reduced, as Hitler had warned them, to little better than vermin as they scraped around for something to eat. The Drittes Deutsches Reich had become a great abyss of darkness into which it had sunk in complete and utter defeat, destitute and alone, as the rest of Europe celebrated and the Allies did, more or less, whatever they chose. As their Führer had once said: "No one argues with the victor. He alone calls the tune." He himself had certainly called it during the years when practically the whole of Europe had lain under his yoke. But now in 1945 there was a different piper, and a different tune.

Germany had paid in full for the aggressive policies which had led to the deaths of millions and millions of men, women and children and enslaved nearly all of the Continent, bringing incalculable misery to an incalculable number of innocent human beings. But now she found herself the unmourned victim of the most devastating and humiliating defeat a nation had ever had to bear.

Overwhelming air power had had more than a little to do with it; in the apt words of Franklin D Roosevelt: "Hitler built a fortress around Europe - but he forgot to put a roof on it."

Chapter 11

PEENEMÜNDE AND THE 'REVENGE WEAPONS'

For some time the Allied leaders had been concerned about the enemy's capability of producing *Vergeltungswaffen* ('Revenge Weapons') or *Wunderwaffen* ('Wonder Weapons'), the latter often contracted by the Germans to *Wuwa*, and which might well bring about an Axis victory. Although blatant lies, for propaganda purposes, were an integral part of Nazi strategy, they nevertheless had noted the Führer's vague but ominous-sounding words contained in a speech made at Danzig (now Gdansk) just after the subjugation of Poland: "We shall have at our disposal a weapon which can not be used against us." They knew that Germany, with her wealth of gifted scientists, probably had the expertise to produce something in the nature of an explosive-filled rocket, a crewless aircraft, a torpedo which homed in on its target, or a beam which could stop engines, or even something far worse -this gleaned from the 'Oslo Report' which had been smuggled out of Norway by scientists living in that country, and was not regarded by anyone as a mere hoax. After all Otto Hahn, assisted by Fritz Strassmann, had split the atom with slow neutron bullets as early as 1938 (although he did not realise it, only that he had achieved something spectacular) and so there was plenty of cause for feelings of apprehension (Chapter 18). The Allies could never be absolutely certain that the Germans were not engaged in the atomic race, even though they knew that Hitler vacillated, and that there was always the possibility of being confronted with lesser, yet still very devastating weapons.

There was much conjecture concerning this potential threat, and also a great deal of rumour from various channels. However rumour started to become fact when, in 1942, members of the Danish Underground sent regular reports to London about what they described as 'frozen lightning' in the sky when some sort of missiles were shot off over the Baltic in the neighbourhood of Peenemünde, a desolate spot on the coast situated some 180 kilometres due north of Berlin. They said that whatever these things were, and they suspected them to be some kind of rocket, they often exploded in the air or when they hit the surface of the water. This information was supported by reports in a similar vein from a Danish scientist working in the Reich, who further stated that the rockets were large and had a range of 300 kilometres.

The existence, or early existence, of a new and frightening weapon was now taken in all seriousness. Plans were made to evacuate the Government from London and with it thousands of essential civil servants, and Duncan Sandys was appointed to head a committee which would investigate the entire situation regarding bomb-carrying pilotless aircraft and rockets. The summary of the committee's findings suggested that the sooner action was taken the better. This would be directed against Peenemünde, a site which had grown from a mere hamlet to a vast industrial complex with 17,000 workers headed by General Walter Dornberger and staffed by a team of physicists such as Werner von Braun (Peenemünde, in fact, is assured a place in history quite apart from its role in World War 2, for it was there that the exploration of space began on October 3, 1942, when the first rocket (a V-2) ever fired behaved perfectly as it was shot out 100 miles over the Baltic). The successful launching inspired Dornberger to remark that the Germans had just produced a weapon which would hit the earth with such power that the impact would be akin to that of 50 express trains pounding along at 60 mph. Von Braun may have been primarily interested in rocket research as a means of probing space, but for the time being Germany was at war and precedence had to be given to developing rockets as weapons which would help his country towards victory. Even so there is little doubt that it was Nazi military requirements which laid the foundations of the development of post-war rocket research and made possible the landing on the moon. As we all know, Von Braun went to America and played no small part in that momentous achievement.

So Peenemünde presented a dire threat and had to be destroyed. Needless to say there was only one person who could see to that. Harris was consulted.

This god-forsaken place lay 600 miles in a straight line from the east of England and the Bomber Chief, ever fearful of daylight exposure anywhere near Germany, was adamant that the target could not be attacked until the nights became somewhat longer and insisted that there must be a delay of about six weeks. This would allow the crews some 20 minutes more cover on both the approach to Peenemünde and departure from it.

This type of operation, a precision attack in darkness was, of course, hardly to Harris's liking, and he still clung to his belief that the best way to defeat Germany, rockets or no rockets, was to keep hammering at

The Great Ingratitude

her cities. Yet at the same time he knew that this was an order which brooked no opposition and that, 'panacea target' or not, it was one which had to be destroyed at all costs; otherwise London and the whole of Southern England, and even areas further afield, would be in for the same treatment that he had in store for all of Germany; he also knew by late July that the enemy was smarting over Hamburg and would be keen to wreak revenge in as devastating a manner as possible. A constant barrage of flying-bombs and long-range rockets could be their answer. Plans of the lay-out at Peenemünde obtained from underground sources and the six-week postponement granted meant that the operation could be prepared in every detail and with typical Harrisian thoroughness and determination. As a full moon was required if success was to be assured, this entailed additional hazards for the airmen taking part. As had happened three weeks earlier in the case of Hamburg (July 27/28), the track was to lie over the North Sea and across Denmark; a 'spoof' raid was laid on for Berlin, where target indicators as well as bombs would be dropped by Mosquitoes. This, it was hoped, would be interpreted as a prelude to a large-scale attack and would lure the night-fighters to the capital. For the first time in Bomber Command history a Master Bomber would control a large raid by radio. There would be three specific aiming-points: the rocket factory itself, the experimental station, and the staff quarters. This was deemed a case where the annihilation of a group of individuals was both necessary and justified. The operation was code-named *Hydra*.

A force of 596 heavies, made up of 324 Lancasters, 218 Halifaxes and 54 Stirlings, took off around 20.30 on August 17, 1943. The target areas were marked by Pathfinder aircraft with different types of flares, including 'Red Spot Fires' which burned in the air and then on the ground for several minutes. Unfortunately some of the indicators landed wide of the mark owing to an unexpected wind change and several crews had released their loads before the Master Bomber could intervene and the Pathfinders could rectify the situation by remarking; thus an appreciable percentage of the total tonnage of 1530 tons of HE and 270 tons of incendiaries fell either in open country in the vicinity of the site or on the ramshackle huts which housed slave labour workers, of whom some 550 were killed. However the remarking carried out by the Pathfinders ensured that many of the bombs were dropped on the right places. The V-2 facilities were completely destroyed although the V-1 installations were left largely untouched.

Bomber Command in World War II

A total of 40 aircraft - 23 Lancasters, 15 Halifaxes and 2 Stirlings -was the cost of the night's work. The majority of them were shot down towards the end of the raid when the fighters arrived to find the clear conditions were ideal for attacking the bombers, and one is apt to wonder what the losses would have been had the German controllers not been completely foxed by the diversionary tactics. The 200 fighters which had remained patrolling over Berlin would almost certainly have caused Bomber Command fearful casualties had they got to grips with the main stream, especially as this was the first occasion on which ME 110s equipped with *Schräge Musik* were employed; indeed it was reported that two of these managed to catch up with the stream on its homeward leg and quickly accounted for half-a-dozen of the RAF machines lost. (There was an interesting episode concerning the fighter squadrons that had massed over Berlin. As they patrolled high above the city General Hans Jeschonnek, German Chief of Air Staff, ordered the anti-aircraft guns to open up and this caused several losses amongst their own aircraft. The following day Jeschonnek committed suicide).

It was a great pity that owing to 'flare trouble' a substantial part of the load was wasted; it was also to be deplored that so many innocent foreign labourers were killed; on the other hand it was estimated that about 180 Germans, nearly all of them scientists, technicians and other highly-skilled workers, perished with them; but severe physical damage had also been done and it was calculated that the development of the *Vergeltungswaffen* was delayed by about two months. This was of vital importance, because it meant that London and the towns of the South ultimately received far fewer 'doodle-bugs' and V-2 rockets than would otherwise have been the case; it was also vitally important as far as the success of the coming Invasion was concerned - the huge numbers of men and vast amount of *matériel* packed into the Channel ports were for the most part already in Normandy when the first flying-bomb landed on June 13 at Swanscombe, about 18 miles to the east of central London, the first of 7488 to reach England (in addition to over 1000 V-2s, the first of which fell on Chiswick in West London on September 8). There is just no telling what might have happened had the Peenemünde raid not been successful and if the Germans had not had to cope with the building of underground factories in the Harz mountains, three hundred miles away, and the transportation of much equipment, including completed V-1s, to the new site. Without the respite that had been gained the outcome might have been very different.

The Great Ingratitude

The attack on Peenemünde was of further significance in so far as it showed that, given favourable weather conditions, Bomber Command was now quite capable of hitting specific targets at night; but weather conditions were much more likely to be unfavourable and Harris regarded Peenemünde as a 'one-off' operation, if an essential one, and no more than an intrusion into his Great Plan. He was still drooling at the mouth over Hamburg and couldn't wait to get back to his cities before nearly all of his Command's resources would have to be committed to *Overlord*.

Although the results achieved at Peenemünde were of paramount importance in the battle against the V-1 and V-2, of almost equal value was a 'normal saturation raid' carried out by 569 aircraft on Kassel on October 22/23, 1943 (a couple of months later), when the city had to undergo the most paralysing onslaught on any large built-up target since Hamburg. A tremendous amount of damage was done both to industrial premises and to living accommodation (110,000 people were dehoused) and one welcome bonus was the elimination of three big Henschel aircraft factories engaged in manufacturing major components for the flying-bomb and rockets. In fact it was estimated later that production of the missiles had again been held up for a period of two months. This raid claimed 25 Halifaxes and 18 Lancasters.

Once the Allied armies had firmly established themselves in Normandy and the assault on the UK by V-1s and V-2s gradually increased in momentum, Bomber Command and the American Army Air Force were compelled to divert much of their attention to the destruction of the launching pads - Operation *No-ball* - set up all along the coastline from France to Holland. The RAF alone took 1¼ million photographs of these sites, which were attacked heavily and regularly, as they were often rapidly rebuilt. Not only were they difficult to identify, but were also difficult to hit as they were small and often constructed in orchards, clearings in woods, and even in large gardens (wooden 'mock' sites of the correct dimensions were installed on UK ranges to enable pilots to recognise them quickly and to practise going in fast and as low as 20 feet); indeed much time and effort went into the bombing of communications to prevent the Germans from moving the missiles up to the pads; and if the flying-bombs and rockets were stored in underground shelters or caves, as they frequently were, the entrances to these were pounded so mercilessly that the enemy could not get the weapons out. Armadas of up to 600 aircraft - Lancasters, Halifaxes and Mosquitoes - undertook operations against *Crossbow* targets, as the campaign against all V-1 and V-2 installations was called, day after day, night after night, and one typical example of the Allied determination to beat the V-weapons was demonstrated on July 4, 1944, when 17 Lancasters of 617 Squadron, accompanied by a single Mosquito and led by Group Captain Leonard Cheshire, dropped 12,000-pound 'Tallboys' on a storage cave at Saint-Leu, 20 miles north of Paris, to which over 7000 V-1s had just been delivered from 40 trains in a single day. Direct hits were scored by these powerful bombs but nevertheless 231 Lancasters and 15 Mosquitoes returned the same night just to make sure that what remained of the arsenal, if anything, would never clatter its way across the Channel. The night raiders peppered the surrounding area with 1000-pound HEs, thus making it impossible for the Germans to move any undamaged weapons to the launching pads. The cost of that venture was 13 Lancasters, all downed by night-fighters. Everything associated with V-weapons was blasted until it was liquidated, no matter how many bombers were required. If it was considered impossible to destroy the deepest subterranean factories and storage caves, all roads and railways and bridges in their vicinity were smothered with bombs and rendered unserviceable; the huge flying-bomb store at Watten (20 miles south-east of Calais) was blown skywards while in the final stages of construction, and when it was rebuilt in a quarry protected by a million tons of concrete, the surrounding area was drenched with HE to ensure that nothing could get in or out. It was hell for the German military - and unfortunately for the French civilians as well. By the middle of August Bomber Command alone had flown over 10,000 sorties against such targets, shattering them with 36,000 tons of HE and losing 100 bombers and 650 personnel in the process, and by the end of that month the Allied Air Forces had hurled approximately 100,000 tons on to the launching sites or the approaches to them - an average of 1000 tons per day throughout a six-week period. Harris reckoned that the results were not commensurate with the gigantic effort involved, and deplored the fact that *Crossbow* had more or less let German cities off the hook for three months. There were other places to which he would have preferred to deliver that massive weight of bombs, other places he would rather have laid waste than rural areas in Northern France, yet he was aware that the relentless measures ordered by the Allied leaders to put paid to the 'Revenge Weapons' was a true reflection of the menace they considered the V-1 and the V-2 to represent.

Nor did the V-weapon blitz end with this mighty assault against it, for we were provided with yet a further example of Germany's ability to carry on producing armaments and to repair industrial plant which had apparently suffered irreparable damage from aerial bombardment. Despite the hammer blows that were dealt everything connected with flying bombs and rockets, these missiles were still being despatched to London as late as March, 1945, and during the entire nine-month period from June, 1944 until then, Bomber Command and the Eighth Army Force flew in all 69,000 sorties and dropped over 122,000 tons of bombs on all types of 'Revenge Weapon' targets. The greater effort was directed against the V-1 (almost 100,000 tons), not a surprising proportion when it is borne in mind that six times more flying-bombs than rockets were aimed at the British mainland.

The significant role played by the Americans is deserving of the highest praise and many of them gave their lives to save those of ordinary citizens of the UK; they contributed half of the total bombs delivered against the sites and half the airmen lost. Nor should the stoicism of the people living in the South of England go unmentioned: if the very name Peenemünde had a sinister ring about it, the same can be applied to the V-1, whose engine, with its distinctive rattling noise, was a fearsome sound to millions, who waited with bated breath, hoping against hope that the noise would continue until the bomb had passed overhead, dreading the 'deafening silence' which ensued as soon as the engine cut, a sure sign that the missile was about to plunge earthwards and erupt in one hellish explosion. Neither should we forget that little Belgium, between October, 1944, and March, 1945, had to cope with 6585 V-1s (of which RAF fighters and ack-ack batteries shot down 2455) and 1712 V-2s, and that the city of Antwerp, an essential supply port for the Allied armies and much smaller than London, alone received 2448 flying-bombs and 1265 rockets. It is interesting to note that as the Allies advanced further eastwards and the launching pads had to be sited in the Eifel area of western Germany, all V-1s were rigorously checked before being fired, and often discarded. The Germans had not worried too much about defective bombs travelling only a mile or two before crashing on French or Belgian towns and villages, but the threat they presented to their own people was an entirely different matter.

For those living in the danger areas a further macabre touch was added when the Germans, dissatisfied with the frequent inaccuracy of the flying bombs - too many were missing even a huge target like London and exploding in open country - converted a number of Heinkel He 177s to carry a piloted V-1 slung beneath their bellies. When the bomb was released the pilot steered it towards its target and then tried to bale out, which was practically impossible because he had no proper escape hatch. To all intents and purposes these pilots were of the Kamikazi breed since they knew that their chances of survival were almost nil; and although almost all of the country's leaders were opposed to the idea of *Selbstopfermänner* (any combatant willing to kill himself to ensure the success of an action) as being a concept alien to the German psyche and quite unacceptable, even in those dire days, Himmler, true to form, advocated that suicide pilots could be recruited from the ranks of the terminally sick or from hardened criminals, but he received little support. In fact the whole project was more or less a waste of time, because the Luftwaffe had few aircraft which could be spared to act as V-1 carriers, and those that did were usually shot down by Allied fighters.

 In terms of final victory the Allies won the battle against Hitler's 'Secret Weapons'. But it was a victory achieved at a tremendous price (not unusual in actions involving Bomber Command and the USAAF): it was estimated that each V-1 (code-named *Kirschkern*-'cherry stone' by the Germans and known to the British as the 'doodle-bug'), which was in effect a 'cruise missile' 27 feet long with an 18-foot wing-span, maximum speed 310 mph, with an 1870-pound warhead powered by an Argus jet and kept on course by a gyroscopic preselector, cost only £115 to produce. The V-2 liquid-fuel rocket, in fact a 'ballistic missile' with a total weight of 13½ tons (including a one-ton warhead) and which reached a height of 50 miles at the top of its curve, was a much more costly proposition, but had the advantage of supersonic speed (3466 mph), which meant it could not be shot down and had to be destroyed while in production, in transport or on the launching pads. It was calculated that in terms of human life the V-weapon programme cost the Germans only a few hundred dead and wounded out of the 7000 manning the sites or working in the factories, compared with over 6000 British civilians killed, 17,000 seriously injured, 23,000 homes destroyed and well over one million damaged, plus the loss of 2900 Allied airmen and 150 Lancasters, Halifaxes and Mosquitoes together with roughly the same number of American aircraft.

 Yet it could have been a lot worse. If the Nazis had been allowed to despatch a regular flow of V-1s and V-2s, life in London and the South could well have become insufferable; Goering's deputy, Field Marshal Erhard Milch, an impassioned Nazi ready to support whole-heartedly the utilization of any weapon which promised wholesale slaughter,

The Great Ingratitude

envisaged one warhead every half-hour 24 hours a day on London alone - which he joyfully announced would have the British 'shaking at the knees'. Even with the more moderate rate of fire Milch did achieve he certainly caused much fear and consternation amongst those threatened by this 'Second Blitz', so much so that Churchill was all for hitting back at German cities by using bombs filled with poisonous gas, and was only dissuaded from doing so by weight of British and American government and military opinion. Thinking of what happened to RAF crews over Germany almost nightly, a crewless bomber, in British eyes in general and in Churchill's in particular, was simply 'not cricket', and deserved an appropriate form of retaliation. As it happened, it would not be long before Harris was once again free to overwhelm the Reich with such a deluge of high explosives and incendiaries that Churchill would be pacified - and then concerned that the country to be occupied by the Allies in the foreseeable future was being transformed into an urban desert. In any case it was an illogical complaint on the part of the Prime Minister, who was no doubt narked by the fact that the Luftwaffe had found an easy, cheap and clever way of threatening to do to Britain what Bomber Command was doing, at such painful cost to itself, to Germany; but you can't really expect to curb inventive genius in the field of weaponry any more than in any other sphere, and one cannot help but conclude that Churchill, who was not renowned for pulling his punches in any circumstances, let alone in his aim to defeat the Nazis, was suffering from a large dose of very sour grapes.

That the UK was spared what could have been a prolonged and pulverizing onslaught by the 'Revenge Weapons' was due in no small measure to factions within German industry, the German High Command and the Luftwaffe, and to Hitler's frequent changes of mind concerning priorities. In fact in his views he was becoming more and more predictably unpredictable and consistently inconsistent. It was the old story of vacillation and indecision which resulted from having too many irons in the fire - flying bombs, rockets, jet fighters, electric-engined submarines, acoustic torpedoes, the mighty 100-ton Maus tank, the 38-ton pursuit tank, the *Pusterohr* ('Blowpipe' bazooka), the 400-feet barrel gun designed to hurl a continuous barrage of huge shells against London (it didn't fire a single one) and whose emplacements swallowed up mountains of scarce concrete which could have been put to better use elsewhere; all these projects - and the list is by no means complete - competed for the inadequate manpower, raw materials and factory space available, all bedeviled by personal rivalries amongst their authors, all subjected to the whims of a desperate and often hysterical Führer who would suddenly order emphasis to be switched from one programme to another, as for instance, when he commanded that production of V-2s should be cut back in favour of increased output of V-1s - and was just as likely to have the decision reversed the following week. It is hardly surprising that all these factors created a detrimental 'stop-go' syndrome, leading to unnecessary delays, wasted efforts, and inevitably a lowering of morale amongst everyone concerned from the scientists right down to those manning the launching pads; yet at the same time their influence in reducing the scale of the V-weapon offensive should not be exaggerated, because what primarily saved the cities of England from a much more severe mauling were the operations against Peenemünde and Kassel and other centres of V-1 and V-2 production such as Fallersleben and Wiener Neustadt; and, perhaps most of all, the heavy unremitting bombing of the launching sites and the destruction of communications all over France and Belgium by both Bomber Command and the USAAF.

Some historians maintain that Germany had every reason to be at least moderately satisfied with the achievements of her *Vergeltungswaffen*, even if these fell somewhat short of turning the tide of war in a definitive manner; these critics claim that, apart from the extensive damage caused in England and the understandable anxieties which spread throughout the population, apart from the colossal effort required of the Allied Air Forces to combat the menace, and apart from the thousands of anti-aircraft guns and barrage balloons and the 22 squadrons of fighters (the Tempest in particular had a 50 mph advantage over the V-1 and shot them down in large numbers, as did the Gloster Meteor jet when it arrived on the scene) that were kept continually in action, they stress that the 'Reprisal Weapons' caused a lull in the Allied Air Offensive against the Reich and for that reason alone, they benefited the Germans. That, of courses, is true, but at the same time the argument is quite fallacious because if the Air Forces had not succeeded in substantially curtailing the number of "doodle-bugs" and rockets which reached England, then neither Bomber Command nor the Americans might have been in a position to carry on with their own offensive - which they later did with such telling effect. The same critics also fail to mention the dreadful possibilities that could have materialised had the Germans been able to employ large numbers of V-weapons against the Allied armies as they struggled for supremacy in Normandy. Victories in war always cost dear and the final one, when it did come in Europe in May, 1945, cost more than any other in history. But the high price paid was acceptable - it had to be - because it was nothing compared to what would have been the unacceptable cost of defeat.

Hitler's attempt to change the whole course of the war by deploying flying bombs and rockets was a classic example of 'too few, too late'; that it could have been many more, much earlier, is a frightening thought - for, let's make no mistake about it, that despite all the hiccups in their production and implementation, the Germans were several years ahead of the Allies in pilotless 'plane development and in rocket technology; and when Hitler announced in Poland, early in 1944 (after he had observed trials of the V-1 and V-2): "First Great Britain, and then the entire world, will soon know all about the destructive powers of German secret weapons", he was making a statement which implied impending disaster for his enemies and which, for once, was not too far removed from the truth - and might have been much nearer it. For it cannot be denied that the "Revenge Weapon" campaign was, for several reasons, a nasty thorn in the flesh of the British. Yet it failed completely in its main purpose, which was to create unprecedented panic in the civilian population and hence a national crisis, and that was because the Nazis failed in both the timing and the weight of their attack, so that when it was finally launched in mid-1944 the Allies were simply too powerful in the air and able to cope with it.

It might be appropriate to conclude this chapter by relating one final little episode in the history of the *Vergeltungswaffen:* namely that at the war's end General Dornberger was captured by the British and taken to London, where it was intended that he should stand trial for the inhuman act of attacking that city and others with V-weapons. Even to the most patriotic of the British, including the Londoners, who had felt the brunt of Dornberger's efforts, this must have appeared to be a rather puzzling course of action, even allowing for the understandable desire for revenge against all things German (which the Holocaust had done much to foster); after all, the V-1s and the V-2s had been filled with HE just like the RAF's more conventional bombs, and there was no significant difference between what Dornberger had done, or had tried to do, to London, and what Harris had succeeded in doing to every town of any size in Germany, not to mention what the Americans, helped by the British, were then doing to Japan. In fact the only basic difference was the method of delivery - and it has to be admitted, as already stated, that the Germans had devised, certainly as far as the V-1 was concerned, a much less costly means of dealing out death and destruction from the air, and no doubt that rankled a little. However - a wise decision perhaps - the trial did not take place and Dornberger ended up where many of his colleagues already were - in the USA - ready to make his contribution to the exploration of space.

Chapter 12

THE MEN WHO MARKED THE SPOT

By the summer of 1942 the higher echelons of Bomber Command, the Air Ministry, and the members of the War Cabinet, had become painfully aware that bombing results left a great deal to be desired and dissatisfaction with the general lack of success was being expressed more and more vociferously; far too often a significant proportion of the night's load fell, at best, on places of little military import, and, at worst, on open ground; too many aircrews and machines were being lost with little to show for it and the situation was being exacerbated by the increasing effectiveness of the enemy's defences. Clearly a fresh approach, based on new devices and techniques, was essential if the deployment of a large bomber force - and this had been the accepted pre-war doctrine in the event of Britain being confronted by a Continental foe - was to play a major part in hitting back in the only way which was then feasible; in other words, Bomber Command, in spite of all its valiant endeavours, had, in the Air Force jargon of the day, to 'get its finger out'. The successful attacks against fire-prone Lübeck and Rostock and the saturation of much of Cologne (Chapter 19) by more than one thousand bombers had been the exception rather than the rule and little impression had been made on the real - and all-important - tough nuts such as Essen and Duisburg and Berlin.

The idea of using certain skilled crews to lead the main body of bombers to the target was not a new one: in fact this had been Bomber Command practice prior to 1942, and still was. However it had been carried out using the old traditional methods of getting there, finding the target if possible, and then trying to hit it. There had been nothing in the way of specially trained personnel, and none of the electronic gadgetry which was now beginning to make its appearance.

It was Group Captain S O Bufton, a former squadron commander (later to become Director of Bomber Operations) who, while operational, had himself experimented with flares and colourful Verey lights as a means of marking targets; and who, once a member of the Air Ministry staff, became instrumental in developing the idea further and in persuading others that a 'Target Finding Force' was an urgent requirement if the overall efficiency of bombing was to be increased.

But to Harris, who had taken over as Chief of Bomber Command only a few months before, the idea of forming such a specialised unit was nothing short of anathema; he wanted nothing to do with introducing a *corps d'élite* into what he considered to be a *corps d'élite* already. He gave several reasons for his objections: the experienced and skilful crews in a squadron were invaluable as tutors by providing guidance to those who had just arrived from Operational Training Units, and squadron commanders would be all against their departure; crews not chosen for the new force and destined to fly for ever - or as long as they survived - in the body of the main stream, would come to regard themselves as 'the poor bloody infantry of the air' and suffer as far as morale was concerned; those selected would, because they were leaders, endure an unacceptable level of casualties, thus reducing the efficiency of the supplying squadrons even further; moreover, there was really no need for such a select force as the new bombing cameras which were on the way would instil a spirit of competition amongst the crews and results would immediately improve. All of these statements were reasonable ones to make, except for the last, which seemed fatuous in the extreme.

But Bufton, refusing to be brushed aside, asked that at least six ordinary squadrons be allowed to experiment, to pool their findings, and to co-operate in the exchange of ideas; he argued that if several experienced and experimental heads were put together regularly the outcome must surely be a step in the right direction. Bufton knew that if better results followed, something much bigger and much better would materialise.

It lay on the shoulders of Sir Charles Portal, Chief of Air Staff, to decide whether or not such a novel force should be created, and although aware that both Harris and his Group Commanders were vehemently opposed to it, he supported his own colleagues at Air Ministry and, like it or not, Harris had to comply - after all the Prime Minister himself strongly supported it. But the Bomber Chief managed to get his own way when he rejected the name 'Target Finding Force' and called it instead the 'Pathfinder Force' (PFF); and demanded that its aircrews, by way of compensation for the high demands to be made on them and for having to undergo a much longer tour of 45 operations (continuity was deemed to be an essential feature of the new unit), should all be promoted by one rank; they would also be privileged to wear a special badge -a metal eagle - but not while engaged on an operation. Thus what was to become the most

The Great Ingratitude

illustrious sub-group within an illustrious Bomber Command, and its ace card in its overwhelming attacks from now on, was given the go-ahead on August 11, 1942.

The courageous and enterprising Group Captain Basil Embry (see Chapter 19, The Jailbusters), was the man earmarked as commander by Bufton, but for some strange reason he was not released from his post as head of a Fighter Command station. The man nominated instead was a 32-year old Australian from Toowoomba by the name of Donald C T Bennett - and superbly qualified he seemed to be from every angle: carved characterwise in the Harris mould - resolute, independent in his thinking, unreceptive to any opposition from those he judged to be less qualified than he - and of those there were many - and of unquestioned valour; for his age he must have been one of the most seasoned and competent fliers of his generation. He had trained initially with the Royal Australian Air Force and later joined the RAF, which he left in 1935 for Imperial Airways, for whom he flew flying-boats and air liners all over the world and made the first commercial crossing of the Atlantic. (On the very day Hitler marched into the Rhineland in March, 1936, Bennett was not too far away from the scene of events as he was that day piloting a plane from Croydon to Cologne). After the outbreak of war he was principally engaged in ferrying military aircraft across the Atlantic from the USA to Britain; he then rejoined the RAF and, as commander of an operational squadron, he took part in several raids over Germany from December, 1941, until April, 1942, and so was well acquainted with the difficulties besetting Bomber Command. Flying from Lossiemouth on April 27, 1942, he was shot down while attacking the Tirpitz (see Chapter 19, Big Bangs) but avoided capture, made his way over the mountains to Sweden, and was back in Britain a few weeks later by courtesy of a Hudson which had gone out from Leuchars to pick him up. Apart from being a highly skilled pilot, Bennett was a recognised authority on navigation, in which he was intensely interested, and in addition had amassed a profound practical knowledge of radio and engineering and of almost everything pertaining to aircraft and flying; indeed there was probably no other person available who was better suited to fill the post of leader of the Pathfinder Force.

Once the decision had been made to appoint him he was asked to call on Bufton, to whom he made it quite clear he was in no way surprised that something tangible was at last being done to improve Bomber Command's generally abysmal performance - not that the aircrews could be faulted in any way because they simply did not have the tools required to do the job properly. Bennett knew he was up against it, but such was the nature of the man that he could hardly wait to bring all his energy and ideas to bear on the single aim of fashioning a group with such technical aids and strategic skills that it would become the guiding force for the great streams of heavies envisaged for the future and guarantee that Bomber Command would go about its job in a clinically accurate manner and end up by being, literally and metaphorically, an earth-shaking weapon in the British armoury.

Harris approved whole-heartedly of Bennett's appointment and assured him that, although he himself had not found the concept of a Pathfinder Force to his liking, he was now committed to it and would leave no stone unturned in his efforts to help its leader make it a success.

No sooner had Bennett taken control than he started to improve navigational techniques: traditional methods such as Dead Reckoning and instruments such as sextants he branded as more or less useless if Bomber Command was to fly in all weathers and achieve its goals; but the co-operation of the scientists was absolutely essential and it was due to him and Harris that research was speeded up and revolutionary aids began to be fitted first of all to Pathfinder aircraft, and ultimately to those in the main stream as well. As far as the manning of the bombers was concerned, it was arranged that each of four groups would supply one ordinary squadron and replace crews when this was necessitated by loss.

When Bennett took over, however, his Pathfinders were not yet supplied with the sophisticated tools it was to acquire only with time; yet they were asked to play the leading role in large Bomber Command attacks just when the Luftwaffe night-fighters were becoming more numerous and much more formidable, when anti-aircraft guns and searchlights seemed to spawn all around the main towns of the Reich; his appointment also coincided with a period of heavy losses, especially during abortive raids on the Ruhr, and indeed from mid-summer, 1942, morale had begun to slump, not as much as it was to do during the Battle of Berlin more than a year later, but it slumped just the same; the increasing number of aircraft failing to return - from 2.5% in the period November, 1941 - February, 1942, to 3.7% from February, 1942 - May, 1942, and 4.3% from May, 1942 - August, 1942 - was the reason. The rate was still climbing when the Pathfinder Force came into being, when the stormy and difficult nights of autumn and winter lay just round the corner.

The Great Ingratitude

The flares available for marking were still rudimentary, but an improvement was made almost right away by filling bomb casings with chemicals which burned with distinctive colours on the ground in the nature of a large incendiary. The purpose of these 'Pink Pansies' was to guide the main body of the bombers - soon to be known as the 'Main Force' - to the target and, limited in scope as the 'Pansies' turned out to be, they were still better than nothing and represented the forerunners of the much more effective target indicators which would make possible the concentrated saturation bombing of compact city areas. 'TIs', as they were called for short, made their appearance when makers of fireworks, who had resigned themselves to redundancy in their own particular trade for the duration, found they were not so useless to the war effort as they had thought, for they were now called upon to employ their wealth of imaginative pyrotechnical skills in a capacity they could never have foreseen; and the result was an apparently endless series of multi-coloured flares of such variety that the Germans had absolutely no hope of copying them on any particular night to use them as decoys. It was a classic example of an innocent peace-time industry being converted to the destructive requirements of war.

Marking was done visually by the Pathfinder aircraft when the target was believed to have been correctly identified (called *Newhaven*); when visibility was poor *H2S* was used; and *Wanganui* (after a place-name in New Zealand) was a system of sky-marking employed when ground flares were difficult to identify because of cloud or fog or smoke. Under such conditions the bomb-aimers dropped their loads on parachute flares after being ordered by the Master Bomber to fly on a prescribed course.

Up until early 1943 (forgetting for a moment about the highly special and exceptional thousand-bomber raids on Cologne, Essen and Bremen around the middle of 1942) an attack by a force of 200-300 night bombers had been considered a large one; but with the birth of the Pathfinder Force the number of planes taking part increased steadily; add to that the replacement of obsolete twin-engined aircraft by the much larger four-engined Stirlings and Halifaxes and Lancasters, and the fact that 5 Group was an all-Lancaster force by the end of 1942 and could drop a greater weight of bombs in a single operation than the whole of Bomber Command a year before, and you had the nucleus of the ever-expanding power that was to end up by laying waste every city and large town in Germany.

Bomber Command in World War II

Bennett's loss rate during the initial stages of operations, that is to say, in the latter part of 1942, rose steadily to 4.6%. Apart from the detrimental effect of the worsening situation on Pathfinder crews' morale it also entailed a temporary diminution in the activities of Bomber Command: too few crews, whose knowledge was *a priori* in the training of new-comers, were surviving long enough to provide this service. Accordingly Bennett insisted on the early implementation of two imperatives: a sufficient supply of the most advanced navigational and bombing aids; the second, but equally important as it was complimentary to the first, was the intensive training of his crews to the point where they would obtain optimum performance from such equipment. After all, it was they who had to tell up to one thousand bombers where they had to drop the bombs they had carried over hundreds of miles. But also high on his list was the bewildering (to the enemy) assortment of flares of which each type would be repeated only at long intervals, if ever repeated at all; these, too, would be constantly improved, as for example when bomb-aimers complained that they were often dazzled at the vital moment by the TIs dropped. Bennett immediately arranged for the manufacture of a hooded version which nullified the glare-back.

Another innovation was the control of the attack by a 'Master Bomber', who kept a vigilant eye on the positioning of the flares and continued to circle the target, giving instructions to main stream crews by radio; in the event of an emergency a 'Deputy Master Bomber' took over; in addition 'Visual Centrers' flew in the body of the main force and replenished markers which were being spent on the ground, thus ensuring that all crews released their bombs on the right spot; and the first of the Pathfinders to arrive over the target were assisted by 'Supporter Crews', whose aim was to distract the defences and at the same time gain experience of marking.

Considering the dominant role the Pathfinders played when the *raison d'être* of the whole operation - the releasing of the bomb loads - was imminent, it is not surprising that one of their tasks was to decide on the route to the target and the diversionary raids to be undertaken. Before each operation they were informed of the number of aircraft taking part, of all relevant details with regard to timing and, having obtained the latest weather forecasts, they worked out what was judged to be the best plan of attack - from which direction to approach the target and which type of markers to use. Each raid involved an exacting preparation for all PFF crews who, apart from taking part in regular training exercises when not on an operation, were compelled to attend long lectures dealing with techniques, emergency measures, and anything that could possibly effect the success or failure of each incursion over enemy territory. They did, as Harris had feared, become *la crème de la crème*, but it is difficult to see how this could have been avoided; and, as far as can be judged, main stream crews in no way felt they were looked upon as second-class operators who simply shovelled out their loads on the instructions of others who were more skilled than they; on the contrary, losses apart, their morale probably rose because they knew they were doing a much better job than would otherwise have been the case. And the growing importance and the expansion of the PFF was acknowledged on January 8, 1943, when it received Group status and became No 8 Group, Bomber Command. Bennett was promoted to Air Commodore, and before that year was out he held the rank of Air-Vice Marshal, having achieved this meteoric rise from Wing Commander in the space of some 12 months.

Bennett did not have to wait long before being granted the means to weld his Pathfinders into a highly efficient unit: the backroom boys at the Telecommunications Research Establishment at Great Malvern worked round the clock to improve upon existing aids and to produce new and increasingly remarkable devices, without which the Pathfinder Force could never have attained its undisputed degree of proficiency; so from the final months of 1942 onwards it could be said that Bomber Command began to cast off its undesired mantel of being a 'hit or miss' force which missed more often than it hit; it was fast becoming a highly technical organisation which transformed the whole methodology of carpet bombing and made it, *à la Bomber Command*, a hugely complex but enormously successful exercise far removed from the haphazard efforts of the early years.

Some of the scientific developments which brought about this transformation have already been mentioned briefly, but it might now be appropriate to describe all of them in greater detail:

Sir Arthur Harris had taken over the leadership of Bomber Command in February, 1942, just when *Gee* was being developed, and it was on the night of August 11/12, 1941, that it was first tested out during an attack by 29 Wellingtons on a railway target in Mönchen-Gladbach (about 20 miles west of Düsseldorf). Two of the aircraft were fitted with the device and it was pronounced to be a success; however, fearful of a *Gee Box* falling into enemy hands before it could be installed in all the bombers, it was decided not to employ it again until it had been produced en masse and become part of the general equipment of Bomber Command.

At this juncture we might be as well to point out that Harris had thought long and hard about the best way in which a given area should be attacked in order to use his resources as efficiently as possible and achieve maximum destruction; not for him a continuation of the accepted practice of his predecessors Ludlow-Hewitt, Portal, and Peirse, who sent mere handfuls of aircraft on the same night to targets as far apart as Berlin and Munich and Essen, with each small formation dropping a meagre load which in no way troubled the defences - or much else for that matter; but from now on, apart from the occasional specific target (Augsburg, Ruhr Dams, Peenemünde, Tirpitz, etc) the great majority of the bombers available would concentrate on a single area of a city and release the entire load in as short a period of time as possible; by so doing they would put anti-aircraft batteries around the target at greater risk and at least some of the guns out of action, resulting in smaller losses amongst the last aircraft to bomb; 4000-lb high explosives (and the occasional 8000-pounder) would rain down from the first of the bombers to go in, so that streets would be blocked with rubble and the fire-fighting services rendered immobile; then into the shattered and roofless buildings would pour thousands of 4-lb incendiaries to start huge fires which would join together and further prevent remedial action by the urban services; yet all this would merely serve as a prelude to a pulverising attack by the main force, which would let loose both HEs and incendiaries. It was an admirable recipe for the destruction of property and human beings alike and the basis for the coming onslaught on Hitler's Germany. But past mistakes would be avoided and no raid would take place unless weather conditions were forecast as at least manageable. Harris had always maintained that thick cloud and fog and high winds constituted a greater danger to his bombers than the enemy defences (but that was in the beginning, when he knew not what lay in store).

The introduction of *Gee* represented the first step towards the realisation of this policy, and offset to a large extent the effects of poor visibility and strong and ever-changing winds, which had often blown aircraft miles away from where they should have been and compelled them either to bring their loads back or to drop them on 'targets of opportunity' - if they ever saw any. Now, thanks to *Gee*, the navigators who had worked themselves to the bone using Dead Reckoning navigation - finding pin-points and working out a change of course by applying, to the new required track, the speed and direction of the wind they had just found, and unable to do very little, except pray, if no landmark could be recognised - could now forget about the sweat-inducing fear of becoming hopelessly lost and feeling responsible for the dire situation in which the crew now found itself; no longer did the navigator have to worry about the ten tenths cloud beneath him because his amazing little *Gee Box* noted the time difference between signals from three stations in England (situated well apart) and immediately told him exactly where he was - all he had to do was plot the position on his chart; and just before he was out of range of the *Box* (fading of signals started at about 5° east of Greenwich, that is to say, when the aircraft reached the middle of Holland or the south-east of Belgium) he was able to calculate the latest wind speed and direction, which would reduce the possibility from then on of straying too far off track; and it was a comforting thought that on the way home he would again come within *Gee* range, find his exact position and work out a course for base. This, in fact, made possible the safe return of many distressed aircraft which might otherwise have been forced down before the shores of England were reached.

Although the use of *Gee* was thus restricted by range limits (due to the curvature of the earth), a bomber about 400 miles from the transmitters still received the signals provided it was flying at a height of around 20,000 feet. This meant that many of the cities of north-west Germany, including the oft visited Ruhr, were well within *Gee* range, but when aircraft dropped below that altitude or were too distant from England they lost the signals, which was not too good when the target was Berlin or one of the towns of Bavaria. *Gee* was first and foremost a navigational aid and was used in bombing only if the target was obscured by cloud (or enveloped in haze, as was so often the case in the Ruhr).

Then, as 1942 was drawing to a close (by which time the Germans had learned how to reduce the effectiveness of *Gee* by jamming), another piece of electronic wizardry was more or less perfected by the boffins at Greater Malvern: this was *Oboe,* which had actually been tried out during a raid on German warships at Brest as early as December 7/8, 1941, and on further occasions, with encouraging results. In contrast to *Gee, Oboe* was a device employed to bomb obscured targets within a range of 350 miles, so to a bomb-aimer it was what *Gee* was to a navigator. The aircraft received signals from two stations in England and used them to maintain the correct track during the bombing-run. One of the stations was known as 'Cat' and the other as 'Mouse'; 'Cat' sent out dot or dash impulses which told the pilot whether or not he was on course, while 'Mouse' transmitted the signal indicating when the load was to be released - simply a matter of pressing the button at the appropriate moment. This often ensured accuracy of between 200 and 400 yards, which represented a gigantic step in the right direction, considering how wild high-altitude bombing had been up till then. While on its bombing-run the aircraft had to maintain steady, level flight for a number of minutes - which seemed an age to its crew as this laid them wide open for longer than usual to attack by night fighters and ack-ack guns; a further drawback was *Oboe's* limited range (as in the case of *Gee,* due to the curvature of the earth) and its restricted use by only 18 aircraft per hour, as the maximum number of stations that could be employed at any one time was three. Because of this limitation Oboe ranked as a device to be put principally at the disposal of the leading Pathfinder aircraft; those without it came in just behind them and increased the effectiveness of the marking by dropping flares of their own.

A special squadron of Wellingtons was formed right away (August, 1942,) to experiment with the new aid and later on it was decided that the Mosquito, with its ability to attain a ceiling far above that of anything else (ensuring that the curvature of the earth played a lesser negating role), was tailor-made for *Oboe*-conducted operations. A further advantage of the fast-flying Mossie lay in the shorter time it required on its bomb-run; hence the much lauded Mosquito was destined to be lauded even more when it was issued to the Pathfinder Force. Ultimately Bennett had several Mosquito squadrons in his Command and altogether these aircraft completed 28,215 Pathfinder sorties out of the grand total of 51,053. Lancasters undertook 19,601, Halifaxes 2106, Stirlings 826 and Wellingtons 305; and of all the PFF aircraft lost (675) only 100 of them were Mosquitoes, although they were used twice as much as all the others combined, proving once again the excellence and versatility of the de Havilland brainchild.

The next marvel to come from the fertile brains at TRE was both a helpful navigational and (at times) bombing aid, and which the PFF received as soon as the first sets were ready: *H2S.* Unlike *Gee* and *Oboe,* it was carried and operated in the aircraft and had unlimited range. The earliest version of the ground scanner which most modern aircraft carry as a matter of course, *H2S* was first issued to Bomber Command towards the end of 1942. Although not so efficient as to induce anything approaching euphoria in the crews, the sets did a useful job - depending on the nature of the topography down below - by depicting it on a small cathode-ray tube in the navigator's 'office', enabling him to pin-point the aircraft's position and therefore especially valuable when the ground was not visible. The 'picture' obtained was invariably hazy and ill-defined, rather like the first black and white TV images; the shapes of sea inlets, lakes and inland waterways usually stood out clearly, but as far as cities were concerned interpretation was difficult unless there were salient features such as, for example, the twin lakes in central Hamburg; consequently *H2S* never worked well over Berlin, which was characterised by too many sprawling, nondescript areas which did not show up well on the screen; the picture also had a frustrating habit of coming and going, but when maximum efficiency was obtained *H2S* provided yet a further invaluable addition to the capabilities of the British heavy bomber. It also contributed to making it a machine of every-increasing complexity - and cost, much to the indignation of some Members of Parliament and top brass in the Army and Navy.

H2S also provided a further example of the countermeasures that usually followed when one side introduced something new: once the Luftwaffe gained possession of a set from a shot-down aircraft, and found out how it functioned, they put the knowledge to good use by applying it to equipment in their own night-fighters, which enabled them to home on to any bomber using it. The order therefore went out to Bomber Command crews that *H2S* was to be employed only when over the target or in an emergency. Nevertheless it was installed in every aircraft of the Pathfinder Force by the end of 1943 and shortly after that every bomber in the main stream was similarly equipped.

In addition to *Gee, Oboe*, and *H2S* there were minor innovations such as *Mandrel* (which disrupted the enemy's ground radar stations) and *Tinsel* (a microphone which allowed the bomber's wireless operator to hear the orders which went out to the German fighter pilots from their ground controllers). Nothing was spared to make the Lancasters and the Halifaxes and the Mosquitoes the most lethal bombing machines that had so far been devised.

The Pathfinder Force cut its teeth on August 18/19, 1942, in an operation which could hardly have been described as an auspicious beginning. The target, the German town of Flensburg, stood on a distinctive sea-inlet of the Baltic (about 90 miles north of Hamburg and on the Danish border), and should have presented no difficulties as far

Bomber Command in World War II

as identification was concerned, but winds had been erroneously forecast and a large number of aircraft strayed over Denmark; other nearby sea-arms apparently caused confusion and many bombs fell on Abenra, 20 miles to the north of Flensburg, on Sönderborg, some 15 miles to the east, and on scattered villages.   Although 16 of the 31 Pathfinder aircraft insisted that they had correctly marked Flensburg and 78 of the 87 others claimed to have bombed the right target, the town itself reported no bombs at all.   Some Danish houses were destroyed and many more damaged, but fortunately no Danes lost their lives and only eight suffered injuries. It was on this operation that the Pathfinders lost their first aircraft - a Halifax, but each member of the crew parachuted safely and ended up in a prisoner of war camp.

The Pathfinder Force was eventually to find itself, inevitably and understandably, right in the centre of the hotbed that existed over and around every German city or town of any size. The few hundreds of night-fighters available to the Luftwaffe in 1942 soon became 1500, then 2000; they too got themselves fitted out with radar gear, and their success with their new equipment signalled the beginning of the hectic battle between the scientists in each camp to try to outdo each other in measure and countermeasure, a battle which was to last almost as long as the war itself.

That, however, lay in the future, and the Pathfinder Force did not take long to make its weight felt. By the spring and summer of 1943 the Ruhr was being dealt with far more effectively, and this was reflected by events in Russia, where the German army was being deprived of a lot of the heavy guns and other equipment it sorely needed. Consequently Bomber Command and its Pathfinder Force were much appreciated by Stalin (who had thought little of British efforts up till then) and in recognition of Bennett's accomplishments he awarded him the Order of Alexander Nevsky.

If operations over Germany were an exacting ordeal for main stream crews - and of that we have already had proof enough - they were even more so for the Pathfinders, who went in first and out last - or at least much later - as they did their utmost to ensure that the raid achieved maximum destruction. Yet there was further evidence of the truth of the old maxim that the exception always proves the rule when Master Bomber Squadron Leader Cranswick was shot down on his 143rd raid over enemy territory, having completed more operations than any other Bomber Command pilot.   'The Reaper', the relentless invisible force whose

The Great Ingratitude

presence was always felt and which usually claimed crews sooner or later, did relent now and again and let someone slip through the small meshes of its net. Yes, now and again ... and usually just for so long ...

Chapter 13

THE NIGHT IT ALL WENT WRONG

The day after 'Happy Hannah's' crew returned from leave following the Berlin operation on February 15/16, Candlish was told to report to the Station Commander.

"Sit down, Ian. Good leave? Good fishing?"

"Yes, thank you, sir. Got a couple of salmon."

"Excellent. And now you've got something else - DFC. Congratulations! It was bound to come but your last trip sealed the issue. You've also got a replacement for Flight Sergeant Whyte. I'll send for him now. And I haven't finished yet - you've also got a brand new Lanc. You'll be trying her out in a day or two."

Candlish was invited by his crew to a little celebration party in the Sickle and Scythe that same night. They went early, when it was usually quiet, and in the snuggery, which they took over, the Skipper went to some pains to try to convince them he didn't regard the award of the DFC as his alone; as far as he was concerned it belonged to all of them. They formed a team, and the best team was the one which was good all through and did not depend on one or two star performers. The gong belonged to 'Happy Hannah' as well - and to Peter, both of whom were no more. All he did personally was to get the big black bugger into the air and bring her back down again, try to keep her steady on the bombing run and take evasive action when required.

"Poppycock, sir!" said Musty Coleman. "It's you who've always brought us back. And look at the last time!"

"Aye, havers," agreed Benny, using his vernacular. "You could have put her doon a wee bit cannier, like, but in the circumstances we forgive you. You had a bit o' an excuse."

The Great Ingratitude

"All right, you all know what I think. Now let's get on with the drinking."

Heads kept popping round the door to see if there were any seats left in the little room, and Candlish felt sorry that the intimate little party was not being held on the station itself. It couldn't, of course, because NCOs and commissioned ranks were segregated in their own messes. He reckoned there should have been a communal 'Aircrew Mess'. He also supported the view, as did many others, that all aircrew, by dint of the special responsibility they had, and of the essentially close relationship which they developed, should have been officers - a proposal strongly advocated by the Royal Canadian Air Force but rejected by the RAF. He held similar views about the award of the Distinguished Flying Cross for commissioned ranks and the Distinguished Flying Medal for others. Why this embarrassing and totally illogical distinction? There was none in the case of the VC, and rightly so.

Candlish spotted a rather hesitant young man looking at them self-consciously from the door.

"In here, sergeant. Glad you came. Come and meet this shower of rogues. This is Sergeant Ronnie Routledge, our new engineer. Just arrived from HCU. Don't know what will happen to him after our tour, but he's one of us for the moment. He might look as if he's not long out of nappies, but he's supposed to know his stuff."

"Bloody hope so." It was Benny, who could bark at those who were on his side, but rarely bit them.

Routledge, whose tender years were accentuated by his fresh, pink cheeks and almost angelic countenance, was put as much as possible at his ease by a hardened crew who could remember their own feelings of inadequacy when they first arrived on an operational station. They would see he was all right. They knew a few tricks.

Inevitably, perhaps, they christened the new Lanc 'Happy Hannah II', and took it on three long training flights. Candlish corkscrewed it and then threw it all over the place, eliciting the remark from the rear-gunner:

"I didnae ken ye were retraining as a fighter pilot, skipper. I've left half ma insides up there. Let me oot! I'm dizzy. Let me oot!"

Bomber Command in World War II

Young Routledge decided that he liked this crew. Candlish had no complaints about the machine. Like 'Happy Hannah I' and all Lancs she apparently loved to be in the air and never seemed to want to land. His customary "Get down! Get down!" was again heard by his crew as he coaxed their new charge towards the runway.

Then to the real thing. They took her to a couple of targets in Belgium and Northern France and she behaved impeccably when assailed by spasmodic but fairly accurate ack-ack fire, and returned with only a few jagged holes and scorches to spoil her pristine appearance. Routledge was not at all shaken, even enthusiastic. Just wait, thought the others. The innocent little bastard would soon learn it wasn't always like that ...

***

The day after their second op. in 'Happy Hannah II' navigator Bob Ainsworth went to see Candlish and asked if he could have a word.

"I'm sorry about this, Skipper, but I just have to speak to you."

"Sure, Bob. What's on your mind?"

"I find this ... very difficult. Oh, dammit, I'm not going to beat around the bush. I've been doing my best to fight it, but ..."

"Scared, Bob?"

"You guessed, didn't you? Look, Ian, during our last trip to the Big City I was in a helluva state. I was shaking all over and my mind just froze. I nearly gave you a reciprocal course after we bombed. All right, you would have noticed the error, but suppose I had calculated the course using a reciprocal wind or something similar? You wouldn't have queried it, but in the circumstances it was all we needed to delay our return and force you to ditch. I'm a liability, I'm ... I really panicked over Berlin. It's these long hauls inside Germany that really get to me now. My God, that last one ... and that's what we're due again next. Maybe Peter hasn't helped ... I'm sorry, Skipper, but it's time you knew. I've tried, God how I've tried, but

The Great Ingratitude

I just can't go on. Don't know what you must think of me. I'm sorry, Ian, I'm sorry.''

''For heaven's sake stop keep saying you're sorry! I'm sorry too, I'm sorry to see a friend suffering as you are, and through no fault of your own. But your condition isn't exactly uncommon, you know, especially during the last few months. No need to apologise for something outwith your control. And I mean that.''

''But you and the others. I...''

''Bob, this happens to the best, and you are a bloody good navigator who has played a big part in seeing us all safely home on more than one occasion. Must say you have kept it well hidden, except that you've been a bit quieter, perhaps, and more introspective than usual. But let's get things straight. First of all there's nothing to be ashamed of, as I keep telling you, and all the more so when you've done 29 ops. You know as well as I do that we're all scared - no, not scared, bloody petrified. The man who says he isn't is a damned liar because on this job even the biggest fool in creation is scared to his boot soles. Trouble is, 30 ops. are far too many for anybody. But, Bob, you've only one to go.''

''That's what I've been telling myself, but it does no good, which just proves what a state I'm in. The mere thought of places like Berlin or Essen gives me the shakes. Suppose it was one of these, or Leipzig or Munich? I couldn't go. Ian, I just can't face it any more. And I would let you all down.''

''No! The mere fact that Bob Ainsworth is telling me all this and not reporting sick with some concocted complaint proves that I'm right. That takes guts in itself. One more, Bob, just one - otherwise I wouldn't ask you. If we got you grounded this very moment you'd be split up from us forever, and I'm positive the rest you're almost due is all you need - it's what everyone needs, and a long one at that. Bob, believe me, this is the best way. Let's leave it now and we'll have a beer in the mess later, OK?''

''Don't expect me to change my mind.''

But Candlish knew his navigator too well: that he was

the type who, despite the 29 ops. he had beneath his belt, would go on feeling guilty and ashamed if he did not lend his support to his colleagues and friends as they tried to surmount this last hurdle before they were let off the hook for a longish spell, and probably for ever if Harris's predictions were correct. He was well aware that the intensity of the man's fear was clouding his reason to such an extent that it made him incapable of foreseeing the anguish that would surely be his lot if he pulled out now. And, even if the worst came to the worst and he didn't survive, he would at least not be condemned to suffer the mental torture that would otherwise lie in store for him.

"All I'm asking you to do is to give it some more thought. If you don't change your mind then so be it."

But Ainsworth ended up by doing just that. Some inward voice seemed to tell him that the Skipper was right. There was only one more, and he prayed and prayed it would be an 'easy' one. He prayed too that it would come as soon as possible, which it did.

***

It came on the night of March 30/31, 1944.

The usual tension was written on the faces of the 125 airmen who crowded into the Briefing Room, but it was written larger on those of 'Happy Hannah's' crew. This was their big one, and the target and its range assumed added importance. Amongst them only Candlish seemed to take it as just one more operation. At least that was the impression he gave. After all, it was part of his job as Skipper.

The curtain swished:

NUREMBERG.

"God!" whispered Candlish, resisting a glance at Ainsworth.

"Christ, Skipper, away doon there! Do they think we're short o' flyin' practice? Oor 30th op. an' they pick a rotten place like that. Must be 1100 fuckin' miles there an' back. Rotten sods! It's no' fair. I'm no' goin'. Calais or Boulogne docks'll do me. I'm no' goin'!" In Bomber Command

The Great Ingratitude

Benny had learnt more about the geographical position of German towns than he had ever learnt at school.

"Wait a minute, Skipper! That's where ye were before the war, isn't it? In that case I'll come wi' ye. I would like to see where ye sowed yer wild - I mean where ye were a hard-workin' student!"

"Quiet, Benny. Stop blethering."

Yes, Candlish reflected, it was where he had been a student. Nuremberg! In his mind's eye he pictured the quaint old alleys of the 11th Century town, the home of Albrect Dürer and Hans Sachs and the Mastersingers, the cosy Weinstuben and the bustling Bierkeller; then the comfortable house in which he had lived near the Wiesenstrasse, south of the centre. He recalled the faces of Herr and Frau Ecker and remembered their two children, one of whom had been only a toddler. How old would she be now? Six? And little Rolf? Nine or ten perhaps. Would their young minds be already poisoned by ludicrous race propaganda? He also saw the other things, the things that had frightened him - the mass parades of strutting, impassioned Nazis, the cold, penetrating eyes of the Gestapo, the kicking-around of the Jews. But the German couple had treated him well, steering clear of politics, and he just hoped they still had that deep cellar and were in it early that night because the RAF was coming with about 800 bloody great bombers. The chances were that Frau Ecker would be on her own with the children and her husband no doubt absent, perhaps already dead on some frozen Russian steppe.

Candlish shook himself. It was time to concentrate on the briefing. The squadron's Commanding Officer spoke about Nuremberg's importance as an industrial centre and especially its munitions factories. They were going to blow them sky-high.

Crews from all groups were to take part. There would be 676 aircraft in the Main Force (462 Lancs and 214 Halifaxes) and the Pathfinders would be comprised of 110 Lancs and nine Mosquitoes, a total strength of 795. Operational height was 21,500 feet and the overall load 850 large and medium-sized high explosive bombs, 18 mines and 32,000 incendiaries. The route was then dealt with in some detail: the waves of bombers would join together to form a continuous stream at a latitude/longitude position about 60 miles east of Harwich; thereafter, in order to avoid the Kammhuber Line - the area patrolled by blocks of fighters to prevent penetration by British bombers into Germany - they would fly a number of dog-legs, keeping to the south of Brussels, Aachen and Bonn and crossing the Rhine near Ramagen; they would then turn east on a long leg to a turning point in the vicinity of Meiningen, from which the final leg of some 75 miles on a course just east of south would take them to the target. After bombing they were to continue almost due south for 30 miles and another four dog-legs would bring them back to base - flying south of Stuttgart, back over the Rhine just north of Strassbourg and carrying on north of Nancy and Châlons; then north of Paris to a point on the French coast east of Dieppe, and finally back across the Channel to Selsey Bill just east of Portsmouth, and from there to their various bases.

The target area was to be saturated within the space of 17 minutes, starting at 0105, which meant one bomber would release its load every one and a half seconds. Crews looked at one another askance. God, what next? They had drenched places in quick time before, but this seemed to be a mathematical impossibility without collision or blowing each other up. They were assured, without feeling reassured, that this threat, likely as it appeared to be to them, would not come to pass and there was no cause for concern. Titters all round; no collisions with nearly 800 of them bombing within the time it took to down a couple of pints? Being reminded that only two aircraft were lost in this way during the 1000+ raid on Cologne in May, 1942, did nothing to convince them either: that particular night the bombing had been spread over 90 minutes and the aircraft hadn't done the run-in like sardines packed in a can.

Some of the Mosquitoes involved would drop diversionary route marker flares near Kassel while others made a spoof attack on Cologne; the Mossies bound for Nuremberg would, of course, mark the real target; Pathfinder Lancasters were to be busy leading the defences a merry dance by drawing false trails all over central and southern Germany. *Window* would cascade down in increasing amounts as Nuremberg was approached, and at the rate of two bundles per minute when they were 30 miles from the city. Somehow it was all made to sound like a Sunday afternoon picnic.

Initially the Met officer gave a mostly favourable report: high cloud over the greater part of the route, and a moon; the cloud was expected to grow thicker as they progressed; over the target itself strato-cumulous would ascend to 8000 feet, with patchy stuff up to 16,000, but no problems for the marking Pathfinders were envisaged; winds promised to be moderate on the whole but might be stronger over Central Europe, especially towards the east - up to 40 knots or a bit more. However a later report from a Met flight Mosquito largely refuted this earlier forecast: skies were likely to be clear right across Germany but thick cloud might obscure the target. Despite those adverse conditions - the hundreds of miles of clear, moonlit sky presented a particular nightmare - the raid was to go ahead. This decision was to prove to be one of the biggest blunders of the entire air war.

A heavy silence hung over the dining-halls as the pre-ops. meal was mostly toyed with. The large number of half-consumed plates ensured that local pig-farmers would be pleased the next day.

During a last minute visit to the toilet after his usual intake of three cups of strong, milkless tea, Benny tried to get steam up:

> *Down the bloody runway,*
> *Into the bloody air,*
> *Goering will be waiting*
> *For us when we get there,*
> *Focke-Wulfs and eighty-eights,*
> *And flak and searchlights too,*
> *But we've got a present*
> *For the big fat slob,*
> *Four tons o' fuckin' TNT*
> *Right down his greasy gob!*

> *And when we get home again*
> *The CO he will say*
> *No screwin' WAAFs to-night, my lads,*
> *No frolics in the hay.*
> *You're off on tour again, my lads,*
> *What lucky boys you are,*
> *Seeing the Reich by night, my lads,*
> *The best thrill that by far.*

***

'Happy Hannah II's' four engines roared into life one after the other, starting at exactly 21.54. The chocks were pulled away eight minutes later and she taxied off. At 22.07 the Aerodrome Control Point flashed the green light to tell Candlish to take up position. Brakes on. All throttles fully open. Brakes off. 'Happy Hannah' trundled forward, gradually picking up speed, and clearing the hedge by a good margin in spite of the heavy load in her petrol tanks and bomb-bays. One minute later Candlish set course for the assembly point. After a further 50 minutes Bob Ainsworth reported that the Belgian coast was just ahead. The Lanc purred on and Sergeant Routledge told his Skipper that his instruments showed that all engines were functioning perfectly. The mainland of Europe now lay beneath.

"Mid-upper to Skipper. Flak to port."

Same voice at 23.37: "Kite on fire ahead."

At 23.41 Tom Courtney spoke from the front turret. "Two aircraft burning on the ground." Then hissed to himself: "Far too much far too soon."

"Skipper to navigator. Our position, Bob?"

"Moment, Skipper ... Yes, Aachen 12 miles to port."

"Roger."

For the next 40 minutes the gunners and bomb-aimer frequently reported the sighting of burning aircraft, and these were reported more and more frequently as they flew on in the bright moonlight. They knew that the fighters were enjoying a bonanza, yet miraculously they had not spotted any so far or been spotted themselves.

"Skipper to crew. They're busy to-night, and no bloody wonder in this light. No dropping off back there, Benny!"

"You know, Skipper, somehow I'm no' very sleepy!"

At 0019 hours:

"Navigator to Skipper. Rhine ahead. Alter course 093. Helluva gale blowing and not too steady either."

"Thank you, 093 it is." Candlish was glad that Ainsworth was being kept busy. The course he had just worked out certainly appeared to be accurate enough. Nor did his voice betray anything, but Candlish could well imagine the churning of his insides - his own weren't exactly motionless. The latest change of course had put them on the 130-mile long leg to the final turning-point near Meiningen, about as near to the centre of Germany as you could get. "Come into my parlour ..." Candlish had the feeling that they were already in it, and that the door had been slammed tight behind them.

He was right. Suddenly the predators were all over the place - Me 110s, Junkers 88s, Focke-Wulf 190s - screaming in on the unmistakeable silhouettes of the big bombers in a sky which was a night fighter pilot's dream.

"Navigator here. Just passed Fulda to starboard. We'll be turning soon for target." The words seemed to come from a dry throat, and from far away.

"Mid-upper to Skipper. We're all making vapour trails that look like tram lines. It's like a bloody air display!"

"Yes, I know. Where's that bloody cloud they promised as we got towards the target?"

A screech from Benny Ramage:
"Me 110 from port!" His guns spat out only a round or two before they fell silent, at which moment the Lanc tottered and staggered under a murderous burst of cannon fire, which came from below. Candlish, untouched, realised it must have been *Schräge Musik* when he glanced back and saw a solid wall of fire and smoke engulf the floor and sweep up to the roof and forwards towards him. An inferno in a matter of seconds.

"Bale out! Bale out!"

Powerless to do anything but try to save himself, he groped for his parachute, knowing he had only seconds, but he managed to get hold of it and clip it on. Struggling to keep his balance against all the centrifugal forces that only an aircraft out of control and in its death agonies can produce, he somehow reached the escape hatch, wrenched it open, and dropped into space.

He felt the welcome rush of ice-cold air and did his best

to count slowly to ten before pulling the ripcord. Then came that welcome jerk on the shoulder, comforting in its fierceness. Once he had regained some sort of mental equilibrium he looked down and saw fires scattered all over the German countryside. Then, transfixed, he watched what was no doubt 'Happy Hannah' spiralling down aflame with one wing trailing behind her, as if it was trying to catch up with the main section. He could see no sign of other parachutes, but knew that if by some miracle any of his crew had got out they could well be outside the range of his vision. He judged that the strong wind was carrying him along horizontally as much as he was dropping vertically. Then his thoughts returned to the others and, remembering the intensity of the conflagration inside the aircraft, he feared that they could not have had a ghost of a chance, especially those behind him, who must surely have been overcome by both the smoke and the flames, not to mention the dangers from exploding ammunition. Benny, in his position in the tail, might have made it if he escaped injury during the attack, but the odds were anything but good.

When Candlish saw the ground appear he pulled his knees up into his chest and clasped his hands round his head in order to cushion the jolt, and on making contact with mother earth he rolled over and over, dragged along by his 'chute which kept on being partially filled by that devil of a wind. Finally he succeeded in arresting it by pulling hard on the cords, then he thumped the release button to free himself of the harness. By that time his right shoulder had been rubbed raw. His right leg also hurt, and part of his outer suit was hot and singeing. He seized a handful of dead grasses and rubbed, just in case, and as he did so he looked around and found he had come down in what looked like a small meadow with houses along one side. He gathered up the unwieldy chute as best he could and stuffed it with some difficulty into a clump of bushes.

Candlish felt very much alone - much more alone than he had ever felt in his entire life - disconcerted, and not a little apprehensive. For the first time he could remember, he didn't know what to do.

His dilemma was cut short by the sound of voices and the beams of electric torches aimed in his direction. These blinded him as the group approached but there was nothing indistinct about the order which rang out:

"Hände hoch, englischer Schweinhund!"

"Jawohl." It was the first word of German he had spoken for nearly five years, yet it surprised him how spontaneously it came. Perhaps he had been subconsciously preparing himself for it. He raised his arms and placed his hands on top of his head, continental style, since he would have been a fool not to co-operate willingly. This was confirmed when someone aimed a kick at him, which did nothing either for his aching leg or his nagging fears of what might lie ahead. He identified the man in charge as a policeman, who led him out of the meadow and into a street, along which they marched, with most of the original group still present and demonstrating their antipathy towards the terror fliers of the RAF by jeering and spitting, by punching and kicking him continually in spite of the official's efforts to persuade them to desist. Finally he ended up in what he took to be the town jail. He was locked in a cell and left alone, having learned that he had come down in a village not far from the town of Bad Neustadt.

Candlish's feeling of extreme disorientation was an experience common to all baled-out aircrew. So much happened so quickly in such traumatic circumstances that the mind had difficulty in grasping the sudden change of situation into which an airman had been pitch-forked only minutes after sitting with his colleagues in at least temporary safety 20,000 feet up in the sky, and often resulted in what could only be described as mental paralysis. He was subjected in a matter of seconds to a series of abject terrors: the tearing of metal as the shells went home, the rapidly spreading flames and the dense, choking smoke, the uncontrollable antics of an aircraft gone mad, the struggle to reach his parachute and get it on; then to find his way to a door or escape hatch as he was thrown from one side of the aircraft to the other, and often injured in the process; throwing himself into space and the agonising wait for the parachute to open; then, as he floated downwards, having to cope with all the terrifying thoughts which hammered at his mind: would he come through unscathed in a sky teeming with bombers and fighters and whizzing bullets and shells? and if, on landing, he avoided bone-shattering buildings, trees and a host of other obstacles, or a drop into deep water, what then? What would he do? What if he was grabbed by hostile civilians driven out of their wits by the bombing, or fell into the hands of Nazi Party fanatics? If, on the other hand, no one came, and his presence on the sacred soil of the Reich was so far unknown, what next? Hide by day and try to travel by night? And where to? Apart from his handkerchief map of Europe and his small compass, he possessed nothing else except his wits and his determination, both of which would be sorely tested in a situation where the dice were loaded 99½% against him. During the first few moments an airman stood on German territory his over-riding sensation was that of being entirely alone in the land of the enemy; he had lost all contact with his home base, his next of kin, his friends and everyone he knew, and abruptly stripped of all ties and personal effects apart from the clothes he wore; he was an uninvited guest and at the mercy of the people in a land he and his colleagues had been terrifying night after night for years. Not a comforting thought in the circumstances, and, as many later reflected with more than a tinge of bitterness, it was a situation for which they had been ill prepared, having received little or no guidance from their commanders as to how they should cope.

Two days later, Candlish was transported to a Dulag (short for *Durchgangslager* - "Transit Camp"), where he was ordered to fill in a form with his name, rank and number. He was asked questions about his squadron and its location but he knew enough about the laws of the Geneva Convention and politely refused. It came as a shock when the Interrogating Officer, with a mocking smile, proceeded to reveal the very details he had requested and many more besides.

But his spirits received an unexpected boost when he was joined soon afterwards by Tom Courtney and Mark Robertson who, like himself, had beaten all the odds and sustained only minor injuries. The three were told bluntly that only pieces of the other members of the crew had been found in the remains of their crashed Lancaster and that these had been buried in Bad Neustadt. A guard also hinted that Candlish had been fortunate in being arrested by a veteran policeman and Courtney and Robertson by the Luftwaffe, explaining his remark by stating that there was an SS training camp in the area. They were also told that the International Red Cross were being informed that they were prisoners of war.

After a few more days in the *Dulag* the three airmen were transferred to a *Stalag Luft* (abbreviation of *Stammlager Luftwaffe*) then in the east of Germany and now in Poland, one of those in which RAF officers were incarcerated.

Once settled in their new surroundings their minds began to straighten themselves out and inevitably their thoughts returned to the raid that had put them where they were.

Quietly but emotionally they mourned their lost comrades: Musty Coleman, the footballing Londoner who had been as quick to shoot at an enemy aircraft as he had at his opponents' goal; and dear old Bob Ainsworth, whose anguish Candlish revealed for the first time, telling them how he had persuaded the navigator to carry on and that he would regret doing so for the rest of his days. But Courtney and Robertson, who had known the sensitive Ainsworth as well as the Skipper, were both convinced - or so they made it appear - that he had done the right thing; at least Bob had been spared future agonies; true, a young mother was without a husband and a child without a father, but Christ, that was what war did to people. And Benny! How had he died? Just a short time ago he had been in their midst and apparently indestructible - tough, lovable, effervescent little Benny, with his rough tongue and his warm heart. It was difficult to imagine such a character reduced to burnt, nondescript pulp; Benny would drive in no more rivets and Clydeside would be the poorer without him; everyone would be the poorer without him. And young Routledge, innocent and willing, who had copped it on his first real trip, and there you had yet one more mother sorrowing for a son who had but too recently still had her milk on his lips. And for three of them the delicately poised guillotine had dropped within a mere hour or two of temporary and perhaps even permanent salvation. Bloody war! Bloody Hitler! Bloody every bloody thing!

They went on to talk of the raid itself, agreeing that it was one of the worst they had known as far as seeing casualties was concerned, and 'Happy Hannah' hadn't even reached the target. They feared the worst for those who had and, if they were still in one piece, were compelled to run the whole damned gauntlet all the way home again. Gloating guards informed them that 134 of their bombers had been shot down, but they refused to believe it could have been quite as bad as that and dismissed the claim as typical Nazi propaganda. They didn't know it then, but Hannah had been one of the 83 aircraft shot down on the outward journey. Fewer were lost on the homeward legs, during which the unusually high winds benefited the bombers by causing the fighters problems while taking off and landing.

Yet their fears for the other Lancs and Halifaxes were justified; on the return trip the wind strength increased and navigators questioned the accuracy of their calculations. One of them refused to believe its speed was 90 mph - and on rechecking he measured it as over 100 mph. They were meeting the gale practically head-on; and above them, that beacon-like moon which turned night into day; all around them, those tell-tale contrails. Just as well the fighters were less active, but they were still active enough, and the bombers continued to fall.

The English Channel had never been a more welcome sight. But the cloud which would have offered them protection over

Bomber Command in World War II

Germany began to amass just when and where they didn't want it; and then at base, or at any base they could find, they were greeted with storms of snow and sleet. Already exhausted pilots of battered aircraft kept losing sight of the runway and had to rely on Standard Beam Approach while their aircraft swung and weaved about and ended up on soft ground rather than on the tarmac, precariously balanced on wing tips at best but in some cases on noses or as near upside down as mattered. Fire-tenders and ambulances were in great demand.

The final reckoning, said High Wycombe, was 96 heavies missing, plus 17 others which had crashed and been 'written off' in England, total 113. This news came as something of a shock to the British public who, to a large degree victims of the 'familiarity breeds contempt' syndrome, had for some time accepted Bomber Command's nightly endeavours as a matter of course, and perhaps needed 'a Nuremberg' to remind them of the continual high price being paid in lives and machines. The operation also served to remind Bomber Command that the Luftwaffe - in spite of earlier massive attacks by the Americans against the German aircraft industry (known as 'Big Week') - still possessed enough sharp teeth to inflict grievous punishment on the invading bombers; in fact during the first three months of 1944 (therefore up to and including Nuremberg), night fighters had claimed 763 Lancasters and Halifaxes, which amounted to 80% of the Command's potential. But the factories and the Operational Training Units saw to it that the gaps were soon filled.

An interesting item appeared in a 1963 issue of the magazine *Jägerblatt* (loosely translated as "Fighter News"): `One of the most calamitous night missions of the RAF was the attack on Nuremberg on the night of 30 March, 1944. The OKW (German High Command) report the following day claimed that 134 bombers were destroyed. Official British statements reported 96 planes as lost or missing and 17 which had crashed near their bases and were beyond repair. The apparent difference between the German and British figures is best explained by a statement issued by the British: "We know that a number crashed into the sea or in the vicinity of their bases. These losses, however, are not included in the official count of missing planes because we know where they are. Therefore they are not missing!"' `

It was certainly the blackest night - ironically, because it was the brightest weatherwise - of the many black nights experienced by Bomber Command. Everything had apparently conspired to make it so, and the presence of fighters all the way along the route raised the inevitable question of a security leak. This was never established. The fact remains that at the breakfast tables on the bomber stations on the morning of March 31, 1944, a record number of well over 700 places remained unoccupied, and large numbers of ground staff waited in vain for the return of their planes and their crews. As 8 a.m. approached and there was no hope left they sauntered off resignedly to their various duties. They were to learn later that the Nuremberg débâcle had cost more airmen's lives than the entire Battle of Britain.

Many believed that Nuremberg was one more nail in Harris's coffin, and according to his severest critics there were not many left to be screwed down. They thought this must surely be the end of his credibility as a strategist and, since the night in question provided them with more ammunition than ever, they didn't hesitate to fire it. But Harris was never without his bullet-proof vest and for the benefit of those who, in his opinion, knew little about such things, he condescended to explain what had happened simply and irrefutably in one short paragraph and which, as far as he was concerned, brought an end to the matter: 'When you're fighting 1000 offensive battles in the course of the longest continual battle of the war, it is difficult to find the changes of tactics every time that will fox the enemy, and one of the changes you have to include is to do what the enemy thinks you would not dare to do - avoid extensive diversionary operations for once and take a fairly direct route to the target, as with Nuremberg.' Harris knew it would be only the most blinkered idiot who would not sympathise at least a little. That might well have been so, but it is worth pointing out that Pathfinder Chief Donald Bennett, who knew more than most about bombing tactics (and whose Pathfinder Force at Nuremberg, 119 strong, lost 11 of its aircraft) did not hesitate to divulge later that the route he and his officers had planned was rejected by the Main Force group commanders and by Harris himself. Indeed Bennett was never one to hold his tongue when he felt strongly about any issue, which he did frequently, and he complained bitterly that the senior officers to whom it was left to make crucial tactical decisions (such as the route to Nuremberg) had no experience of operational flying in the new concept of air warfare such as was being waged by Bomber Command; but this blatant weakness in the latter's organisation, Bennett explained, was due to the decision by the Prime Minister and the War Cabinet that such officers were barred from operational flying.

The wind speed, which had been so grossly underestimated, had played havoc with navigation and especially with the

Pathfinders' flares, many of which were blown away to the east of the city, and the number of fatalities amongst the Nurembergers - only 69 in the urban and surrounding rural area - testifies to the inaccuracy of the bombing, further impaired by a "creep-back" which started on the northern fringes and eventually extended 10 miles back along the track from Meiningen. Further confusion had developed when one or two Pathfinder aircraft had mistakenly marked Schweinfurt, about 50 miles short of Nuremberg. More than 100 bombers had spotted the flares and released their loads, which fell mostly outside the town and killed two civilians. It had been a long and trying haul, culminating in a night of catastrophe.

Once again Harris was saved to a certain degree, on this occasion by the imminence of the Invasion and by deploying most of his force, albeit as unwillingly as always (but only, he reckoned, temporarily) on what were considered by his superiors to be more relevant targets than German cities. Eisenhower and his deputy Tedder might say for a time how the bombers would be used, but as soon as the invading armies had gained a firm foot-hold on the Continent, Harris would forget about army co-operation and get on with the main business, with the added advantage of having his electronic aids transmitters positioned a lot nearer the enemy homeland, which meant both greater bombing accuracy by his crews and greater personal safety for them. He still licked his lips in anticipation of the day when, under the renewed onslaught of his bombers, the Nazis would scream for peace long before the Allies had reached the Rhine; and if he had further criticism hurled at him for his 'wanton' annihilation of their cities his answer would still be the same, namely that he 'didn't consider all the towns in Germany worth the bones of a single British grenadier.'

At the same time it is difficult to escape the thought that perhaps Harris himself was not as confident as he wanted others to believe, and he came near to hinting that all was not right when he demanded night fighters to protect the bombers. It had been proven long before that big bombers flew over Germany in daylight at their own peril and now it was beyond doubt that they were in extreme danger no matter when they went.

The exhilarating prospects created by Hamburg had failed to materialise. Berlin, in the eyes of many, had been a failure; and now Nuremberg, in the eyes of all, an unmitigated disaster.

The Great Ingratitude

Chapter 14

FESTUNG EUROPA

There obviously came a time in the course of the Second World War when British and American endeavour focused mainly on the daunting task - strategically and logistically "the most difficult and complicated operation that has ever taken place" as Churchill described it - of preparing for and successfully carrying out the invasion of the Continent of Europe, of Hitler's so-called *Festung Europa* ('Fortress Europe'). It requires no great stretch of the imagination to appreciate the enormity of such an undertaking and of the numerous problems which had to be overcome by meticulous and imaginative planning. Any major hitches could have resulted in abysmal failure which, at best, would have delayed final victory for years; and, with the Japanese fighting tooth and nail to retain every island in the Pacific and thereby taking a heavy toll of the Americans, the possibility of a catastrophe in Europe was one that could not be contemplated. The Invasion had to succeed, no matter how great the effort required, no matter how long and complex and costly the preparations; it had to be as little of a gamble as was humanly and materially possible.

The Allied High Command knew that every possible ruse had to be employed to confound the enemy, that all sorts of complicated and ingenious devices had to be fashioned if success was to be ensured. The main concern was the landings themselves and no stone was left unturned to deceive the enemy into believing that these would be effected in the Pas de Calais; a fictitious American army was based in Kent, with General Patton in evidence to bolster its authenticity - and when the latter did go to France he was replaced in England by another senior American general to give credence to the German belief that the real landings were yet to come; dummy airfields and military installations of various kinds were erected and double agents played their part by disseminating false information; a British army was assembled in Scotland to point to an imminent invasion of Norway; old ships and massive blocks of concrete were to be towed across the Channel to form an artificial *"Mulberry Harbour"*; a few weeks after D-Day, *PLUTO* ('Pipe Line Under The Ocean') would be laid to provide a regular and adequate supply of fuel; and a host of smaller ploys and inventions, too numerous to mention, were all designed to make certain that nothing, absolutely nothing, was overlooked. At the same time the Allied Commanders realised that the ruses, no matter how original, could not be guaranteed to work, that all their weaponry and numerically superior strength would count for little if they did not get off the beaches and gain a foothold as soon as possible; and that this was so because of the presence, not far from the coast, of highly trained and dedicated Panzer and Waffen-SS divisions, battle-hardened after long experience of the slaughter-house syndrome in Russia and which could be rushed to the landing areas speedily enough to inflict severe losses, if not even worse. The chiefs, both military and political, feared a Dunkirk-like retreat, but a Dunkirk rendered a thousand times worse with acres of water and sand stained with the blood of their soldiers; they even had visions of Somme-like casualties; and, in the deep recesses of their minds there existed the distinct possibility that the enemy might, at the appropriate moment for him, introduce a weapon of such devastating power that the known threat from V1s and V2s would be nothing in comparison. So the towering priority was the safe passage of the armies and their equipment from the sea on to the beaches - always a tall order in circumstances where even a small defending force can massacre a large but very vulnerable one - and then getting them off the sand as soon as possible and establishing a solid foothold in the first fields of Normandy. That was the *Schwerpunkt* which presented itself in stark and awesome reality on the morning of June 6. Failure spelled unmitigated disaster: they simply had to make it.

So the Commanders did everything militarily possible, and even some things verging on the impossible, to crush all immediate opposition and advance rapidly into Normandy. They knew only too well that in launching the Invasion they were hovering dangerously on the capricious wings of fate. Eisenhower and his deputy-supreme Commander, Air Chief Marshal Sir Arthur Tedder, and their immediate subordinates, must have had recurring nightmares in the period leading up to D-Day. Not too unfavourable weather was also of the utmost importance and on June 5, when strong winds still blew in the Channel, Eisenhower found himself faced with a decision the weight of which few lesser mortals could have borne; but there was a host of other anxieties besides and no doubt unforseen difficulties would have to be tackled from the moment the anchors were raised in the ports all along the south coast of England.

But behind all this lay one undeniable and comforting fact which would go a long way to ensure that this, the greatest single

The Great Ingratitude

enterprise in the long history of war, would not fail: the Allies had at their disposal, and had had at their disposal, what was to be the dominating force in deciding wars from then on - superior air power, and in this case superior to such a degree that, compared to their opponents, they possessed what almost amounted to an embarrassment of riches.

As far as Bomber Command and the USAAF were concerned, the Second Front had been opened and the Invasion had started long before June 6. Operation *Pointblank* (Chapter 4), to which, for many months, they had been compelled to devote most of their endeavours (in the case of Spaatz practically all of them) had been the prelude without which the storming of *Festung Europa* would have been out of the question: *Pointblank* had seen to the destruction of communications from Holland right to the Atlantic and of a huge part of the enemy aircraft and synthetic oil industries, which had left the Wehrmacht and the Luftwaffe bereft of vital resources. Throughout Northern France itself the bombers had continually blasted coastal batteries, bridges, railway and road junctions; now it was their duty, not only to continue in the same vein, but to attack and destroy everything which would in any way impede the actual Invasion - just before it, during it, and as long after it as was required to facilitate the advance eastwards through France and beyond.

But it should not be assumed that all this passed off smoothly and without dissent amongst the Allied Commanders. On January 13, 1944, Harris had written a letter to Portal, bemoaning the fact that he was committed to *Pointblank* and *Overlord* and stressing his conviction that Bomber Command would play a far more effective part in supporting the Invasion if it intensified, rather than drastically reduced, its attacks on German industrial centres; the destruction of communications and arms dumps, beach defences and gun emplacements were not the right kind of targets for Bomber Command, whose crews were trained with a vastly different concept in mind; attacking such small specific targets would be a blatant misuse of its great power and would give only a 'specious appearance of supporting the Allied armies', and umpteen bombs would be wasted in trying to hit small targets, whereas the same bombs would miss little if they were emptied out over a city.

One can understand Harris's frustration; here he was (he believed) on the brink of hammering the enemy into final submission and yet obliged to divert his crews to the task of trying to find things like railway and road bridges and small piles of shells dumped here and there. General Carl 'Tooey' Spaatz, as Commander of the US Strategic Air

Bomber Command in World War II

Force, was of similar mind: he wanted no respite for the Luftwaffe and believed he now held Germany in a death grip, thanks to the damage he was doing, and wished to go on doing, to her aircraft and synthetic oil industries. Like Harris, he too thought he could win the war in his own way and he was haunted by the fear that Bomber Command might achieve its goal by carrying on as usual while he was told by Eisenhower where his B-17s must go and what they must do. It bothered him continually that his RAF counterpart seemed to get off with ignoring *Pointbank* directives - blaming the weather for instance as being too poor for precision bombing but still good enough for saturation attacks on cities - and would perhaps succeed in forcing Germany to capitulate (*Rankine* was the code-name for the sudden collapse of Germany under bombing) before the Invasion, while he had to toe the line. In this context it is interesting to note that Harris and Spaatz had basically the same aims, both believing that their bombers could do the necessary, if by different methods.

But it was made abundantly clear to both Bomber Chiefs that the requirements of *Overlord* took first priority and that consequently Harris and Spaatz would carry out strategic operations only with the Supreme Commander's consent; and it must be said that, once committed, they applied themselves to the task with great zest and determination. Bomber Command, for instance, completed almost 16,000 sorties in the summer of 1944, the majority of which were effected by smallish formations which flew all over Europe destroying airfields and radar installations, marshalling yards and military camps. And Bomber Command's pronounced success in attacking small specific targets appeared to belie everything Harris had said about its inability to do so.

During the months preceding D-Day it was of paramount importance that the thousands upon thousands of troops being assembled in bases all along the south coast of England, together with their mountains of equipment, should be protected at all costs from enemy aircraft or fast-moving surface vessels such as E-boats (a number of the latter caused havoc on one occasion during US Army exercises off the Devon coast); on the great day in question men and *matériel* had to be transported across the Channel without losses that could prove to be crucial; the beach landings had to be unmolested as far as possible; then, with the soldiers ashore but still very vulnerable, every step had to be taken to prevent the Germans rushing reinforcements to the relevant sectors (it should be remembered that the Wehrmacht had 60 divisions, 11 of them armoured, in the Low Countries, and that in Normandy alone there were six infantry divisions with another in reserve, plus a parachute regiment, and, near Caen, a Panzer division). It was going to be no 'Sunday afternoon picnic', as Stalin was wont to describe the Normandy campaign.

If Bomber Command and the USAAF had been active from the Atlantic to the Elbe in *Pointblank* operations, during which they had dropped the best part of 200,000 tons of bombs and lost 2000 aircraft in the process - let us not forget that for the aircrews the 'Invasion' had begun much earlier - in the days immediately preceding D-Day the heavies seemed to spend about as much time in the air as they did on the ground (many crews flew twice in 24 hours) and unleashed on the enemy forces stationed on the coast of Normandy and some way inland such a maelstrom of high explosives that it must have made the German defenders wish they had been posted to somewhere more peaceful such as the Eastern Front. One of the best examples was the bombardment (Operation *Flashlamp*) by well over 1000 Lancasters and Halifaxes, of ten huge gun emplacements sited in a commanding position overlooking the Channel. Before midnight on June 5 (D-Day-1) 100 aircraft were assigned to each battery and showered down upon it a shattering 600 tons (total 6000 tons). The enemy gunners who experienced this hellish crescendo were frozen into a state of immobility and it was said that some of the survivors ran around berserk and hovered for weeks on the verge of insanity. This is believed to have been the most ferocious bombardment ever undergone by soldiers anywhere.

Less intense but still highly devastating was the attack, by almost 1600 American bombers, on the Utah, Omaha, Gold and Sword landing beaches, which was halted only minutes before the first troops jumped ashore early on June 6. They destroyed many mines, machine-gun nests, tank traps and booby-traps and barbed wire barriers with their 3500 tons of high explosives. In the skies above 5500 fighters patrolled the Channel and the beaches from Ostend on the Belgian coast to Cherbourg in the West, a gigantic operation which guaranteed that few, if any, hostile aircraft were able to attack the 3908 ships and 2500 landing craft, and so conspicuous was the Luftwaffe by its absence (no more than 70 sorties were flown by its fighters on D-Day and they shot down only one Allied aircraft) that the fleet was virtually unchallenged, as were the 2400 transport planes being towed by gliders. At the same time the skies were further blackened by the mightiest bomber armada ever to take to the air, a total of 5200 machines which flew on unchallenged and provided indisputable proof of Allied might and Axis impotence. Altogether 13100

Bomber Command in World War II

British, Commonwealth and American aircraft flew over the Channel on June 6. It is difficult to say who were the more awestruck - the soldiers and sailors in the ships as they gazed up at the endless procession of aircraft, or the airmen in the aircraft as they gazed down upon the endless procession of ships. Such a spectacle had never before been witnessed and is not likely ever to be witnessed again; and it goes without saying that the enormous umbrella directly above the soldiers' heads did more than a little to bolster their morale as they were about to be pitched into the fray.

On D-Day-1 and on D-Day itself Allied aircraft of all types flew a phenomenal 14,000 sorties for the loss of some 130 (another 60 were damaged). Considering the major role they had played in facilitating the landings this was, in military terms, a small price to pay.

A further operation carried out by Bomber Command was the elimination of most of the 90-odd Luftwaffe radar stations strung out along the coast from Holland to Cherbourg. They were attacked before D-Day and by D-Day itself each and every one of them between Le Havre and Barfleur on the north-east tip of the Cherbourg peninsula had ceased to function. The few that remained in working order elsewhere were rendered more or less ineffective by Allied aircraft which flew over the Channel with special jamming equipment.

And, of course, you couldn't keep 617 Squadron out of the action; for once this élite band of airmen were called upon to effect an operation which, if vastly boring compared to their usual assignments such as bursting dams or sinking battleships, still contributed much to D-Day success. As we have already noted, the Allied High Command had endeavoured, in many subtle ways, to convince the Wehrmacht that the Invasion would take place in the Calais area, and during the night (June 5/6) immediately before the landings, an example *par excellence* of precise air navigation was illustrated when eight of the squadron's Lancasters circled the Channel all night long to simulate the passage of a convoy of slow-moving ships towards the shoreline in the vicinity of Calais, the idea being that any enemy radar still working would have their screens filled with convincing blips which would dupe the Germans into concentrating both their forces and their attentions in the wrong place.

The British and American armies and the Royal Navy made an excellent job of the invasion of Europe but the air forces' colossal contribution before, during, and after D-Day, cannot be overemphasised. There is no doubt whatsoever that without it all those involved, on the sea and on the land, would have had a much harder time of it - especially on

The Great Ingratitude

June 6 when the losses incurred were far lower than expected and 150,000 men were put ashore with negligible harassment from enemy aircraft; if any of these did appear, such as the four Heinkel 111s which managed to drop a few bombs on Juno beach, they were soon shot from the skies by patrolling Spitfires and other fighters. On Omaha, where it was for a time touch and go for the Americans, even a moderately sized force of Luftwaffe fighters or bombers might easily have tipped the scales and forced a messy retreat back into the sea; and attacks by large formations of German aircraft on the four landing beaches could feasibly have stopped the landings in their tracks and produced the blood bath that the Allies dreaded.

Those generals and admirals who up till now had always shown themselves to be sceptical and even bull-headed about the potential of aircraft in general and of the bomber in particular, surely couldn't have remained so any longer. They saw with their own eyes what the airmen could achieve and were to go on seeing it all the way to the Lüneburg Heath. Of the near three million Allied troops involved in the push through France, Belgium and Holland and into the Reich, it seemed nothing short of miraculous that just over 200,000 were killed, wounded, or taken prisoner. But it was no miracle, simply irrefutable proof of the effect of the monstrous tonnage of bombs with which Bomber Command and the USAAF had wrecked the enemy's war industries, drained her oil supplies and severed her lines of communication in the first half of 1944; and of the support the bombers continued to give until the whole of the Third Reich collapsed. Day after day they attended to targets which had literally to be blasted apart, while the Tactical Air Force Spitfires sprayed enemy troops with their cannon and machine-guns and rocket-firing Typhoons mauled the Panzers as they tried to hit back in fierce counter-attacks. The men in the thick of it on the ground were by no means slow to acknowledge their heart-felt gratitude to those above them in the air; whenever they needed help they got it, and usually it meant the early destruction of whatever was threatening them.

Such requests were frequent. In the early hours of July 8, for example - just over a month after the landings - 450 aircraft of Bomber Command, with a total load of 2500 tons, flattened the area around Caen as a preliminary to a major assault on the city by British and Canadian troops. The very accurate bombing was concentrated on an area 2.5 miles long and a quarter-of-a-mile deep, and lasted for only 40 minutes. Like their colleagues in the shore gun emplacements on June 6/7, the German defenders were stunned by the weight of the bombardment; the Allied soldiers were able to move into the suburbs, thanks to the destruction of most of the enemy guns and to the shocked condition of those manning what was left. Such pulverising onslaughts from the air had this additional advantage of severely reducing German morale and indeed SS Panzer General 'Sepp' Dietrich, who commanded the Sixth SS Panzer Army and was as tough and competent a leader as any on either side, described the aerial bombardment of his armoured units as something against which there was no defence, something which reduced his men, all seasoned veterans of the Russian Front, to quaking, numbed apologies for the fine soldiers they undoubtedly were.

Such bombardments were commonplace. Whenever a difficulty was encountered which would hold up the advance and cost the lives of many Allied soldiers, the formula was the same: call in the bombers. Another typical example was the situation at Wesel, on the right bank of the Rhine about 12 miles north of Gelsenkirchen. This was a heavily defended town of moderate size (population 25,000) and Montgomery, desperate to get across the river and open the door to all of North-West Germany, asked Harris, on March 23, 1945, if he would do the needful (Wesel had already been heavily bombed on February 16 and on March 6). The Chief of Bomber Command never lost an opportunity to demonstrate what his bombers could do to a built-up area and despatched 195 Lancs and 23 Mossies; the outcome was the reduction, in twenty explosive minutes, of what had been a town to a vast pile of rubble. The soldiers went across the river and what remained of Wesel, which was very little, was easily captured. Ironically the job had been done so well that when Montgomery's men arrived they had the greatest difficulty in moving forward as all the streets were choked with masonry. (The author visited the town a few months later and could not find a single undamaged building or a single human being - nothing seemed to live there except rats).   (#)

No one who knew Harris was in the least surprised when, soon after peace came, he claimed that the bomber had won not only the greatest air victory of the war (the offensive against German cities) but the greatest land and sea victories as well (the Invasion and the sinking of enemy ships). Extravagant as this claim might have appeared to many,

---

(#) The Germans later reported that the pre-war population of 25,000 had been reduced to less than 2000 by May, 1945: that Wesel, with 98% of its buildings in ruins, could, for its size, lay claim to being the most heavily bombed town in the Reich.

The Great Ingratitude

it was generously substantiated by Montgomery's assertion - and that from a man not inclined to be too appreciative of others - that the bomber had been the most influential weapon of the lot, while Eisenhower himself proclaimed that the air forces had achieved 'the impossible'. German commanders, so starved of air power themselves, readily concurred.

All this was so because in the manifold preparations for the largest scale - and one of the most critical - military campaigns in history, the bomber destroyed the enemy's vehicles of war, both those in production and those in being; it destroyed the fuel supplies that were necessary to keep mobile those which he still possessed, and disrupted the vital communication links, which prevented these from getting through; it annihilated strong German positions by relentless and continuous pounding, so that the armies were able to land and move on with far lighter losses than would otherwise have been the case.

Hence the part played by Bomber Command and the USAAF in the storming of Hitler's *Festung Europa* can never be overestimated. Without it everything could have come to grief on the beaches of Normandy.... and then?

Chapter 15

WHERE TONIGHT - WHAT ABOUT THIS PLACE *DARMSTADT?*

As the summer of 1944 passed into autumn and Germany was subjected to more frequent and more violent bomb storms, the Command had to start looking around for targets in a country which had the largest concentration of big towns in Europe. *L'embarras du choix* of the years up to 1943 had gone for ever; the long sought-after means - bombers aplenty - were now available, enabling Harris to lay on two major attacks on different centres the same night, but the ends were in somewhat short supply. That was the measure of the devastation and there were still some eight months to go.

The town of Darmstadt, which had blossomed from the middle of the 16th century onwards as the capital of the grand-duchy of Hesse-Darmstadt, was the home of 125,000 souls and situated on a sloping plain between the forested plateau of the Odenwald and the Rhine, and 25 miles due south of Frankfurt. It was a pleasant provincial centre with the lovely rural region of the Spessart just to the east. Life was far from hectic in a milieu characterised by museums, theatres, magnificent churches, pleasure grounds and parks, and with a 300-year old castle sitting plumb in the middle of the Altstadt (Old Town). Darmstadt had been a recognised cultural centre from the 18th century onwards and boasted an established artists' colony on the Mathildenhöhe, a park created in 1830 by Grand Duke Ludwig II. It possessed famous landmarks such as the 108-feet high statue of Ludwig X, the Kranichstein Hunting Lodge and the Russian Church commissioned by Tsar Nicholas II. It was the home of the German Academy for Language and Poetry and the venue for the annual presentation of the Georg Büchner prize, the most prestigious German award for literature; living each day in such a civilized ambience meant that its inhabitants were perhaps as untainted by Nazism as any it was possible to find in the Third Reich.

Not many of Bomber Command's crews had ever heard of Darmstadt and at briefing the air-gunner who immediately exclaimed "Yeah, another damned Stadt like all the rest of them!" received some guffaws for his pains to produce a somewhat corny joke.

The Great Ingratitude

The town had some pharmaceutical and electronic industries, a diesel engine plant and was renowned for its fine printing works, but its contribution to the nation's war production was so small as to be almost unworthy of calculation; and fewer than one in five Darmstädters were employed in the handful of factories scattered here and there.

Over the years Darmstadt had received the occasional stray bomb dropped by aircraft which should have aimed them elsewhere, or when, early in the war, the surrounding forests and ripening wheat had been set alight in a puny attempt to deprive Germany of essential commodities. The death rate had been negligible and the townfolk's main experience of raids had been the frequent fiery glow in the sky above Mannheim and Frankfurt and Ludwigshaven, and the thumps and bumps which had rippled over in their direction when these cities were undergoing heavy attacks. In fact they had been spared for so long that they bathed in complacency, convinced that neither the British nor the Americans would bother with a town like theirs, which offered so little in the way of bomb-worthy targets. Moreover the British, they were wont to say, especially when one of the neighbouring cities were being paid a visit by Bomber Command, had a soft spot for Darmstadt in view of the fact that the Prince of Hesse, who lived not far away, had consanguinity with the British Royal Family; it did not occur to them that Harris had probably never heard of the Prince of Hesse, and even if he had and was aware of the relationship claimed, it is extremely doubtful whether he would ever have consulted Buckingham Palace while planning any operation, and that even if the Prince had been related to God himself it would not have made any difference. But it was a little story which made the Bomber Chief smile when he heard it after the war, eliciting from him the remark that he thought the citizens of the Reich knew him better than that. They should have.

Many Darmstädters also comforted themselves with the thought that their town was such an attractive place that the Allied armies, now only 80 miles from the stretch of the Rhine nearest to them, would no doubt want to use it as an area headquarters when the fighting stopped. As a consequence of these various factors they hadn't bothered to build air-raid shelters, arguing that if a few misplaced bombs landed in their midst their cellars would afford them protection enough. On the other hand there was a small minority who wondered if it would not soon be the turn of the smaller, untouched towns to become the object of Bomber Command attacks; and, of course, they were right, because there were no big ones left. They feared it was the RAF's aim to destroy everything in Germany and endeavoured each day to get the latest news about the progress of the British and American armies, praying that their arrival would not be long delayed.

But such worriers were few and far between and it was a direct result of the general *laissez-faire* attitude, abetted by Darmstadt's insignificance as a manufacturing centre, that its defences were feeble, practically non-existent.   There were no municipal bunkers, the fire-brigade was small and ill-equipped, and most of the ack-ack guns it had possessed had long since been removed to places where they were regularly required. Hardly any children had been evacuated and the Nazi Party had left it to the civil authorities to provide safeguards in the unlikely event of bombardment from the air.

This nonchalance was to receive a rude shock and to be blown sky-high with much of Darmstadt itself when Bomber Command decided to make good its neglectfulness on the night of September 11/12, 1944. The visiting party consisted of 218 Lancasters and 14 Mosquitoes. By Bomber Command standards this appeared to be a force of very moderate proportions, but considering the relatively small target area it was the equivalent of despatching between 1200 and 1400 bombers to a large city like Hanover or Cologne. In the circumstances, therefore, it is questionable whether any precautions taken by the Darmstädters would have made a great deal of difference.

It would not have made a great deal of difference because September 11 was the night that Hamburg came to Darmstadt. It all happened in the space of 51 minutes, starting just four minutes before midnight and ending at 00.47.

At this stage of its history Bomber Command could afford to indulge in some experimentation, trying out new methods of marking and saturation techniques. A town such as Darmstadt, virtually unscathed, suited its purpose admirably: it was an ideal guinea-pig.

Was this the main reason for the choice of target or were undamaged urban communities of even average size now so much of a rarity that it seemed illogical or inexcusable to leave one out? Or had it come to the point, some critics asked, when it was just a matter of more or less closing one's eyes and sticking a pin into the map of Germany until it picked something that would do? It could have been any one of these or a combination of each of them; but it did typify a situation in which

The Great Ingratitude

Bomber Command had begun to act like a bulldozer gone berserk, with the throttles jammed fully open. This was perfectly understandable because it now possessed the brute force it had craved for so long and at the same time was faced with diminishing danger from an impoverished Luftwaffe. Darmstadt was one of the unfortunates - another much larger and better known city was to get similar treatment some five months later, thereby creating a hullabaloo which is with us to this day - which lay in the bulldozer's path when it was howling for revenge for the battering it had received during the two frightening and bloody years which had all but brought about its downfall. It was also justifying the gigantic outlay, all the effort required by vast numbers of factory workers as well as ground-staff and the trained crews, all the time spent by scientists engaged in a frantic struggle to improve its complicated equipment in order to nullify German counter measures and reduce the Command's losses. Somebody or something had to suffer.

Harris's deputy, Air Vice Marshal Sir Robert Saundby, gave the operation the code-name *Luce* and it was planned with the usual thoroughness, including diversionary tactics. A squadron of Mosquitoes was ordered to attack Luftwaffe airfields and 47 others went to Berlin. A further 18 Mossies patrolled the route of the main stream, their remit being to attend to any night fighters which might harass the bombers.

The Lancasters took off on the near 1100 mile long flight - considerably increased due to the dog-legs - with 400 tons of high explosives, many of them 4000-pound cookies, which would open up the buildings before the 580 tons of incendiaries were shovelled in to light all the inflammable material which would then be exposed. The famous Kavallerie Exerzierplatz (Cavalry Parade Ground), a little to the west of the town centre, was chosen as the aiming-point. Bomber Command was now in a position to cash in on its now not inconsiderable experience of sowing death and destruction and was gradually bringing things down to a fine art in what was, perhaps paradoxically, not a very delicate business. So on the night in particular it was not a case of the normal approach of the main stream along a straight line and with all the aircraft flying at the same altitude. This time they came in at various heights between 12,000 and 16,000 feet to implement a new bombing technique calculated to cause more widespread damage than anything practised up till then. No longer was it a simple matter of 'drop the bloody things and get out quick'; in order to ensure that the loads did not all fall within the same small area around the Exerzierplatz each individual aircraft released its bombs at a given moment, timed to a second and thus permitting a more even distribution over the whole town. This experimental tactic proved to be highly successful and was later referred to by surviving Darmstädters as *der Todesfächer* - the 'Fan of Death'. It was a most appropriate description.

The Lancasters had become airborne just before 21.00 hours and followed a route which took them over Luxembourg, to give the impression that they were heading for one of a variety of more likely targets such as Saarbrücken, Kaiserslautern, Karlsruhe or Stuttgart. The German radio crackled out its customary messages reporting different formations of enemy aircraft apparently all over the north and north-west of the country. And the listeners wondered. Not that those in Darmstadt were greatly perturbed. This happened more or less every night of the week, but they were rarely molested in their cosy country surroundings.

The flare-dropping Mosquitoes caught up on the Lancs around 23.30 and the German radio announced that they were heading fast towards the south-west. Then the main force made a sudden and radical change of course to the north - straight towards Darmstadt, whose sirens began to emit their plaintive cries. Its citizens, although practically certain that the aircraft would simply be passing over as they normally did, trooped down to their cellars, just in case, some of them even laughing at the oft-repeated jokes about Darmstadt not appearing on RAF maps of Germany. There would be little jocularity for a long time to come.

Fourteen minutes before midnight parachute flares began to fall and within seconds both town and sky were lit up by that weird and ominous glow of which its inhabitants had heard, but happily until now, had never witnessed except from a distance. Those still above ground looked out, and were numbed by a feeling of foreboding. The highly improbable had happened: Bomber Command had come to Darmstadt.

All the target indicators landed on or within 400 yards of the Exerzierplatz and consequently accurate bombing was incredibly easy for the main stream. The few decoy fires which had been hastily lit, chiefly in adjacent woods, were totally ineffective and the attack was later announced to have been a complete success. Further, the loss of only 12 Lancasters (and no Mosquitoes) was considered quite acceptable after a long penetration over one of the most heavily defended areas of enemy territory.

The bombing of Darmstadt was the most hellish nightmare for its unsuspecting inhabitants, and would have been an ideal subject for the future makers of popular horror films - had it been possible

The Great Ingratitude

to produce on celluloid scenes of such spine-chilling proportions and had they been permitted to present them for public 'entertainment'. The Darmstädters had been told about the terrifying aspects and indescribable consequences of fire storms, but they were now about to undergo at first hand an experience in which the realisation far outweighed the most fearful anticipation: rivers of flame poured from the houses into the streets and from the streets into the houses; people cried out in agony as they literally burned to death as they ran, stumbling over the corpses that littered the roadways before adding their own to swell their number; in the cellars of the Rheinstrasse and the Elizabethstrasse and the Heinrichstrasse families sat paralysed by the earth's convulsions, and then by their own, and were reduced to cinders in the furnace which ensued when flaming doors and ceilings collapsed on top of them and ignited the coming winter's fuel which was stocked all around; if they did get out more or less unharmed it was merely a matter of moments before they were enveloped in a roaring, blinding sea of fire, and became part of the funeral pyre.

No one could help anyone else. All the streets were impassable and the small fire-service never got into action - not that it mattered, as it would have been no more effective than a child's water-pistol. Everything was destroyed including all lines of communication. To rub salt into the wound an ammunition train blew up, hurling more burning debris everywhere and adding to an inferno which was small by Hamburg standards only in area, certainly not in intensity.

Just over an hour after the last plane had departed a fire-laden wind of hurricane force roared through the town, demolishing everything that still stood and sending a 5000 foot column of flame shooting upwards with a fiendish howl, unnerving even further those still with wits enough to hear it and driving them to the brink of insanity. Small wonder that pregnant women gave birth prematurely. The temperature was said to have reached an unbelievable 2000 degrees Centigrade and what couldn't burn, melted. Bodies sank into the thick layer of ashes and disappeared. And, amidst all this, the heart-rending screams of the dying. But at least they did not scream for long.

Macabre features were there in plenty and one of the most harrowing scenes followed the detonation of a 4000-pound 'cookie' in the cemetery. Both long and recently dead Darmstädters were blown high into the air and, to add to the normal ritual of burial in the ground, they were belatedly cremated above it.

The ashes of one single human being could be swept into

a dustpan, and the shrunken remains of entire families were removed in wheelbarrows. The streets were strewn with parts of the human anatomy and multi-coloured arms and legs pointed grotesquely skywards out of the piles of blackened masonry, as if to indicate the origin of their owners' demise. Corpses were taken away by the cartload by anyone fit enough to help, and were either thrown into heaps to be set alight once again or into mass graves in a cemetery already in a state of chaos. Sickening scenes, almost identical to those of the extermination camps which were soon to turn the stomachs of hardened Allied soldiers, were witnessed all over Darmstadt, but with Germans themselves the victims of this holocaust. Nor did the similarity go unnoticed by Bomber Command's critics when the full horror of the town's agonies became universally known. There was no basic difference, they claimed - the British aircrews had been guilty of the same crimes as the Germans. But more of that in a later and, perhaps, more appropriate chapter.

The Darmstädters had suffered and died and no one was able to do anything about it. No one could help because it was physically impossible to get anywhere near the fire-stricken area. Groups of would-be rescuers who had been rushed over from Frankfurt and Mainz could only stand on the autobahn and watch as they choked and sweated and were forced to move further and further back.

Apart from the death of 12,000 of its citizens and the grievous burns which disfigured and incapacitated many for life, and all the houses and shops which had been devoured by flames, Darmstadt lost a wealth of art treasures of all kinds, valuable paintings, books and engravings.

When the fire storm had consumed all there was to consume, and was finally abating, the Bomber Command crews were landing back at base. Probably some of them would have eaten a less hearty breakfast had they been able to glimpse the ghastly scene they had left 500 miles behind them. But - apart from 84 of their colleagues - they were back on terra firma and that was all that mattered to them. Their thoughts were on their 'kips' and a good sleep. Then an evening in the pub. The morality of altitude ...

Those who visited Darmstadt in the days following its cataclysmic experience were affected not only by what they saw but by the audible silence which hung over the town. As they waded through the ashes - the ashes of everything, of human beings and material mixed in some sort of gruesome *pot-pourri* - there was no birdsong, no chatter of voices, no dogs barking, no shouts from children at play. There was no greenery either, nothing. It was like a scene from another world, an uninhabited world, a world of ghostly gloom; and those Darmstädters who were still there could have done without the ghoulish-minded who came in from outlying villages to see for themselves what Bomber Command had done to a town and its people.

The survivors, suddenly shorn of everything they had held dear, looked like zombies and those still capable of rational thought tortured themselves further with the question: Would the bombers come back, as they had done in the case of other places? Some tried to convince themselves that they wouldn't, there being so little left to destroy; others had succumbed to such a depth of apathy that they no longer cared, while for some the prospect of a second attack was just too much and they fled, no doubt encouraged to do so by the total lack of services and amenities, because all water supplies had been cut, there was no electricity, no gas, no medical care, no postal deliveries or collections, no telephone; and, ironically, nothing with which to make a fire ...

As for those who perished, German records show that 15 in every 100 died from blast, the same percentage from incineration, and a horrifying 70 in each 100 from suffocation. One in five was a child. Of nearly 8500 private dwellings, approximately one half were completely destroyed and nearly 500 so badly damaged as to be uninhabitable. 70,000 people found themselves homeless and many tens of thousands left the town to aggravate problems of accommodation elsewhere. Of the Altstadt there was absolutely nothing that remained; it was just a huge, empty space knee-deep in greyish-black ash.

The United States Strategic Bombing Survey, published in 1945, stated: 'This was an area raid of the classic saturation type, which had so efficiently razed Hamburg. Darmstadt was virtually destroyed'.

But there was something else which the report did not mention: the destruction of Darmstadt proved beyond a shadow of doubt that Bomber Command could now do to the Reich what Harris had planned from February 22, 1942, the day on which he had taken office; in other words it could, as he had promised, 'wreck Germany from end to end' with the means it now had at its disposal.

With the annihilation of a place with as little military significance as Darmstadt, it certainly looked as if that plan was well on the way to being fully implemented; and the fact that Germany no longer presented a target-rich environment did not augur well for what was left.

Chapter 16

HITLER ERRS AGAIN

Home, sweet home! There was nothing more comforting to the crew of a bomber returning from a long night trip over the Reich than the sight of their own airfield beckoning just ahead. It was a moment, if not of elation - because that was an emotion seldom experienced - but of quiet satisfaction; one more, one less; a moment to savour the agreeable thought of a meal of bacon and eggs and strong, hot tea, and then of falling blissfully into a warm bed. At such times the airmen were usually too tired to bother thinking about what might be in store that same night or the one after.

Home, sweet home - or was it? For there were at least two periods during the offensive when it was 'home' all right, but when the reception was not quite as 'sweet' as it might have been.

We have already noted (Chapter 1) Hitler's hostile reaction to the desperate pleas made to him by experienced Luftwaffe officers to be allowed to base their fighters mainly in Northern France, so that the bombers could be attacked while they were taking off for the night's operation or while landing after it. This was quite in accordance with German pre-war air theory on the tactics required to deal with any bomber fleet employed against the Fatherland. The intruder aircraft, originally termed *Klebeflugzeuge* ('adhesive aircraft')would pounce on the bombers when the latter were unable to take evasive action - because of the close proximity of other members of their own squadron or for one of the other obvious reasons. General Kammhuber explained the ploy admirably when he said: "If I want to kill wasps I go to their nests and smoke them out. I don't swat them in the open one at a time. I visit the nest when they are in it". He made it clear to the Führer that it was often difficult to locate and destroy a bomber stream, especially in adverse weather conditions; the Luftwaffe seldom knew exactly where the aircraft were, except when they were attacking the target, but they certainly knew where they were based in England.

But the Führer remained for the most part unimpressed by the logic of the argument; and although he did yield now and again to

The Great Ingratitude

the men who were in charge of the Reich's air defences, he did so most reluctantly and did not appear to want to know that the RAF used Mosquitoes regularly in this way to shoot up German fighter stations before or during large Bomber Command operations against the Reich.

The first time he relented was in the autumn of 1940, when, on the night of October 20/21, the first British bomber lost to intruders was a Whitley based at Linton-on-Ouse. It had just taken off on the long flight to the Skoda Works at Pilsen in Czechoslovakia when it was raked by Hauptman Karl Hulshoff and crashed, killing four members of the crew and injuring the fifth.

When these intrusions over English airfields did take place they were generally successful and a typical foray was that of February 10, 1941, when a raid on Hanover by 222 bombers claimed only three over Germany, while five were lost in the proximity of their bases; and in spite of the fact that these *Fernnachtjäger* (long-range night intruders), mainly Junkers Ju 88s and Dornier Do 175s, had accounted for 86 British aircraft over England by October, 1941, Hitler gave the order that such operations should be discontinued, insisting once more that it was preferable that his people should see RAF planes crashing with their own eyes rather than be told about this happening elsewhere, which they might or might not believe. The next intruders were not to appear in British skies for more than two years, much, it might be said, to the relief of Bomber Command. But the Führer, vacillating as he did in so many spheres, allowed the resumption of such sorties between August 1943 and April 1944, and during the first four months of 1945. The most punishing night of all for Bomber Command was on March 3/4, 1945, the 2000th of the war, when approximately 200 night fighters followed back to England the various formations which had been raiding Kamen, the Dortmund Ems canal, Berlin and Würzburg, or taking part in mine-laying or diversionary sweeps. This Luftwaffe operation was code-named *Gisella* and ironically (considering the war had but two more months to run) the biggest and most destructive of the lot; it was believed to have accounted for 32 aircraft - 15 Halifaxes, 11 Lancasters, three Fortresses, two Mosquitoes and a Hudson, while only eight bombers were shot down over Germany or German occupied territory. It was during this operation that one of the participating Ju 88s, which came down near Elvington, was the last German aircraft to be lost over Britain during the War. Before the end of March four other British aircraft fell victim to Luftwaffe intruders.

Bomber Command in World War II

It was calculated that these night stalkers destroyed five British aircraft in 1940, 86 in 1941, four in 1943, 40 in 1944 and 36 in 1945, a total of 171. These included 32 Wellingtons, 24 Lancasters, 16 Halifaxes and four Mosquitoes, but 21 different types were lost altogether - even a few Spitfires and Hurricanes, dear old Annie Ansons and Oxfords and Tiger Moths. When the *Fernnachtjäger* were on the prowl nothing was safe.

Yet it could have been much, much worse; had Hitler listened to the voices of experience and reason the night intruders could have become a real thorn in the flesh of Bomber Command. This would have been particularly the case in 1943 and 1944 when damaged Lancasters and Halifaxes were often compelled to keep on circuiting their bases as they awaited permission to land. Frequent attacks would have added a further dimension to the already perilous business of taking a bomber over Germany and bringing it back. The morale of the crews during that period was, as we have seen, low enough, especially at the time of the Battle of Berlin, and further demands would have been put on their sorely tested resilience as they approached what should have been the succour offered by their own coast and mainland, only to find they could be sitting ducks. They had quite enough to contend with over Brandenburg and Westphalia without having their trials prolonged over Lincolnshire and Norfolk.

But once again, by overruling the wise advice of others who knew better than he, Hitler showed that he could often be his own worst enemy, and for this tactical blunder on his part Bomber Command, by its own admission, was more than a little grateful. Had the intruders been employed regularly and on a large scale, the Command might have been forced to make radical (and impairing) organisational changes, even to the point of moving its bases much further to the north and thus causing no end of disruption and delay. Harris, determined as he was to give as little respite as possible to Germany's cities, would not have been at all pleased.

Chapter 17

FLEETING THREAT

The principal enemy fighters which Bomber Command and the USAAF had to face were the single-engined Messerschmitt Bf 109 and Focke-Wulf 190, the twin-engined Messerschmitt Bf 110 and Junkers 88, and their variants. These were all reliable piston-engined machines (the FW 190 was the only new conventional fighter produced in effective numbers from 1939 onwards) with good performance and fire-power, and they accounted for the great majority of bombers shot down by the Luftwaffe squadrons. The exact figure will never be known, but it ran into thousands.

Yet these losses would have been all the greater had German fighter design and production not been obstructed in ways similar to those that afflicted the V-weapon programme (Chapter 11). A typical example was the incomprehensible vacillation concerning the Heinkel He 219 *Uhu* ('Eagle Owl'), a machine which, had it been given the chance, would have presented to Bomber Command in particular a further deadly peril when it was finally issued to Luftwaffe *Nachtjagdgeschwader* (night fighter squadrons) in the summer of 1943. (On the night of June 11/12, when 783 aircraft attacked Düsseldorf, a single Uhu shot down five Lancasters one after the other). A twin-engined two-seater, it boasted a maximum speed of 416 mph and, with its radar and heavy armament (by 1944, just when it was most needed, it carried the devastatingly effective *Schräge Musik* twin 30 mm cannon) it possessed the potential to inflict severe damage on the large bomber formations. Fortunately for them, only 268 Uhus left the factories.

But an even more worrying threat to Bomber Command loomed on the aeronautical horizon. As early as the late thirties, aero-engine designers were aware that the petrol-driven aircraft had been developed almost to its maximum performance. This was because of the large disproportionate decrease in a propeller's pulling power as speed increased, quite the opposite in the case of a turbo-jet or rocket engine, since the power did not have to be converted elsewhere (to a propeller) and the flow of air entering the compressor produced more forward thrust the faster the aircraft flew. The Germans were amongst the first to experiment in this new and exciting field.

While the war was still in its infancy they spent a lot of time and effort in trying to produce jet aircraft and, considering the fact that test pilot Fritz Wendel made the first flight in a turbo-jet fighter on July 18, 1941, in a Messerschmitt Me 262, and that on August 8 the same year, a Messerschmitt Me 163, destined to be the fastest fighter in existence in early 1945, was flown from the airfield at Peenemünde with Heini Dittmar at the controls, it is perhaps surprising that Bomber Command, when at the height of its endeavours from 1943 until early 1945, did not find itself assailed by a new menace which might have made losses unsustainable, especially about the time of the Battle of Berlin when it was going through its worst patch and crew morale was giving cause for grave concern. That the unthinkable did not materialise was due to several reasons.

Hitler, dismissing the views of his experienced air officers in his customary intransigent manner, ordered that the Me 262 be developed as a fighter-bomber - the *Blitzbomber* as he called it. He insisted that the conventional fighters in service with the Luftwaffe had proved themselves a match for any of the aircraft the Allies possessed, and that time and resources should not be wasted in producing aircraft without which he could win the war in any case. He maintained that developing jet fighters would delay victory rather than hasten it. Even if it is argued in his favour that in 1941 the Luftwaffe was still the most powerful air force in existence and that the Reich had not yet experienced the relentless bombing that was to descend upon it, he still ought to have realised from various sources (including Churchill himself) that an onslaught on Germany from the air was the avowed British intention. But the man was not for turning. Even impassioned pleas from the much respected fighter ace Adolf Galland, who knew a thing or two about air combat - he had flown the fourth prototype of the Me 262 and pronounced its performance as dazzling - failed to influence the Führer. Nor did reports of jet research in Britain, and the growing intensity of the Air Offensive against the Reich do anything to make him change his mind. He still claimed that the piston-engined fighters were doing an admirable job and he displayed growing impatience to see the Me 262 appear as a bomber which would play a decisive roll during the impending Allied invasion by sweeping in on the beaches and wiping out the enemy troops and equipment as these were landed. London too, was in his sights. Hitler was always obsessed with

The Great Ingratitude

attack - fast, unstoppable attack - which after all had made him master of nearly all of Europe, and took an anathematical view of anything relating to defence.

Yet one or two top Nazis had at times the guts to oppose their Leader and, once out of range of his blustering and raving, quietly did what they considered to be apposite. Field Marshall Erhard Milch, for instance, ignored Hitler's commands and organised the development of the Me 262 as a fighter. Willi Messerschmitt also played his part by not manufacturing the aircraft as a bomb-carrier, and when the eighth prototype took to the air in December 1943, it was armed with four 30 mm cannon. This formidable machine, it was confidently believed, would be the answer to the expected arrival in German skies of the huge American B-29s and B-32s, reputed to have a ceiling of about seven miles. The Me 262 (or *Schwalbe* - 'Swallow') would be able to get up there in no time and annihilate them through speed and fire power. No other Luftwaffe fighter was remotely capable of doing so. In fact the USAAF did not plan to use their massive new machines in the European theatre - they were intended for the Far East. Nevertheless the Me 262 represented a dire threat to all bombers and, provided it was delivered to the squadrons in adequate numbers, seemed quite capable of turning the tables in the air war over Germany.

But the problems connected with the twin-engined, single-seat Me 262 were manifold and apparently never-ending. Although the ninth prototype was air tested in late January, 1944, umpteen difficulties arose with regard to engine construction, due mainly to the enforced use of ersatz materials, and engine life amounted to no more than a few flying hours. The Me 262 was a difficult aircraft to fly, especially when in the hands of inexperienced pilots (which, of necessity, many of them were). 'Flame-out' often occurred on take-off, resulting in a crucial lack of power and a crash-landing - or worse, and the loss of pilots the Luftwaffe could ill afford. This fault, however, was largely rectified when the Jumo engines were replaced with power-units from BMW. Such delays and drawbacks were most frustrating for the Germans as the aircraft could climb at almost 4000 feet per minute, travel at nearly 550 mph at 20,000 feet, and had a range of 500 miles. Me 262 pilots soon learned that their fantastic speed precluded the normal combat method of infiltrating the bomber stream and picking off individual Fortresses and Lancasters; so they adopted the practice of streaking right through the enemy formation and spraying one or two, or even three, bombers with savage cannon fire. The American and RAF pilots and gunners had no time to react (sometimes they didn't even get a glimpse of the 262s) and for a spell this new menace did Allied crews' morale no good at all.

Yet the Me 262 could have appeared much earlier, which would also have allowed more time for ironing out its faults; but the old dissensions and envies kept raising their ugly heads and a prime example was the feud between Milch and Willi Messerschmitt: the latter, thoroughly peeved when Milch turned down his piston-engined Me 209 in favour of his Me 262 jet, told the Führer that the jet had a significantly higher fuel consumption than the 209, and thereby obtained a peremptory *Führerbefehl* ('Order from the Führer') to produce the propeller-driven aircraft. But Messerschmitt had conveniently omitted to mention to Hitler that the jet required only low-grade fuel and not the high octane of which stocks were low. The Führer's order was later rescinded - but only after it had delayed development of the Me 262 by 6-9 months.

Hitler gave vent to his usual display of histrionics when he learned early in 1944 that, contrary to his orders, the Me 262 was not being produced as the bomber he had ordered as a means of coping with the now imminent Allied attack on his 'Fortress Europe'. He later relented to a certain extent - no doubt because of the overwhelming air assault which was in the processing of shaking his Reich to bits - but still insisted that work on the aircraft as a fighter should not slow up its appearance as a fast bomber, and indeed stipulated that only one in twenty be allocated to the fighter squadrons. But by the time the Invasion came these squadrons possessed pitifully few Me 262s - perhaps a couple of dozen. The troops were landed successfully on the Normandy beaches and a great opportunity was missed; nor did the jets play anything but a very minor part in the ensuing battles which raged in France.

Production slumped as fuel shortages worsened and as aircraft factories were pulverised by Allied bombs; also, RAF and American fighters employed a very effective tactic to lessen the threat from the Me 262: when carrying out a large bombing operation they sent swarms of Spitfires, Mustangs and Typhoons to patrol above the jet airfields and to attack the fighters as they took off or landed. A number of German jets were destroyed in this way - ironically a method scorned by Hitler when Luftwaffe officers wanted to do likewise to Bomber Command on its own bases (as we have seen in the previous chapter).

Although more than 1400 Me 262s were turned out by the factories by early 1945, only some 200 of these actually ended up on

The Great Ingratitude

operational service. As a consequence of the regular bombing of communications in the Reich itself, many of the aircraft lay marooned in sidings for lengthy periods, their existence apparently forgotten, and a quarter of the total number built were lost either through writing themselves off in accidents or by Allied fighters. Yet in spite of all the set-backs and manufacturing troubles which dogged it constantly throughout its erratic career, the Me 262 accounted for approximately 400 aircraft, mostly American Flying Fortresses. But Bomber Command also experienced its undoubted capabilities: the conventional German fighter had long been Harris's main enemy, and enemy enough, and when crews fleetingly observed their first Me 262 their initial surprise quickly gave way to a feeling of intense unease. They had been led to believe that the Luftwaffe was more or less a spent force - their own recent experience had tended to confirm this view - yet here they were being confronted by a new and frightening menace of which they had heard but for which they were not prepared. Veterans of pre-jet operations who had thought they had a fairly good chance of surviving what must surely be the closing stages of the war, now began to have second thoughts: pilots had not time to take evasive action, gunners no time to align their sights because all they saw, if they saw anything at all, was a dark streak which had come and gone in the batting of an eye. They did not know that both jets and pilots were in short supply. Had they been plentiful many more aircrews would have shared the fate of some of their unsuspecting colleagues - all too clearly demonstrated during the daylight attack by 469 aircraft on the new U-boat pens in the Blohm & Voss shipyards in Hamburg on March 31, 1945 (see Chapter 1). The last wave of bombers had arrived behind schedule, missed its protective screen of Mustangs, and found itself pounced upon by small, strange-looking fighters which went past at lightning speed, but not before they had consigned seven out of 20 Lancasters and Halifaxes to oblivion. Even the high-flying, hard to catch Mosquito was no longer safe: for the first time it could be confronted by an adversary which it was unable to meet even on equal terms. Inevitably Mosquito losses increased. Bomber Command, which had thought that the Luftwaffe fighter force was all but dead and buried by the late autumn of 1944, was rudely jerked out of its ever-growing feeling of security. Yet, worrying as the new jet phenomenon was, High Wycombe also knew that the end of the war was in sight and wisely regarded this belated menace as a last flicker of the candle. It is not difficult to imagine the possible consequences had such a situation arisen even a year earlier but, mercifully, as with the V-1 and the V-2, it was a case of too little, too late.

The Luftwaffe continued to send up Me 262s as late as April, 1945, and by so doing continued to claim British and American bombers. By then the factories were still turning them out - only God knows how they managed to do so - and some did get through to the few jet bases that were left. Small indeed was the reward for all the effort expended on research and for the loss of Germany's best remaining pilots.

Although the Me 262 represented by far the main hazard to the Allied bomber fleets as far as the new concept in fighters was concerned, the tiny, stubby Messerschmitt Me 163 (or *Komet*), which went into action in the summer of 1944, had a unique claim to fame: it was the first operational rocket-powered interceptor aircraft. Single-seat, and tailless, with a maximum speed in level flight of almost 600 mph, this singular advantage was far outweighed by its inability to stay airborne for a practicable length of time (maximum 12 minutes), and the part it played in combat was negligible. In fact it was credited with the destruction of less than 10 enemy aircraft. Its negligible role resulted from a host of manufacturing problems, and after the Messerschmitt plant at Regensburg had been pulverised by the Americans on August 17, 1943, further serious disruption was caused that same night when Bomber Command attacked the rocket sites at Peenemünde (Chapter 11), where the Me 163 was continually being put through its paces and its fuel was produced. The latter was a highly volatile mixture of hydrogen peroxide and alcohol/ hydrazine which could never be relied upon not to explode prematurely - or to remain stable when the aircraft was affected by the slightest of bumps. Both taking off and landing an Me 163 was a frightening experience, and accidents were commonplace. With the Regensburg factory out of action the plane's manufacture was taken over by a smaller firm which lacked the expertise to iron out its faults. Nevertheless the machine had tremendous potential and, like the Me 262, could have become an effective part of the Luftwaffe armoury if the Germans had had the required resources and had time been on their side. Just as well they didn't, and that it wasn't.

The only other German jet fighter to enter service was the single-seat Heinkel He 162, called the *Salamander* or *Volksjäger* ('People's Fighter'). Powered by a BMW turbo-jet (mounted on its back), and armed with two cannon, it could reach a height of 20,000 feet in less than seven minutes. Test flown for the first time as late as December 6, 1944, in a last desperate effort to produce, as quickly as possible, a fast, mass produced fighter which could play havoc amongst the huge Allied

The Great Ingratitude

bombing fleets, the prototype was flying just over five weeks after the designers had got to work. Semi-skilled, and even unskilled labour, were put to the task (mostly underground to ensure protection from air raids), using whatever materials were available. With such an approach it was inevitable that faults abounded; apart from trouble with the wings the Salamander was a most disagreeable aircraft to fly and the depths to which the Reich's resources had fallen was illustrated further by the decision to have the plane piloted by fanatical members of the Hitlerjugend (Hitler Youth), whose only experience had been on gliders. Goering, in one of his rare intrusions into Luftwaffe matters at this point in the war, but as bombastic as ever, promised 1000 Salamanders each month by early 1945, but like many of his pledges this one too fell wide of the mark, and only 116 entered service out of about 275 actually completed. By then the Allied air forces had destroyed practically all the remaining fuel stocks and it is doubtful if a solitary Salamander ever took off to intercept the bombers. No British or American crews reported that they had ever encountered such an aircraft.

***

Basing their argument on the huge losses sustained by Bomber Command and the USAAF from conventional fighters alone, some students of the Air Offensive have voiced the opinion that the war could have taken a very different course had Germany's jet fighter programme not been plagued by so much bungling and disruption. They are possibly right. Certainly there can be no doubt whatsoever that had the Luftwaffe possessed these aircraft somewhat earlier, and in sufficient numbers, the big bomber formations might have been carved to pieces; the Normandy landings would have been an infinitely more hazardous undertaking, with abject failure more than a possibility; the jets would have protected Germany's synthetic oil plants and the factories in which the machines themselves were produced; their pilots would not have been subjected to such hurried and inadequate training and would have been all the more proficient at their job. Anything could have happened.

But the jet fighter programme was typical of the chronic administrative ineptitude which characterised armament development in the Third Reich. Just as Hitler had extended himself territorially in Europe, which brought him extra problems, he allowed the same situation to arise as far as the development of the tools of war was concerned, which was as good a way as any of sapping stocks of scarce materials and causing rivalry and jealousy amongst those involved in the projects. Concentration on either the V-1s or V-2s, or the jets, carried out in an organised manner, and bereft of wrangling, would have been a far better policy - and almost undoubtedly with far more rewarding results.

Chapter 18

"BANDS AND SHEPHERDESSES"

Operation *Thunderclap* and the unimaginable agonies to which it subjected the city of Dresden is as well known as the attack on the Ruhr Dams; but as well known, unhappily, for vastly different reasons. The raid itself has been fully described in David Irving's book 'The Destruction of Dresden' (Irving is now, some would say, an unashamed apologist of Hitlerism and a darling of the neo-Nazis) and in Alexander McKee's 'Dresden 1945' and I do not intend to give a detailed strategic account of an operation which, more than any other, tarnished the name of Bomber Command in the eyes of many and including some who, until that fateful night, had whole-heartedly supported the Bombing Offensive. So it would not be amiss to examine its origins, the circumstances surrounding it, what it did to the city, and the arguments advanced by those who decried it as totally unnecessary and a brazen outrage.

Back in June, 1944, the Chiefs of Staff had agreed that 'the time might well come in the not too distant future when an all-out attack by every means at our disposal on German morale might be decisive' Portal believed that there might come 'a moment at which the balance can be tipped by an attack directed against the morale of the High Command, the Army and the civilian population, rather than against objectives immediately related to the battle'. He thought Berlin, with its many governmental and Nazi Party offices, would be a suitable target. The plan was to rain down on the capital, within the space of a few days, a petrifying 25,000 tons of bombs to cause unheard of terror and confusion, and thereby to bring about a massive exodus of the survivors following a complete breakdown of amenities and civil order; in other words it would be a raid which would prove that 'the unbearable' could not always be borne, not even by a people which so far had shown itself to be unbelievably tenacious in the face of constant and heavy attack from the air. Portal must have known that the Battle of Berlin had come nearer to shattering the morale of Bomber Command than that of the Berliners, but, to give him his due, he was suggesting that such an all-consuming blitz would take place only when all Germans surely realised that defeat was staring them in the face and there was no way back; a bombardment on the scale envisaged would perhaps be the final straw and break the spirit of the nation.

However at the Yalta Summit, held between February 4 and 11, 1945, and attended by Churchill, Roosevelt and Stalin - Portal too was present - the Soviets wanted to know if their allies would help them in their advance westwards by using their bombers to raze Leipzig. Harris, never enamoured with the thought that cities in the east of the country had seen less of Bomber Command than those elsewhere, was all for extending his campaign to the farthest-flung corners of the Reich - as were the Americans, who opened *Thunderclap* by hitting Berlin and Magdeburg. But in the end it was Dresden, close to the Czechoslovak border and right in the path of the Red Army, which was selected as the place destined to go down in the history books as, up till then, the most frightening example of what could happen to a large town which had been selected for annihilation from the air. Yes, Dresden; it could so easily have been somewhere else - in such apparently whimsical fashion was the fate of great cities decided...

Beautiful old Dresden which, as Harris was wont to say of many towns in Germany tailor-made for Bomber Command's undeniable ability to create conflagrations of a size and intensity hardly envisaged before his waves of heavy bombers showed what could be done, was 'built more like a fire-lighter than a human habitation'. Its nucleus, the Altstadt (Old Town), formed a concentrated mass of ancient wooden buildings, inflammable as tinder and a recipe for disaster. With a population well in excess of half a million and situated on the Elbe 350 miles south-east of its estuary at Cuxhaven on the North Sea, Dresden had been the capital of Saxony since 1485. Those who later maintained that they found it difficult to find terms adequate enough to express the depths of their disapprobation were not altogether correct when they claimed that the city possessed little by way of military targets: apart from its importance as a centre of communications with national and international railway routes and a frequent rallying-point for German troops and *matériel* bound for the Eastern Front, it had precision instrument, engineering and chemical industries which had sprung up in the 19th century and had long contributed to the demands of war. All this, however, was either outside the knowledge of the censurers or conveniently overlooked by them. It was no Essen, certainly, but neither was it completely devoid of important factories.

Twenty minutes before 10 pm on the evening of February 13, the first wave of 270 Lancasters, led by a few Mosquitoes, droned over the city on their 1600-mile round trip of 9½ hours duration at the unusually

The Great Ingratitude

low altitude of 10,000 feet, but the presence of a layer of cloud beneath them spoiled the accuracy of the bomb-aiming and only moderate success was achieved; but about four hours later - the purpose of the time interval had been to ensure that the defences and emergency services were thoroughly disrupted - a second formation of 530 Lancs arrived at 01.30 hours in clear weather, to create a fire storm of awesome proportions. Altogether 1480 tons of HE and 650,000 incendiaries - only about half the normal bomb load for a force of this size because of the large amount of petrol required - fell on Dresden. The following day 400 American heavies threw more fuel into the inferno - one wonders why - and again the day after that - which is even more astonishing. The end result was a scene of such limitless desolation that it would be something of an understatement to say that Hamburg had come to Dresden; rather was Dresden a foretaste, in the physical sense at least, of the ultimate at Hiroshima for, if six months later you had placed photographs of the remains of each city side by side, you would have had difficulty in telling which was which. In fact, on learning the full details about Dresden, Portal must have concluded that the prediction he had made in 1940, when Bomber Command was woefully weak and capable of causing the enemy only slight inconvenience rather than serious problems, ranked as one of the greatest underestimations of the entire war: 'We have not yet reached the stage of desiring to burn down a whole town, but when this stage is reached we shall do it by dropping a large quantity of incendiaries first and then carry out a sustained attack with high explosive to drive the fire-fighters underground and let the flames get a good hold'. It is doubtful whether Portal, or anyone else, ever envisaged the creation of the galloping ocean of fire which consumed everyone and everything that lay in its path.

Although other towns in Germany had known the horrors of such attacks - up till now principally Hamburg and Darmstadt - it was Dresden, on account not only of its size but of the nature of its structure and its population swollen by countless refugees desperate to keep ahead of the Red Army, which became the prime example of the method of destruction outlined by the Chief of Air Staff five years before; and since it was civilians who suffered in the Second World War more than anyone else, and German civilians more than anyone else at the hands of Bomber Command, and especially at Dresden, it might be in context to describe the experiences of one or two individuals who were caught up in the most devastating fire storm of the lot, a nightmare of nightmares which on that fateful night in the city's history was shared by thousands of others, many of whom, unlike Eva Beyer and Annemarie Waehmann, did not come through.

Typical were the further traumas to which Eva, a young bakery assistant, after a night of indescribable terror, had to endure when she began to search the smouldering or still flaming ruins for members of her family as soon as it became daylight on February 14:

'I came upon scenes which defied description; everywhere you looked you saw parts of bodies, arms, legs, heads, hands and torsos which were being gathered together and piled up by the air raid defence people and soldiers. They threw petrol over the huge heap and burnt it, and lorries kept bringing more parts to add to the pile. I just stood there, rooted to the spot. Was my mother somewhere amongst that obscene mess?

Later I used to wake up screaming during the night. We were also scared out of our wits at the approach of the Russians.

At one stage I dropped to my knees, shaking like a leaf and sobbing my heart out. This was when I arrived at what had been the women's clinic. Women lay on the ground with new-born babies. Some of the mothers had their stomachs burst wide open and half the babies were hanging out; many of them were mutilated. After a day or two, pools of evil greenish liquid began to form and spread out under the bodies, and this happened with all the bodies in all the cellars all over the city. Then the SS Pioneers brought in flame-throwers and burnt out the cellars with their contents; of all people they knew best what the next stages of decomposition would be as the days went by and temperatures rose; great clouds of flies hovered over the human remains and masses of maggots crawled about all over the flesh and bits of burnt clothing that were left.'

Annemarie Waehmann, 20 years of age, fled from the Friedrichstadt hospital where she had been a patient and somehow survived by running and just keeping ahead of the racing wall of fire. When morning came she saw, in the company of another patient (a 15-year old refugee), things she said she would never have imagined possible:

'Thick, choking smoke everywhere. We had to climb over burning roofs and walls which had collapsed and flaming material was falling all around us - and everywhere lay corpses shrunk to half their life-size. At one point I saw a number of people sitting nonchalantly on the ground. Why were they so still? Then we realized why - they were all dead.

There were no streets left, nothing but piles of débris. Then, to crown all, another air raid warning, announced by army men in the vicinity as the sirens were all kaputt. We decided to try to get through

The Great Ingratitude

the station to the Räcknitzer Höhen - higher ground - and on the way we found corpses piled up in great heaps about five metres square and two metres deep. A lot of these people had been on fire and had jumped into reservoirs, only to be drowned when others leapt on top of them.

As if all this was not enough, low-flying American planes came at us with their machine-guns firing and screams rent the air everywhere. I believe these planes then went to the Elbe meadows, where crowds of people were seeking shelter from the flames, and did the same thing there. Who ordered that to be done? Had the whole world gone mad?'

If, up until then, anything had happened on earth which, more than anything else, came nearest to resembling Hell, then surely it must have been Dresden; if, up until then, a city had ever died a horrible death - and we can think of the great natural disasters at Pompeii, Lisbon and San Francisco amongst others - that city was Dresden. But this time the unstoppable elemental force, terrifying in its dimensions, had been the result of essential ingredients provided by man - to create a fiendish concoction so far unknown even in modern warfare. The heat reached an estimated and unimaginable 3000 degrees and, since some types of stone can withstand only just over 1000 degrees, buildings simply collapsed even if untouched by fire or high explosives. This is what happened to the imposing Kreuzkirche, the 'Church of the Cross', where all the valuable paintings but one were completely destroyed. Some surviving inhabitants still maintain today that as many as 250,000 people perished, supporting that figure by claiming that not enough importance was attached to the unknown thousands of refugees who had scant knowledge of their whereabouts and were unable to find a refuge; others assert that without a shadow of a doubt at least 70,000 civilians lost their lives. A tourists' guide published in 1977 stated that more than 35,000 died a violent death and this figure is now accepted as possibly being the most accurate - but the chaos was so vast that it, too, can be regarded as only an approximation; the same guide put the total number of dwellings reduced to little more than dust as 80,000 (out of a total of 220,000, with only 45,000 undamaged) - in other words roughly four out of every five houses were rendered unfit for human habitation. More than a quarter of a million citizens became homeless; 15 square miles in the centre of the city were reduced to an unbroken sea of grey ash.

The theorists of the pre-war Trenchardian school had been proved right in the end, for if any doubts still existed about the potentiality of air power and of the heavy bomber in particular, these were finally and irrevocably dissolved at Dresden. It was the heavy bomber which had caused, first of all, death and material destruction on an unprecedented scale and then, as far as we can judge, for the first time under the Nazis, a slight but perceptible decline in social discipline, manifested mainly in the form of looting, for which the penalty was death. It is worth pointing out that following this cosmic upheaval in a large German city many of its survivors secretly blamed Hitler for the tragedy and for their suffering. So perhaps at last, at long last, unmistakable signs of civil disorder were there to be seen. But how much the Dresden experience contributed towards an effective undermining of that people's steadfastness in the face of growing adversity (apparently the main aim of Portal and the Chiefs of Staff in laying on the operation) must remain very much open to question. It seemed to have made little impact on military personnel and in spite of the disorderly behaviour on the part of some of Dresden's citizens (the looting just mentioned) few outward signs of decreasing resilience revealed themselves and indeed, as far as the ordinary townsfolk were concerned, British prisoners of war, compelled to clean up amongst the still smoking ruins a week after the attack, paid tribute to their stoical attitude and to their spirit of defiance. This was illustrated in the slogans painted on walls in large, bold letters just a day or two after the raid: *'Nie wieder ein 1918! Sieg!'* ('No repeat of 1918! Forward to victory!') and *'Deutschland muss leben, auch wenn wir sterben müssen!'* ('Germany must live, even if we have to die!'). The prisoners, who hadn't been having too easy a time of it themselves, could not help but admire such pertinacity in such appalling circumstances. But these rallying cries might well have been the work of monomaniacal Nazis or of those who still had faith in Hitler's ability yet to produce a devastatingly powerful 'secret weapon'. And of course it goes almost without saying that for their own safety the Dresdners, like all their compatriots, had at all times to suppress their innermost thoughts if these could be interpreted, however slightly, as prejudicial to the well-being of the régime; defeatist talk was highly dangerous talk, not only as late as February 1945, but even when the Russians had penetrated well into Berlin; therefore it must not be assumed that the absence of any united effort to rebel against the continuation of the war indicated a wish to carry it on, or that morale had not been lowered. The citizens of the Reich, indoctrinated and browbeaten to a degree possibly unparalleled anywhere in any era, did not object because objections would simply have aggravated their already miserable lot - it was as simple as that. That alone explains why it is quite inconceivable that an experience such as Dresden, coming when the tide heralding imminent defeat was surging in relentlessly from both East and West, should apparently have been accepted without complaint by those who had endured it and by those who feared their own town might be the next to be singled out for similar treatment; and if Portal and his colleagues did not realise their goal by inflicting what they had hoped to be the *coup de grâce* to German morale and the immediate collapse of the nation, then they had simply miscalculated the extent of that people's tenaciousness - or of its impotence to act - not an unpardonable error of judgement on their part in a conflict in which mistakes were numerous on both sides and often of far greater significance; and we have already noted that the whole question of German morale was extremely difficult to assess, thanks to the nature of the régime itself - the grip in which the populace was held was just too tight; and undoubtedly Hitler's repeated warning that the Allies demand for 'Unconditional Surrender' would plunge their land into a great dark abyss in which they would become the slaves of the subhuman hordes from the East (whom the Führer himself had intended to enslave on a permanent basis) was a powerful factor in sustaining them in their ordeal, especially as it was strengthened by their deeply ingrained loyalty to authority, no matter how perverse, an attitude which was beyond the comprehension of all democratic peoples and even of that of their leaders, who failed to realise that not for a moment had it occurred to the politically naïve Germans that it was also in the selfish interests of the Nazi hierarchy to postpone for as long as possible the day of reckoning; that way they would have more time to prepare to lose themselves amongst the wandering masses or to arrange their escape to other, welcoming lands.

With regard to the American attacks on Dresden and the machine-gunning of its hapless citizens, it appeared that the policy of Arnold and Spaatz and Eaker 'not to throw the heavy bomber at the man in the street' had been abandoned; further confirmation of this radical change of mind was provided on March 2, just a fortnight later, when 407 four-engined planes of the USAAF, carrying 940 tons of HE and 140 of incendiaries, set off for -Dresden. On this occasion the target was said to be a specific one - the marshalling yards, but again many more Dresdners died. The German press found it difficult to find adequate terms to express their anger vis-à-vis the bomber crews of both air forces and words such as *Terrorflieger*, *Luftgangster* and *Kindermörder* screamed from their headlines. But it was the RAF which had done by far the greater part of the damage (for the loss of only nine Lancasters, two of which crashed in France and one in England) and the British man in the street did find it rather surprising that the Germans of all people should have the effrontery to describe others as 'terror fliers', 'gangsters of the air' and, of all things, 'child murderers'. But not so those who unequivocally denounced the raid, many of whom were well known national figures, and the furore erupted like an irate volcano: Members of Parliament thundered out their disapproval in the House, and cries of horror issued from countless lips when the rumour got around that as many as 150,000 men, women and children could have died. So Dresden provided all the ammunition required for the heaviest salvo ever directed at Bomber Command; the old questions were raised, and the old condemnations were voiced, but this time much more vigorously and much more persistently: how could this most recent and unambiguous example of bombing policy be anything but morally indefensible, especially now that the end was in sight? Why, only a few days before the massacre the Allied leaders (at Yalta) had thought the moment ripe to plan the political reorganisation of post-war Europe! (But that, as we shall see shortly, might well have had something to do with the raid). Why this utterly pointless example of overkill? (It seemed to have been forgotten that overkill had started with the invention of gunpowder). Surely it was an acceptable fact that Dresden, by no stretch of the imagination, could have been classified as an important military target? And had it not been overflowing with panic-stricken refugees? Had it not been virtually defenceless, nearly all its guns having been removed to try to stem the threat from the East? Had it not been renowned as one of the finest cities in Europe, a seat of learning and culture, often referred to as the 'German Athens' or 'Florence on the Elbe'? Had Bomber Command not put its all-consuming torch to what this great city was more than anything else, a huge treasure house, a plethora of museums, art galleries, libraries and scientific institutions? Had Bomber Command not once again revealed its insatiable appetite for wanton destruction by reducing to white-hot ash the most exquisite examples of Baroque and Rococo architecture, and priceless and irreplaceable specimens of Meissen china? Others, on hearing that the purpose of the raid was to 'break German morale', claimed that as far as Bomber Command was concerned 'breaking morale' was merely an overstretched euphemism for indiscriminate slaughter. Those expressing the most extreme views, and who went on doing so long after the surrender, found little to distinguish between the incineration of the pitiable citizens of Dresden and the pitiable inmates of the extermination camps. What else had the city been but the greediest oven of the lot, consuming tens of thousands in a matter of an hour or two? Some agreed with Hitler's customary denunciation of the bomber crews and, when the War Crimes Trials opened at Nuremberg about nine months later, the same people were not slow to point out that if Germany had been the victor and had established her own 'Nuremberg' in Bath or Oxford, then she would have been meting out the same punishments for 'crimes against humanity' as the Allies were, and Portal and Harris, to name but two, would have been hanged. The point is, of course, that there was no 'British Nuremberg' and it was due to a large extent to Harris and his crews that there wasn't.

Churchill, turning his back on the very man who had been entrusted with implementing the policy of which he himself had heartily approved and described as 'the only way through', appeared not to want to know about the operation and hurriedly changed the subject whenever it cropped up. Harris, as might be expected, caught it right on the chin, but, unperturbed as always, said the target had been a mass of munitions factories and a key transportation centre for the East, and swept the wave of criticism aside with muttered references to sentimental droolings from those who associated Dresden first and foremost with 'brass bands and china shepherdesses'. In his eyes the raid had been eminently successful - and that was all that mattered. They hadn't all been so.

Other detractors held the view, although according to them it constituted no valid reason for the enormity of the crime committed, that the primary aim of the operation had been to sound a clear warning to Stalin, whose territorial ambitions, revealed to Churchill and Roosevelt at Yalta only a few days before the attack, bore a striking resemblance to those of the megalomaniac they were all struggling to depose; hence Dresden was intended to provide the Russians with a practical demonstration of the overwhelming air power the Allies could deploy if the occasion demanded. Taking into account the strained relations that were already developing between the British and the Americans on the one hand and the Soviets on the other - just as Hitler had predicted - and the undeniable possibility of an even more horrendous extension of the conflict which had been tearing Europe apart for five and a half years, then it could be argued with some justification that if this was indeed the case then the operation against Dresden might well have averted a situation too frightening for words.

To refute the charge that the destruction of Dresden was unnecessary, a simple analogy might be appropriate: in a big professional boxing match, with much at stake, a participant does not hold back, no matter how much he seems assured of victory; there always exists the danger, until the contest is over and the winner has been declared, that the apparent loser may pull out something special and unexpected. That was something of which the Allies were very conscious in early 1945, when the sudden appearance of German anti-aircraft and anti-tank beams was considered by them not to be outside the realms of possibility, while an even greater source of uneasiness derived from an awareness that the Germans - who had shown, with their introduction of original and powerful weapons, that their inventive genius could never be underestimated - had been investigating the field of nuclear fission (Chapter 11); and the Allies could never be certain about the extent of the progress they had made. They did know that Otto Hahn (later to be awarded the Nobel Prize for his work) had found, in December 1938, that the atom could be split; they also knew that Werner Heisenberg, responsible for nuclear research throughout the greater part of the war, had also received the Nobel Prize as early as 1932 and that his team included the very talented Carl Friedrich von Weizsacker and Eric Bagge; they were further aware that the Germans were well ahead of anyone else in their experiments and that the Wehrmacht was eager to have the 'ultimate weapon' developed.

The Allies' apprehension had increased when the Danish scientist, Niels Bohr, with whom German physicists had been in close contact, escaped to the United States in 1943 with a drawing, possibly of a nuclear reactor, which he showed to Robert Oppenheimer, the son of a German immigrant and the foremost American engaged in this work. The Americans could hardly be blamed for fearing that the Germans might be well on their way to producing a bomb and consequently attached extreme urgency to their 'Manhatten Project' as they were determined to have the weapon at the earliest possible moment. Moreover their bomb, once ready, was intended for Germany (primarily for Berlin), not for Japan. They were obsessed by the possibility that a Nazi bomb would be used on London and on big cities along their eastern seaboard.

Their anxieties might have been lessened to some extent had they been aware of the paucity of the resources, financial and otherwise, which the Germans required for this kind of research; and that the Wehrmacht had announced at the end of 1941 (after the first setback in the Russian campaign) that unless they had the bomb in their armoury within a year at most (and not the two or three years forecast by the scientists) they. were not interested; a wonder weapon was required in a matter of months; not years, and they believed that the rocket programme (Chapter 11) could be implemented much sooner and probably have the same end result. The Allies were ignorant of these facts and for all they knew the Germans could have been well on the way to success. The war had to be brought to a conclusion as soon as possible and Operation *Thunderclap* was one of the efforts made in this direction.

British and American fears were proved to be well founded when, a matter of days after the Nazi surrender, Allied soldiers came upon a nuclear reactor underneath the foundations of a church at Haigerloch in Bavaria. They also learned that by May 1945 the Germans had been three-quarters of the way towards completion of the bomb and that 125,000 personnel had been active in nuclear research. Erich Bagge, when interrogated later, claimed that if he and his colleagues had received the resources poured, often haphazardly, into a host of other projects, such as rocket development, they would have got much nearer their goal much sooner, perhaps even before hostilities ceased. In other words, thank God, the project was plagued with the conflicting interests and the bureaucratic squabbling to which we have already referred in Chapters 11 and 17. Hitler, for instance, was more or less kept in the dark about the entire nuclear programme, because the scientists and the Wehrmacht realised that with such a tantalising prospect before his eyes their Führer would more than likely have dropped everything else and demanded that the weapon be ready for use in a month or two at most, which would have been quite impracticable and would have put unbearable pressures on all concerned.

The Allies were aware towards the end of the war that the Reich was alive with rumours that Germany was about to drop an atom bomb - far from the truth, as was to be learned later, and probably disseminated by the Nazi propaganda machine to boost morale in the darkest days the Party had ever known and to retain the usual blind allegiance to it - but the casual dismissal of such a dire threat, at a time when victory appeared to be just round the corner, would have been an act of the grossest irresponsibility.   (#)

(#) On November 19, 1942, two Halifaxes took off for Norway from RAF Skitten, a Hurricane station near Wick whose aircraft protected Scapa Flow. The aim of the operation was to blow up the heavy water plant at Vemork. Each bomber towed a Horsa glider carrying 16 soldiers who, once their mission was accomplished, were to be escorted into Sweden by Norwegian freedom-fighters. Unfortunately the Halifaxes could not find the beacons placed in position by the Resistance and became lost. One of them with its glider, crashed into a mountain, the other glider did likewise when its tow-rope severed. Of the 48 men who participated only the crew of the second Halifax survived and returned to Wick. Those airmen and soldiers not killed in the crashes were executed by the Gestapo after being interrogated. The plant was eventually destroyed by members of the Special Operations Executive in conjunction with the Norwegian Resistance.

Bomber Command in World War II

In the spring of 1945 there also existed the belief, mistaken to be sure and in retrospect perhaps rather hair-brained, that large Hitler-worshipping units of the SS were planning to hold out in an unassailable Bavarian 'Redoubt', but it was taken seriously enough by Eisenhower to cause him to swing his main armies towards the South, thus needlessly slowing up the advance through the heart of Germany. That was of minor importance compared to the possibility of an atomic attack, but the rumour about these mythical legions still helped to convince the Allies that the sooner the Nazis were forced to lay down their arms the better.

In the light of these facts the final onslaughts carried out by Bomber Command and the American Air Force, including the holocaust created at Dresden, might be best explained as precautionary measures intended to bring an end to the war before anything drastic could possibly occur to reverse the then favourable situation; and at that moment in early 1945 the destruction of a city of such beauty and historic and cultural significance as Dresden, callous as it may sound, counted for little in the eyes of the Allied commanders; add to all the worries mentioned above the growing impatience of Britain and America, both war weary after their long, prodigious efforts and with Japan still to conquer, to put an end to the whole sorry business in the European theatre without further delay (earlier they had had reason to hope that it would be all over by Christmas 1944, but the surprise German offensive in the Ardennes - the 'Battle of the Bulge' - and other setbacks on the drive to the Rhine had put paid to such aspirations). Therefore if Dresden shortened the war by a single day or prevented the death of a single Allied combatant, then it was justified, and in this context it falls into the same category as the dropping of the atom bombs. The fact that Hiroshima and Nagasaki saved many more Allied lives than Dresden, is irrelevant, because the underlying principle is the same: when you wage war you do not spare the enemy at the cost of your own; as American General 'Blood and Guts' Patton put it: 'It's not a matter of dying for your country but making sure some other poor bastard dies for his'. In the circumstances Dresden was an act of *amorality* rather than of *immorality*, as are the majority of deeds done under the protective umbrella we conveniently label 'war'. Because 'war' is murder in uniform.

In February, 1945, no one knew that hostilities in the European theatre would be over three months later, and on the night of February 13/14, May 8 was not a fact. It became a fact only on May 8. That is, in my opinion, the main argument in defence of the bombing of Dresden and I cannot see how it can be refuted; and let's be perfectly frank

The Great Ingratitude

and perfectly honest - one could also question how much the Allied war leaders or how many of their countrymen were unduly perturbed over the death of a large but indeterminate number of civilians in what, amidst all the upheaval, was just another city belonging to the nation which had deliberately laid an entire continent in ruins and was responsible for a war which had already claimed an estimated 60 million lives, 40 million of them civilians. In fact many of them viewed Dresden, if they bothered about it at all, as a fitting form of retribution for the long catalogue of German misdeeds. Some recalled the eloquently worded propaganda poster, composed by J B Priestley, which had been displayed on walls all over Great Britain early in the war:

THE SECRET BEAST

In the middle of a great civilised continent, far from the sea which brings a breath of the outer world to freshen men's minds, a secret people dwell.

Ever and ever again they become crazed with a spell of hero worship. A leader arises among them who tells them they are greater than the other peoples of the world. Knowing nothing of the world's vastness and of the seas which link land to land, they believe - and march out to slaughter and destroy.

The secret people of the Germanys are worse than fools in their folly. When their madness comes upon them, out leaps a primitive, barbarian beast-like instinct. They kill without pity, rejoicing in blood, as animals kill. They know no law, as animals know no law.

They are Europe's secret beasts, roused to senseless fury. It is all Europe's mission to cower them and cage them today, as all Europe has had to do before.

The Hun is at the gate. He will rage and destroy. He will slaughter the women and the children...

Out then and kill ... the extermination of the wild animal let loose on Europe is the plain business of Europe's citizens.

***

Bomber Command in World War II

At Dresden, and in the Air Offensive in general, Priestley's beast was exterminated in the same way as he predicted it would exterminate others, and that, to Britons in general, was fair enough. And those of literary bent could quote Shakespeare's Macbeth and confirm, that as far as they were concerned, Dresden was simply a further case of '... those who teach bloody instructions which, being taught, return to plague th'inventor' - and in essence the same pronouncement as Harris's less poetic but crisp 'they are sowing the wind' as he watched London burn in 1940. In other words the British public in general believed that the instigators of dastardly acts had no room for complaint when they received a goodly dose of their own brand of medicine. These people may not feel that way now, but they did then, and that is a very relevant point, because the facts must be examined with eyes that saw things as they were in early 1945, not with eyes spared the sights and minds spared the traumas of 1939-45 and not blessed with the convenient and sanctimonious hindsight of 1950, or 1980, or the year 2000. That is why it is quite unacceptable that some historians, mere children during the war or born after it, should come along - because they were not there - and condemn the raid as an unnecessary act of out-and-out brutality and an eternal stigma on those who authorised it; and that this antipathy should be extended to the aircrews themselves, to whom Dresden was just a further operational order to be carried out like all the others, reveals a degree of irrationality that in no way assists their case. If such recorders of events wish to go beyond the reporting of bare historical fact and enter the realm of ethics (to be sure not always an easy task when you are dealing with 'total war'), then their assessment will carry weight only if they are thoroughly acquainted with the diverse pressures, including those of the political climate, which were prevalent at the time and can be evaluated only by those who had been entrusted with the direction of the war and who were in a better position than most to decide how it could best be conducted; and certain historians fail to realise, or to disregard the fact, that Dresden was no more than the logical culmination of the policy formulated by senior airmen in the thirties, the inevitable outcome of a strategical expertise which had been painfully learned and developed to a state of near perfection and could not be abandoned till peace was won; that Arthur Harris, as Commander in Chief of Bomber Command, was merely implementing the strategy laid down by his superiors. If Sir Richard Peirse, his immediate predecessor, had still been in charge, the formula would have been exactly the same, though probably carried out with less

The Great Ingratitude

commitment. That is why Peirse was sent elsewhere and Harris was given the job.

The determination to pursue that policy until the bitter end was clearly demonstrated as Operation *Thunderclap* continued. On the night following Dresden, where the fires still raged, neighbouring Chemnitz (later to be renamed Karl-Marx-Stadt and to revert to 'Chemnitz' with the collapse of communism in East Germany) underwent a heavy attack, as it did again on March 5/6; the total number of aircraft involved in the two raids, which were almost of equal size, was 1477, comprising 997 Lancasters, 474 Halifaxes and six Mosquitoes, of which 22 Lancs and 13 Halifaxes were lost over Germany and a further nine Halifaxes crashed in England soon after take-off due to severe icing, one of them killing civilians in York. Although the first of the attacks did not fully attain the desired results the second inflicted severe fire damage on the central and southern districts of the city (no casualty figures are available). During the same period (up until March 27), large raids were also carried out against Dortmund (514 Lancs and 14 Mosquitoes on February 20/21), Duisburg (362 Lancs and 11 Mosquitoes on February 21/22), Essen (342 heavies and 18 Mosquitoes on February 23, and 1079 aircraft - 750 Lancasters, 293 Halifaxes and 36 Mosquitoes - on March 11), Dortmund again - it received a record tonnage of bombs on March 12 (4851) during a visit by 1108 aircraft, the force being made up of 748 Lancasters, 292 Halifaxes and 68 Mosquitoes, Wuppertal-Barmen (334 heavies and 20 Mosquitoes on March 13), Würzburg (Chapter 19), Witten (324 aircraft) on March 18/19 and Hannau (277 Lancasters and eight Mosquitoes the same night), Hildesheim on March 22, and Paterborn five days later (again Chapter 19). And these were not the only raids by any means - they were simply the largest and most destructive. Yet it was always Dresden which preoccupied the critics, even although many of the large centres quoted had already been bombed into rubble.

At this juncture it is apposite to point out that it was invariably Bomber Command which drew the heaviest fire from those who abhorred the whole idea of carpet bombing and fire-raising on a gigantic scale, and this despite the fact that a Dresden-type operation was repeated on several occasions by the Americans on the mainland of Japan. On May 9/10 (less than a month later and when the hue and cry over the firing of the German city was at its height), 280 Superfortresses released 1650 tons of incendiaries on Tokyo - and incendiaries were used because the majority of its houses were made of wood and paper. The death toll lay somewhere

Bomber Command in World War II

between 80,000 and 120,000, larger than that following the atom bomb attacks on either Hiroshima or Nagasaki (discounting, of course, subsequent fatalities due to the effects of radiation). Tokyo was set ablaze a further six times in April, again with horrendous casualties on each occasion, and the same fate befell Kawasaki and Nagoya. In May, Superfortresses poured down 24,000 tons into different cities - Nagoya suffered two fire storms in the space of three days and Tokyo was once more aflame after a visit by 502 aircraft towards the end of the same month. Other places attacked were Otaka, Tokuyama and Oshima. Then in June 42,000 tons were dropped, mainly on Osaka and Kobe but also on Tokyo and Nagoya. In July the story remained the same, the victims being Osaka, Kure, Akashi and Kumamoto - and Tokyo, which underwent a further fire storm after an onslaught by 1022 bombers. In early August, and not forgetting that the unconditional surrender was to be accepted on August 14, Japanese cities were still being burned down; even after the first atom bomb had fallen on August 6 and the second on August 9, Tokyo found itself subjected to yet another fire raid on August 13, just one day before Hirohito decided enough was enough.

The USAAF had been quick to note the effect of fire-raising raids by Bomber Command on Germany and had followed suit both there and in Japan. Hundreds of thousands of Japanese town dwellers must have died horrible deaths - and right until the last day of the war, not just till several weeks before it ended - but this did not provoke the same hullabaloo as Dresden. Why? Was it because Dresden was in Europe and well known to many, whereas Tokyo and her sister cities lay in far-off Nippon, known to few, and with a culture which was alien to western minds? The difference in attitude could hardly be ascribed to Japanese atrocities since in that sphere the Germans required lessons from no one.

I think it should also be pointed out at this stage that it is difficult to recall a single dissenting voice being raised concerning the 'accidental' but unavoidable killing by RAF bombs of thousands of civilians in the occupied countries, especially in France - something which worried Churchill continually. (On the whole the victims' families and the subjugated peoples accepted such tragedies as a necessary evil, as a price to be paid for their eventual liberation).

On the fortieth anniversary of Dresden in February, 1985, newspapers published articles and letters, most of them deprecatory, and a TV programme recalled the raid in a manner which definitely would not have met with the approval of the Chief of Bomber Command.

The Great Ingratitude

Viewers, with ex-operational aircrew amongst them, watched what many of the latter considered to be a nauseating spectacle when an ageing participant in the operation apologised to two elderly lady survivors, in Dresden itself, for what he and his colleagues had done to their city and its inhabitants so many years before. No doubt the subject will be discussed with renewed vigour when the fiftieth anniversary of the war's end is celebrated in 1995 as the controversy seems fated, like Bomber Command's activities in general, to go on for ever (see Appendix 2).

Perhaps one final personal reflection: as one who took part in the exhumation of missing aircrew in the Ruhr at the war's end, as Candlish did (Chapter 23), I have often wondered since how I was able to perform, day after day and month after month, such a gruesome and disturbing task amidst endless gloomy desolation and remain more or less normal; no doubt because at that time I had been hardened, toughened - call it what you will - by what I had witnessed over a lengthy period. Whether we like it or not that is what war does to normal, civilised human beings, and Dresden was just one example amongst many - Warsaw, Coventry, Belgrade, Hamburg, Tokyo, Hiroshima - of what they do to each other when they become involved in it.

Chapter 19

EVEN THE SMALL SHALL NOT BE SPARED ...

With all of Germany's largest industrial centres virtually reduced to ruins by the early winter of 1944, senior airmen realised it was an expensive and largely non-productive exercise to revisit those where only small areas remained untouched; further attacks simply moved the rubble and caused inconvenience only to those dwelling in cellars beneath wrecked buildings. Although there were notable exceptions - old favourites such as Nuremberg, Duisburg, Hannover, Stuttgart, Dortmund, Essen, Cologne, Hamburg and Bremen were yet to take more heavy poundings - the Command, when not engaged in attacking oil plants (which Harris did far more often than he is given credit for) and other military targets, looked around for medium-sized towns, some of which had never heard the drone of approaching bombers. More often than not the places selected possessed little in the way of industry, or at least of industry on which the German war effort depended. It was also a period during which the enemy fighter force was in rapid decline, even if it did demonstrate now and again that it still had a sting in its tail, and daylight operations became more frequent if still in a minority. The smaller towns which suffered all had populations of between 90,000 and 130,000.

On the night of December 4/5, 1944, while a force of 535 Lancasters was raiding Karlsruhe, the rather insignificant town of Heilbronn, standing some 30 miles to the north-east and engaged mainly in the wine trade, was attacked by 282 Lancs and 10 Mosquitoes (12 of the heavies were lost). The 1254 tons of bombs which suddenly rained down on its unsuspecting inhabitants razed 82% of the built-up area; intensive fires did most of the damage and there is every reason to believe that a mini-fire storm developed - ''mini'' when compared to others, but which would probably have been described as ''major'' two years earlier, so terrifying and devastating were its effects on a town of this size. The death-toll was 7000.

***

The Great Ingratitude

A fortnight later, on the night of December 17/18, it was the turn of the ancient town of Ulm on the Danube, about the same size as Heilbronn, the birthplace of Einstein and which could also boast that its Gothic cathedral had the highest stone spire ever built anywhere (530 feet). As was the case with Heilbronn, the raid took place concurrently with another major attack - on Duisburg by 523 aircraft. Lying half-way between Stuttgart and Augsburg, its citizens had heard the ominous sound of Merlin engines often enough, but this was its first and only raid, carried out by 317 Lancasters and 13 Mosquitoes. Ulm was the location of the Magirius-Deutz and Kässbohrer factories, which produced lorries, also of other industrial plants, military barracks and military hospitals, all of which were destroyed or severely damaged. During the operation, which lasted less than half-an-hour, almost 1500 tons were dropped on the centre and its immediate vicinity. Again there was a mini-fire storm which claimed the same acreage of destruction as had occurred at Heilbronn. Fortunately for those who lived in the town a large-scale evacuation had been ordered following the experience of Heilbronn and had this not taken place there is little doubt that the figure of 600 killed, of whom roughly 500 were women and children, would have been a great deal higher; about the same number were injured and almost 25,000 of Ulm's inhabitant had no home to which they could return. Somewhat miraculously the cathedral spire remained intact.

***

Of similar size to Heilbronn and Ulm was Pforzheim, standing on the northern fringe of the Black Forest and originally the site of a Roman settlement (its name derived from the Latin *porta*). It was the proud possessor of a famous medieval Latin school and the birthplace of the humanist Johann Reuchlin in 1455.

Its earlier inhabitants had suffered untold horrors on two occasions; when their town was sacked during the Thirty Years' War (1618-48) and again during the War of the Grand Alliance (1689-97). During the Second World War the Pforzheimers had witnessed a large number of heavy raids on their larger industrialised neighbours - Karlsruhe, 15 miles to the north-west, and Stuttgart, 27 miles to the south-east, but they had remained cradled comfortably between them. Like Darmstadt, Pforzheim offered little in the way of targets of military importance and so, again like Darmstadt, the majority of its citizens had believed themselves to be fairly safe. Why should the RAF take any interest in a place which was the innocuous centre of the German jewellery trade and the watch-making industry, and was characterised mainly by schools and workshops engaged in teaching and implementing these crafts? True, it did produce some electrical equipment (and paper), but only on an insignificant scale. And Darmstadt, after all, had been a much larger town; most of them conveniently forgot, or tried to forget, about Heilbronn and Ulm, yet at the same time there were those who, like others elsewhere, feared that no town in Germany, irrespective of the extent of its contribution to the war effort, was now immune to a violent onslaught by Bomber Command. Such anxieties increased when Pforzheim was visited by small formations of Mosquitoes (never more than six) on half-a-dozen occasions between October 3/4 and November 8/10. Then came a period during which they seemed to be forgotten once more and which allowed them to regain, in large measure, their earlier sense of security; understandable, but unwise. It was merely a lull before the storm.

And a long lull at that, because no more Mosquitoes arrived over Pforzheim until the night of February 23/24 - 10 days after Dresden, of whose torments the Pforzheimers knew - but there were a few more Mossies this time, 13 in all to be exact - and immediately behind them came 368 Lancasters. Pforzheim's hour had come.

Even more so than in the case of Darmstadt such a large force was out of all proportion to the size of the target. There could be only one result.

The Mossies marked with a high degree of accuracy and the Lancs, coming in as low as 8000 feet, shed their load of more than 1800 tons in the space of 20 minutes. The ensuing fire storm reduced to red hot ash an area two miles long by one mile wide and wiped out 82% of the centre of the town. In so doing it killed 17,600 citizens, a number surpassed only in Hamburg and Dresden and far exceeding both of these when the figures are related to the total number of inhabitants, because one quarter of the Pforzheimers died in the flames.

It is perhaps strange that Pforzheim in particular did not cause the same uproar amongst the critics as Dresden, coming as it did only a week later and suggesting that Bomber Command had similar treatment in store for many other places in Germany which were still more or less untouched and of minor or no importance. In fact few British people had ever heard of a town called Pforzheim or the fire storm which had engulfed it, at least not until September, 1991, when, seven years after Harris's death, plans were announced to erect a statue of the Bomber Chief in London. But more of this in Appendix 2.

***

A fortnight after Pforzheim, on the night of March 16, while Bomber Command was effecting the very last of its 22 major attacks on Nuremberg with 277 Lancasters and 16 Mosquitoes - and losing almost one in ten of the former on an operation to a city which had few happy memories for either Harris or his crews, including Candlish and his two surviving friends - the old cathedral town of Würzburg, 55 miles to the north-west, slightly larger than Heilbronn and Ulm and Pforzheim and whose industries (on rather a small scale) consisted of engineering, brewing, wine-making and printing, was the next small town candidate for annihilation. It had witnessed an attack by 32 Mosquitoes just less than a couple of weeks before, but the Würzburgers were praying that that had been their quota and, before anything bigger took place, the war would be over. It wasn't, and the visit by 225 Lancs and 11 Mosquitoes showered down 1130 tons in 16 hellish minutes, ravaging 90% of the built-up area and obliterating a number of beautiful historic buildings. Almost 5000 of the town's inhabitants perished.

***

Six days later it was the turn of Hildesheim, a score of miles south-east of Hannover, to be drawn out of the Harris hat. It had been a free city of the Holy Roman Empire in the 13th century, contained rather more industry than the others, and was linked to the important Mittelland Canal, but it is extremely doubtful whether these factors had anything to do with its selection. The railway yards were purported to be the target, but the 227 Lancasters and eight Mosquitoes carried out what was virtually an area attack; 70% of Hildesheim was destroyed and this included several historic buildings with the Cathedral and churches amongst them. Some of the worst devastation occurred in the residential quarters and 3000 blocks of flats (more than 10,000 apartments) either completely collapsed or were rendered uninhabitable. Almost 1650 people died.

***

Bomber Command in World War II

On March 27, the Americans were advancing eastwards in North-Rhine Westphalia and the market town of Paderborn, they said, was in their way: enter 268 Lancasters and eight Mosquitoes, and needless to say the old town did not remain in their way for long; high explosives and 3000 separate fires virtually removed it from the map in 14 minutes. Yet the number of townsfolk who died totalled only 330.

By this time the Allied armies had penetrated well into Germany and Paderborn was the last smallish town chosen as a target for Bomber Command. The citizens of many others must have heaved a deep sigh of relief when they finally saw the soldiers enter their streets ...

Chapter 20

ONE-OFFS - OR 'CIRCUS ACTS'?

If the term 'circus acts' was sometimes disparagingly used to describe certain one-off operations, far removed from the main stream syndrome which convulsed extensive urban areas, it was, generally speaking, quite an inappropriate epithet and had a possible ring of truth about it only where one or two such targets were concerned. And these inevitably begged the question - where did theatricality end and worthwhile endeavour begin? The reader will be left to judge for himself. Critics questioned whether the continued existence of a fjord-bound battleship or a large viaduct would, in late 1944 or early 1945, have prolonged the war even by a single day; they blamed Bomber Command for not pulling in the reins, for not harnessing its thirst for destruction and for indulging, merely for its own satisfaction, in smart 'show-off' tricks till almost the very last minute. It was accused of destroying targets just because they were destructible, not because their destruction was desirable. As we have already said, it was understandably difficult for Bomber Command to reduce the impetus, for now with its revolutionary Wallis bombs and all its magical electronic gadgets it was capable of achieving just about anything, and felt obliged to prove it. Then again, if such an accusation is true - and there is probably just a little evidence to suggest that in certain cases this might well be so - it should be remembered that it was only comparatively late in the war that Bomber Command began to have things more or less its own way; it hadn't always been like that, far from it; and the traumatic days, or rather nights, of 1943-44 had left deep physical and psychological scars which were still obvious; and it was a far cry from the days of its birth pangs when it had encountered great difficulty in finding the right city, never mind a specific target, till it had become a huge, well-equipped and complex organization which could annihilate a large town in less than twenty minutes or select something as small as a ship or a bridge and blow it to smithereens from a height of four miles - or 50 feet.

It should further be borne in mind that even if Germany was on the brink of defeat, Japan was still very much a contestant and that Bomber Command expected to be transferring itself to the Far East in the not too distant future. Hence it was keen to try out new navigational and bombing aids and to perfect new techniques, and there was generally much more to the so-called 'circus acts' of the final months than simply swashbuckling around Europe looking for something to bomb; 617 Squadron, for instance, already had their programme all mapped out: they would depart for Okinawa and use their Tallboys and Grand Slams to facilitate the landing of American forces on the mainland of Japan.

They did not go, of course, as there was no need. The two most powerful bombs of the lot, the only two in existence, had been dropped before they could set off.

1   A LESSON LEARNT

In early 1942 the U-boat offensive in the Atlantic was at its height and exacting an ominously heavy toll of Allied, and particularly British, merchant shipping. The Royal Navy, with demanding commitments elsewhere, was being extended to its limits, even beyond them, and so critical had the situation become - more than 1400 ships had gone to the bottom in the space of 16 months - that it was fast approaching one of touch and go. Every possible effort had to be made to scale down the losses and it was only logical that Bomber Command should be asked to play its part. Attempts were made to destroy the submarines in their fortified underground pens at places such as Brest, Lorient and St Nazaire, but these proved to be useless with the bombs then available, which just bounced off the massive concrete structures like ping pong balls and did about as much damage. Individual factories, however, though still a difficult proposition, offered more chance of success.

Harris chose the large Maschinefabrik-Augsburg-Nürnberg plant, known to the Germans as MAN, and which claimed to produce every second U-boat diesel engine made for the *Kriegsmarine* (MAN had other plants dispersed around Europe). If it could be destroyed the submarine menace would be reduced to a considerable extent.

Augsburg, because of its extreme distance from England, would have been a most unlikely target for Bomber Command a year or so before, but the new Avro Lancaster had been issued to some squadrons early in 1942 and had immediately shown its capabilities on March 3, when four aircraft had dropped mines in the German Bight and two had bombed Essen on March 10/11. Now, still in its infancy, there was no better way to find out its full potential than by sending it off on a low-level

The Great Ingratitude

experimental attack on what would prove to be the longest operation undertaken by Bomber Command in daylight throughout the entire war - owing to the relative smallness of the target a night attack was out of the question. The distance that would have to be flown across Central Europe in those days was quite phenomenal; this would be no quick low-level incursion into Northern France, in and out again and back across the Channel before the defences had time to get to real grips with the bombers, and it would be a lot further than the Ruhr; Augsburg entailed an overall flight of 1250 miles over heavily defended enemy territory and, to get under the radar, at a height of zero feet. The difficulties of piloting and navigating at such a low altitude have already been mentioned when dealing with some Mosquito operations, and it would have been difficult to find a more daunting task for the new bomber and the airmen selected for the trip.

The 12 crews detailed for the raid, six from 44 (Rhodesia) Squadron at Waddington, and six from 97 (Straits Settlement) Squadron at Woodhall Spa, made long, tiring practice flights all over the British Isles to get used to the high mileage involved in the actual operation and carried out numerous dummy bombing runs on suitably sited and similarly sized 'targets', as extreme accuracy was essential. The raid was to be led by Squadron Leader J D Nettleton of 44 Squadron, a South African, who was to be awarded the Victoria Cross for the gallant rôle he played in pressing on with great determination in the face of frightening odds. All the other survivors would also be decorated.

On April 17, each aircraft, weighed down with 2150 gallons of petrol, took off in sections of three at 3 pm, so that the first would arrive over the target a little over five hours later, with still enough daylight to bomb and assured of the cover of darkness for the long haul home. Each Lanc carried four 1000-pound HE fitted with 11-second delayed action fuses. Several fighters and 30 Bostons were sent to attack airfields in Northern France, the idea being to destroy enemy fighters on the ground or engage them in the air while the big bombers sped through the gap hopefully created in the German defence system. The ploy was largely unsuccessful; in fact it was later stated - and all the evidence available confirmed this - that the Lancasters might have fared better without the support of the RAF fighters and Bostons, whose presence had alerted the Me 109s and got them into the air, ready to engage the Lancs as soon as the latter reached the French coast.

On leaving Waddington and Woodhall Spa the aircraft

Bomber Command in World War II

made for Selsey Bill (just east of Portsmouth) then across the Channel to Dives (on the coast 15 miles north-east of Caen). They then flew south-east, skirting Paris and making for Ludwigshafen on the northern tip of Lake Constance. There they turned north-east and headed straight for Augsburg. At least that is what the survivors did, because four of the Lancasters of 44 Squadron had been shot down by fighters before they had penetrated 100 miles into France, and for much of the way Nettleton and his only remaining colleague, Flying Officer A J Garwell, were sorely tested as they had to contend both with obstructions rising from the ground and attacking fighters, which disappeared from the scene only when they were short of fuel or out of ammunition. The two aircraft, both badly damaged, limped on and dropped their bombs on the factory. Garwell, however, tore into the ground immediately afterwards. Then the six Lancs of 97 Squadron, who had got through relatively unscathed while the 109s were being refuelled and rearmed, roared towards the factory at roof-top height and the crews could see the tops of buildings being blown off by the ack-ack gunners, but all of them managed to bomb before two of their number spun into the ground in flames.

Although five of the 17 bombs had failed to explode, a fair amount of damage had been done to the diesel engine workshops. But much of the plant remained untouched and the overall effect on production was minimal. The cost - seven Lancasters out of 12, and 49 skilled airmen - was high, far too high, and, according to Harris, in no way compensated for what had been achieved.

Any illusions about low-level attacks offering protection against marauding fighters and preventing effective fire from anti-aircraft batteries - the belief being that the latter had hardly time to fire at all - were rudely dispelled. After Augsburg Harris swore that none of his bombers and crews would ever be sacrificed again in long, daylight flights to precision targets, or daylight flights to any target for that matter (the successful Dambuster operation took place in the dark and had Harris's approval for various reasons). He was more certain than ever that an important point had been rammed home, namely that the losses occurred in such operations proved beyond all doubt 'that daylight attacks on Germany could, at that time, be carried out by Bomber Command only at a prohibitive casualty rate'. Any raid was a failure if the enemy inflicted more damage on you than you did on him. Moreover, Germany's enormous industrial output, which streamed out from her thousands and thousands of factories sited here, there and everywhere, could never be significantly curtailed by daylight precision attacks. Even if that were possible - and it certainly was not - Bomber Command alone and not German war production, would be badly mauled, and fatally so. It could therefore be said that the Augsburg experience went a long way in fashioning what was to be the *opus operandi,* with only rare exceptions, from then on: fly at night, fly high, and fly in huge numbers so that a large area could be swamped; that would take care of any 'precision targets' it contained, and that would be the predominant role of the British heavy bomber and especially of the promising Lancaster when it became available in sufficient numbers.

As we shall now see, the 'Thousand Plan', implemented only six weeks after Augsburg (and ignoring for the moment its political implications), was to provide a realistic demonstration of what was to befall the Third Reich. Harris had made up his mind: no more foolish Augsburgs - and woe betide Germany ...

2   THREE THOUSAND BOMBERS IN THREE NIGHTS

ACT 1: OPERATION *MILLENNIUM*

This, the apt code-name for the attack on Cologne on May 30/31, 1942, was one of the most singularly decisive raids ever carried out by Bomber Command, yet took the form of an 'act' or 'show' put on for a very special purpose; and since a show of any kind - particularly an ambitious one like this - is designed to impress, Operation *Millennium* was no different. The British and American audience for whom it was intended included those occupying the highest rungs of the political ladders, and was huge; as was the cast: the leading part played by Air Marshal Sir Arthur Harris, with able assistance from many thousands of others, amongst them more than 6000 young airmen; and the raid in question, which turned out to be the first of a dramatic trilogy to be enacted in the space of a month, was by far the most dramatic of the three.

To the British public, the vassalized peoples of Occupied Europe, and a host of sympathisers elsewhere, this attack by 1047 bombers was an event which gave much cause for satisfaction and even jubilation. The news that such an unprecedented force had spilled its lethal load on to one of Germany's foremost cities, with the promise of much more to come, was welcome news indeed, and regarded as just retribution for the earlier Blitz on the UK and for the Nazi record of slaughter and mayhem from the western shores of France to the Arctic and the Black Sea. It was also regarded as a victory - and a victory was what was required to uplift those who so far had tasted only the bitter pills of an apparently never-ending string of reverses (losses in transatlantic convoys were approaching the critical stage and Montgomery's success at El Alamein was still six months away). Hence Cologne provided a shot in the arm just when such a fillip was sorely needed. Moreover it became immediately obvious to everyone that this new man who had taken over as Chief of Bomber Command had meant what he said: "One cannot win wars by defending oneself."

But, unknown at that time to the stoical citizens of the UK, the first great onslaught undertaken by Bomber Command did much more than destroy 600 acres of a famous German city. Irrespective of how commendable such a blow to the enemy was, its real significance lay in the attainment of higher aims which were the main reasons for its prosecution.

These aims were profoundly political, the operation against Cologne being in fact a last-ditch attempt to prove to all the doubters and vehement objectors that Bomber Command could be a telling weapon in Britain's armoury. In early 1942 the Command's reputation - mainly because of inadequate resources - stood at an abysmally low ebb. Certainly it had carried out successful fire-raising raids on Lübeck and Rostock in March of that year, but its critics had been quick to point out that these towns had been both easy to find and easy to set alight, and did not present the same challenge as the vital centres of German war industry in the Ruhr and elsewhere, which so far had been no more than slightly dented by the bombers which had tried to destroy them. So great and widespread had become the repudiation of the Command in various quarters that the moment was ripe for it to justify its very existence in order to keep itself together as an independent force capable of implementing an independent and viable policy; otherwise it looked destined to be classed as a mere ancillary organisation placed at everyone's beck and call for attacks on whatever the Army or Navy or anyone else might decide; an odd-job body with no programme of its own and a mere shadow of the force envisaged by its Commander, with less than a ghost of a chance of getting at Germany's throat. The Americans, too, were watching, and if Bomber Command went on failing to produce the goods then other tasks would be found on the other side of the world for the Flying Fortresses and the Liberators now rolling off the assembly lines. Nor would the hard-pressed Russians be at all pleased if considerable pressure could not be brought to

The Great Ingratitude

bear on Germany from the West. In May, 1942, the Command stood at a crossroads and ·if it was going to take the right turning it had to act decisively - and soon. It was time to grasp the nettle - firmly and hard. Harris, with his customary resoluteness, did just that.

He needed no telling that the risk he was running by committing his entire force - and more, because he would have to include several trainee crews and instructors to attain the magical figure of at least 1000 bombers - to a single town on a single night could be nothing short of suicidal; in the event of a catastrophe, which was quite possible, there would be little left. At the same time, considering the low regard in which Bomber Command was then held and the opposition to its expansion, he knew that if something momentous was not done he would lose the fight in any case. That was the stark truth of the matter: nothing less than a devastating attack on a well known German city would keep all sorts of mouths shut and win him the support of the War Cabinet and the industrial backing which was essential. If he succeeded the way would be open for Bomber Command to become the mighty weapon of which he dreamed, the pulverizing force which would batter the Reich into surrender. If he failed then that would be it. But he knew he could delay no longer - the mutterings were becoming louder, the protests stronger. It was now or never. (#)

Yet he derived comfort from one important fact: no one needed to tell the British people of the brutal nature of the enemy who confronted them and what the price of defeat would be. The bombing of their own cities - let us not forget that for three months in 1940 an average of 300 bombers had disrupted London alone every night - had resulted in the cry "Give it 'em back!" If he could do just that, and on a grand scale, the nation would applaud, and demand even more; and that, propaganda-wise, would be a factor the waverers within the government would judge as a valid one in the argument for the retention and the furtherance of Bomber Command.

Together with his deputy Sir Robert Saundby, Harris had now to decide on the identity of the German city which was doomed to be reduced to smoking ruins and to go down in history as the first to have to cope with more than one thousand bombers; but, more importantly, the one which was destined to decide the fate of RAF Bomber Command.

(#) One of the instructors "roped in" for the raid was Flying Officer Leslie Manser. Already a veteran operational flier at only 20 years of age, his Manchester was hit by flak just after bombing and began to lose height rapidly. When the port engine burst into flames he ordered his crew to jump and carried on alone in an attempt to bring the aircraft home, but it crashed in Belgium in a great ball of fire. His posthumous VC was auctioned at Christie's in April, 1992, for £57,200.

Bomber Command in World War II

It had to be large and easily identified, otherwise the whole operation could become a complete fiasco and achieve exactly the opposite effect to the one intended. This meant that a highly desirable target in the Ruhr conurbation was out of the question as the last thing wanted was a diffusion of loads over a dozen different centres. Harris at first favoured Hamburg, easily found on the Elbe with its myriads of docks and the two tell-tale lakes extending right into the city centre - and it was fire-prone. But it lay outside *Gee* range and if weather conditions changed for the worse its effects could be calamitous. No, he reluctantly decided, it couldn't be Hamburg (its turn, as we know, was to come 14 months later in the nature of a cataclysm), and finally concluded that Cologne was the best bet. *Gee* would assist the navigators and the prominent bend on the Rhine on which the city stood would ensure correct identification. But moonlight and the absence of cloud over the target were prerequisites. Much depended on the elements, and these could be foreseen only to a limited extent.

The planners of a raid by such a large number of aircraft were working in the dark with regard to certain factors, and one of the problems which loomed large was the danger of collision. However, the mathematical experts who were consulted and had been provided with details of the plan of attack - varying heights, time intervals between waves and other information, estimated that losses incurred in this manner would be negligible, even although all the bombing was to take place within the space of 90 minutes. It was further calculated that if any collisions did occur these would be more than compensated for by the saturation of the ack-ack and searchlight batteries by the first group of aircraft to go in; also, the different altitude and timing levels would substantially obviate chances of being hit by 'friendly' bombs from above.

After a phenomenal amount of liaison between Headquarters, Groups and Station Commanders, everything was prepared as thoroughly as was humanly possible. But the force had to be kept on standby while Harris awaited the weather he needed. Magnus Spence, a reticent Orcadian who held the position of Command Met Officer and had proved himself to be as accurate as anyone in what was a very difficult field, gave a gloomy forecast on the morning of Wednesday, May 27, and the operation was cancelled. Thursday 28 was no better - still thick cloud and thunderstorms over Western Germany. Next day - same report. The nights with a full moon were beginning to run out and, with such a huge air armada, good, clear conditions were essential, not only over Cologne but over the English 'Bomber Country' when the aircraft returned. Further, with so many trainees taking part risks had to be reduced wherever possible, not increased.

Each postponement had its dangers, not least the possibility of the enemy beginning to wonder why Bomber Command had been so inactive for several days; a security leak was also within the realms of possibility, since the intense activity on so many bomber stations naturally made people, RAF personnel and civilians alike, wonder what on earth was afoot. With such things in mind Harris sent about 150 aircraft to targets in Northern France on May 29.

At least the delay had given the ground crews more time to check and recheck the bombers, some of which (especially the Hampdens and the Whitleys and some of the Wellingtons) were somewhat antiquated and had been brought in solely to make the figure of 1000+ possible.

On Saturday, May 30, Spence reported that adverse conditions still prevailed over Germany; thunderstorms were widespread but there was at least half a chance that the target would be clear of cloud around midnight; visibility on UK bases was expected to be satisfactory provided the weather did not deteriorate by the time the last aircraft had returned. Harris weighed up all the facts: if he had to wait for the next moon Bomber Command's fate might by then be sealed by politics; and in any case yet another postponement, and a long one, would do little good for the morale of either airmen or ground staff. It looked as if they had to go that night.

After due consultation with those present at the morning conference - including Saundby and Spence - Harris finally jabbed his finger at a place on the map spread out before him:

"Thousand Plan to-night. Target Cologne."

Then he walked out into the open air, tugging out another Camel cigarette and thrusting it into his mouth. There was little he could do now but hope ... and hope.

On 53 different bases from Hampstead Norris in the South (near Reading) to Middleton St George in the North (seven miles south-east of Darlington) and including other famous names such as Scampton, Waddington, Woodhall Spa, Coningsby, Mildenhall and Stradishall, Saturday, May 30, was a day of intense activity and feverish excitement - but tinged with apprehension or worse if you were aircrew - the longest day most of them could remember; but the thousand and one tasks which had to be performed to make sure that the aircraft were completely airworthy and to prepare them for the operation - petrol, oil, bombs, ammunition, oxygen and so on and so forth - had all been completed by take-off time.

The airmen had been living on their nerves for rather too long and the atmosphere at briefing was both tense and electric. Station commanders themselves took on the job of being the first to address the crews, and the target was revealed in the usual manner amidst a silence that could be heard: COLOGNE. It could have been worse, a lot worse, and gasps of what could best be termed semi-relief were audible all over each briefing room between Hampstead Norris and Middleton St George.

"To-night you will attack the city of Cologne *with more than one thousand bombers.*"

This announcement was followed by further gasps, and this time they were gasps of *incredulity. More than one thousand bloody bombers!* They would pulverize the place -even if the ground defences were not entirely liquidated the men manning them would be numbed into inaction by the sheer weight of the onslaught. Crews jumped to their feet, shouting and cheering. *Over one thousand bombers!*

Then came full details of the route to be followed and of the method of attack. They would cross the coast of Holland just to the south of Rotterdam, and then fly via Eindhoven and Mönchen Gladbach; thereafter all they had to do was follow the Rhine upstream to the target, and once they had bombed they would proceed on a southerly course to Euskirchen (24 miles from Cologne and 13 from Bonn) then straight back over north-east Belgium to the North Sea and home. The city was to be attacked in waves going in at three minute intervals, with the *Gee*-equipped aircraft in the lead and dropping incendiaries to light up the old part of Cologne to act as a beacon for those coming in their wake. The second wave of aircraft would drop their loads one mile to the north of the conflagration and the third one mile to the south; it was believed that, if this procedure was carried out successfully, the fires would join together to form the biggest any of them had yet seen; they were also told that, in order to saturate the defences and make their own lot much easier, all the bombing had to take place within 90 minutes.

The Great Ingratitude

It was this latest announcement which quelled the initial excitement and enthusiasm of the crews. If there was anything they dreaded more than anything else, whether on a training flight or on an operation, it was the fearful possibility of making physical contact with another aircraft. Some of them had witnessed collisions with their own eyes and all of them knew what a horrific and normally fatal experience these were. To-night, they thought, must be pregnant with danger from this quarter. More than one thousand bombers shedding their loads within the space of 90 minutes? How near were they going to be to each other? How could a large number of collisions possibly be averted?

Inevitably the question was raised in every Briefing Room, and inevitably the answer was the same: "We have it on expert authority that the risk of collision is so small as to be almost negligible provided you all stick rigidly to the plan of attack. Keep to the times and heights given and you'll have nothing to worry about. Only one collision is expected."

An outburst of nervous, derisive laughter was the reaction to what those taking part in the raid considered to be a bland and unconvincing answer. They knew only too well that adhering accurately to times and heights was by no means as simple as it was made to sound by an officer standing on the floor of a Briefing Room. With such a huge number of aircraft converging in tight array on a single target, some blinded by searchlights, others taking evasive action, yet others hit and either wallowing or out of control, they judged such attempted reassurance quite preposterous and worthy of all the contempt it deserved. Yet typically dry aircrew humour was never far away:

"Excuse me, Sir, but these experts, did they say which two aircraft it will be?" was the delightfully sardonic question respectfully put by one of the participating airmen on one of the bases.

The Briefing Officer laughed with the others. Then he became serious again:

"I repeat that the figure is valid if you follow all the instructions. If we spaced you out more and took say, two hours to complete the bombing, you would be in far greater danger. Cologne boasts more than 150 searchlights and not far short of 600 ack-ack guns. The way you are going to do it will overwhelm them. Please don't worry about collisions.''

A further item of news was designed to make the crews feel more secure. As the force would be passing through an area - it could not be avoided - where about 150 enemy fighters could pounce on them in the bright moonlight, every effort was to be made to curb such interference: 49 Blenheims of 2 Group were detailed to attack airfields in Holland and Belgium, and down as far as Bonn, and a further force of 40 Havocs and Hurricanes (the latter equipped with extra fuel tanks) would try to engage the Luftwaffe fighters both on the bombers' outward and homeward legs, and would bomb the bases into the bargain. The first of the intruders were scheduled to take off at 22.45 hours so that they would be ahead of (or would overtake) the first wave of fire-raising Wellingtons and Hampdens and Whitleys and thus make the latters' passage through the danger zone less perilous. This may have been welcome news to the crews, but in actual fact these back-up forays were to do little to reduce the scope of the night-fighters. The number of intruder aircraft was too small to make a real impression; moreover they were badly equipped and possessed few aids to help them find the fields; the small bombs some of them managed to drop on the latter did little damage as the enemy fighters were well dispersed - the Germans had learned in their campaigns in North Africa and Russia that it was prudent in the long term, if impracticable in the short, to keep large gaps between their parked aircraft. But the crews bound for Cologne did not know of all this, only that any additional support would be most acceptable.

The airmen's morale, high as it already was in anticipation of the telling blow they were about to deal the enemy, was further bolstered by a signed message from Harris which was read out to all crews at briefing:

'The force of which you form part to-night is at least twice the size and has four times the carrying capacity of the largest air force ever before concentrated on one objective. You have an opportunity therefore to strike a blow at the enemy which will resound, not only throughout Germany, but throughout the world. In your hands lie the means of destroying a major part of the resources by which the enemy's war effort is maintained. It depends, however, on each individual crew member whether full concentration is achieved. Press home your attack to your precise objective with the utmost determination and resolution in the foreknowledge that if you individually succeed, the most shattering and devastating blow will have been delivered against the very vitals of the enemy. You are a

The Great Ingratitude

thousand strong. Let him have it - right on the chin!'

The first bombers (Wellingtons and Stirlings) took off at 22.30 and the sirens in Cologne began to emit their chilling wail at 00.17; not until 01.55 did the all-clear sound, and within that space of one hour and 38 minutes the inhabitants of the historic city, who had already undergone 106 (mainly abortive) attacks by Bomber Command, were introduced to something quite different, something conducted on a scale they had hitherto never imagined. What they experienced was the first great bombardment from the air of any city in history, and one which was to be repeated again and again in the next three years until all the other cities and large towns of their homeland existed as such no more, only as proof of the power of the aerial bull-dozer that Bomber Command had become. They were the first real witnesses of a new phenomenon in modern war - the attempt by a large force of aircraft to saturate a congested urban area, thereby causing what, by 1942 standards, was monumental destruction, and at the same time to deprive its inhabitants of essential amenities, severing communications and spreading fear of more of such trials to come. And it was from Cologne that the first great exodus of panic-stricken citizens took place in the wake of a visit from Bomber Command: about 140,000 of them fled immediately.

This was not surprising, considering that a chosen area of the city had absorbed 864 HEs, 20 aerial mines and more than 456,000 incendiaries, amounting to an overall total of 1455 tons dropped by the 898 aircraft which claimed to have bombed the right target (some 15 released their loads elsewhere). After the final wave (Halifaxes and Lancasters) had sent down their HEs it was estimated by the German authorities that 2500 separate fires had resulted, many of which joined together to create one vast burning area three miles long and two miles wide, in which few buildings remained unscathed. The force of 602 Wellingtons, 131 Halifaxes, 88 Stirlings, 79 Hampdens, 73 Lancasters, 46 Manchesters, 28 Whitleys - totalling 1047 - had apparently done all that could have been expected of it.

For the operation was, in general terms and for that era during which the Command was largely without the electronic aids that were to come later, a success, and the loss of 41 aircraft (29 Wellingtons, four Manchesters, three Halifaxes, two Stirlings, one Hampden, one Lancaster, one Whitley), although the highest number so far for a single operation, was judged to be acceptable in view of the revolutionary nature of the raid and the good visibility which favoured the enemy fighters and anti-aircraft batteries. The Cologne defences themselves were estimated to have shot down 20 of the bombers (16 to the guns, four to fighters, while two were victims of the one predicted collision - yes, the boffins had got it exactly right, although how much this was due to their expertise or just mere chance will never be known!) The other losses were incurred, mainly from fighters, when the bombers were en route to and from the target. Bomber Command theory about the importance of the early pounding of the ground defences was proven to be largely correct: the first wave suffered 4.8% of the total losses, the second 4.1% and the third wave 1.9%. To everyone's surprise the 368 aircraft (17 lost) flown by crews from Operational Training Units sustained fewer casualties than the experienced crews from operational squadrons. 'Sprog' crews were always much more likely to 'get the chop' than hardened veterans, and this apparent anomaly could be ascribed to the shortage in many operational crews of one or two members whose places were filled by recruits just as raw as those from OTUs.

If 41 valuable aircraft and about 230 invaluable airmen was the cost of the night's work, what appeared on the credit side of the balance sheet? A large amount of damage had been done to the city of Cologne, as was revealed the next day on the photographs brought back by five small and very fast wooden aircraft which, during their visit, had added their own little contribution by chucking down a few bombs themselves. The Mosquito had gone to war. Germany, as we know, was to see - or hear - an awful lot of it in the three years that lay ahead.

Although no great ocean of fire had developed on the lines of Lübeck and Rostock (much smaller and more combustible compared to Cologne with its great size and wide thoroughfares) the blaze must have been a substantial one just the same as it was seen by the last crews of the force when they were approaching the Dutch coast - and 300 aircraft had yet to add their considerable load. German records retrieved at the end of the war stated that 3330 buildings had been destroyed and nearly 10,000 damaged, mostly by fire. 2560 were industrial or commercial premises; 36 large plants were put completely out of action and a further 292 had their productive capacity cut by 50-80%. More than 13,000 homes were no more, and almost 29,000 suffered damage; some 470 citizens and military personnel died and more than 5000 were injured. 45,000 people were dehoused. The raid followed the pattern which was to be characteristic of all saturation bombing because, in addition to hotels and shops, 9 hospitals, 17 churches and 16 schools were totally razed; and, inevitably, widespread

The Great Ingratitude

disruption was caused by the destruction of water and gas mains, electricity supplies and public transport.

The blow dealt Cologne was a heavy one, but only relatively so in view of Bomber Command's rather inept performances up till then. Although it gave the Germans only an inkling of what was going to befall their major towns in the not-too-distant future - Cologne included - the effects of the raid were enough to qualify the city to occupy the premier spot in the bombing league, well ahead of the other unfortunates such as Guernica, Warsaw, Rotterdam and Coventry. And even if it was learned at the war's end that Cologne had been hurt a lot less than was at first believed and that life and work there had practically returned to normal long before the month of June was out, that is now of little consequence; that Harris would have to wait till 1944 and early 1945, before the wholesale devastation he promised became a reality, is also of little consequence; yet one is tempted to reflect on what would have transpired had it been known then that the Germans were quite capable of coping with and quickly repairing damage wrought on the Cologne scale - and achieved only after a prodigious effort by so many bombers. No doubt this would have led to further controversy and at best an extension of the probationary period allotted to Bomber Command, and the outcome may not have been in Harris's favour. But that is merely interesting conjecture, and the fact remains that the 1000-bomber raid on Cologne served its purpose by acting as the catalyst which won the Bomber Chief the approval he needed and set the bomber-building machine in motion. In that sense it was a resounding victory. 'The Strategic Air Offensive against Germany' (HMSO) officially stated: 'The exertions and the risks to which Air Marshal Harris had exposed his Command had been justified by the event.' A practical and convincing demonstration had been given in support of the argument for a great and speedy expansion in the front line strength of Bomber Command. As Harris himself wrote in his 'Bomber Offensive': 'My own opinion is that we should never have had a real Bomber Offensive had it not been for the 1000-bomber attack on Cologne.'

It might not be out of place to pause here and point out that in Second World War bombing, it was often, although not always, inherently impossible to evaluate with more than a rough degree of accuracy the damage inflicted on the enemy's resources as a result of any individual raid, and therefore to know whether one's own efforts, losses of aircraft and crews, had been justified. Notwithstanding it would be true to say that, up until Cologne (apart from the few notable exceptions just mentioned), the balance of Bomber Command's account after each sortie had been predominantly in the red - and those responsible for financing the campaign had not been too pleased. But Cologne put it, according to all the evidence then available, clearly in the black; and with more numerous and far heavier saturation attacks to come, in the black it was chiefly to remain - which was invariably a correct assessment if Berlin and Nuremberg are forgotten. The Air Offensive was phenomenally expensive - as all war is, whether you win or lose - but it was more expensive to the enemy and, pragmatically, that was all that mattered.

It was only natural that Harris derived intense satisfaction from the letter he received from the Prime Minister immediately after the raid:

'I congratulate you and the whole of Bomber Command upon the remarkable feat of organisation which enabled you to despatch over a thousand bombers to Cologne in a single night and without confusion to concentrate their action over the target into so short a time as one hour and a half. The proof of the growing power of the British Bomber Force is also the herald of what Germany will receive, city by city, from now on.'

The last few words in particular must have had Harris smacking his lips. And he must have felt an extra layer of icing had been added to the cake when General 'Hap' Arnold, Commander of the USAAF, sent his own tribute:

'As Commanding General of the US Army Air Forces I desire to extend my congratulations to you, your staff and combat crews for the great raid last night on Cologne. It was bold in conception and superlative in execution. Please convey to your officers and men my admiration for their courage and skill, and say that our air forces hope very soon to fly and fight beside them in their decisive blows against our common enemy.'

(And all this despite the fact that the American remained resolute in his opinion that area bombing was the wrong way to go about things and strongly advocated attacks on specific targets - Chapter 18).

So Harris had triumphed. Or at least he had cleared the first and most important hurdle, for the raid had other consequences, as yet largely unforseen. It had shown the Nazis what Britain's intentions were and they reacted in the same way, if with less urgency and on a smaller scale - because Cologne, although shaken and momentarily disrupted, was anything but grievously injured - as they did after the Hamburg holocaust just over a year later. In May, 1942, German industry was far from being fully extended, and Cologne fired a warning shot. War production was immediately stepped up a gear or two, and with amazing speed and thoroughness; and thus after Cologne, just as it was to be after Hamburg, Bomber Command became to a certain extent the victim of its own success. At this bombing game it sometimes appeared that you just could not win ...

It was an ominous outlook for the bomber crews. Up till Cologne all German forces - land, sea or air - had been overwhelmingly concerned with attack. This was no longer so, and it worried the Nazi leaders that the German people were about to experience something quite new - the defence of their very homes and work places. Up till then they had been told again and again about the glorious exploits of the Luftwaffe in both neighbouring and far-off lands; now they were to see it operate at first hand because its future rôle was to be that of a defensive force; and what it had to defend was Germany itself.

**

ACT II: DRAMATIC FAILURE - OR WAS IT?

The engines of the aircraft making up 'The Thousand Force' had hardly had time to cool down or the ground crews to complete essential repairs or maintenance when Harris made a further striking decision: two nights after *Millennium* a second enemy city was destined to undergo similar treatment. Coming as soon as it did, it appeared to be a somewhat surprising decision, but it was also understandable: the crews were geared up and in buoyant mood, the huge force was still arrayed in battle order, and the moon still shone. Harris had decided there was nothing like striking while the iron was hot, and an early repeat of Cologne would dispel any lingering doubts about the capability of a large bomber formation to sow destruction on an unheard-of scale. Two German cities laid waste in such a short period would not be something that could be ignored - either by friend or foe - and would provide indubitable proof - if that was still needed, of the regular show Bomber Command could put on if given the means.

Bomber Command in World War II

The intended victim this time was Hamburg, which he had already been compelled to reject in favour of Cologne, but the abominable weather conditions prevailing over the Hanseatic port would simply have invited disaster. The choice fell upon Essen, the heart town on the west-east axis of the Ruhr, Europe's greatest industrial conurbation (Chapter 10) and a name which was to be matched only by Berlin in emotiveness amongst the aircrews, a place better to avoid if you could. This, too, was a surprising decision because Essen, although arguably the most worthwhile city target in all Germany, was at that time perhaps also the most intimidating; its fearsome defences, its perpetual smog and haze, its indeterminate outlines in the middle of a vast built-up area which was a mapmaker's - and a navigator's - nightmare. But Essen it was to be. That would silence the critics.

At briefing the crews were reminded of the giant Krupp complex and of what it meant to Germany's war effort; and that practically the whole of Essen was a mighty arsenal and if they could do to it what they had done to Cologne ...

A force, not quite of 1000, but of 956 (not of course including the 48 Blenheims which were sent out to German fighter bases), and composed of 545 Wellingtons, 127 Halifaxes, 77 Stirlings, 74 Lancasters, 71 Hampdens, 33 Manchesters and 29 Whitleys, set off for the city which had always been, and always was to be, right until the spring of 1945, one of the biggest thorns in Bomber Command's flesh - and a hell of a place to live if you were a German.

The weather forecast, which had been judged to be reasonable, was well off the mark, with low cloud over Essen adding further to the difficulties of identification. Masses of flares were dropped by the leading Wellingtons, but exactly where these landed is highly debatable. Reports from returning crews were soon found to be grossly exaggerated. Although only 189 said they had failed to find the target area, the others - 767 of them - claimed to have 'definitely' bombed the city. But 'definite' was a dangerous word to use in respect of recognition of any town in the Ruhr, especially in the dark and under adverse weather conditions and, sincere in their reports as the crews no doubt were, it was shown that out of a number of photographs taken during the raid only a few revealed that bombs had fallen within five miles of the target; and it was not by mere chance that more damage had been done in eleven other towns, of which Oberhausen, Mülheim and Duisburg suffered most. These three all lay to the west of the prescribed aiming-points, and it was queried whether this was the first example of 'creep-back', but could perhaps be more accurately ascribed to misidentification. The number of dead in Essen - 15 out of a population of 750,000 - and the number of houses destroyed - seven - would certainly seem to be unlikely figures after a claimed onslaught by 767 bombers! And since 150 people were killed in Oberhausen, Mülheim and Duisburg alone, and others in eight other places, it would appear reasonable to assume that many of the crews *thought* they had hit the right target. In other words, as a saturation raid against a single, compact area, which cost 31 aircraft and 212 airmen, Essen was something of a disaster for Bomber Command and a clear victory for the Luftwaffe defences.

But at least the operation confirmed Harris's belief that the carpet bombing of a target in an area like the Ruhr, under conditions of poor visibility and for the time being at any rate, presented insurmountable difficulties and was far too much of a hit-or-miss business with emphasis on the 'miss'. *Gee* was helpful but it was not enough and such places could not be profitably attacked on most nights without improved electronic aids. 'Raid Leaders' had done all they could to light up Essen, or what they thought was Essen, but the boffins would have to be given the resources - and quickly - to produce the necessary gadgets which would defeat both the elements and human error.

The Essen raid begs the question - what would have been Bomber Command's fate if Harris had chosen it in the first place instead of Cologne? He must have thanked his lucky stars he didn't. Yet ironically, Essen rated as a further victory; the true facts, at least those that were known, were not revealed by High Wycombe; and there were few who believed that one thousand bombers could fail to leave behind them anything but a trail of unparalleled destruction, no matter where they went. Hence Essen was assumed to be a repeat of Cologne. The '1000-bomber' tag did infinitely more for the future of Bomber Command than the actual bombing results, irrespective of how poor these could be.

***

ACT III: THE THOUSAND PLAN FINALE

The third and concluding act of the triad took place just over three weeks later, on the night of June 25/26. It would be gratifying to say that the finale was suitably climactic and largely dispelled memories of the previous débâcle; but although it was much more profitable than the attack on Essen - it could hardly have been anything else - the overall results fell well below those at Cologne.

This time the city chosen was Bremen, Germany's second-largest seaport standing 35 miles up the River Weser and with a population of 575,000. A highly industrialised centre with shipyards, engineering, oil refining, and a large Focke-Wulf aircraft factory, it had no large neighbour with which it might be confused; and it produced U-boats - at that time a real threat, not only to the Atlantic life-line which kept Britain from starving but to the passage of the growing numbers of American military personnel and increasing amounts of *matériel* bound for the UK (on this account Churchill insisted that the Admiralty should play its part in attacking a target with which it was very much concerned, and accordingly Coastal Command contributed 102 Hudsons and Wellingtons). The Prime Minister was sharply conscious of the powerful American lobby which demanded that Japan should be attended to first, and that heavy Atlantic losses of US shipping bound for the European theatre would only provide these lobbyists with more ammunition in support of their argument.

Bomber Command despatched 960 aircraft which, together with those from Coastal Command and five from Army Co-Operation Command, brought the total up to 1067. This was the largest force numerically so far to be concentrated on one city - and surpassed only by the 1079 sent to Essen on November 3, 1945 (Chapter 10) but not by any means the greatest in bomb-carrying capacity as 57% of the bombers were still twin-engined machines. The Bremen raid was also unique in the diversity of the types operating - no fewer than 10, and consisting of 472 Wellingtons, 124 Halifaxes, 96 Lancasters, 69 Stirlings, 51 Blenheims, 50 Hampdens, 50 Whitleys, 24 Bostons, 20 Manchesters and four Mosquitoes. In this connection it is interesting to note that in the Hamburg fire storm raid just over a year later only 74 twin-engined types took part (all Wellingtons) out of the total of 787. Bremen was the only occasion on which such a miscellany of aircraft was used and the raid was a far cry from the nights yet to come when Lancasters, Halifaxes and a handful of Mosquitoes would be the sole machines used. But Harris was still scraping the barrel and although he had hoped to be able to allow OTUs to get on with their own programme, once more he had to commandeer well over 200 old aircraft considered to be fit only for training exercises.

The 142 bombers from 5 Group were detailed to aim at the Focke-Wulf factory, 20 Blenheims at the AGW Weser shipyard and

The Great Ingratitude

the Coastal Command Hudsons and Wellingtons at the Deschimag yard. The others, totalling 803, would carry out an area attack on the town and docks, and all loads were to be shed in even a shorter space of time than at Cologne - 65 minutes. By now the crews were getting used to this high concentration of aircraft, and the titters were subdued.

As often as not Bomber Command's luck with the weather, when the weather was all-important, was just too bad to believe. On this occasion the cloud which had blanked out Bremen during the day was expected to disperse later in a strong west wind, but the latter dropped just at the worst possible moment and the cloud remained stationary over the target. *Gee* came partly to the rescue, however, and the fires started by the leaders were used as aiming-points by the main force crews. Nevertheless the effects of the bombing by so many aircraft could only be described as disappointing. True, one of the large assembly buildings belonging to the Focke-Wulf factory took a direct hit from a 4000 lb 'cookie' dropped from one of the Lancasters and was blown to smithereens, while other parts of the plant were severely damaged. Other industrial complexes and dockside warehouses also suffered, but it was learned later, as was so often the case, that the raid had not been as successful as at first thought, and this despite the fact that the wind had risen again during the attack and worked in Bomber Command's favour for a change by helping to spread the fires. 572 houses were gutted, more than 6000 sustained various degrees of damage, and roughly 6000 people were left without a roof over their heads; but if 696 crews bombed Bremen, as they claimed, then they ought to have left much more evidence of their visit. The relative failure of the raid was further emphasised by the loss of 44 aircraft of Bomber Command in addition to four Hudsons and one Wellington of Coastal Command - and 291 aircrew. Moreover 22 of the 65 bombers damaged returned in a sorry state and many of them had to be scrapped. These figures represented the highest losses so far incurred by Bomber Command on a single operation. An additional worry was the high casualty rate amongst instructors and pupils (over 40% of those taking part). It was all too evident that such a depletion of the Command's 'seed corn' could only bring about a dearth of experienced crews in the near future; it also meant the end of 1000-bomber raids for the time being.

Air raid officials in Bremen stated that 80 aircraft had attacked their city, of which they claimed 50 shot down. The BBC announcement that over 1000 had participated was, said the same officials, merely to make the huge losses appear more acceptable. But although

Bomber Command in World War II

Nazi propaganda did intend at times to be so overdone as to appear quite incredible, even to German ears, the Bremen operation left some room for doubt as to its cost effectiveness. It was in no way a failure like Essen, but neither was it a victory like Cologne, and, everything considered, the three raids constituting the 'Thousand Plan', involving the loss of 134 aircraft and nearly 800 aircrew, had taken a grievous toll of Bomber Command's resources. Germany had been stung, but it was a sting which had generally lacked in venom; and yet, evaluated from the point of view of British morale, the story was a different one: the cry "Give it em' back!" had been replaced by "They're getting it back - and how!" Harris and his crews were hailed by a public which was not cognizant of the true facts (although these, admittedly, were then known in detail only by the enemy) and was easily swayed by the thought of the terror and turmoil they assumed must have reigned in Cologne and Essen and Bremen. The man in the street, and others besides, just did not know that the despatch of 1000 bombers was not synonymous with unlimited destruction. At the same time there were still some military strategists, members of the War Cabinet, and prominent figures from various walks of life, who were not easily duped and remained sceptical; just as his severest critics were to lambast him later (already pointed out in Chapter 10) as he proceeded on a course whose aim seemed to be - and was - the systematic annihilation of everything in the Reich, he was even at this early stage and in the wake of the "Thousand Plan", accused of showmanship and sensationism , of gambling with airmen's lives and valuable aircraft. But the number of fault-finders had perceptibly diminished, and that was all that mattered; Bomber Command was on its way.

Initially Harris had believed that the most effective policy would be a one thousand raid per month, plus 'small sundry operations', but after Bremen he changed his mind; he told Portal that four raids once a month by one thousand aircraft would be more likely to bring better results; and having drawn up a list of major towns doomed to undergo this type of assault, he insisted that enough had been done to ensure that Bomber Command should be able 'to dispose of a weight of air attack which no country on which it can be brought to bear could survive.' Now he felt he could, and did, demand a huge step-up in the production of four-engined bombers. Given an adequately-sized force he would liquidate the Ruhr and Berlin and every town of note in Germany. But the Command must be allowed to operate in accordance with its own concepts, in its own way, and after he had eliminated the U-boat bases for the Navy, he wanted

The Great Ingratitude

no more interference from that quarter, or from any other quarter, which would divert his precious aircraft and crews from the primary aim (although he must have known that when the Invasion did come he would be called upon to play a prominent part, but that was well into the future).

When asked by Churchill to give a detailed written account, for the information of the War Cabinet, of the intended aims of Bomber Command, he submitted this two days after the Bremen raid and did not miss the opportunity to complain yet again about the lack of official appreciation of the work done by his bombers:

'What incredible assumptions of an early end to the war would follow upon the destruction of a third of Cologne in an hour and a half by some swift-moving mechanical force which, with but 200 casualties, withdrew and was ready to repeat the operation 24 hours later! What acclaim would greet the virtual destruction of Rostock and the Heinkel main and subsidiary factories by a naval bombardment! All this, and far more, has been achieved by Bomber Command: yet there are many who still avert their gaze, pass on the other side, and question whether the 30 squadrons of night bombers make any worthwhile contribution to the war.'

But anyone who believed such a tempo could be maintained on a frequent and regular basis was outrageously optimistic, and no one knew that better than Harris. The 'Thousand Plan' had been a temporary expedient to attain a certain goal, and had succeeded in so doing. Both airworthy bombers and proficient crews were in short supply and any prolongation of the Plan would have entailed further, and perhaps fatal, erosion of Operational Training Units. So after Bremen there came a lull, with large-scale attacks from then until the first months of 1943 the exception (600 aircraft went to Dusseldorf on July 31/August 1, 1942, and 479 to the same target on September 10/11, and what was significant was the growing proportion of Lancasters participating in each operation). The great winner from A V Roe was steadily making its mark; the Pathfinder Force was about to be formed (Chapter 12) and the all-important and long-awaited electronic aids were beginning to appear in greater numbers and becoming more and more sophisticated.

Although Saundby had assessed Cologne as 'the beginning of the end' for the Third Reich, it would perhaps have been more accurate to have described the situation, using the famous Churchillian phrase, as 'the end of the beginning'.Bomber Command had still a long way to go, but the days of dithering and general ineffectiveness were over, and it was undisputedly the end of that very inauspicious beginning. A new and, in Harris's estimation, a true course had been set, and it was one which he would pursue relentlessly, vigorously, uncompromisingly. The throttles would soon be fully opened and locked in position, and there they would remain until Germany lay in ruins.

After the lull would come the first signs of the gathering storm ...

3   THE 'FRENCH KRUPPS'

It was indeed a rare occurrence when Harris softened his attitude towards attacking precision or 'panacea' targets, and consequently all the more incomprehensible that he appeared to raise no strong objections when, just six months after Augsburg, the decision was taken to attempt to destroy the huge Schneider plant at le Creusot; perhaps this was due to the fact that this target was of unusually large dimensions and could therefore be 'carpet bombed' on a minor scale; that it did not lie in Germany; also because le Creusot represented the French equivalent of Krupps of Essen and was engaged in turning out large numbers of anti-aircraft, anti-tank and much heavier guns, in addition to locomotives and military vehicles, including tanks. Again it was an ambitious and daring raid and deserving of more recognition than it received; Augsburg was well known to the British public, while le Creusot was not.

The first of two attacks took place - as in the case of Augsburg, low-level and in daylight - on October 17, 1942. Intensive training was carried out by nine squadrons of Lancasters, about 100 aircraft in all, from 5 Group, inland of the Wash and under the command of Wing Commander L Slee. It further resembled the Augsburg raid in that the operation entailed a long flight which demanded great concentration and determination by the crews as they sped 300 miles across almost the whole breadth of France just above the tree tops, having made a time-consuming detour westwards to the Atlantic and crossed the French coast south of St Nazaire in a bid to confuse the enemy and keep him guessing as to their likely destination. It was akin to travelling from London to Peterborough via Bristol.

The Great Ingratitude

94 Aircraft were despatched, of which six were detailed to attack a transformer adjacent to the factory and from which it obtained its power. The Lancs flew without escort and on reaching Nevers, about 70 miles short of the target, they climbed to various heights between two and eight thousand feet. So far they had remained unmolested by either fighters or flak, but four aircraft were damaged and two airmen injured when they flew into flocks of birds; they all returned safely apart from one of them which tried to hit the transformer - it came in too low and crashed into a roof-top.

Although 140 tons were dropped many of the bombs fell short of the target. Some of them did land on the factory and its immediate precincts, but results were poorer than had been hoped. Unfortunately the workers' quarters received their share of high explosives, but it has never been revealed how many Frenchmen lost their lives or suffered injuries.

Eight months later, on June 19/20, 1943, it was decided to send to the same target a much larger force of 290 aircraft, and this time at night. 181 Halifaxes, 107 Stirlings and two Lancs set off. No target indicators were dropped by the Pathfinders - only flares - a strange decision since it was not a practice to which main force crews were accustomed. Many of them failed to identify the plant, a task rendered more difficult by the large amount of smoke rising from the flares which had been intended to light everything up, not the reverse. Only one crew in five actually hit the Schneider complex and once again some of the bombs fell on workers' accommodation. As in the earlier raid the number of French casualties was not divulged.

But one crew in five meant that 58 aircraft had shed their loads where it mattered and although it proved difficult to obtain accurate information about the amount of damage, a great deal of havoc had been wrought and production of armaments substantially reduced for a time at any rate. Yet a force of nearly 300 bombers should have blown the factory to bits, big as it was, and we are forced to the conclusion that if the Pathfinders had used target indicators instead of smoke-inducing flares such a large stream of heavies might have achieved a great deal more.

After each of the le Creusot raids it was reported that Harris went away muttering obscenities about 'these damned panacea targets' and swore if he had anything to do with it few such attacks would take place in the future, and certainly not until Bomber Command possessed the technology which would more or less guarantee a high degree of success. And in the main he struck rigidly to his guns and demonstrated in vivid fashion only five weeks after the second visit to le Creusot what he considered to be the most effective way of crippling Germany by opening the Battle of Hamburg. No more of this nonsense of trying to hit a few hundred square yards of barely discernible factory buildings; from now on the target would be several square miles of a major city. A city was something they couldn't miss.

We know what happened to Hamburg, and to the others

4   UNINVITED GUESTS

The Air Offensive was a grim business and often a very bloody one, with the nearest thing to elation of any sort perhaps a faint smile of satisfaction after a successful trip. But there was one operation - as far as I know the only one - which had definitely a comic touch and caused a great deal of mirth on RAF stations and in British homes from Land's End to John o' Groats.

The British Government had learned that the egotistic Hermann Goering and the loathsome Minister of Propaganda, Josef Goebbels, were to address a huge rally on January 30, 1943. The occasion was the tenth anniversary of Hitler's accession to power and the celebration was to take place in the impressive Sportspalast in Berlin. Goering would be the "star turn" in the morning, Goebbels in the afternoon. Unfortunately Mr Wonderman himself could not appear - he was probably too engrossed in his worries about the Russian Front.

Here was a God-sent opportunity to singe the beards of two of the top Nazis in their own backyard.   There was no real malevolence intended - although no one on the British side would have been terribly upset if the principal performers in particular had had their breeches torn or their heads blown off.   This, of course, was what the Germans thought the RAF was trying to do, as they never did come anywhere near to an understanding of the British sense of humour.   The main intention was to poke a finger in the eye of the Nazi hierarchy and give the world a good laugh.

All the usual instruments used to create euphoria and mass hysteria were present: military bands, a grand parade, featuring the smart black-uniformed SS and crack Wehrmacht units, other Party big-

The Great Ingratitude

wigs, fresh-faced Hitler youth and Hitler Maidens (*Bund Deutscher Mädel*); the huge banners portraying swastikas and German eagles; everything designed to whip everyone into a patriotic frenzy and to remind any doubters of the invincible power of the Third Reich and its demigod Adolf Hitler (Paulus was to surrender at Stalingrad three days later).

The scene was set. The grateful tribute to the Führer for the ten glorious years he had given the Master Race was about to be paid.

At exactly 11 am the ample figure of Reichsmarschall Goering, resplendent in a new uniform richly bemedalled, would address the multitude ...

Dead on time, and just as the latter was about to deliver his oration, the thousands present were treated to an unexpected fly-past (led by Squadron Leader R W Reynolds) and a few celebratory fireworks. There was a sudden deafening din as three Mosquitoes, with their six Rolls Royce Merlins screaming at full throttle and with freshly painted RAF roundels, streaked over the Sportspalast on Bomber Command's first ever daylight visit to Berlin, the city which, Goering had promised, would never play host to an enemy bomber. Hardly anyone in the audience had seen an RAF aircraft before, but they were seeing some of them now.

Panic and chaos ensued. Back at base all those who knew about the raid had their ears glued to the radio. Sure enough, right to the minute, a mighty thump drowned out everything else being transmitted; then came shouts of "Achtung! Achtung!" from frightened and high-pitched German voices. Eventually it was announced that the Reichsmarschall would be delayed for a minute or two. The 'minute or two' stretched to a good hour, by which time the Mosquitoes were roaring back over the North Sea well on their way home. The bands had played stirring German music to try to calm the crowd until it was at last considered safe for Goering to make a belated reappearance.

And the comedy was not yet over. The same afternoon a second trio of Mossies (led by Squadron Leader D F Darling) which had flown low-level to Lübeck and then turned through 40° starboard for Berlin, gaining altitude all the time, arrived over the city, and only moments before Dr Goebbels was due on the rostrum the bombs went down. It is believed that the Propaganda Minister, who was also Gauleiter of Berlin, chose to make his speech from an underground bunker. Not that the crowd on the surface would feel any better for that.

Listeners to the BBC news bulletin the same evening heard a recording of the entire proceedings. They were also given a description of the entire operation by one of the aircrew who had taken part. All ten of the airmen who returned - sadly Squadron Leader Darling and his navigator, Flying Officer W Wright were shot down - were congratulated personally by the Chief of Air Staff, Sir Charles Portal, and then went on to have a whale of a party in London. All those who participated were decorated.

5   THE DAMBUSTERS

Few people are unfamiliar with the Dambusters' raid (Operation *Chastise*) of May 16/17, 1943, when the Möhne and Eder Dams east of the Ruhr were breached. Many will have seen the film, which has appeared several times on TV, or read one of the books describing it in detail. Hence it is not considered necessary to repeat a lengthy account of it here. Suffice to say that, praiseworthy as the feat was, and a testimony both to the genius of Barnes Wallis for his 'bouncing bomb' and to the skill and courage of Wing Commander Guy Gibson and his highly-trained Lancaster crews of 617 Squadron, who held a steady course as they flew at 60 feet above the water into the teeth of murderous ack-ack fire, the degree of disruption it caused the German war machine, albeit substantial, was only temporary.

Although the reservoirs were reputed to supply the vital Ruhr area with most of its electricity and water, the damage was soon repaired and within a short space of time the factories were back in full production. Rather was the raid a morale-booster which, like Cologne, excited an admiring British (and foreign) public and won their acclaim, but its heavy cost helped to confirm Harris's conviction, if it needed confirming, that such operations, without guaranteeing anything in the nature of a lasting blow, took far too heavy a toll of his precious airmen and aircraft. This was not the line he intended to pursue, and Hamburg would prove him right only a couple of months later. At the same time he did not object to the favourable publicity that Bomber Command enjoyed following the raid. It drew attention to the spectacular achievements of which it was capable and he no doubt appreciated part of Churchill's speech to the United States Congress only two days after the operation:

"The condition to which the great centres of German war industry, and particularly the Ruhr, are being reduced is one of unparalleled devastation.

The Great Ingratitude

You have just read of the destruction of the great dams which feed the canals and provide power to the enemy's munition works. That was a gallant operation, costing eight out of the 19 Lancasters employed, but will pay a very far-reaching part in reducing the German munitions output. Wherever their centres of war industry exist or are developed, they will be destroyed.''

The bursting of the Möhne and Eder Dams was an excellent example, in fact perhaps the example *par excellence*, of a precision raid where it was quite impossible to assess the damage done in terms of disruption to enemy war production. Bearing in mind the number of imponderable factors, a very rough assessment is all that can be made. In this case we must place on the debit side the long hours spent in training, the cost of producing Barnes Wallis' revolutionary bomb and of the eight Lancasters lost with their 56 airmen, who had been amongst the most highly skilled crews in Bomber Command. On the credit side the breach made in the Möhne, nearly 300 feet wide and 70 feet deep, unleashed such a solid wall of water that two days after the raid the reservoir's storage capacity was reduced from 140 million tons to about 15 million. Obviously such a violent flood, moving at great speed (but slowing as it began to fan out) left a trail of disaster in its wake; it played havoc with roads, railways and waterways and cut off electricity and water supplies; the damage to factories was very difficult to calculate, but it is known that 125 were destroyed or partly put out of production; 300 homes were swept away or ruined beyond repair; an estimated 1294 people were drowned, 859 of them in Neheim-Hüsten, and the others mostly in Arnsberg, Soest and Iserlohn (of those who perished it was calculated that 493 were female farm labourers from the Ukraine and some were prisoners of war); 7000 cattle and pigs were lost; 46 bridges lying directly in the path of the torrent were swept away or rendered unsafe; 2000 men had to be employed to rebuild the Möhne.

The breaching of the Eder did more damage in the large city of Kassel than it did in the Ruhr, but this was more or less confined to the canal system. It became clear later that had the Sorpe been burst instead of the Eder, a great deal more destruction would have been wrought in the industrial centres of Dortmund and Bochum in particular, and would have rendered the operation of far greater value. But amid the euphoria created by the radio news bulletins and the newspaper headlines the British public knew little of these facts. As far as they were concerned the bursting of the Dams was a momentous achievement carried out by brave and clever young men and certainly worthy of the Victoria Cross and the 34 other decorations awarded; but, perhaps more importantly, it was also proof of the growing capability of Bomber Command.

Regarding the much-shown film it might be appropriate to mention the unrealistic and totally erroneous methods used over the years by makers of war films in general and perhaps of RAF and USAAF operations in particular. Too many members of aircrew bear that 'devil-may-care' look and tend to speak, if they are British pilots or navigators, with Oxford accents, and if air-gunners or wireless-operators, with pronounced regional brogues; but, worst of all, they display a sang-froid and a cheerfulness which are entirely out of place; they are invariably quite unperturbed and even seem to relish situations fraught with the most frightful danger. Certainly there were exceptions, but high spirits were often feigned, and when the airmen and their aircraft were in the thick of it and liable to be consigned to oblivion at any second, the reality was far removed from what is usually presented on celluloid. If the fears and tensions and general atmosphere of the German film 'The Boat' were applied in future cinematographic productions of the war in the air, then perhaps the public would get a much more accurate impression of what it really was like to take part in a bombing mission. Happily there now seems to be a tendency in this direction, recently exemplified in the American film 'Memphis Belle'. Certainly not before time.

The Dambusters raid, taking place when it did, was definitely no 'circus act' - Bomber Command could not afford to indulge its Lancasters in such luxuries at that stage of the war. The operation was an honest and calculated attempt to deal a single heavy blow at the main arsenal of the enemy's war industry. If results did not quite measure up to expectations, that in no way detracts from all the effort, skill and courage which made the attack at least partially successful. But due to the very fact that it was one of Harris's detested 'panacea targets' - yet attractive to him nevertheless as a way of putting Bomber Command on the map - and achieved, at a high price in blood and sweat, less than had been hoped, the Bomber Chief was now one hundred per cent sure that this was the wrong way to go about things; indeed it could be said that the breaching of the dams and the reluctant and expensive attacks on other specific targets were in part responsible for the flood of bombs which would engulf every sizeable town in the Reich from then on.

Hamburg, remember, was just round the corner.

6   THE JAILBUSTERS

But dams weren't the only things that could be burst.

During the winter of 1943-44, the Gestapo in Northern France had enjoyed something of a bonanza in rooting out and arresting a large number of Resistance leaders. In fact they had been so successful that the entire Resistance organization in that area was virtually in a state of collapse and no fewer than 120 of its members were languishing in Amiens prison as they awaited imminent execution.

With the approaching Invasion and the Allies' growing need of a steady flow of the latest information about German troop movements and defences, plus the co-operation of the Resistance in harassing the enemy just before and after the armies had landed, it was the worst possible moment for such a thing to happen; and there was another significant factor - the rocket sites which were springing up all along the Channel. These, as we have already seen, constituted a dire threat both to the civilian population of Southern Britain and to the large concentrations of men and equipment building up all along the South Coast. It was therefore imperative that the Allied Air Forces should know where the sites were and wreck each and every one of them.

When British Intelligence learned the facts about Amiens and were asked by the Resistance if something could be done to free the prisoners, the only feasible method seemed to be an air attack on the jail. It was blatantly obvious that this would be an extremely tricky and hazardous operation for all concerned. Some had strong reservations about killing innocent people (the captive *résistants*) and others charged with crimes ranging from minor offences such as black-marketeering to those entailing murder and rape (which were none of the RAF's business), but what finally swayed the balance was the inevitability of the early death of those already doomed: they would have more chance of living by being bombed than by facing a firing squad.

It was decided that it was a job tailor-made for Mosquitoes. No 2 Group Commander Basil Embry wanted to lead the raid himself, but was forbidden to do so by senior officers, who knew only too well that should a man of his rank and standing be captured he would be pumped by the enemy for all sorts of information, including Invasion plans, and that there was no guarantee they would not get it by resorting to the foulest possible means. Another strong argument against Embry's participation - a man as resourceful as he was courageous - was the huge reward advertised by the German High Command for his capture. He had flown over enemy territory under a pseudonym and when his aircraft was shot down he had attacked and killed his guards and got back to the UK via Spain. Reluctantly Embry nominated another fine and experienced pilot, Group Captain Percy Charles Pickard, to lead the raid.

The operation was aptly code-named *Renovate* as that, they hoped, was exactly what the Germans would have to do to Amiens prison after their visit.

The Resistance supplied every obtainable detail about the building and its environs and even a plan of its lay-out, including the height and thickness of the walls. A small model was made for the many briefings that were held and a scale model for crews to study from the air. They flew over it time and time again so that on seeing the real thing they would instantly recognise the exact spots where the bombs had to land.

The most propitious moment for the attack, advised the Resistance, was at noon when most of the German guards and personnel were having lunch in the dining-hall, which should therefore be one of the main aiming-points - if it was hit fewer of the enemy would be available to pursue and round up escapees. Resistance workers would be in the vicinity of the prison to help their colleagues make their getaway and escort them to safe hiding-places, and to provide them with food, shelter and civilian clothes.

The Resistance was duly informed of the RAF's plan of attack: a first wave of six aircraft would try to burst open the outer prison wall in two places and destroy the dining-hall. The second wave, three minutes later, would bomb the main prison walls and the guards' quarters. The third was ordered to hold back in readiness and would release its bomb load, thirteen minutes after the second wave, only if the other attacks had failed. 11-second delay HEs were to be used. It was estimated that the blasts would also shake the cell doors from their hinges. Split-second timing and extreme accuracy were essential.

The difficulties and the dangers for all concerned were so numerous that grave doubts were raised as to whether such a raid could succeed. As someone remarked, it could turn out to be the biggest eff-up of all time. But when the Resistance sent the news that the day of execution was now very close, it was decided, in spite of the atrocious weather - heavy snow showers all over Western Europe, during which no 'postponable' operation would ever have taken place - they had to go on February 18. Low-level flying in falling snow creates conditions just about as bad as you can get; nor does such weather make map-reading - more demanding the lower you fly - any easier either. It was on days such as this that Bomber Command was inclined to the belief that it was the Devil who was Lord of the Skies.

Surprise was all-important. Not too far away at Abbeville, just a few kilometres inland from the coast and only 40 from Amiens, was a fighter base commanded by a man long known to the RAF and much respected by it - Adolf Galland - credited with a huge number of air combat victories. Galland was a force to be reckoned with, as were his pilots, who had all been inculcated with his theories about how best to shoot down the enemy in all sorts of situations. His Me 109s and Focke-Wulf 190s would be off the ground and after them like greyhounds out of a trap.

To avoid detection by radar the Mosquitoes roared across the grey waters of the Channel, just skimming the wave tops. They were not much higher when they arrived over the flat countryside of the Pas de Calais. They had to lift their wings to avoid roofs and treetops, and startled villagers caught a fleeting glimpse of them as they stood with mouths agape or threw themselves to the ground. As they approached Amiens, by which time visibility had thankfully improved, and tore down the long, straight road from Albert and the village of Querrieu, they climbed a few hundred feet and by so doing easily picked out the large Gothic cathedral and then the prison. They swooped down again, one or two of them coming in lower than some of the buildings, and both the Armenois and the Germans, although quite used to having the RAF over the town (it was an important railway junction and frequently visited) wondered what on earth could be brewing this time. They had never seen RAF aircraft so low before.

The earsplitting noise of the engines was followed by a few seconds of almost complete silence before the bombs rocked the prison. Exactly the same sequence was repeated three minutes later when the second wave attacked.

As had been feared from the outset, some prisoners were killed, also several Germans, but a substantial number of the Resistance fighters got out. Although quite a few of them were recaptured once the uninjured soldiers had regained their senses and reinforcements had arrived - the snow-covered terrain did nothing to help the runaways - others remained at large and were able to regroup and recommence their activities in the Allied cause.

The Mossies, some of whose crews had seen prisoners

running across the fields adjacent to the prison, wasted no time in beating it back over the Channel. Two of them were lost, including that of Group Captain Pickard.

When the Normandy landings took place some four months later the Allies were in possession of many items of useful information which, without the brilliant attack on the prison, would almost certainly have been denied them.

7   BIG BANGS

The 12,000 lb Tallboy and the 22,000 lb Grand Slam high explosive 'earthquake' bombs were further examples of Bomber Command's indebtedness to Barnes Wallis for providing it with weapons of hitherto unprecedented power of destruction. The only regret was that these awesome additions to its armoury did not become available till fairly late in the war, and one cannot help but reflect on how they might have influenced events had they been produced somewhat sooner and launched against such resilient targets as Krupps in Essen and the submarine pens. Harris would probably have offered his right arm in exchange for a few hundred of them a couple of years earlier.

Yet delivery to the enemy of Tallboys and Grand Slams would have been quite impossible at any time without the superlative lifting qualities of the faithful Lancaster. The bomber, which had begun its career some four years before with a full operational weight of 24 tons, was, in the later stages, after certain modifications had been carried out, capable of becoming airborne at a full fighting weight of 32 tons. To achieve this additional potential two of its gun-turrets - mid-upper and front - had to be removed (obviously less of a hazard than in the days when the Luftwaffe fighting force was at its zenith) and its bomb-bays extended towards the tail; it was also refitted with Merlin 24 engines to enable it to get these massive loads into the air and, in the case of the Grand Slam, to hurl at the enemy what was the penultimate weapon of the Second World War - the ultimate was to shock Japan and the entire world in August, 1945.

Crews stared aghast at this colossus as it was winched into the gaping belly of their aircraft and, despite all the assurances received, they felt that getting off the ground with the monster must at best be a matter of touch and go. But the Lanc lived up to its name. Admittedly it groaned and moaned a little as it struggled to get its apparently punctured tyres off the tarmac, and its wings continually altered slightly in shape under the tremendous strain. But, ever willing, it did it.

The success of the big bombs was partly due to their abnormally thin casing, which allowed for a much higher proportion of high explosive content, and to their beautifully streamlined contours which increased their earthbound speed to something bordering on the fantastic. For optimum results they had to be dropped from a minimum altitude of three miles. An exploding Tallboy, some 10,000 lb lighter than the Grand Slam, dislodged something like 5000 tons of earth.

A clear example of the destructive force of even the smaller Tallboy was demonstrated on June 8/9, 1944, when a formation of 20 Lancs attacked the railway tunnel at Saumur on the River Loire, about 40 miles east of Tours. The aim was to halt the passage of reinforcements northwards and hence to delay their participation in the battle of Normandy. The raid was led by Group Captain Leonard Cheshire, the Bomber Command pilot who had completed so many operations that his VC was awarded for displaying unflinching courage in the face of the enemy over so long a period. Flares were dropped with great accuracy and no fewer than 19 Tallboys were released. One of them was particularly effective as it dug deep into the elevated ground above the tunnel mouth before exploding. Several weeks later liberating Americans stood and gawped at the gigantic mountain of earth which still blocked the tunnel - a whole hillside had literally collapsed on top of it.

***

The 45,000 ton battleship Tirpitz was a continuous source of worry to the Admiralty during the last two years of the war, when she was normally hidden away in narrow Norwegian fjords but poised, no doubt, to break out at the opportune moment. It was therefore difficult for the Royal Navy to get to grips with her; and it had to have her kept under constant surveillance, knowing that she could appear at any time and wreak havoc amongst the Allied convoys bound both for the UK and Northern Russia.

After her transfer to Norwegian waters on January 15, 1942, she had occasionally left safe anchorages - to intercept Convoy PQ-12, for instance - and been attacked, unsuccessfully, by various naval units. British midget submarines which penetrated Altenfjord put her out of

Bomber Command in World War II

action until March, 1944, and on April 3 she suffered further damage from Barracudas operating from aircraft carriers. Other attempts were made to sink her, not just as a target *per se*, but also in support of deception plans for D-Day (Operation *Fortitude North*) to suggest imminent landings in Norway. Three British carriers, escorted by the battleship Duke of York, had tried again on July 17 and on August 22, and the aircraft, without scoring any hits themselves, were repulsed with heavy losses from her guns and also from fighters stationed on nearby airfields. Further attacks on August 24 and 29 also failed.

It was time to enlist the help of Bomber Command.

In Harris's eyes Tirpitz was a 'panacea target', but no doubt chuffed that the Admiralty should request such a favour, agreed to comply, saying that he would attend to it 'when he had a spare moment'. No one could censure him for such a prickly response: he hadn't forgotten the Navy's derisive dismissal of the heavy bomber if confronted by a battleship. Changed days indeed.

Enter 617 Squadron.

Due to the extreme distance of Alta fjord, where Tirpitz was moored, from the nearest British airfield at Lossiemouth in the North of Scotland, 28 Lancasters set off on September 10 for the Russian base at Yagodnik, a mere 300 miles from the target compared to the 1300 from the Scottish base. The operation was scheduled for September 15 but on that day they found the battleship obscured by a huge smokescreen. The Tallboys were aimed at the shell detonations from Tirpitz's guns and only one hit (on her bows) was thought to have been obtained.

The ship was moved to Tromsofjord (200 miles nearer Lossiemouth) and, on November 12, a force of 30 Lancs took off before dawn from the Scottish airfield to make the round-trip of some 2200 miles. Their mid-upper turrets and other weight-saving items of equipment had been dispensed with so that extra fuel tanks - which increased capacity to just over 2406 gallons - could be fitted. While still several miles short of the Norwegian coastline the crews could see Tirpitz lying festooned in her anti-submarine nets. This time the inevitable smoke was pumped out too late on a morning with perfect visibility and Wing Commander Tait, who led the attack, reported on his return that so many Tallboys had exploded

The Great Ingratitude

on or in close proximity to the battleship that it was most unlikely she was still afloat.

She wasn't. Tirpitz had gone down, taking most of her trapped crew with her. Over 1000 men perished.

No doubt the Admiralty, at last relieved of this sinister menace to convoys and capital ships alike, swallowed its pride and expressed its grateful thanks to Bomber Command and the crews of the bombers which, they had said, would never be a match for a battleship.

In fact Bomber Command sank 19 of Germany's heavy warships, the final operation taking place on August 9/10, when, in a raid on the harbour area of Kiel by 591 Lancasters and eight Mosquitoes, the remnants of the once proud *Kriegsmarine* were put out of commission; the *Admiral Hipper, Admiral Sheer* and the *Emden* were either sunk or suffered irreparable damage, auguring what was about to happen to the nation which had produced them.

***

The Tallboy's big brother, Grand Slam, was deployed in cases where an even greater blast was required. One typical example was the bombing of the Bielefeld Viaduct (between the marshalling yards town of Hamm, just outside the Ruhr, and Hanover, one of Germany's main industrial cities). The huge viaduct was therefore a key communications target, and one which had witnessed many futile attacks from early on in the war and taken a heavy toll of the planes involved. But it wasn't old Hampdens and Whitleys which went there on March 14, 1945, with puny loads which were quite incommensurate with the task in hand. This time it was the latest Lancasters, one of which carried a Grand Slam. The bomb bored 30 feet into the ground and caused a mini-earthquake which shook the entire structure to bits. It simply collapsed like a pack of cards.

In all 854 of these Tallboys and 41 Grand Slams fell on enemy targets. They were used by 617 Squadron to blow flying-bomb installations (often underground) to smithereens and at Hamburg-Blankenese on the Elbe, and on the west coast of France, they lifted blocks of reinforced concrete as big as houses (protecting the submarine pens) into the air as if they had been made of cardboard. On April 1, with only three weeks of the war left, Bomber Command despatched 949 heavies (mostly Lancasters) and 20 Mosquitoes to Heligoland, and just to make sure that nothing was left of the airfield and the naval base after their visit,

Bomber Command in World War II

36 Lancasters returned the next day to drop six Grand Slams and 27 Tallboys. The island fortress wasn't a good place to be and if some of the more fanatical Nazi personnel stationed there still entertained hopes for Führer and Fatherland, then these, even for them, must have been largely dispelled.

***

On April 25, 1945 - just five days before Hitler cheated the Allies out of taking his place in the dock at Nuremberg with his erstwhile abettors - the curtain could hardly have come down in a more fitting manner to mark the final operation by the aircraft which had contributed more than any other to his downfall. The target was the *Adlernest* ('Eagle's Nest'), his retreat at Berchtesgaden which he had visited regularly, and especially when he had felt the need for solitude and a few revitalising gulps of Bavarian mountain air; nor could the weapons themselves have been more appropriate - they were Tallboys.

When an apparently oversized force of 359 Lancasters, accompanied by 16 Mosquitoes, approached the lofty redoubt, the surrounding peaks played havoc with the *Oboe* equipment carried by eight of the Mosquitoes, and, in spite of the latters' altitude (39,000 feet), they were unable to operate satisfactorily. The presence of much mist and snow did not help either, but direct hits were scored with the 12,000 lb bombs, the explosions echoing and reverberating the length of the Alpine valleys and bringing home to the elderly mountain dwellers what they had been missing for the previous 5 years. The raid was most effective as both the chalet and the SS barracks were severely damaged. On the debit side Bomber Command lost its last two Lancs of the total of 3431 claimed by enemy action during the three years since the spring of 1942.

Barnes Wallis had invented, and Bomber Command delivered, weapons to which the strongest and thickest building materials were no longer immune; in fact there was no substance on earth which could withstand the devastating explosive power of these tremendous bombs. They were scheduled for Japan, by courtesy of 617 Squadron, but, by courtesy of the Americans, the Nipponese got something else, and they were not required.

The Great Ingratitude

8 'GUTEN MORGEN, HERR HIMMLER!'

During the first years of the occupation of Denmark the German forces generally behaved themselves, leaving the administration of the country to the Danes, but as Resistance groups formed and began to make their presence felt by early 1943, their attitude changed completely. By September they tried to round up all the Jews (over 6000), but about 90% of them managed to reach Sweden, thanks to the efforts of an irate Danish populace. Resistance to the Nazi jackboot increased rapidly and by the autumn of 1944 the Gestapo files were so full of incriminating evidence concerning individual saboteurs that it was feared massive retaliation would soon be effected to demonstrate to others in an unambiguous manner what happened to those who committed 'crimes' against the Greater German Reich. Accordingly the Danish Underground had asked the Air Ministry if the RAF could do them a good turn by destroying all the evidence, which was stacked away in the university of Aarhus, on the east coast of Jutland. This was agreed and the six Mosquitoes despatched did such an excellent job that early in 1945 a further request was made for a similar raid, this time on the former Shell Petroleum building in Copenhagen, which, like Aarhus, contained accusatory information certain to put a number of citizens in dire jeopardy. In addition several Danes, for whose lives they feared, were incarcerated on the top floor, and such an attack would at least give them a chance to escape.

With recollections of Amiens the Air Ministry pondered long and hard, but was finally persuaded to undertake the operation when an almost frantic second appeal was made. What helped to swing the balance was the reported imminent meeting (which would last a few days) of a large number of high-ranking Gestapo officers in the same building. This was regarded as a further incentive: two birds (but, it was hoped, many more) with one stone or, rather, several bombs. Operation *Carthage* was on.

At this stage of the war it was considered safe to allow Air Vice-Marshal Embry (who had been forbidden to take part in the Amiens attack) to lead, under the pseudonym of 'Wing Commander Smith', the entire force of 18 Mosquitoes and 28 escorting Mustang fighters to a point just short of Copenhagen, when Group Captain R Bateson would assume command. They took off around 08.00 hours on March 21 and sped straight across the North Sea at 250 mph at wave-top height in order to avoid radar detection. With the Danish coast in sight they climbed to 150 feet and increased their speed to 280 mph. Over the Jutland peninsula, the largest of the three mainland areas forming Denmark, the formation sorted itself out into three waves and flew on at one minute intervals, heading for Zealand and Copenhagen on its east coast.

At 11.15 hours (when it was reckoned that all the Gestapo officers would be in the building) Bateson easily picked out the Shell House and went in, with his colleagues on his heels. The 16 500 lb, 11-second delayed action bombs and an equal number fitted with 30-second fuses were all dropped within the space of six minutes. As 32 of the captives were detained on the top storey, this meant the bombs had to hit the building as near to the ground as possible. This was achieved, and before the entire structure became a raging inferno and totally destroyed, most of the Resistance members had made their escape, many of them hurt and severely shaken, but still very much alive. However, eight of them had perished. The Danes reported that the Gestapo suffered 74 fatalities. An unexpected bonus was the capture of the Gestapo's official list of Danish collaborators.

As almost always happens, and is expected to happen, in operations of this nature which involve such unpredictable results, some Danes lost their lives in the bombing and an unforseen tragedy occurred when one of the Mosquitoes collided with power lines and crashed in the Frederiksberg Allé, near the Shell House. Following crews saw the huge blaze caused by the ignited fuel and took it to be the target. Some of the bombs landed on the adjacent Jeanne d'Arc school, killing 112 people, 88 of them young pupils and the majority of the others nuns. It said a lot for # the Danes that in the next edition of their clandestine newspaper, while profoundly sympathising with all those who had lost dear ones, especially children, they paid tribute to the crews who had carried out such a daring and dangerous attack, and to the RAF fliers who had died.

Apart from the Mossie lost over Copenhagen itself, another crashed into the sea, a third ditched and a fourth made for Sweden, a mere 20 miles away. Two of the Mustangs also failed to return. The others landed at base only a minute or two behind schedule after a gruelling trip in excess of 1100 miles and lasting well over five hours.

Many factors had to be weighed up and agonising decisions had to be made in carrying out operations of this typewhich

The Danish Resistance Movement 1940 - 1945 by Aage Roussell, 1962.

could easily end up with undesirable results and even in unmitigated disaster. Was it justifiable to kill a few prisoners so that others might go free? Was it right to put the lives of innocent Danish or French civilians at risk in order to kill Germans or hamper their war effort? How did you arrive at an acceptable balance? Some of the traumas arising from such experiences during the Second World War did not go unheeded in similar circumstances which occurred on frequent occasions later - for example when air liners were highjacked or when no pre-emptive strike was effected to free hostages held by Saddam Hussein before the start of the Gulf War..

9   MANNA FROM THE BOMB-BAYS

In the many thousands of sorties flown by Bomber Command there were perhaps only two which succoured instead of destroyed, which the crews found pleasant to perform and where the results were immediately known to them.

Operation *Manna* was carried out in late April and early May, 1945, when operationally hardened airmen found themselves taking off on a very different kind of mission: instead of sending earthwards tons of death-dealing bombs they dropped nearly 7000 tons of life-saving food in an area in Western Holland which was still occupied by the enemy and where the population was on the brink of starvation. In the space of nine days 2835 Lancaster and 124 Mosquito flights were made before the German surrender.

10   'PASSENGER' LANCASTERS

The second was quite an emotional and a highly satisfying experience for the crews. After 30 Mosquitoes and seven Lancasters had flown to eight different camps to deliver instructional leaflets to British prisoners awaiting liberation, Operation *Exodus* got under way. It lasted from April 26 till May 7 and during that time 75,000 servicemen were brought back, mainly from a collection centre at Brussels, but from other airfields as well. Remembering that at the end of the First World War nearly two months had elapsed before all the prisoners were home again, and aware it was intended to use lorries and ships once more, it was the RAF who suggested that Lancs be used to ferry the men back. It was in fact the Pathfinders who made an experimental run to a camp on the Baltic and it was so successful that the following day nearly all of Bomber Command took part - and everyone was home in 'Blighty' in no time.

The crews participating found it a strange experience to be landing their Lancasters on soil which, during the long years of night bombing, they hadn't really ever seen and had associated only with the streams of flak sent up to destroy them.

Each Lanc carried 22 passengers away from the dreary misery of the camps. Those liberated were mostly exhausted in mind and body, some of them emaciated after more than five years behind the wire; on the other hand many became as sprightly and excited as schoolboys as they climbed aboard the great black bombers, the sound of which had done so much to sustain their morale throughout their captivity and which were now taking them home. Cramped and uncomfortable as they were in a machine which had hardly been built with passengers in mind, they couldn't have 'cared less' - to use typical RAF jargon - and many of them were later proud to say that they had flown in a Lanc.

Some of the Bomber Command aircrew amongst them - and there were quite a few of those - renewed temporary acquaintance with the aircraft they knew so well. Recently captured pilots asked if they could take over for a short spell, navigators did a spot of map-reading and gave a progressive account of their position to other passengers, engineers kept their eye on the instruments recording what was going on in the four engines, gunners peeped into turrets if these hadn't been removed and recalled frozen fingers and feet and nightmarish nights that would remain with them for ever. As the English North Sea Coast came into view there were broad grins and back-slapping and plans hatched to enter into the biggest binge of all time.

They came home in their tens of thousands, members of the British Expeditionary Force captured in France as long ago as 1940, sailors who had fallen into enemy hands even before then, Desert Rats and soldiers taken in Greece and Crete and Italy and Normandy; commandos and marines who were far from being the fine physical specimens they had been; and, of course, fighter pilots and bomber crews. Their war and their time of waiting was at last over, but now they had another fight on their hands as they sought to rehabilitate themselves as civilians after the stresses and strains of battle and prison camp life. For each and every one of them it would be anything but easy, for some there would be real problems, but they would soldier on notwithstanding. There was not much else they could do, and, after all, they had had plenty of practice.

11 THE CURTAIN FALLS

Operations *Manna* and *Exodus* were still being carried out in early May and Bomber Command crews naturally thought that they would never again fly with bombs to Germany; but the Allies had got hold of information about large numbers of troops still at the disposal of the Wehrmacht being assembled at Kiel for embarkation to Norway, where the nature of the terrain (as in Bavaria, Chapter 18) was highly suitable for a determined last-ditch stand which would have meant a continuation of the war and further loss of Allied military and Norwegian civilian life. Thus was Kiel destined to be Bomber Command's final target in the Third Reich - on May 2/3, two days after its leader had died by his own hand. His successor, Admiral Dönitz, who, like Harris, had believed he could win the war on his own - in his case with his U-Boats in the Atlantic - was known to be in the Kiel area at the time, a fact which lent credence to such an eventuality. No one intended to take any risks when victory was only days away and Bomber Command, once again and for the last time, was asked to step in.

The first phase of the operation was the strafing and bombing of airfields in the area of the port by 53 Mosquitoes (one of which crashed while executing a low-level napalm attack, killing Flying Officer R Catterall, DFC, and Flight Sergeant D Beadle). Then followed two formations of Mossies, flying one hour apart and totalling 126 aircraft. Nine-tenths cloud lay over the docks but *Oboe* and *H2s* were used and the glow of large fires could be seen penetrating this barrier. Many buildings surrounding the harbour collapsed, 18 civilians lost their lives, and soon after the raid was over a large convoy of military trucks and other vehicles set off for Flensburg - on an alternative route to Norway? Allied troops arrived in Kiel 36 hours later and the German personnel and equipment heading north towards Denmark were overtaken and captured.

The last Bomber Command aircraft of the 8953 lost in the Second World War were the Mosquito just mentioned and two Halifaxes sent as support and believed to have collided over the target, claiming altogether 15 airmen when hostilities were all but over - the very next day German officers came to Montgomery's headquarters on Lüneburg Heath and surrendered all German forces in the north-west of the country, in Denmark and in Holland. For an unfortunate few it was the old story of being so near and yet so far ...

So the curtain finally descended on a Bomber Command

stage which had laid on some of the greatest dramas in 5½ dramatic years of war, and quite a number of its most poignant tragedies. And the Reaper too, apparently, was still there, right to the very end, having his final say ...

Chapter 21

"WE MIGHT HIT SOMEONE ON THE HEAD!" - PROPAGANDA FROM THE SKIES

The propulsion of propaganda sheets into the ranks of enemy armies, with the intention of eroding their desire to fight, has been a regular practice since the 16th century. In his book *The War against France, 1870-71* the German writer Theodor Fontane described a new method of delivery - leaflets dropped from balloons. During the First World War the Germans considered the dissemination of propaganda to be a military weapon of such significance that they ordered the summary execution of any captured British airmen engaged on such a mission. Lenin went so far as to say that such 'news-sheets' were the most important of all forms of literature in either peace or war.

It was not until the Second World War, however, that the propaganda leaflet, thanks to the availability of aircraft with much greater range, was used on a gigantic scale; and although still aimed at military personnel on the battle fronts it took on a further dimension when it was extended in large measure to civilian populations, partly (but certainly not entirely) because it was believed they were more likely to succumb to it than those imbued with a soldier's discipline.

The leaflet dealt with the latest 'news' (the veracity of which depended on its national origin), reported blatant lies and misdeeds on the part of opposing governments, made threats of what was to come, or took the form of an illustrated sheet cleverly captioned and depicting scenes designed to strike fear into those in the other camp. Often a leaflet's credibility did not, surprisingly, depend so much on its objective, truthful content, but on the probability that the events forecast might occur.

Allied leaflets, if taken chronologically, provide a broad and, for the most part, an accurate summary of the course of the War. There might be slight distortions here and there, but this was generally due to misinformation at the time rather than to a deliberate attempt to falsify the facts. It is not recommended that German leaflets be assessed on the same lines!

Bomber Command in World War II

The first British leaflets fell on German soil on the night of September 3/4, 1939, when the War was only a few hours old, and by December 31 of the same year 34 million had been dropped, with three or four new versions each month. By 1943, 50-60 different leaflets existed in 10 different languages, and altogether Bomber Command delivered approximately 1500 million during the War, 1362 million of them after June, 1941. On D-Day the RAF and the USAAF let loose 27 million over France and by May, 1945, the tally in Western Europe (by both air forces) had reached the astronomical figure of 6500 million in 29 languages. The area covered then had a population of about 200 millions, which meant 32 leaflets for each and every inhabitant. It is worth noting that to make capital out of the turning tide of battle 75% of British and American leaflets were dropped after the Invasion.

As will be seen from the examples which follow, psychological content demanded changes in the light of events and by 1943 this had become as different from what it had been in the 1939-42 period as the delivering aircraft were as different from the Whitleys and Hampdens and Wellingtons which had acted as the first distributors. Thanks to the greater ceiling of the four-engined heavies 75,000 copies could now be spread over an area of 15 square kilometres from a height of 20,000 feet at average wind speeds - the stronger the wind the longer they remained airborne and the more widespread the circulation. Such extensive scattering did not please the Nazis, who feared it would convince their subjects that Bomber Command could, and did, go everywhere. Apart from the leaflets released by trainee aircraft (OTU crews benefited from these exercises which served as a preliminary to later bombing excursions into more hazardous parts of the Reich) the Command also employed special units which either flew on their own or accompanied the big bomber fleets.

A substantial proportion of the leaflets were delivered to occupied countries, especially France, and these were of definite value in boosting morale by reminding those enslaved that Gt. Britain had not fallen under Hitler's yoke and was determined to fight on; later they enlightened information-starved peoples about the progress of the war, encouraged subversive activities against their overlords and, finally, gave essential instructions to the French underground and ordinary citizens as to what they must do once the Invasion forces had landed. Equally useful were the instructions which drifted down to Allied prisoners of war in their camps just before these were liberated.

The Great Ingratitude

Unfortunately the same cannot be said for the hundreds of tons of paper with which Germany itself was 'bombarded' and Harris was right when he so fervently ridiculed the dropping of leaflets on the Reich as an utter waste of men, machines, petrol, paper, endeavour and everything else (Chapter 6). In the immediate aftermath of the War, I questioned several German civilians on this point and they were practically unanimous in their opinion that these propaganda sheets made little impact. Like Harris they had derided them. This was even the case after crushing defeats such as El Alamein and Stalingrad and while the Air Offensive was at its height and it was clear that only a miracle, or a series of miracles, could stave off defeat. I was told that some of those with near relations at the front, particularly in the East, were temporarily affected when they gazed at pictures of the massed German dead on the Eastern Front or the horrors of Stalingrad; similarly Wehrmacht soldiers everywhere became distressed on seeing the wreckage of their home towns and wondered about the safety of their next of kin. Often they were told by their officers that the photographs could be of any town, perhaps not even a German town, but when the Air Offensive really got going they saw the growing chaos with their own eyes each time they went on leave. On the other hand some Germans informed me that such experiences stiffened their resolve rather than the reverse.

Harris's crews were inclined to agree with their commander in his assessment of the value of leaflet raids and felt they were risking life and limb to little purpose. But their unique sense of humour never deserted them and witticisms were commonplace: "There's always the possibility of a parcel failing to open and hitting someone on the head!"; "See that you check the parcels before you chuck them out to make sure they are properly undone -otherwise you might hurt someone!" "I'm going to throw mine out over a village soon after take-off so that they can be used for making fire-lighters."

Yet if the propaganda leaflet fell a long way short of demoralising the civilian population the German authorities took the whole matter very seriously and spent much time and energy on precautionary measures. They were also deeply concerned about the dropping of counterfeit banknotes, food ration coupons, army leave chits and vouchers of all types whose purpose was to create social and economic havoc. The Nazis reacted very strongly right from the beginning and every citizen was quickly informed of the consequences of being found in possession of a British leaflet of any kind. Himmler himself ordered that the national press quote the case of a 20-year old factory girl in Nuremberg who, while at work on the night of September 10/11, was reported by an overseer to have had in her possession a leaflet which she had read and treasonably passed on to others - as requested at the foot of the page by the enemy - and was arrested at the factory the next day. She received a sentence of four months imprisonment and had to pay all court costs.

As the number of leaflets continued to increase the Reichsführer SS saw fit to issue an edict on February 29, 1940, which stated that in view of the apparent confusion amongst the populace as to the procedure to be followed after a drop, no one was to be left in any doubt about the steps to be taken by any person finding a leaflet: he or she would notify the local police immediately. The latter would begin a thorough search after informing the Gestapo, who in turn would keep in close touch with the Gauleiter (Nazi Party boss for the district). Himmler placed much stress upon smooth and timeous co-operation amongst all concerned. 30 copies (if possible) of each new leaflet were to be retained for record purposes by the Gauleiter, whose duty it was to ascertain right away over how large an area the offending material had spread and to inform his counterparts in adjacent districts that a drop had taken place.

German apprehension vis-à-vis this type of propaganda was further demonstrated by a second decree from Himmler dated February 2, 1944. With the War going badly for the Nazis they feared more than ever that the leaflets could have an adverse effect on the nation's morale: 'In the present struggle for Germany's and Europe's survival the enemy will employ every imaginable means to annihilate the German people. By using leaflets he is trying to grind down our spirit to resist and with false ration cards and banknotes he is trying to generate disorder in the Reich. This enemy propaganda thus hopes that Germany - militarily invincible in 1918 -will fall apart from within'.

By February, 1944, it is doubtful whether the Germans required leaflets to tell them that the Reich was falling apart, both from within and without. Harris would have chuckled over that one and probably considered Himmler to be as stupid as those in the British government who insisted that the damned things should be loaded in millions into his bombers. He would certainly have appreciated the pun in connection with the German word for 'drop' -*Abwurf*, which also means 'offal' or 'refuse'; (and it is unlikely that the humourless head of the SS did so either, otherwise he would have made use of it).

The Great Ingratitude

It was hardly surprising that the Nazis resorted to their customary ruthless methods by announcing in the same decree that anyone passing off, or trying to pass off, a fake banknote or ration card would be regarded as a 'war economy criminal', a 'national parasite' of the lowest order and severely punished.

Fully aware that dissuasion by terror was an almost infallible weapon when dealing with his own people, Himmler went on to state in the same decree:

'I announce such sentences with a clear conscience. We have no wish to condemn people to death, but when this is necessary for the well-being of the Reich we cannot afford to show mercy'.

He then promised 'special treatment' for the worst offenders and in less serious cases incarnation in a concentration camp. 'Special treatment' usually meant a bullet. Himmler, artful as always, pointed out that the fakes could readily be distinguished from the genuine article by those who were in the know and hastened to add that the tell-tale characteristics would not be revealed to the public. In other words, if you found any sort of leaflet or voucher you handed it in - or suffered the consequences.

Bearing in mind that the French and the Belgians (up until they succumbed in 1940), the Russians and the Americans were also engaged in extensive leaflet-launching campaigns, it was only to be expected that the psychological approach varied somewhat according to its origins. As we are dealing with Bomber Command we shall naturally concentrate on the material produced by the British, but at the same time it might be interesting to have a glance at others as well, including some of Germany's own efforts.

On the whole British propaganda aimed at Germany itself was, particularly in the earlier years of the war, somewhat unconvincing, but then, one might ask, how could anyone conjure up effective propaganda against a traditionally militaristic nation which had carried all before it and really believed itself to be invincible? Goebbels, on the other hand, had long practised the art and become highly skilful in its execution, having realised early on in his Nazi career the value of the mass media (he was the first propagandist to fully appreciate its potential) as an instrument for fashioning the malleable German mind. Although his written material, much less in volume than that of the British, was on the whole sharper and more penetrating, it no more succeeded in weakening British morale than did the efforts of the Political Warfare Executive to weaken that of the Germans. Goebbels simply did not understand the never-say-die attitude of a freedom-loving people like the British when faced with possible defeat at the hands of the monstrous tyranny represented by Nazism; and as for Britain's own weak attempts to make the Germans believe, up to the third year of the War, that all was not as rosy for them as it looked, it should be said that the Political Warfare Executive received little assistance from their government's ministers about how they ought to go about their task; and this was because the government had initially no clear conception as to how it intended to conduct the War.

However, raw German nerves were touched now and again, as in a British leaflet which claimed - true or false? - that large sums of money had been deposited by top Nazis in remote foreign banks, just in case their dreams of world hegemony were shattered and they had to seek asylum in sympathetic lands. The RAF information sheet in question told the people that Goebbels and Goering had each more than 30 million marks stashed away in South America and Japan.

The first British leaflets were both honest and optimistic - but, as things were, what else could they be? They repeatedly told everyone all over Europe, including the Germans, that Hitler could not and would not win the War. Perhaps the majority of Britons believed this, or tried their level best to believe it, but on the Continent such pronouncements were regarded merely as empty waffle from a proud nation which would soon fall as all the others had fallen; and in the summer of 1940, when it was assumed by those already vanquished that only a narrow strip of water temporarily delayed the bludgeon which had pounded them into rapid submission, they could hardly be censured for thinking as they did.

But, as the dust began to settle after Dunkirk, as London began to suffer as Warsaw and Rotterdam had done, and as the RAF began to hit back, the attitude of the conquered peoples underwent a change. Leaflets (and BBC broadcasts) took on a new meaning as they now came from a nation which was no longer unfamiliar with Hitler's war machine - and was fighting back, apparently with more determination and success than they had done. RAF Fighter Command had actually repulsed the hitherto indomitable enemy and Gt. Britain had thereby gained a new respect; here was a country which did not intend to lie down, a country which represented the last bastion of freedom in Europe and was at that moment the only hope - not much, but some, and it was a hope which

Ref. page 281

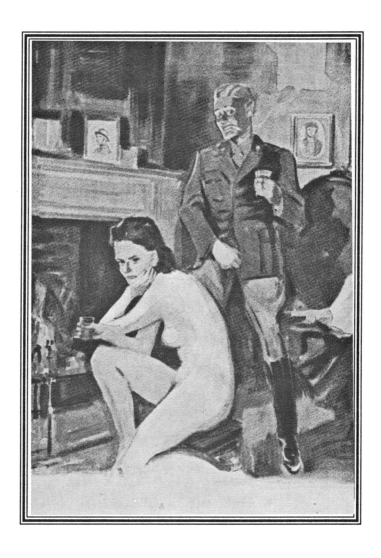

Ref page 281

Ref page 281

increased as the sound of RAF engines in European skies was heard with growing frequency ...

The first British leaflet dropped on Germany carried the heading:

WARNING!

and beneath it the words:

A MESSAGE FROM GREAT BRITAIN TO THE GERMAN PEOPLE It began by stressing Hitler's broken guarantees and the British government's obligation to declare war when Poland was invaded; and went on to quote from the speech the Führer had made in the Sports Stadium in Berlin in September, 1938:
'We have no further territorial demands in Europe'.

It was then pointed out that the war was totally unnecessary as Germany was threatened by no one; no one had objected to the reoccupation of the Rhineland, to the *Anschluss* or the bloodless return of the Sudetenland to the Reich. But after that Hitler had impinged upon the independence of non-German peoples and by so doing had condemned Germany to what was going to be a costly and ghastly war which she could not hope to win. He had completely deceived everyone, his own subjects included. Yet the British felt no animosity towards them, the German people.

The leaflets which followed in close succession concentrated on Germany's inability to wage a prolonged war because she already stood on the verge of bankruptcy. Gt. Britain and her allies, on the other hand, possessed immeasurable reserves of manpower, armaments and raw materials and were much too strong to suffer defeat. (#)

The German people had the right to insist on peace. Britain and France wanted the War to stop and were prepared to negotiate with a German non-Nazi government which was similarly disposed.

The few Polish leaflets which were dropped over the German armies in the short-lived *Fall Weiss* campaign ('Plan White', Hitler's code-name for the invasion of Poland) were written in the same

(#) It was not known then that the German manpower problem would be solved to a large extent by the recruitment of slave labour from all over Europe and that foodstuffs and raw materials would be seized at will.

The Great Ingratitude

vein, and even more naïve, as they asked the rapidly advancing German soldiers to demand that the War should end, that they should throw away their weapons and surrender. By so doing they would get rid of that madman Hitler and the tyranny he represented. French leaflets told the Germans that the whole world was rising against the Führer, who would be struck down eventually, no matter how long it took.

In those early days it appeared that the Allies failed to appreciate the situation and, propaganda-wise, were merely banging their heads against a solid wall. They insisted on distributing material meant to reveal Hitler's lies at their very worst. A good example was an extract from a speech he had made on October 20, 1933 (leaflet delivered in November, 1939):

'Do you really believe we are bringing up our young men, on whom we all depend for the future, to have them slaughtered on the field of battle? Not one single person amongst us has any intention of going to war with Poland over the Corridor'.

Then a quotation from his address to the Reichstag on May 31, 1935:

'Germany has a non-aggression pact with Poland which is a worthwhile contribution to peace in Europe. We have only one desire, and that is to strengthen our bonds of friendship with the Poles'.

The Germans, of course, were well aware of such utterances. But they had raised no objections to the rape of Poland, and were unlikely to do so in November, 1939, when it was all over. One monotonous leaflet followed another, more or less repeating the same theme: Gt. Britain's aim was the establishment of a new and peaceful Europe, but who prevented this? The Nazi government, because it had robbed Germany's neighbours of their freedom and enmeshed Germany in a war. Gt. Britain's goal was the annihilation of the brutal and aggressive spirit of Nazism, which craved for the conquest of other peoples; if the Germans really wanted freedom, they had to rebel against the Nazi system and elect a peace-loving government.

German leaflets often tried to play one ally against another. At the beginning of 1940, during the so-called 'Phoney War', French troops in their defensive positions were inundated with a sheet showing on one side a wounded Frenchmen sheltering in battle with dead or dying comrades all around him as he held a photograph of his wife or girlfriend in his hand. At the top was written: 'Où le Tommy est-il resté?' ('Where is the Tommy?') and the second side showed exactly where the Tommy ref pages was - in a bedroom with the (now naked) lady depicted on the photograph. 276/277 He stood with a glass in one hand and with the other was manipulating his flies. The Germans seemed to think that such an approach demoralised Allied troops and led to friction amongst them.

In March, 1940, Bomber Command crews tossed out a big batch of a leaflet of which the title was both clever and apt:

GESTAPOLEN

(a juxtaposition of 'Gestapo' and 'Polen' (the German for 'Poland'). ref page 278

The text began by quoting the words of Gauleiter Greiser: 'The fate of the Poles will be hard but just'; and then went on to describe what was really happening to them: the reign of terror conducted by the Gestapo and the SS - thousands of innocent citizens murdered, the whole land laid waste, starvation rampant, fathers imprisoned, children transported to the Reich as slave labour, mothers to Central Poland, concentration camps everywhere. The reverse side of the same leaflet, also headed 'Gestapolen', showed a huge, gorilla-like member of the SS, wearing the cruellest of expressions as he strode down a burning Polish street, a revolver in one hand and a whip in the other and with dead civilians in his wake. Above the picture appeared the words: 'They devastate whole countries and this they call peace', and beneath it: 'Is this the kind of *Lebensraum* you are fighting for?'

In May, 1940, the Germans again indulged in their then frequent practice of trying to jeopardise Anglo-French relations and to create breaches between French and British troops. One leaflet asked the French for whom they were fighting and told them it was better to live for France than to die for England. They should surrender - they would be well treated. When their situation became desperate another leaflet told them that their government was making them continue the struggle only so that many of its members could escape across the Channel. Why didn't they show the white flag? (It was, of course, not long before they did so).

Once Gt. Britain stood on her own Bomber Command

The Great Ingratitude

leaflets underwent a change both in tone and content and sought to remind the Germans of the untapped power that the UK had at her disposal. One which was delivered in August, 1940, just before the Battle of Britain, was addressed to the citizens of the capital of the Reich:

CITIZENS OF BERLIN!
Are you not yet aware of the situation?

It went on to ask if they had lost their powers of reason. Did they really believe (as they were told by their rulers) that Britain, with a population of 47 millions, faced the Axis' 200 millions? Had they forgotten there was such a thing as the British Empire, in which 492 millions were united against Hitler? Did they not realise that out of Hitler's claimed 200 millions at least 80 millions were conquered peoples who loathed their oppressors and were waiting for their chance? Had they also forgotten that the entire industrial and agricultural production of North and South America would be mobilised against Germany? Did they really believe Goebbels when he told them that Gt. Britain was powerless and starving and cowed and would submit in a matter of days? Had they forgotten that the Royal Navy was mightier than all the rest of Europe's navies put together? That the Royal Air Force was flying all over Germany and in July alone had dropped 27,000 bombs on military targets in the Ruhr and the Rhineland? The bombs which fell with the leaflet they were now reading provided them with proof that the war, which Hitler had started, was being continued and that if they hoped to defeat Gt. Britain by means of blockade, they should consider certain facts: the blockades were not working. For almost a year Raeder and Goering had been making great efforts in this direction, yet the Royal Navy, the Merchant Navy and the RAF were all much larger than they had been in September, 1939 - and food stocks, too, had increased substantially.

It was then pointed out that the British could hardly believe that Hitler was stupid enough to attempt to invade the UK. Gt. Britain was not Norway. Such a foolhardy attempt would signify the end of the war and the end of Adolf Hitler; and when and how the war ended would be decided by Gt. Britain - and with her the entire world!

This was because Hitler had blundered; supported by his military might and Gestapo brutality he expected everyone to admire him as a great 'conqueror'. But everyone detested him and his national

WANTED

FOR INCITEMENT TO

MURDER

Ref page 286

The Great Ingratitude

The Battle of the Atlantic is being lost!

The reasons why:

1. German U-boats, German bombers and the German fleet sink and seriously damage between them every month a total of 700 000 to 1 million tons of British and allied shipping.

2. All attempts at finding a satisfactory means of defence against the German U-boats or the German bombers have failed disastrously.

3. Even President Roosevelt has openly stated that for every five ships sunk by Germany, Britain and America between them can only build two new ones. All attempts to launch a larger shipbuilding programme in America have failed.

4. Britain is no longer in a position to secure her avenues of supply. The population of Britain has to do with about half the ration that the population of Germany gets. Britain, herself, can only support 40 % of her population from her own resources in spite of the attempts made to increase the amount of land under cultivation. If the war is continued until 1942, 60 % of the population of Britain will starve!

All this means that starvation in Britain is not to be staved off. At the most it can be postponed, but whether starvation comes this year or at the beginning of next doesn't make a ha'porth of difference. Britain must starve because she is being cut off from her supplies.

Britain's losing the Battle of the Atlantic means Britain's losing the war!

Ref page 287

socialist dictatorship would perish because the entire outside world was hostile to it and the hate of the millions suffering under his yoke was increasing all the time.

The Berliners were reminded that they used to be respected and perhaps they could now consider how they might work towards Germany's salvation. In the coming winter of war, as in many war winters yet to come, they would see that Gt. Britain had been right when she said:

'The war will last as long as Hitler's régime!'

The back of the leaflet outlined a number of facts - 'known to the world at large' - which were designed to make the Germans realise the hopelessness of their position. British Merchant Navy tonnage had increased by seven million tons in less than a year; between mid-June and August, 450 German aircraft had been shot down over England; in an attack on a convoy on August 8, 60 out of 400 Luftwaffe aircraft had been destroyed for the loss of only two small ships and 16 RAF fighters (in OKW communiqués these figures had been reversed); the Berliners were reminded of Goering's promise that not a single bomb would fall on the Ruhr or Berlin, but the text named 24 cities or towns already attacked by Bomber Command, including some in the Ruhr; it was then announced that it would be Berlin's turn soon (this came along on August 25/26 in the form of the 'summer-house raid', Chapter 4); the RAF had dropped 37,000 tons of bombs on Germany in a month and the Luftwaffe a mere 7000 tons on Britain during the same period; heavy contingents of troops had arrived and were continuing to arrive regularly in Gt. Britain from Canada, New Zealand and India - and not a single man had been lost; Canada was building her own warships, bombers, fighters and tanks; India's manufacture of weapons was rising and the same applied to South Africa; additions to the Royal Navy outnumbered losses; in the USA 88% of the population supported rearmament against Hitler irrespective of the cost; the Senate had approved of the calling-up of men between 21 and 31; newspaper baron Hearst, earlier opposed to American intervention in the War, had announced that the USA was on Britain's side against Hitler; the American finance minister had promised Gt. Britain 3000 more American planes every month; US General Pershing had ordered the immediate transfer of 50 US destroyers to the Royal Navy, a piece of news which the American press had warmly welcomed; the pan-American conference held in

The Great Ingratitude

Havana had decreed that no territory in the Western Hemisphere would pass out of the possession of a nation engaged in the War to that of another - that is to say that the Germans would not be allowed to take over French or Dutch or Danish colonies; the leaflet then described what was 'a taste of the cost of war' for the Italian Fleet with its loss of 18 U-boats, two destroyers and two cruisers including the *Bartolomeo Colleoni*, reputedly the world's fastest, but not fast enough to escape the old Australian cruiser *Sydney*.

Finally the leaflet mentioned the bad harvests which were threatening parts of Europe with starvation in the approaching winter. Hitler guaranteed that Germans would not starve - because he intended to plunder food from all the occupied lands - and according to the Hague Convention conquerors are obliged to provide for the conquered. Hitler alone was responsible for the food crisis.

As an invitation to acquire the information denied them by their own rulers the times and wave bands of the BBC's daily transmissions (seven) from London in the German language were listed in the bottom right hand corner.

The great majority of Germans looked on propaganda of this kind as quite laughable and it certainly did not succeed in making any of them quake in their shoes. In August, 1940, they had every reason to believe - and who could have blamed them? - that as a military power they were invincible and no propaganda nonsense from the beleaguered British was going to make them think otherwise. Their illustrious Wehrmacht had swept everything before it and it would continue to do so as it surged across the Channel to deal with the last obstacle that lay in its all-conquering path.

Sometimes German leaflets dropped on Britain were ultimate models of hypocrisy. One of these, dated September 1940, showed a full picture of Churchill, wearing American-type gangster garb and with a machine-gun tucked under his arm (and, of course, with a large cigar in his mouth). It was captioned:

WANTED
FOR INCITEMENT TO MURDER

ref page 2

The reverse side bore the words:

Bomber Command in World War II

'This gangster, who you see in his element in the picture, incites you by his example to participate in a form of warfare in which women, children and ordinary civilians shall take leading parts.
This absolutely criminal form of warfare which is forbidden by the HAGUE CONVENTION
will be punished
according to military law
Save at least your families from the horrors of war!'

The propagandists (British, not German!) did try to display a sense of humour now and again. In December, 1940, when the threat of invasion was diminishing but by no means over, Bomber Command delivered a voucher entitling the holder to a single outward journey from France to England (the word 'single' was emphasised). It stated:

'Members of the German Army, Navy and Air Force are hereby courteously invited to make use of this voucher. A very warm reception with music will be provided, there will be a big fireworks display, a free swimming pool and Turkish baths.   Numerous other forms of entertainment will be laid on and all of these will be put at the disposal of the revered visitors. In consequence of the extremely kind reception planned it is expected that only a handful of the distinguished guests will return home'.

Contrast that with the soberly worded German leaflet of early 1941:

The Battle of the Atlantic is being lost! ref page 284

A British leaflet in April, 1941, describing the tragedy of Belgrade following upon the indiscriminate bombing of Warsaw and Rotterdam, blamed the Germans for 'the invention of total war'. The point was made that weak nations could do little to strike back, but Gt. Britain was not one of those; moreover, the enslaved countries were beginning to rebel and cause the Nazis a multitude of problems:

WHOEVER SOWS THE SEEDS OF HATE
WILL REAP REVENGE

The Great Ingratitude

In FRANCE, so blatantly plundered by the occupiers, they called the Germans 'Colorado beetles', 'grasshoppers' and 'bugs'. The little children in the seaports shouted 'dead fish' to them - in reference to the unsuccessful invasion attempts carried out the previous autumn; and the farmers in Brittany reviled them as 'dung for the next harvest' - assuming further invasion attempts.   **(#)**

In HOLLAND, where in undefended Rotterdam alone Luftwaffe bombs had killed 30,000 civilians in a few minutes the previous May, no German dared to venture alone on to the streets at night. The numerous canals were very deep and had no railings - and hence the German solders and other enemy personnel were referred to as 'corpses on leave'.

In NORWAY, the German Summary Court of Justice had had ten more patriots hanged. The Germans were called 'Christmas tree decorations' because the Norwegians intended to string them up on the big fir trees of their forests when the time came ...

In POLAND, SS terror had been raging since September, 1939. In recent weeks 154 members of the SS and Police - including a Police general - had died in fights with Polish guerillas. On such a foundation Hitler intended to build his 'New Order'. All Germans were asked to think about the situation and never to forget that WHOEVER SOWS THE SEEDS OF HATE WILL REAP REVENGE!

In May, 1941, Bomber Command sent down masses of sheets giving details of the times and wavelengths of all radio transmissions from London in German. Content of each broadcast was included and this ranged from news bulletins to programmes for the soldiers of the Wehrmacht, regular lists of German prisoners of war in British hands (no doubt to encourage people to listen), music, even a magazine programme for women. These transmissions went on practically non-stop from 11.00 until 02.15. The following advice was also given:
'We know that in Germany - in contrast to Gt. Britain, the USA and other

---

(#) In Britain too there were rumours of unsuccessful attempts by the Germans to land troops on the east coast of England, but this was never officially confirmed.

free countries - it is forbidden to listen to foreign stations. But
YOU TOO CAN TUNE IN WITHOUT RUNNING ANY RISKS!
All you need do is take the following precautions:
Close all windows! Place the receiver on a cushion! Don't put it near a
wall! Keep the volume low!
There is no secret way of finding out who is listening to foreign broadcasts.
Be assured that we are constantly broadcasting on several wavelengths, all
of which cannot be jammed at the same time. If it should happen that you
cannot hear us clearly on the station you normally use, then you will find
us on the official German broadcasting service! It's easier still if you have
a separate loop aerial which you can turn to receive the desired station,
because all you have to do is keep on turning it till you hear our
transmission much more distinctly than the one which is trying to disrupt
it. Remember too that the best position changes from time to time'.

During the month which followed a four-page leaflet in
newspaper form headed:

AIRMAIL
Delivered by the Royal Air Force

dealt mainly with the flight of Rudolf Hess to
the UK. It said:
'Hess knew the facts and he saw Germany's defeat as inevitable'.
It then went on to give details about the Deputy-Führer's
journey: during the late evening of May 10 he had landed in the South of
Scotland after flying an unarmed Me 110 from Augsburg. Since then the
entire world had been asking why. The leaflet claimed to provide them
with the answer:
**'You in Germany have been asking the same question and
your government has tried to dismiss the matter by stating that Hess
is mentally deranged, that he is obsessed with idealism and imagines
he can intervene to save England from defeat.**
**Some may believe that but the correct answer is known only
in Gt. Britain, not in Germany; and if it is true that Hess really hoped
to save a nation by his intervention, then that nation is certainly not Gt.
Britain!**
**Of course we already know the answers to many questions
which are bound up with the flight to England, and these are known**

only in Gt. Britain and in Gt. Britain alone, and probably no one will know what they are apart from those who are occupied with the direction of the war against Germany.

As Hitler's second-in-command Hess was familiar with every detail concerning the war, with all the Führer's plans and intentions. Just a few weeks ago, on April 27, this was confirmed in your newspaper the *Essener National-Zeitung*, which reported that there was no facet of German public life with which Hess was not concerned. He had all the figures about the state of production in Germany, about the Battle of the Atlantic, about the present and the future striking power of the RAF, about the British blockade, about the mood of the subjugated peoples and the mood in Germany itself. For these very reasons he was convinced of two things, firstly, that this war will be a long one, and, secondly, that Germany cannot win a long war.

Hess is no welcome guest here in England. We know all about his past and we won't forget it. But he is a useful guest - because *he knows the facts'*.

The front page then gave details about the training of RAF airmen in Canada (Chapter 3) - 67 flying schools were turning out 30,000 graduates per year, who would eventually be posted to all combat areas. After this there was information about what was going on in other parts of the Empire: Australia had trebled her armaments production in six months; little New Zealand had already sent 1430 fliers to the theatres of war; Indian troops had taken 14,000 Italian prisoners in the first few days of the British December offensive in North Africa for the loss of 28 dead and 80 wounded; then came a pronouncement from President Roosevelt: 'The Axis Powers will not win this war. My judgement is based on the latest and most reliable information'.

Page 3 was devoted mainly to the new British 'area bomb' and how it threatened Germany, since its explosive power was five times greater than that of any other bomb in existence. An American journalist, who had witnessed it being tried out, called it an 'area bomb' because one alone was capable of annihilating a huge acreage. A few German cities - so far not many - had already had a taste of this mighty weapon.

A picture showed a 'relatively old and small bomber' - a Whitley, with an example of the huge new bomb lying beside it. The text then warned that the latest British and American aircraft, the Short Stirling

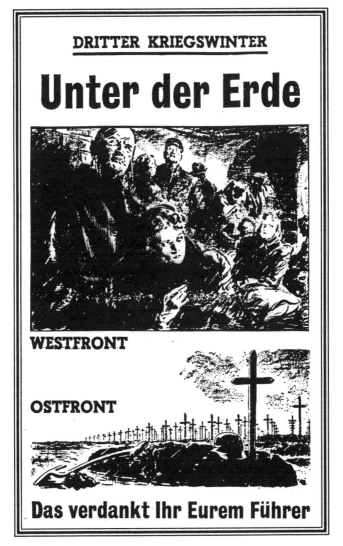

Ref page 294

and the Liberator, for instance, some of which had already flown on operations to Germany, were machines with twice the wingspan of the Whitley and could carry four times her bombload. Further, they could fly from England to Warsaw and back without refuelling.

The Germans were then invited to read the account of an RAF pilot who, from the air, had observed the explosion of one of the new bombs:

'When it exploded a huge jet of flame shot upwards to form a red crown of fire about half-a-mile across and a volcano-like eruption sent buildings up into the air. Even at a distance of 10 miles it was a frightening sight. I have already taken part in 31 bombing raids but have never witnessed anything to compare with the destructive power of this bomb'.

And what about the German bombers? How were they faring? In their night attacks on British towns they were suffering increasing losses each week. In March (1941), 49 had been shot down, in April 87, and in the first fortnight of May the figure had soared to 141.

Another item referred yet again to the bombing of Warsaw and then of Rotterdam on May 13, 1940, when 30,000 men, women and children were needlessly killed. But this time they quoted the reason for such atrocities as explained by two German generals. First of all General Quade on Belgrade:

"We must not underestimate the effect on morale of the masses of the civilian population when they have been subjected to attacks by the Luftwaffe".

Secondly, the words of Field Marshal Kesselring on April 25, 1941:

"In my opinion the goal of total war will have been attained by the Luftwaffe when the will to resist amongst civilian population has been so broken that occupation of their country can be achieved more or less without fighting".

In May, 1941, savage losses were being suffered by British merchant shipping at the hands of the U-boat wolf packs in the Western Approaches, so Page 4 of the same leaflet made much of the fact that the British navy had sent the boats of the three ace captains,

Bomber Command in World War II

Kretschmer, Prien and Schepke, to the bottom. A picture showed the first of the trio, the 'Wolf of the Atlantic', stepping ashore in a British port as a prisoner of war. Once again play was made of the *Wir fahren gegen England* theme ('We are marching against England'), to which was added 'But they didn't return home'. Then the leaflet asked what had happened to the other two illustrious commanders, whom Hitler had also decorated with the Knight's Cross and Oak Leaves. Just as they hadn't known about Kretschmer's fate, they didn't know that Schepke was dead. And as for the most famous of them all, Prien? Where was he? Recently no one had heard anything about him. (The inference was obvious).

While the German armies were racing across Russia in apparently unstoppable fashion the Soviets dropped a leaflet addressed to the ordinary soldiers which was intended to inform them of Hitler's deplorable behaviour. He had accused the Russians of not adhering to the non-aggression pact, which, they said, was a blatant lie. The soldiers were then told that many of their comrades were turning their backs on the Führer and deserting to them. The great Red Army guaranteed their safety and even offered them the hand of friendship.

A sheet which may have had more effect fell amongst the hard-pressed and suffering German troops in that dreadful first winter of the campaign. It showed a picture of a German soldier knee-deep in snow in an endless white wilderness and asked what on earth he was doing there:

'Through snowstorms and fire you are marching eastwards. Your comrades lie in countless graves behind you. With each passing hour the numbers of your dead are mounting and with them the numbers of widows and orphans in your homeland. Each day the frost gets keener, the cold is becoming unbearable, your sufferings are becoming more acute. Where do you think all this is going to end up?'

In January, 1942, an Anglo-American leaflet was distributed over France in order to boost morale. It consisted of a picture of the Statue of Liberty with the words:

'To the country which gave us "la Liberté" we shall give it back'.

In the spring of 1942 a Bomber Command leaflet entitled:

THIRD WINTER OF THE WAR BENEATH THE GROUND ref page 29

provided two illustrations. The first was of the Home Front, with the German civilians cowering in a deep 'bunker', and beneath it and captioned 'Eastern Front', lines of endless German graves which stretched to the horizon. At the foot of the page were printed the words:

'For all this you can thank your Führer'

Another, delivered at about the same time, showed a picture of a German city in 1918, busy with people and traffic and with an explanatory note:

'In 1918 Germany surrendered when the war was obviously lost. The German Army returned home to an undamaged Fatherland. Germany had lost a war, but it had not sacrificed its life and its future'.

Immediately beneath it a second illustration, this time of a city in ruins:

'This is what many German cities now look like and what all German cities will look like if Germany allows Hitler to continue this war to the bitter end'.

By June, 1942, the Allies could rub home to the German population one or two of their victories and the big attack on Cologne was no exception. The leaflet was headed in huge letters:

THE LUFTWAFFE'S HEAVIEST RAIDS FAR EXCEEDED BY THE RAF MORE THAN 1 0 0 0 BOMBERS IN A SINGLE OPERATION

The text ran:

Ref page 296

The Great Ingratitude

'During the night of May 30/31 the RAF launched an attack against Cologne with well over 1000 aircraft. The operation was concentrated into 90 minutes and the German defences were simply unable to cope with the onslaught.

Prime Minister Churchill said in a message to the Commander in Chief of Bomber Command on May 31:
...This proof of the growing strength of British air power is a warning of what is going to happen to one German city after the other...'.

The leaflet ended by reporting that two nights later the RAF had attacked the Ruhr with a second 1000+ bomber raid. Then the ominous words:

'The RAF Offensive in its new form has begun'

An interesting Russian leaflet cascaded in large numbers on to German lines in the summer of 1942. It depicted an encaged gorilla, unmistakably a caricature of Adolf himself, wearing a mad expression, with blood-stained paws, Nazi insignia and all. The cage carried an identifying label - 'Gorilla Adolf' - and warned that this creature was rabid.

ref page 295

At the bottom were printed the words:

'THIS IS WHERE HE BELONGS. THIS IS WHERE HE'LL END UP!'

In January, 1943, as more and more evidence of Nazi crimes came filtering through, a further attempt was made via the RAF to inform the German people of what their rulers were doing in Occupied Europe. Entitled 'MASS MURDER' the leaflet gave details of the diminishing Jewish populations in Germany, Austria, Czechoslovakia, Poland, Holland, Belgium, France, Yugoslavia, Romania, Greece and Norway through mass murder in camps and elsewhere. The situation was summarised by stating that well over a million European Jews had already been extirpated. But the whole civilised world stood in judgement and the Allies had, on December 17, 1942, published a declaration signed by representatives of Gt. Britain, America and the Soviet Union which ran: 'From every country occupied by Germany, Jews are being transported to Eastern Europe under the most hellish conditions imaginable. In Poland, which the Nazis have made their greatest slaughter-house, the Jews, apart from a few skilled workers who can be employed in the armaments industry, are being driven from the ghettos established by the invaders. Nothing has since been heard of the deportees. Those who are fit are slowly worked to death in forced labour camps, while the aged and the frail are starved to death or executed in large numbers. Hundreds of thousands of men, women and children have become victims of the vilest atrocities committed in cold blood.

This bestial and systematic extermination of innocent human beings only serves to strengthen the resolve of all freedom-loving peoples to eradicate completely this barbarism practised by Hitler. The governments which have signed the afore-mentioned declaration swear to ensure that no person responsible for these crimes will escape punishment'.

Page 1 of the leaflet ended by quoting, in heavy print, the words written in the political journal *Zeitschrift für Politik* by SS Brigade Commander Dr K W Best in June, 1942:

'The extermination of foreign nationalities is quite acceptable if it is carried out in its entirety'.

The reverse side of the same leaflet dealt with Hitler's maniacal obsession with 'the Jewish problem' and some of the principal reasons for it:

STRENGTH THROUGH FEAR

'Why does Hitler, after he has plundered and decimated the Jews, wish to wipe them out with hunger and gas and fire and sword?
These mass murders, unparalleled in history, are smearing the name of Germany in monstrous fashion. And the numbers of those responsible is so large that it will be impossible for the victors to distinguish between the guilty and the innocent. That is the intention of Hitler and his SS. The Nazis aim to kindle the hate of the whole world against the whole German race so that they can say to the German people: "The world will give you tit for tat. If you do not wish to be exterminated, as we are exterminating the others, you must fight for Hitler".
Hitler's propaganda tells you that you have all made

common cause, that the German people as well as the SS are up to their eyes in it. It is Hitler who intends to implicate every individual German in the outrages committed by the SS.

Because the German people are beginning to doubt the victory they have been promised, then the German people have to be 'united', united in the fear of the consequences which will result from the most dreadful crimes ever perpetrated.

The Allies are not waging a war of annihilation of people against people, of race against race, as the Nazis are doing. Unlike the Nazis, they are not trying to wipe out foreign nations and their cultures. But whoever supports the theory and practice of the SS puts himself in the same category as they, and will answer in the same way. Justice demands that no one, whether guilty of a crime or an accessory to it, will escape.

Therefore: Every German must now decide if he wants to share the fate of the Nazi criminals. We are keeping accounts.'

Two months later a leaflet showed a burning Stalingrad and beneath it the frozen corpse of a German soldier lying in the snow. On the other side, in huge heavy capitals:

GAS

and following it, the words:

'On April 21, 1943, the British government made this announcement: ...According to reports we have received from various sources Hitler is preparing to use gas on the Eastern Front. The British Government is therefore repeating the warning it issued last year: each time poisonous gas is employed against Gt. Britain's ally Russia the same weapon will be used extensively by Gt. Britain on centres of German armament and against ports and other military targets throughout Germany. Britain's preparations for launching gas attacks are now complete and the measures required to combat any German retaliation have been put into effect all over the country...'.

Bomber Command in World War II

In early 1943 German troops on the Eastern Front read a news-sheet dropped by the Russian Air Force which was intended to demoralise them further at a time when they were retreating almost everywhere:

'THE SECOND FRONT IS COMING!
GERMAN SOLDIERS!

DID WE NOT TELL YOU, that Hitler's blitzkrieg in Russia would fail?
THAT IS EXACTLY WHAT HAS HAPPENED.

DID WE NOT TELL YOU, that Hitler would never take Moscow?
In the winter of 1941-42 Hitler's army was crushed and thrown back hundreds of kilometres.

DID WE NOT TELL YOU, that Stalingrad would become the grave of hundreds of thousands of German soldiers?
Indeed Stalingrad has become the grave of two German armies, Paulus's Sixth Army and the Fourth Panzer Army.

DID WE NOT TELL YOU, that Hitler's spring and summer offensives would only mean that more of you would be sacrificed needlessly?; that we would win back much of the Russian territory you had occupied and your divisions would be wiped out?

THAT TOO IS WHAT HAS HAPPENED.

You have lost your elite divisions. The Romanian, Hungarian and Italian armies in Russia no longer exist. In the autumn of 1942 and during the winter that followed the Red Army not only liberated the territory occupied by the Germans in 1942, but a whole string of towns and districts which had been in your hands for about 18 months.

DID WE NOT TELL YOU, that Germany would become the theatre of the war in the air?
THAT TOO HAS COME TO PASS.

DID WE NOT TELL YOU: don't delude yourselves that the Americans will not come.

The Americans have landed in Africa and with the British they are defeating Rommel.

AND NOW WE ARE TELLING YOU:

THE SECOND FRONT IS COMING!

DON'T BELIEVE what Goebbels tells you - that the Allies do not possess enough ships to effect a landing in Europe. They already have more than 56 battleships, 150 cruisers, 480 destroyers and thousands of merchant ships which will be used as military transports. In 1943 America alone will launch 2500 vessels totalling 20 million tons.

DON'T BELIEVE that German U-boats will be able to wreak havoc amongst the ships of the huge Invasion fleet. THE U-BOATS PROVED TO BE QUITE INCAPABLE of preventing the Americans and the British from transporting a great army across the Atlantic to Africa. They completely failed to thwart the passage of one million men and thousands of tanks, aircraft and guns from the USA and Canada to England. THEY WILL BE EVEN LESS CAPABLE of obstructing the landing of Allied troops on the coast of Europe.

DON'T BELIEVE that an 'Atlantic Wall' will render the coast of Western Europe 'impregnable'. The history of this war has shown that there are no fortifications in existence which can withstand modern artillery and heavy tank divisions. The coastline which stretches from Narvik to Crete is 1500 kilometres long and all of it is open to such an attack. And there are no 'Walls' which will be able to cope with it.

DON'T BELIEVE all this tittle-tattle about misunderstandings and disagreements amongst the Allies which, you are told, will jeopardise the Second Front. The close bonds that exist between Russia, Britain and America have been forged not only through co-operation and mutual aid, but also in the blood spilt in the battles in Africa and at Stalingrad, and now these bonds will be strengthened even further as we batter Hitler both in the East and the West. Besieged on all fronts

Bomber Command in World War II

HITLER WILL COLLAPSE
GERMAN SOLDIERS!   THE SECOND FRONT IS COMING
Hitler and his gang have already lost the War.   Free yourselves from
these ruffians, before it is too late.

PUT AN END TO THE WAR!
GIVE YOURSELVES UP TO THE RUSSIANS!'

One of the most interesting leaflets delivered by Bomber Command (in July, 1943) was in fact German in origin, and entitled 'A GERMAN LEAFLET'. In their own introduction the British propagandists explained that it was actually a text written by student members of the banned anti-Nazi *Weisse Rose* ('White Rose') group and distributed by them (3000 copies) around Munich University on February 18, 1943. Six of the students involved, including Hans Scholl and his sister Sophie and Christoph Probst, were hanged just five days later, while others were imprisoned or sent to the Eastern Front.   Somehow or other a copy of the proscribed material found its way to England and subsequently millions of them were dropped all over Germany.

The 700-word **'Manifesto of the Munich Students'** was printed in full.   Here is a brief summary:

'Our entire nation is shattered by the defeat at Stalingrad, where 330,000 of Germany's sons were needlessly and irresponsibly sacrificed, thanks to the ingenious strategy of the First World War corporal . Führer, we thank you!

The German people are restless.   Are we going to go on trusting such a dilettante with the fate of our armies?   Are we going to keep on losing our German youth just to satisfy the lust for power of this vile clique who govern us?   No, not any longer!

The day has come when accounts must be settled, when an end must be put to the most abominable tyranny which our people has ever had to endure.   In the name of the entire German people we demand to be freed from Adolf Hitler.   In our most formative years the SA and the SS have sought to reduce us to uniformity, to anaesthetize us, to prevent us thinking as individuals in order to create in us blind and stupid allegiance to the Führer.

The Great Ingratitude

We have only one message: Fight against the Party! Get out of all Party organizations, whose aim is to seal our political lips. What we want is to be able to learn the truth about everything and have freedom of mind and speech! We shall not be put off by threats or the closure of our universities. Every single one of us must fight for our future, our freedom and our honour.

Freedom and honour! For ten years Hitler and his cronies have debased the meaning of these two noble words as only dilettantes can. The frightful bloodbath for which they are responsible has opened the eyes of even the most stupid German and the name of Germany will be reviled for ever if German youth does not finally rebel, seeks revenge and crushes its tormentors, and helps to build a new Europe.

Students! The German people is depending on us to inspire the eradication of the national-socialist terror. Those who died at Stalingrad are imploring us: Go to it, the signal fires are already smoking!

Our people are ready to rise up against the enslavement of Europe by national-socialism. They want to see freedom and honour restored!'

With the growing Allied initiative on all fronts leaflets now tended to concentrate on Germany's approaching doom. In August, 1943, one dropped by Bomber Command and entitled *Kölnische Zeitung* (name of the famous Cologne daily, the idea being to provide the Germans with the true facts which they ought to have been given by their newspaper) listed setbacks as they occurred each month:

NOVEMBER 1942	Defeat at El Alamein The Allies land in North Africa Russians advance towards Stalingrad
DECEMBER 1942	Russians break through on the middle Don
JANUARY 1943	Tripoli falls Caucasus evacuated by Germans

Bomber Command in World War II

FEBRUARY 1943	Sixth Army liquidated at Stalingrad 240,000 dead, 91,000 prisoners Russians break through at Woronesch
MARCH 1943	General retreat in Russia Annihilation of Ruhr industry begins
APRIL 1943	Defeat at El Akarit 10 Million kg of bombs fall on German industrial targets
MAY 1943	Panzer Army wiped out in Africa, 248,000 prisoners The whole of North Africa in Allied hands 12 million kg of bombs fall on German industrial targets
JUNE 1943	16 million kg of bombs fall on German industrial targets Russian counter-offensive begins Sicily invaded Fall of Mussolini

In December, 1943, the first side of an American leaflet consisted of a few words in large, bold type, stating that two years earlier, on December 11, 1941, Adolf Hitler had declared war on the USA. The reverse side showed what he had let himself in for:

'Hitler's declaration of war means that the military might of a nation of 130 million people is rallied against him. In two years the American Army has grown rapidly in strength and now numbers 7,700,000 men.

Hitler's declaration of war has mobilised America's huge industrial production to full capacity. Every five minutes the USA turns out one aircraft and every day it builds five merchant ships. Between January, 1940, and October, 1943, 65,000 tanks left the factories together with a million military vehicles, 170,000 pieces of artillery and 1½ million machine guns.

Ref page 306

Hitler's declaration of war means that the American Navy, with over 800 warships and 2,000,000 men, will now fight alongside the British Navy.

TO-DAY THE USA ARE FIGHTING WITH THIRTY-THREE

OTHER NATIONS AGAINST HITLER'S GERMANY'

Naturally the Invasion, not an opportunity to be missed, inspired quite a flood of Allied propaganda. Shortly after the landings the USAAF dropped a leaflet headed 'The Opening of the Fourth Front' showing pictures of troops storming up the Normandy beaches and of some of the senior British and American officers standing on French soil - General Eisenhower, Air Marshall Sir Arthur Tedder and General Sir Bernard Montgomery. Beneath the picture was printed the announcement made by the Supreme Allied Command in London on June 6:

'Under the command of Supreme Commander Eisenhower the landing of Allied Armies began this morning on the north coast of France'.

A description of the operation followed, no doubt intended to reveal to the Germans the huge armies and the vast amount of *matériel* possessed by the Allies, all of it, or at least most of it, now on its way to Germany:

'Just one day after the liberation of Rome over 5000 ships, supported by 11,000 aircraft, took part in the landings. Air bombardments unparalleled in their ferocity were effected by 1000 heavy RAF bombers against large batteries on the Atlantic Wall during the preceding night and large numbers of airborne troops and paratroops were landed behind the German lines. Infantry, protected by 640 warships, were brought ashore by landing craft and moved forward under a huge umbrella of fighter aircraft. The crew of a Liberator bomber, there to observe the scene, reported that the sky was practically invisible owing to the density of aircraft and that the Channel appeared to be bridged by ships from one side to the other'.

The leaflet then went on to describe the action in some detail, stressing that opposition from the Luftwaffe was inconsequential and that the presence of U-boats was hardly noticed. Considering the magnitude of the task, Allied losses in both personnel and equipment had been extremely light. The already large Allied armies were being reinforced with each passing day and Hitler simply did not have the means to stop them.

A few days later a map of Europe, Anglo-American in origin and with the caption:

FOUR-FRONT-WAR

ref page 304

made it abundantly clear to the Germans that they were being assailed from all sides and on four fronts. Armies were pressing towards them from Italy (Southern Front), France (Western Front), Russia (Eastern Front), while Germany itself (Home Front) was depicted under a deluge of bombs.

The second page sized up the German position:

'EASTERN FRONT.....HOME FRONT......SOUTHERN FRONT
....and now -W E S T E R N   F R O N T

1. EASTERN FRONT
On October 3, 1941, Hitler declared: "Russia is finished". But, just like Napoleon, Hitler was forced to retreat. Now the Russian armies are only 500 kilometres from Königsberg and 650 kilometres from Breslau, and are awaiting the order to begin the last and decisive offensive.

2. HOME FRONT
Four years ago Hitler said: "The war in the West is over", and started a total air war against Gt. Britain. At the same time his U-boats tried to sever the British lines of supply. But the Luftwaffe was defeated and England became the Allies' unsinkable aircraft carrier. Now it is the RAF and the American Air Force which are on the offensive. They have opened a front, a front which so far has never existed: the front above the German homeland, on which, according to the assurances given you by Goering, not a single bomb would fall.

Day and night, from the West and from the South, great Allied air armadas are attacking Germany's heavy industry, her aircraft factories, her oil refineries and the internal lines of communication on which the German plan of defence depends. And now American bombers are also coming from the East. Encirclement of Germany from the air is complete.

<u>3. SOUTHERN FRONT</u>

In the third week of May, Cassino was still being talked about in Berlin as an 'impregnable fortress' and Anzio as a 'second Dunkirk'.

In four weeks the Allies stormed Cassino and defeated Kesselring's army, inflicting losses of 40-50,000 men and taking more than 18,000 German prisoners, including a substantial part of the First Parachute Division. The Allies smashed through the Gustav Line and the Adolf Hitler Line, which had been built up for months on end, overran German positions in the hills and occupied Rome.

Thanks to prolonged and lightly opposed air attacks nearly all road and rail communications were cut. British, American and French warships are operating unopposed along the Italian coast and firing on the German positions. And Italian partisans, who are cutting the German lines of communication in the rear, are showing what men are capable of when they are fighting for their freedom.

Together with the 'impenetrable' Eastern Front and the 'impenetrable' Home Front, the 'impenetrable' Southern Front is falling apart in exactly the same way.

CATASTROPHE IN THE EAST

CATASTROPHE AT HOME

CATASTROPHE IN THE SOUTH

AND NOW THE ALLIES ARE LANDING IN THE WEST

THE FOURTH FRONT HAS BEEN OPENED'

One could hardly blame the professional Allied propagandists for believing that the last three leaflets in particular might have gone some way to convince the Germans that there was no point in continuing with the War. Most of them no doubt agreed, but that was a far cry from being able or willing to do something about it.

The next month (July, 1944) and just after the attempt on the Führer's life, the sorely-pressed Wehrmacht legions in Russia were inundated, by courtesy of the Russian Air Force, with a message from the 'A Free Germany' movement (League of German Officers):

The Great Ingratitude

PEOPLE OF GERMANY!
MEMBERS OF THE WEHRMACHT!
THE DIE IS CAST.

'Brave men have risen against Hitler. They rebelled against his intention to drag his lost war right into the heart of the Fatherland. Further, 20 generals on the Eastern Front have said that they want no more of 'this pointless shedding of rivers of blood', and, with their troops, have laid down their arms.

And now, in Germany itself, responsible-minded generals have joined in the revolt against Hitler. The signal has been given. The uprising of the people over the senseless continuation of a war already lost has found its first expression in the assassination attempt. Now the fire must be fanned throughout the whole nation. Germany must be saved from Hitler and his accomplices.

Hitler empowered the executioner Himmler to annihilate these pioneers of German freedom. That kind of power can be nullified only by the power that lies in the hands of the German people. The latter must not forsake those who took steps to get rid of Hitler. Every blow struck against Hitlerism, no matter who delivers it, is a blow struck against the mortal enemy of our nation, a blow struck in the name of patriotism.

It is only in this way that we can avoid the great misfortune now threatening our people: the continuation of the war and with it the complete ruin of Germany.

Whoever, whether at the front or at home, carries out another order from Hitler or from Himmler, is helping to destroy Germany.

On the other hand all of those who refuse to obey such orders, whether generals or privates, whether managers or workmen, are fighting for Germany's salvation. Everyone must realise that:
If Hitler remains in power, it means war and chaos in Germany. It means that you will all bleed to death.

Hitler has led Germany up a blind alley. In order to divert judgement from himself and his gang, he is ordering Germans to fire on Germans.

Our people must show that they do not wish to be associated either with him or his crimes.

The fight to get rid of him has begun and the thoughts of every honourable German are with those who tried to do so. Do not leave them in the lurch!

Generals, officers, soldiers - all those at the front - stop fighting against the Allies and direct your weapons against Hitler!

Workers and employers engaged in war production - throw down your tools! Germans at the front and at home! Unite yourselves to be free of Hitler! Obey the commands of those who are leading you against him!

WE ARE WITH YOU TO OVERTHROW HITLER!
WE ARE WITH YOU FOR FREEDOM AND PEACE!'

Then came the signatures of the members of the National Committee, including those of such well known personages as the President, Eric Weinert, the Vice-President General Walther von Seydlitz, General Alexander Edler von Daniels, Major Karl Hetz and Lieutenant Heinrich Graf von Einsiedel.

A further plea later the same month arrived from Field Marshal Paulus, who had wished to surrender at Stalingrad long before he did, but was prevented from doing so by Hitler, and felt bitter about the needless loss and the extended suffering of so many of his soldiers:

'A MESSAGE FROM FIELD MARSHAL
PAULUS
TO THE GERMAN PEOPLE
GERMANS!

As a Field Marshal in captivity I feel it is my responsibility to tell my

The Great Ingratitude

comrades who are still fighting, and the whole German nation, that
there is only one way out of the dire situation in which we find
ourselves:
Removing Hitler and ending the war!
The highly professional General von Seydlitz, who was a member of my
Sixth Army, did not, I assure you, desert his troops and go over to the
enemy. That was a wicked lie broadcast by German radio. The truth
is that in the ruins of Stalingrad the General was in a hopeless position,
bereft of ammunition and supplies of all kinds. With the rest of the
Sixth Army he had no option but to surrender.

Herr Himmler is also lying when he tells you that German prisoners
in Russian hands are treated inhumanely and that they are compelled
to concoct propaganda against their own country because a whip is
dangled before them or a gun is pointed at the back of their head. In
spite of the bestial treatment of countless defenceless men, women and
children in the occupied zones of Russia (crimes for which Himmler
is responsible) German prisoners in the Soviet Union are treated   (#)
humanely and correctly.

Here in Russia fatherland-loving Germans of all ranks and stations
have joined the 'A Free Germany' movement to avert further misery
to our people and to show the world that we Germans utterly denounce
Hitler's crimes. One of the first to support this view was General von
Seydlitz who, thanks to the respect in which he was held by his
comrades, became one of the leaders of the movement. With a
common goal in mind - to help the German people in its misery -
hundreds of thousands of German prisoners of war have voluntarily
joined the movement, including thousands of officers and more than
30 generals. The aim of 'A Free Germany' is to re-establish the honour
of the German nation, of a free German nation, so that once more we
can be accepted amongst the civilised countries of the world.

(Signed): Paulus
Field Marshal
Former Commander of Sixth Army'

(#) Bearing in mind the relatively small proportion of Wehrmacht prisoners who returned from
Russia, one is apt to wonder if Paulus had a gun pointing at his own head.

Even with the Nazis' days so obviously numbered German propagandists insisted on appealing to paternal and husband/wife emotions, well exemplified by this picture of the little girl and her letter to her daddy (dropped on American troops in December, 1944).

They still seemed to attach a great deal of importance to creating spite and jealousy, a good example being a leaflet dropped on American troops in France. It compared the high wages of the American factory worker with the miserable lot of the man at the fighting front, and ended with the question:

WHO WANTS THE WAR IN EUROPE TO LAST?
YOU OR HE?

Others were crude and even distasteful:

TWO WAYS OF SPENDING THE WAR

re pages
317/318

depicted a gory battle scene with wounded or dead Americans and on the reverse side an American civilian (identified by the lit-up skyscrapers visible through the window) in the act of seducing a girl on a bed:

When it became abundantly clear that the War could not go on for very much longer leaflets were used to give instructions to the German civilian population, to tell them what was coming and how they were to behave. The following example was a combined effort by Gt. Britain and the USA:

MILITARY GOVERNMENT - GERMANY
PROCLAMATION FROM THE SUPREME COMMANDER
TO THE GERMAN PEOPLE:
'I, General Dwight D Eisenhower, Supreme Commander of the Allied Forces, make the following pronouncement:
1.
The Allied Forces, which are under my Command, have now stepped on to German soil. We come as a victorious army, but not as an

oppressor. In Germany we shall eliminate National Socialism and the German militarism which so often has disrupted the peace of the world. Leaders of the Wehrmacht, officials of the Secret State Police (Gestapo) and all persons who are suspected of having committed crimes and atrocities will be tried in court and, if found guilty, will be punished.

2.

All authority and power is invested in me as Supreme Commander of the Allied Forces and as Military Governor. The Military Government will carry out its duties in accordance with my instructions, and every citizen will obey instantly and without opposition all orders and public announcements made by the said government. Military courts will be set up to convict anyone who breaks the law. Any opposition to the Allied Forces will be severely dealt with.

3.

All German courts and educational establishments will be closed until further notice. People's Courts, Special Courts and SS-Police Courts and all other Courts will cease to function. The resumption of activity in criminal and civil courts and the re-opening of educational establishments will be sanctioned as soon as circumstances allow.

4.

All officials are obliged until further notice to remain in their posts and to observe and carry out all orders issued by the Allied Military Government. This also applies to all workers and employers of all public and private enterprises and to all persons engaged in essential occupations.

DWIGHT D EISENHOWER
Supreme Commander, Allied Forces'

And then, the last leaflet of all, delivered by Bomber Command and the USAAF during the first days of May:

THE END!

GERMAN ARMIES IN HOLLAND, DENMARK AND NORTH-WEST GERMANY SURRENDER UNCONDITIONALLY

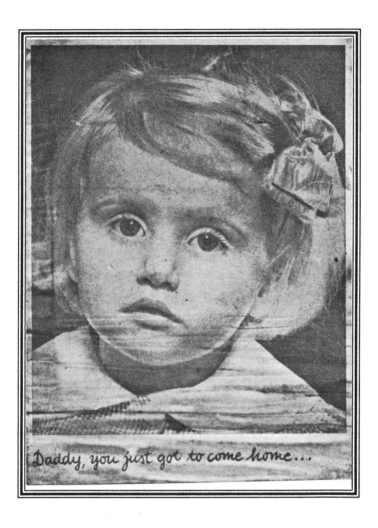

Daddy, you just got to come home...

The Great Ingratitude

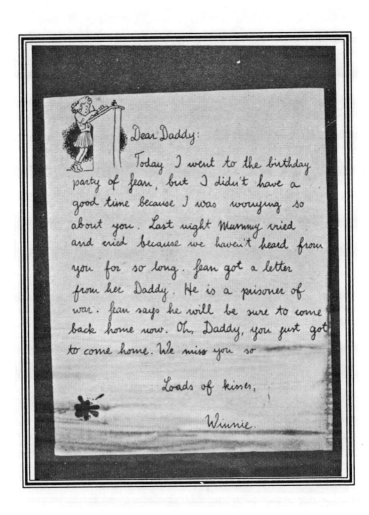

Dear Daddy:

Today I went to the birthday party of Jean, but I didn't have a good time because I was worrying so about you. Last night Mummy cried and cried because we haven't heard from you for so long. Jean got a letter from her Daddy. He is a prisoner of war. Jean says he will be sure to come back home now. Oh, Daddy, you just got to come home. We miss you so

Loads of kisses,

Winnie.

Ref page 311

The Great Ingratitude

Ref page 311

Bomber Command in World War II

Officially hostilities were to cease at 8 pm on Saturday evening, but long before that German troops had called a halt and laid down their weapons. The official Allied communique, issued at 20.15 hours, stated:

'Field Marshal Montgomery has announced to the Supreme Allied Commander that all enemy forces in Holland, North-West Germany and Denmark, also in Heligoland and the Frisian Islands (over one million men) have surrendered to 21st Army Group with effect from 0800 hours on Saturday, British Double Summer Time.'

An accompanying photograph showed Montgomery receiving Admiral von Friedesburg (Admiral of the Fleet and Donitz's right hand man) and his aides outside his tent on Lüneburg Heath, to which they had come to sign the capitulation.

* * *

(#)

So ended what, as far as the Reich itself was concerned, must be labelled a fruitless campaign. Although Bomber Command crews were inclined to grumble that the paper they carried would have accomplished much more had it been replaced by bombs, in actual fact the 1000 million leaflets dropped by them on Germany itself weighed only some 400 tons, and the same weight of high explosive or incendiaries would have contributed little to the damage done by Bomber Command's overall figure of 955,044 tons. At the same time the 5½-year long leaflet delivery entailed much extra effort and organisation apart from the substantial cost in men and machines.

Like the bombing, or in conjunction with it, the leaflets failed to encourage the insurrection which was their aim. But at the time the British, like the Americans and the Russians, had no conception of the degree of mental strangulation in which all but a handful of Hitler's subjects were held. For too many years the Germans had had a plethora of blatant untruths rammed down their gullible throats by the sharp and scheming minds of Goebbels and his underlings; they had become brainwashed into unquestionable obedience to Nazi authority and to it alone; and, as doom approached, they were by then cocooned in a sea of apathy, and by and large no longer cared.

(#) This was followed on May 7 by the unconditional surrender of the Wehrmacht in Eisenhower's headquarters in Rheims and the act of capitulation was repeated on May 8 at the Soviet headquarters in Berlin-Karlshorst. Final and total capitulation took effect from 23.01 hours on May 8.

Chapter 22

WAS IT ALL WORTH IT?

Throughout its short but momentous history Bomber Command seemed fated from the outset, from one source or another, to be a constant target for heated controversy which has not abated with the passing of half-a-century. Moral arguments apart, its most uncharitable opponents questioned the validity of its whole strategy and the extent of its contribution to final victory.

Over and over again the question has been asked whether the policy it adopted and, with a few exceptions, pursued relentlessly until the very end of the war - saturation bombing - and the results achieved therefrom, justified the loss of tens of thousands of valuable young lives, and of thousands of expensive machines with all their complicated electronic equipment (some historians assert that Bomber Command *alone*, not the entire RAF, swallowed up one third of the total wartime budget); whether this policy justified the long training procedures which necessitated the transportation of cadets half-way across the world (Harris estimated it cost an average £10,000 to bring each of them up to operational standard, in present day terms at least £300,000); or the gigantic human and logistical effort required nearly every night, over a three-year period, to launch a big attack against some German city (roughly 70,000 personnel were involved in preparing and executing an 800-heavy bomber raid); whether it crippled the Reich to such a degree as to markedly curtail her war production and bring hostilities to an earlier conclusion than would otherwise have been the case; and did its wrecking of hundreds of barges in 1940, in harbours all along the coast from Holland to Normandy, make Hitler realise what he was up against and help him to decide that he should postpone his conquest of the UK for the time being and first of all dispose of the Soviet Union? Did Bomber Command really play a significant role in sustaining the nation's morale in the dark depressing days up to early 1943? Did Operation *Pointblank* save countless Allied lives during the 1944 landings and thereafter? Did the Command, in Operation *Crossbow,* prevent London and the South-East, the Invasion bases and the Allied armies in France from being pulverised by the V-1 and the V-2? Did its sowing of the waters of the Baltic, the North Sea and parts of the Mediterranean with approximately 50,000 mines, which kept one third of the German Navy engaged in an effort to render these harmless and sent to the bottom or damaged more than 1000 enemy ships, contribute to the ultimate success of the Allied land forces in North Africa and on the Continent of Europe? Did the same operation prevent Swedish ore from reaching Germany and German supplies from reaching Russia? Apart from the general devastation of enemy industry did the dehousing of hundreds of thousands of essential workers, and the regular disruption caused in the lives of millions, adversely affect war production? Was such an authority as Albert Speer right when he said the bombing of German cities tied down, on the homeland, at least 20,000 pieces of artillery and hundreds of fighter aircraft, and caused such a drain on manpower alone that had the raids been much less severe the Nazis might well have knocked the Russians out of the war before the Allies invaded France, with dire consequences for that event? (In this connection we might well note the words of Field Marshal Milch when he addressed a gathering of senior RAF officers after the war: 'The Russians were wrong in complaining at the lack of a Second Front, because the Second Front existed in the form of Bomber Command's Air Offensive. If we had had available in the East all the 8.8 to 12.8 mm guns required at home then the Soviets would have been incapable of carrying out their successful tank attacks and the results would have been disastrous for them. Of the 19,713 guns produced from 1942 until the end of 1944 only 3172 of them went to the army because the rest (84%) had to be diverted to the defence of German cities against the bombing. It is a most interesting point because although the damage your bombers did was very heavy I think the damage you caused by weakening the German army was much more significant'); did the continuous drone of heavy bombers en route for the Reich give hope to the millions enslaved in the occupied territories of Western Europe and encourage them to organised resistance? And finally - perhaps the most significant and certainly the most interesting - question of all: would the Air Offensive against Germany have eventually won the war, with no need for an invasion, as Harris claimed it would?

In view of what he has read in this book so far the reader himself might feel he is in a position to answer all these questions, except the last, to which none of us can know, or ever will know, the definite answer; at the same time it is difficult to accept that, if the Invasion had not taken place till later than it did, and had the weight and ferocity of the bombing been continued for a few weeks - a few months at the most - longer, how any nation on earth could have endured such a cataclysmic experience, especially when there existed not the slightest hope of any respite. Apart from the ultimate effects on morale - although we have already indicated just how resilient the German populace proved itself to be - it became exceedingly difficult, if not downright impossible, to provide 75 million people, of whom 13 million had lost their homes, with even the bare essentials of life when shortages were increasing daily and transport was in a state of chaos. All we can say is that *Rankine*, the code-name for the sudden collapse of Germany as a consequence of the bombing, might well have become a reality had the war gone on for just that little bit longer. An intriguing question but, alas, unanswerable.

Hitler, outlining to his architect Speer in the middle thirties his grandiose plans to rebuild Berlin and all the major cities of Germany on monolithic lines - which, in his view, would serve the twofold purpose of ensuring that his subjects maintained their respect for authority and of intimidating any foreign diplomats who arrived with ideas too big for their boots - ended up by saying: "In ten years from now no one will recognise the Reich." How right Bomber Command was to prove him to be. And even his timing was incredibly accurate, for by the late spring of 1945 Priestley's ravaging `beast' (Chapter 18) had been caged and destroyed; and this time, perhaps, it would never again be allowed to rise like a Phoenix from the ashes of its cities to plague the nations around it ... not in the military sense at any rate.

For it was mainly Bomber Command which turned Germany into a desert. In doing so, from its very first operation when the war was just 45 minutes old and a lone Blenheim took off to reconnoitre shipping along the North German coast and poke a challenging finger at a powerful enemy, till its last operation, the attack by Mosquitoes on Keil on May 2/3, 1945, it flew 389,809 sorties against the enemy and dropped more than 900,000 tons of bombs in the process. It lost 8953 aircraft and 47,268 men killed, with a further 4200 seriously injured. In addition 8300 lost their lives during training - in those days all flying was fraught with danger and it is a sobering thought that one airman in seven died on non-operational duties. It can be calculated that 107 tons of bombs were dropped for every aircraft lost. And what proportion of that load fell on 'worthwhile' targets, or on no targets at all? 80 tons, 70 tons? Perhaps only 60 tons? Worth it? Yes, if the yardstick, the only one, was the significant extent to which they reduced the Nazi potential to continue the War.

Bomber Command in World War II

Of the 23 cities or large towns attacked in the Reich itself (out of the 60 on Harris's 'hit list' and all of which had substantial areas devastated), Bomber Command destroyed a total of almost 35,000 acres with nearly 330,000 tons of bombs - an average of 54%. We have already mentioned what happened to the industrial centres in the Ruhr (Chapter 10) and will confine ourselves here to stating the acreages of destruction wrought in some other towns: Würzburg 89%, Hamburg 75%, Darmstadt 69%, Ludwigshafen 64%, Hanover 60%, and Berlin 33%. When it is considered that the Luftwaffe wrecked only 400 acres of London and 100 of Coventry compared to the 6427 laid waste in Berlin, the 6200 and 2003 respectively in the much smaller cities of Hamburg and Düsseldorf, and between 1000 and 2000 acres in a host of others, some idea of the extent of the total damage might be appreciated. The fact that more than 600,000 civilians were killed and nearly a million injured - although in those trying times no one on the Allied side bemoaned the death of war workers - was quite coincidental and not part of the policy of Bomber Command. Nor was it its intention to hit hospitals and churches and schools, but when you set out to flatten a chosen area in order to curtail the resources being used against you, then it is quite impossible to avoid doing so. As Harris said: 'If you hit everything you will hit something'. And it was by hitting everything that Bomber Command hit the things that mattered. That was how it operated - generally speaking it knew no other way, for harsh and costly experience had taught it that there was no other way - and the critics of its methods ought to be reminded that, as Candlish pointed out, it is war itself which is evil and obscene and, as Dr Noble Frankland maintained as long after the war as 1961, the greatest obscenity of all would have been Great Britain's defeat by one of the most vile régimes ever known. The Second World War had to be won at all costs, which is saying that no punches could be pulled. Bomber Command did not pull any - which sometimes caused it to operate at the extreme limits of sustainability.

It should not be forgotten that in the sombre days of 1940-41, when Britain's armies were suffering reverses everywhere and her Atlantic life-line was in extreme jeopardy, Britain knew she was engaged in a war to the death because defeat loomed like a great black chasm as she teetered close to its edge; hence the creation of a large bomber force was regarded as the only way of hitting back by attacking the enemy beyond the Rhine. At that time practically every nation on earth would have backed Germany to win and the maxim 'war does not always decide who's right - only who's left' had a particularly ominous ring about

The Great Ingratitude

it in the face of Germany's apparently indomitable military strength. The might of right was then a frail reed to clutch and there was little doubt in most minds as to who would be left.

We have just discussed above what might have transpired had the Air Offensive gone on for a further few weeks, and by the same yardstick it could be argued confidently, almost indubitably, that had Harris had at his command in 1942 or 1943 the bomber strength he possessed in late 1944 and early 1945, Europe would have known peace much earlier than May 1945; and his prediction that the function of the Allied armies would have been reduced to that of a mere occupying police force could have been realised. Although it is generally accepted that it was the two atom bombs dropped on Hiroshima and Nagasaki which brought about a sudden end to the struggle in the Far East, these added only a minimal 3% to the already existing devastation (Chapter 18) and it is well within the realms of possibility that a few more heavy raids with conventional bombs would have achieved the same purpose. I think we should realise that America's strategic carpet bombing of the Japanese mainland, conducted on a massive scale against fire-prone targets, was reminiscent of Hamburg and Darmstadt and Dresden and a belated but categorical admission that the destructive power of huge saturation attacks was the most efficient means of bringing an enemy to his knees, of rendering it no longer capable of 'bearing the unbearable'. By adopting this policy the American Air Force, which throughout most of its European campaign had advocated the greater efficacy of bombing specific targets, conceded that Harris had been right all along.

Bomber Command occupies a very special and indeed a unique place in military history. All in the space of a few but hectic years it made a faltering debut, not knowing quite what to do or how to do it; but once it had decided upon the course it had to steer and gradually grew in size and perfected its expertise, it became the most powerful organisation of its type the world had ever seen, and then, with the advent of nuclear weapons, it found itself suddenly and irrevocably obsolete. *Veni, vidi, vici.*

When peace finally came in May, 1945, the Royal Air Force had an overall compliment of 1,079,835 officers and men, including WAAF personnel. Of these 193,313 were aircrew, a number which was greater than the entire strength of the service at the beginning of the war, and of that total 125,000 flew with Bomber Command. But we must not forget the vast army of 'erks', those who, outside in all weathers, faithfully and tirelessly toiled on the Wellingtons and the Mosquitoes, the Halifaxes

Bomber Command in World War II

and the Lancasters, ensuring that everything worked, and worked well, and in so doing formed a close bond with the aircrews, for whom they had a deep and lasting admiration.

As for the fliers themselves I do not think that much more needs to be said. They were a special breed of youngsters, *la crème de la crème* amongst fighting men, indulging in a type of combat which, by its very nature, could be appreciated fully only by those who took part in it. The crews of Bomber Command gave their all - literally in so many cases - and the refusal to award them with their own campaign medal must rank as one of the most blatant travesties of military justice of all time and an eternal condemnation of those who decide on such things. All operational aircrew, irrespective of the Command to which they belonged, received the Air Crew Europe Star up until June 5, 1944, and thereafter the France and Germany Star; a private who dug latrines in the desert got the Africa Star, the clerk in Rangoon the Burma Star, while the men who regularly took a bomber into the heart of the Reich received nothing of any consequence - the same in fact as anyone who set foot in Europe between the Invasion and the surrender. That was a cruel rebuff (in RAF circles believed to be mainly due to the destruction of Dresden) which will go on rankling Bomber Command's diminishing band of survivors until the last of them joins his comrades in the peace which only eternity brings.

While on this subject it might not be out of place to note that, apart form the large number of DFMs, DFCs and DSOs with which Bomber Command airmen were decorated, 19 of them received the Victoria Cross (eight posthumously); and God alone knows how many acts of selfless heroism were performed and known only to the crews of the bombers which spun vertically into the ground or exploded in the air in the customary ball of fire; no survivors, no witnesses, no reports - no gongs. Only *Nirvana* for the only ones who knew.

Of the Allies, Great Britain had fought longer than anyone else, from the first day, September 3, 1939, to the last, May 8, 1945; and of the British Armed Forces, RAF Bomber Command had fought longer than either of the other two services, never stopping from the moment that solitary Blenheim became airborne when the war was just minutes old, till the final attack by Mosquitoes on Keil on May 2/3, 1945. It had suffered - how it had suffered - and anyone arguing that it played no significant part in re-establishing peace in Europe is skating on the thinnest of ice. When the broad spectrum of its achievements are examined, and digested, it might even be questioned whether victory would ever have

The Great Ingratitude

been possible without it. To denounce or even to belittle or underestimate the accomplishments of its leader and its crews would be - regretfully has been and still is - one of the greatest ingratitudes ever inflicted on those who have offered their services in war.

Chapter 23

GOERING'S GUESTS

As Bomber Command expanded and its raids became heavier and more frequent, with correspondingly greater losses, the Luftwaffe had to accommodate a large number of aircrew - by the end of the war 29,000 - in prison camps sited almost exclusively in Silesia and Poland. The fact that Goering would have none of them in the occupied countries of Western Europe was due to the relative proximity of the UK, the assistance escapees received from resistance groups, and to the unquenchable adventurousness of the airmen themselves. Whereas the vast majority of army and navy personnel were quite content to sit out the war in the camps, irrespective of how miserable a life it was - and this is in no way intended to be a criticism of their attitude - the young aircrews invariably displayed a much more rebellious spirit and were far more likely to attempt to escape than members of the other Services. The last thing Goering wanted was to have the same men flying against him for a second time: he had quite enough opposition from the RAF as things were. It is not surprising therefore that the famous Colditz fortress, in which habitual escapers were incarcerated, housed more flying personnel than soldiers or sailors or anyone else.

Perhaps the sudden transition from their almost unrestricted freedom when not on flying duties, and their generally comfortable billet in the UK, to the depressing, cooped-up atmosphere of a Stalag Luft, accounts to some extent for the RAF attitude; but rather more significant was their dislike of inaction and of a tedious, regimented life of utter boredom. Furthermore they had become so accustomed to living on a razor edge and of continually flaunting death in the face that they just could not give up the habit of dangerous living, and the very planning of escapes helped to satisfy their craving for something meaningful and exciting to do, especially if it caused disruption to the enemy; moreover they had not known, nor did they want to know, the rigid and, in their opinion, nonsensical discipline of their own army or navy - nor that of the Luftwaffe. The rumbustious life they had led in the air bred within them a feeling of restlessness, a crying need for positive action which had to be realised somehow and somewhere on the ground; if it had to take place

The Great Ingratitude

behind the barbed wire of a prison camp, so be it... Or, better still, outside it.

Aircrew became notorious amongst their captors for their frequent 'goon-baiting' - 'taking the mickey' out of anybody and everybody on the staff, and showing little respect for rank as they did so. Indeed their ploys often landed them in serious trouble when German Camp Commandants reached the end of their tether. The crews were disparagingly outspoken in their denunciation of everything German, made rude references to Hitler and his chief associates and gave their hosts the unmistakable impression that they considered all Germans to be the absolute dregs of the human race. The unique and close camaraderie that had been fostered in the bomber transferred itself naturally and smoothly to the new situation in which they found themselves; and in all their escapades they supported each other to the hilt.

With such a broad cross section of men representing all trades and professions there was no end to the number of skills that could be tapped both for recreational and more serious purposes. Prisoners became expert at improvisation and disguise artists provided a source of entertainment which was all the more enjoyable if it hurled abuse at the enemy. A German NCO or officer coming in to inspect a barrack room might suddenly be confronted by a man for all the world looking like the Führer, swastika armband and all, who would lambast the visitor, ranting and raving at him for not paying due respect to his Leader by jumping to attention and giving the Nazi salute; or, in full view of guards, prisoners would pin a large drawing of the Führer's face, with great mad staring eyes and coarse hairs from a black broom attached as a moustache and dripping with saliva (dirty water) to the outside wall of a hut and proceed to attack it with balls of mud. Sometimes the Germans were so taken aback they simply did not know how to react - they found themselves quite unable to cope with this alien and thoroughly Ungermanic type of humour and their unconcealed embarrassment was an eternal source of enjoyment to their tormentors. These RAF boys had a cheeky, confident way of committing highly provocative acts which seemed to flummox the guards completely; had Russian or Polish prisoners indulged in similar behaviour they would probably have been shot on the spot.

The guards were often nonplussed not only by general RAF behaviour but in particular by the airmen's reaction to punishment. Even when severely hauled over the carpet for some misdemeanour aimed at rankling the camp authorities, for which they usually received at least three weeks solitary confinement, such painful exclusion from their comrades was accepted with a blend of stoicism and humour which was quite incomprehensible to the unimaginative German mind. This was especially the case when the miscreants, 'free' again after paying the penalty for their sins, took immediate retaliatory measures which only led to further and longer periods in the cramped confines of the 'Hole'. In fact the prisoners' undisciplined conduct might well have resulted in far more serious consequences had their guards not been in the main rather aged and slow-witted members of the Luftwaffe, and one cannot help but wonder what would have happened had the SS been put in charge of the camps, for never before had guards had to put up with prisoners such as these. If the aircrews were the unwilling guests of the Führer and his Reichsmarschall and showed it, then their captors were not too happy with them either; for the airmen could, and often did, make their lives something of a disciplinary hell with their continual taunts and the uproar they created to drown out shouted commands; a fair analogy would be the mental turmoil undergone by a school teacher incapable of maintaining an acceptable degree of order in his class, and had the guards been of a higher mental calibre the prisoners might have fared a lot worse.

In spite of the latters' behaviour, and, in part at least, probably because of it, an undeniable respect was shown towards them by the Luftwaffe personnel, inspired both by the admiration they felt for their own aircrew and by the fact that they had been nurtured on a propaganda diet which emphasised overwhelming German military might; and, since the aircrews from 1943 onwards had taken part in the most awesome demonstrations of air power the guards had ever witnessed, it was only natural that they should hold them in high esteem, enemies or not. Nor did the Luftwaffe personnel castigate them too severely for destroying their cities - after all they had done their own share of that all over Europe - although relations were frequently soured after a big saturation raid with huge civilian casualties or when new prisoners arrived in the camp reporting that some of their own crew members had been lynched before their very eyes by revengeful mobs, or when news of similar atrocities leaked out, such as the execution of 50 RAF officers on Goering's orders following the large-scale escape from Sagan. Indiscipline also erupted when NCOs (they were held in different Stalags from commissioned ranks and were forced to work whereas officers were not) were formed into squads to clean up local bomb damage and forbidden to run for shelter if an air raid started. Tensions reached dangerous proportions when

The Great Ingratitude

they were escorted to crashed bombers and ordered to remove the bodies still inside. This was a rather indelicate German method of showing them what happened - as if they didn't know - to many of their comrades, while at the same time reminding them that they were lucky still to be alive and ought to show their gratitude to their hosts for looking after them by behaving themselves at all times.

The Luftwaffe took every imaginable precaution to ensure that any escape plans were thwarted as soon as possible and hence the prisoners were strictly guarded at all times, partly because of the guards' fear of the fate which undoubtedly awaited them if they became lax in their supervision. Apart from the numerous watch-towers with their continually manned machine-guns, armed patrols, usually accompanied by Alsatians and Dobermans, were never far away. Sometimes a prisoner, acting out of sheer boredom or frustration or perhaps momentarily mentally unbalanced, would rush the wire in a gesture of defiance and the machine guns would fire a few rounds to warn him to get back - or else. Punishment for such unruly conduct was invariably a spell in the 'cooler', an experience, rather surprisingly, to which some men were not averse because it gave them a break from the crowded huts, where card games such as bridge went on for hours on end and were apt to prey on the nerves of non-participants; and everyone was plagued by the loud-speakers which blared out propaganda about Axis victories and Allied defeats. But these announcements were made in German, (indicative of the generally low educational standard of the camp personnel, even of officers) and only a handful of prisoners understood any of them. Those who did sometimes informed friends of what had been said, more as a diversion than anything else. But they did often learn the truth when a recently shot-down colleague joined them. This bothered the Germans but there was little they could do about it.

Most prisoners suffered periods of depression, brought on by a general feeling of uselessness and the tedious lives they were forced to lead. Some of them, if they had the energy, found short games of cricket and even of soccer or rugby of real therapeutic value, while others walked endlessly round the camp perimeter, discussing all topics under the sun from their future ambitions in 'civvy street' to more immediate plans to escape from their present confinement - the latter invariably being highly original but also highly unlikely to succeed, even hair-brained - and condemned by the Camp Escape Committee as impracticable. But then that was the first reaction to the idea of building a wooden horse! **(#)**

(#)*The Wooden Horse* by Eric Williams, published by Collins.

Bomber Command in World War II

Another means of alleviating boredom was the 'shows' in the form of short sketches and pantomime which they rehearsed diligently; these were very popular and much appreciated by the German personnel, who hardly lived an exciting life themselves. The Red Cross did their best to supply reading material and the camp library was reasonably well stocked.

The multitude of skills available in such large groups of intelligent and knowledgeable prisoners were turned to other pursuits apart from entertainment: radio experts bribed guards for parts then constructed sets which were concealed in ingenious ways and important BBC news was soon relayed to everyone by word of mouth; rough escape maps were produced and official rubber stamps for false documents were fashioned from shoe heel rubbers; in fact the amount and variety of useful items that could be produced was quite incredible.

Satisfying one's hunger was one of the greatest problems which beset prisoners of war. Very little food was provided by the Germans, and what there was consisted mainly of old soggy potatoes and onions and 'soup' which could only be described as nauseating, even to a starving man. There is no doubt whatsoever that far fewer POWs would have survived, or survived as well as they did, had it not been for the regular supply of food parcels supplied by the Red Cross. These contained principally tins of bully beef, condensed milk and biscuits. Unfortunately the Germans adopted the habit of opening the tins before handing them over, thus rendering their contents less durable - they didn't want the airmen to save the containers for use on escape bids - but this ploy was beaten at least in part by spreading a layer of margarine on top of the food to preserve it.

Apart from the food parcels the arrival of a letter from home did a lot to brighten up what would otherwise have been yet another long, bleak day (the prisoners themselves were permitted to write two letters per month on a special form). However *Kriegies* - an abbreviation of the German *Kriegsgefangene* (''prisoners of war'') - sometimes received what could only be described as rather bizarre and pathetically funny letters. One air-gunner eagerly tore open the first he had been sent, from his father, a regular soldier, to find the latter had disowned him on the grounds that he was the only member of the family ever to allow himself to be captured. As the gunner had been practically blown out of his aircraft on a particularly trying night over Berlin, the nature of his reply to pater might easily be imagined. Then came the sequel - the airman eventually escaped, made it back to the UK and on arriving home was greeted with the news that his father had been taken prisoner in Normandy.

The Great Ingratitude

Another *Kriegie* who had become engaged to a girl not long before parachuting on to German soil received from her some time later a few words informing him that she had married his father. He wrote back 'Dear Mum....'.

A navigator gave vent to some rather strong language when a demand for unpaid Income Tax arrived from the Inland Revenue. He enjoyed concocting a suitable reply, which was rendered even spicier by the inclusion of some suggestions made by others in his hut. As far as they knew no other prisoner in the camp received a tax demand thereafter.

Correspondence from home often emphasised the prisoners' isolation when next of kin mentioned people or places their sons or husbands or sweethearts should have known but of whose existence they had completely forgotten. This was one of the worrying and lesser known effects of being shut up behind the wire.

A further enemy was the extreme cold in winter. In many camps temperatures remained below freezing point from November until March and could drop as low as -24C. Prisoners tried to combat this hazard - rendered more serious by the lack of heating and proper food - by going back to bed immediately after morning *Appell* ("roll-call") and staying there until about noon. Their wooden, double-tier bunks were equipped with mattresses filled, not too generously, with straw, and as they were provided with only two very thin blankets they used their clothes as extra covers or simply kept them on all the time. There were showers of a sort (when not frozen) but no hot water, and latrines were primitive in the extreme. The prisoners sat on a narrow, wooden beam over a hole (emptied when full and the contents loaded on to trucks) and had to be careful not to tip over backwards. Going to the toilet was a humiliating business which did nothing to improve the airmen's relations with the enemy.

The Germans produced standard paper 'money' for prisoners' use. The notes were printed on only one side of very poor quality paper, and measured about 3 inches by 1½ inches. They displayed a swastika and German eagle in the bottom left hand corner, were of various denominations, and warned the holder (in German) that the voucher was valid as currency only to POWs and was restricted to purchases within the camp, or outside it on fatigue parties; it could be tendered only to members of the camp administration, and any prisoner contravening these rules or producing forgeries would be punished. The notes bore the signature of the Supreme Commander of the Wehrmacht. Money that could be used only to buy items in camp? What items? There was nothing worthwhile to buy. And forgeries? Prisoners were unlikely to try to forge something which was of no value while they could be far more profitably engaged in turning out fake identity cards and other documents which they would need if they managed to escape. The 'money' was a joke, and rather a poor one at that - about as valuable to the POWs as the immediate post-war currency was to the German civilian population, and for the very same reasons.

***

Candlish and Courtney and Robertson found the world into which they had descended - both literally and metaphorically - a strange one indeed, but after the passage of a few weeks they had more or less succeeded in coming to terms with it, even with the disgusting food which was almost totally lacking in nutritious value. Like the majority of their colleagues they at times dreamed of mouth-watering five and six course dinners and liqueurs and cigars in top London hotels and restaurants; on wakening up they were soon brought back to reality with a nibble at a Red Cross biscuit, but they did experience moments of elation on hearing reliable news of Allied progress or of another city which had received the full Harris treatment; and they celebrated the Normandy landings with an extra brew of slightly stronger tea than they could normally afford to make. At first they were inclined to talk about the others in their crew who had not made it, and were inclined to mention Benny most of all, knowing what a morale-booster his presence would have been in any NCO camp; but, they reflected ruefully, he would no doubt have spent most of his time in solitary ...

The trio were fortunate, like other small groups in the Stalag Luft, of being blessed with the type of friendship which stems from shared adversity and interdependence over a period of time. They knew quite a lot about each other - their respective families, their interests and their aspirations - and consequently they found they could while away most of an afternoon or an evening in quiet and at times intimate conversation; but it was noticeable how the restricted quarters of a prison camp provided a milieu which was very much a double-edged sword: it could draw men even closer together and give them added strength; on the other hand it is understandable that in a situation in which they lived on top of each other, day after day, with little to do, it gave ample opportunity for moments of friction and even outbursts of invective. So the first signs of any fracas was immediately stamped upon, and usually successfully, by

The Great Ingratitude

a senior officer, thus keeping the peace. It was wisely accepted by all that a far better outlet for their frustrations and their energy - such as the latter was on their inadequate diet - lay in any kind of accepted activity they could conjure up. Candlish himself offered to teach German and received a response which, one could say, was at first rather negative - "What? Learn these bastards' fucking language?" - but after reminding his colleagues that it was not only Nazis who spoke it, and that it was one of the most important tongues used anywhere, he won some of them over and soon had an enthusiastic class of about a dozen pupils for half an hour each day, most of whom had been quick to realise that an ability to understand and speak the language could be useful if they wanted to eavesdrop on guards or if and when they managed to escape. With textbooks unobtainable Candlish adopted an almost entirely oral approach - which, ironically, was to be the revolutionary and obligatory method some 25 years later - so that pedagogically he was unwittingly away ahead of his time. He would have been the first to admit, however, that his way of teaching was dictated by sheer necessity rather than by a realisation of how a foreign language was to be taught in later years.

While Courtney continued to worry about his wife and small son in Manchester and did fall into the occasional fit of depression, he did manage to cope quite well on the whole, thanks largely to his close rapport with Candlish and Robertson. The latter remained for the most part his cheerful self but never ceased to complain about the camp rations, continually telling the Germans that huge men like himself should qualify for double helpings, notwithstanding the doubtful culinary worth of the 'food' which was dished out to them. He had no doubt that Reichsmarschall Goering was favoured in this way, but it was a jocular remark which was not altogether appreciated by his hosts. Yet all three of them were thankful that they had not been shot down until early 1944, by which time it was fairly obvious that they were on the winning side and that the end of the war must surely be in sight.

Candlish had decided right from the outset that he wouldn't fritter away his time waiting for it to pass. He conversed with the guards regularly, which certainly helped him in everyday conversational German, but they were almost exclusively an illiterate bunch, speaking dialect with pronounced regional accents and frightful grammar; his chats with them - or, more accurately, brief exchanges of words - were always mundane and gave him little opportunity to learn anything new or to embrace subjects which would provide much needed practice in educated speech.

His crying need was for good books, especially literary texts, and procuring these did not turn out to be as difficult as he had feared. Tempting offers from his invaluable Red Cross parcels, reluctantly as he parted with such titbits in a country where everything produced seemed to be 'Ersatz', ensured that the more tractable of the guards obtained for him useful titles from the nearest town library; and by increasing his bribes substantially with the more audacious personnel, few and far between as they were, he even managed to get his hands on the occasional work by Jewish writers such as Heinrich Heine, which proved that not all such proscribed books had been burned on the orders of the Führer. Where they came from he knew not, nor did he care, but took the precaution of concealing them safely. He could not help wondering about the possible punitive aspects of a situation where an RAF officer was found in possession of such forbidden literature: as he was British he considered that he should have nothing to worry about but also realised only too well that the Nazis had no respect for others' views, and the danger of discovery was always on his mind. He also felt he had to be protective towards the men who had supplied them, which they had agreed to do only after much persuasion on his part and had made it clear to him that they would certainly be for the high jump if the secret was revealed. Very few of them were prepared to go as far as to bring him outlawed 'Yiddish trash', not even for a whole wagon-load of Red Cross parcels, as they knew full well that if caught they could well be on a wagon themselves and bound for a destination they would rather avoid.

Candlish also managed to consult histories of literature, books on philosophy, philology, painting and music, and learned treatises on grammar, from all of which he took copious notes on any scraps of paper he could get hold of, usually with a lead pencil obtained from a German for a couple of cigarettes. Sometimes, to keep his language flowing and to enhance it with the high standard of literary German a university demanded of its students, he wrote essays on topics such as life in a Stalag Luft and on his experiences as an operational bomber pilot. Some of the pieces he wrote he was to translate into English back at St Andrews and sell to various papers and magazines. Searching for *le mot juste* and trying to develop an attractive style was a far cry from aiming a Lancaster at the heart of a German city and at first he found concentration difficult, but as his brain gradually got back on to its former literary rails the work became easier and he tackled each self-allotted assignment with zeal. He did everything

The Great Ingratitude

he could to amass knowledge of things German, aware that this would stand him in good stead on the last lap towards that cherished MA Honours degree; he knew the course demanded great staying power, that it was akin to running an academic marathon during which many fell by the wayside.

Thanks to his long absence due to the war, and his age, he would be what was to become known as a mature student, but trusted that the studies he was completing in the prison camp, combined with his experiences in other fields, would more than make up for any blunting of his intellect. Strange how at that time people only in their mid-twenties often thought they were past the studying age. It was a concept that was soon to be changed.

So what for the majority of prisoners was a life of the most stultifying monotony bedeviled by an overwhelming feeling of purposelessness, was utilised by Candlish to great effect and helped immeasurably to keep him on an even mental keel - but that does not mean to say he could have put up with it indefinitely, profitable as it was for his future. He was fortunate in having a definite goal which went a long way towards alleviation of the trials of an irksome and stressful existence, but he renounced his studies almost completely in the final few weeks, when the growing excitement engendered by the approach of the Allied armies, from both East and West, was hardly conducive to concentration on anything at any level.

Then, with the Russian armies advancing ever and ever closer, there came a glorious day when the entire camp was suddenly ordered to prepare for immediate evacuation westwards; after trudging along for several kilometres, a march during which, for some strange reason, those prisoners who had indulged regularly in sporting activities found the going tougher than those who hadn't, they were bundled on to a train which, after several hours (there were long delays), deposited them near to an abandoned military barracks. The next day the GIs came bursting in, bombarding them with cigars and cigarettes and candy bars and gum and demanding to know if there were any of those sons-of-bitches of guards they wanted them to bump off. The American advance had been so unexpectedly rapid that the great majority of the German staff had been taken by complete surprise and only one or two of them had had time to make a quick exit and to disappear into the surrounding countryside.

Ecstatic as the newly liberated were, their spirits were somewhat dampened not long afterwards when they heard of the thousands of prisoners from other camps, including a number of RAF men, who had

Bomber Command in World War II

been forced to march much greater distances than they and had been machine-gunned by low-flying American fighter-pilots, who seemed to think it was their duty to shoot up anything and everything that moved. Some of these unfortunate souls had been more than five years behind the wire and the reaction of their more fortunate colleagues is not difficult to imagine. Candlish judged it to be one of the cruellest acts of fate he had ever encountered in what had been a long, hard and bloody struggle, and his mind went back to instances when RAF bombers had been attacked in the same way, if in less lamentable circumstances, but with the same fatal consequences.

Trigger-happy bloody Yanks! (#)

(#) The much publicised killing of some British soldiers in the Gulf War by American aircraft half-a-century later reminded ex-members of all three Services of the frequency of such "errors" in World War II.

Chapter 24

RUINS AND RATS, RIP-OFFS AND REVELRIES

After the last shot had been fired and the last bomb had been dropped the Allies faced the onerous task of creating administrative order out of chaos of a magnitude hitherto unknown in any vanquished state. Not the smallest of the problems was the welfare of the millions of German homeless, of returned, and returning prisoners of war - and of the latter there were still countless hordes in camps from the northernmost tip of Norway to North Africa, from Canada and the USA to the wastes of Siberia (although many of those captured in the Soviet Union never saw the Fatherland again). Add to the POWs the endless streams of displaced persons, many of them ex-slave workers and concentration camp survivors from almost every country on the Continent of Europe, and one can appreciate the Herculean proportions of the mess and the muddle and the numerous problems with which the occupying powers were confronted; and all this in a land largely bereft of shelter, of food, of medical services, of almost all essential amenities, and inhabited by a people as benumbed and demoralised as it seemed possible to become, and fully conscious of the fact that it was loathed and despised by every civilised nation on earth.

Germany was divided up into four Zones of Occupation - the British, American, Russian and French. The re-establishment of an orderly and more acceptable way of life was fraught with particular difficulties in the area to be governed by Great Britain, and the situation was admirably sized up in the then popular phrase: 'America got the scenery, France the vineyards, Russia the farmlands and Britain the ruins'. Perhaps it was due to more than a trick of fate that it fell to the British to administer the North-West of the country, an area extending roughly from Hamburg down through Hanover to the Ruhr and Düsseldorf and Cologne. We all know what happened to those cities, and newly arrived soldiers, and civilian advisers, appalled at what they saw, were quick to remark that the part of Germany inherited was just retribution for the activities of Britain's Bomber Command; non-RAF personnel chided aircrew with the question: "Did you need to go as far as this?"

Bomber Command in World War II

The physical picture which Germany presented in 1945 has already been described in some detail in previous chapters. It is much more difficult to convey an atmosphere which reeked of depravity, of utter human misery, of humiliating defeat. The Master Race had become a race of servants, ordered to carry out all sorts of menial chores for their new overlords, but were usually glad to comply if it earned them a crust or two. Their degree of subservience, feigned or not, knew no bounds and in fact often embarrassed soldiers and airmen when civilian males, many years their seniors and often crippled, respectfully doffed their caps or saluted as they hastily stepped off the pavement to let them pass. The initial policy of non-fraternisation underlined the contempt in which it was considered all Germans should be held, but this was soon abolished as it was found to be quite unworkable.

De-Nazification centres sprung up everywhere, and in nearly all towns of any size route signs pointed the way to courts, often make-shift, where war crimes trials were being held. Civilians were marched into cinemas and halls and forced to watch film depicting the enormity of the atrocities committed at Auschwitz and Buchenwald, at Belsen and Dachau; not for a moment were 75 million Germans allowed to forget the misery and the agony which the Third Reich had inflicted on a significant proportion of the human race. Yet observers noted that the expressions on the faces of those who had just witnessed these horrors on celluloid betrayed little, if any, emotion. Perhaps they had been so hardened by their own suffering, by what they had seen in the big bombing raids and by the general devastation and confusion around them that they remained quite unaffected; death and decay was, and had been, everywhere, and they were mainly concerned with their own survival.

In the towns people eked out a sorry and precarious existence in cold, vermin-infested cellars, often beneath the ruins of buildings designated by a black cross to indicate that bodies still lay buried amongst the rubble - hence the huge and escalating rat population. Town-dwellers in particular simply clung on to life and their day-to-day struggle surely gave them some conception of the depths of degradation to which fellow Germans had reduced much of Europe's population. In these cellars they ran a never-ending risk, especially during periods of high winds, of being bombarded yet again by lumps of masonry, bricks and wooden beams. If they were hurt or became sick - epidemics were a constant worry to the occupation authorities - few hospitals were left standing and those that did exist were poorly equipped and staffed.

The Great Ingratitude

Any shops that still functioned had pathetically little to offer apart from useless junk and food was so scarce (some of the more audacious, driven on by hunger, tried to stop and plunder trains carrying anything that was edible) that almost any kind of meat was coveted and a living dog was a rare sight. In fact British guard dogs, invariably Alsatians, would habitually disappear from requisitioned houses as soon as they were fully grown. No one bothered to go and look for them as their fate was almost certain.

Herbs were gathered from roadsides and hedgerows to make 'soup', acorns from woods turned into 'coffee', seeds of dock plants were smoked as tobacco and the smallest birds' nests were robbed of their eggs. Harris's prediction in 1940 (Chapter 1) had proved to be correct: what ye sow ye shall also reap.

With German marks of little value as hardly anything could be bought with them, a job as cook or waiter or cleaner on military premises, especially in officers' messes, was what everyone craved. The scraps which could be salvaged from kitchens or unfinished meals (or more palatable food sometimes given to employees by sympathetic soldiers and airmen), were worth their weight in gold. Luxuries such as British and American cigarettes, coffee and chocolate acted as the real currency and few servicemen, including officers, drew any pay and could live sumptuously for a week on the Black Market proceeds of a 10-packet of Players. In the messes a Scotch whisky cost the equivalent of two old pence (less than one new penny) and a bottle of British beer about the same. These drinks were paid for in German marks, which to all intents and purposes meant they were gratuitous. In fact officers often took it in turn to pay the total monthly mess bill, and it did not bother a non-drinker too much that he was coughing up for those who imbibed regularly. The cheap cost of all the alcohol and tobacco and many other concessions was, of course, borne by the British tax-payer.

Hardly any of the servicemen had ever lived better in their lives and saved their pay into the bargain. If the lack of withdrawals from their pay-books was queried, which it seldom was, the answer was always the same - no one ever lost in a card game! To help curb the drain on the British Exchequer a special military currency was introduced in the summer of 1946 for use in messes and, although that may have clipped the men's wings a bit, it did not effectively reduce their comfortable life style.

Black Market activity was rife. Typical rendezvous were main railway stations, but transactions went on everywhere. British personnel handed over much sought after commodities and received in exchange fountain pens, watches, binoculars, cameras, jewellery, even gold and silver ornaments and exquisite works of art. For the majority of them it was a pleasant and profitable way of relieving boredom, more in the nature of a diversion, but there were those, including Control Commission officials, who made practically a full-time profession out of it - almost *à la Goering* - and acquired items of great value from starving Germans for a mere pittance, usually *objets d'art* which they sneaked back to Britain when going home on leave, not obstructed too much by Customs officers who were not over conscientious and even kindly disposed if you wore army ribbons or the wings of RAF aircrew on your chest. There were even stories of large pieces of superlative furniture - and on one occasion a racehorse - going back in Dakota transport aircraft. During that shambolic period of so much to-ing and fro-ing just about anything was possible.

To offset the ghostly gloom and atmosphere of their surroundings those stationed in urban areas held parties which often degenerated into orgies. As a further means of escape officers took themselves off regularly in their military transports (petrol by courtesy of HM Government) to spend weekends in places like Brussels and even more distant Paris, where all sorts of diversions were available, where night clubs functioned and drinkable beer could be bought in establishments frequented by civilians (impossible in Germany). However most of the Army and Air Force personnel just stayed where they were, indulging themselves to the hilt if they so wished, for it was not only dogs that were few and far between in Germany at that time. A new-arrival in the country was immediately struck by the shortage of able-bodied males in the 17-45 age group, and this, together with the undeniable attraction of the man in uniform for the opposite sex, especially one who could provide the little comestible or nicotinic pleasures denied for so long to the fräulein or young widow, created for many a situation which came close to absolute moral depravity. All the young ex-combatant had to do was dangle a small but desirable bait before his intended victim's eye, and the only thing that kept him in check was the fear of contracting VD, a much more serious and publicised disease than it is now, and about the high incidence of which members of the occupying forces were repeatedly warned. They were regularly obliged to sit through ghastly films portraying the ghastly consequences of infection, strongly advised to use condoms if they must indulge, then to keep a look out for any symptoms and, if these did appear, to report sick immediately. It was a strategy which possibly got the

The Great Ingratitude

message through as well as the authorities dared hope, a fact illustrated when young men, having succumbed to temptation, turned up at the military hospital with all the signs of a good dose of gonorrhoea but were declared quite free of the malady. After intercourse they had worried so much about having been smitten with something awful that discharges had in fact occurred. Others devised methods of satisfying basic instincts with the minimum of risk: as female German servants in the employ of British forces had to undergo regular medical check-ups, some enterprising officers availed themselves of the necessary information and grabbed the girls immediately they had been given the all-clear and before they could possibly become infected.

In the dystopia to which the once proud and meticulously organised Third Reich had been reduced, the Allies worried about outbreaks of civil unrest or even out-and-out rebellion. RAF aircrews in particular were judged to be at risk and all officers were issued with revolvers and told not to go out unaccompanied. Thankfully these fears proved to be unfounded. The population had seen enough of violence and living, if you could call it that, from hand to mouth, and had no heart for insurrection which, after all, would have merely served to land them in deeper trouble. They were too much concerned with personal survival, with channelling their energies, such as they were, towards goals which would make life a little easier. At the same time the Occupying Powers had failed to fully appreciate the unquestioning obedience of the politically naïve Germans towards authority - of any kind -and of the inbred respect they showed for uniforms (a symbol of authority). This was exemplified in the attire worn by minor officials such as country station-masters, who sported as much gold braid on their caps as a Marshal of the RAF.

Yet amidst all the physical and moral decay the Germans' penchant for hard graft stood out for all to see - they simply had to be up and about and doing something. Squads of women (*Trümmerfrauen*), many of them of anything but tender years, attacked mountains of rubble with their bare hands and removed it in wheelbarrows, tenants of cellars endeavoured to embellish the entrances with something resembling a front door, and men carrying brief cases walked business-like along the streets early in the morning as if on their way to some important meeting. Where were they going? And to do what? British observers habitually asked themselves these questions without ever arriving at an answer. Perhaps the answer came only a few years later in the form of the so-called *Wirtschaftswunder* ('Economic Miracle'), a prime example of German assiduity (even if generously financed by the Marshall Plan) and determination to make a good life for themselves in the face of what, in the late spring of 1945, looked like unsurmountable odds.

Germany, which had turned a Continent upside down and inside out only to eventually suffer the same fate herself, became, in what seemed no time at all, that same Continent's strongest economic force. To be sure a different situation this time, a different goal; but the basic fact remains: the German phoenix had done it again.

So Germany's cities, well-planned and glistening new, were all back on the map within roughly the same period of time it had taken Bomber Command to remove them from it.

Chapter 25

EPILOGUE

IN SOME QUIET CORNER ...

They ran a ghastly gauntlet
They wavered not, nor fled,
They soldiered on regardless,
They trembled, and they bled.

Now they lie in foreign soil,
Far 'neath their starry sphere,
At which they gaze eternally,
Released at last from fear.

After a lengthy leave Candlish spent a few weeks as an instructor until the sudden collapse of Japan following the dropping of the atomic bombs in August, 1945. With all aircrew training now over he became redundant, and after clicking his heels for a couple of months on a disused airfield in Cheshire he was sent to St John's Wood in London, where he and half a dozen others were supposed to act as interpreters for a foreign delegation due to arrive in the city in the late autumn. However it never appeared, and, just as he was becoming rather bored with nothing to do, a Group Captain arrived one morning and asked him, and those of his colleagues who knew German, whether they would be willing to go to Germany for an unspecified period 'to search for missing aircrew'. They were told that although an accurate figure could never be ascertained, it was estimated that, of the 47,268 airmen of Bomber Command reported killed or missing in Europe, or who had died in prison camps, the exact fate of some 25,000 personnel was not known (this figure included a small proportion from other Commands). A considerable number had presumably been claimed by the waters of the North Sea, or consigned to oblivion in such minute pieces over the European landmass that the Germans were unable to provide any information about them whatsoever. But many had been buried by the enemy and, if identified, had a cross bearing their names

Bomber Command in World War II

over their graves; if unidentified only three stark words on the cross told the world that here lay an *Unbekannter Englischer Flieger* ("Unknown British Airman"). It was the task of the newly formed RAF Missing, Research and Enquiry Service (MRES) to comb the Continent, but mainly Germany, since that was where most of the "Missing" were, in an effort to find and positively identify the bodies of as many as possible of those who had been lain to rest in those unmarked graves and to have the wooden crosses suitably inscribed with rank, name, service number and date of death. In successful cases next of kin would be immediately informed so that they might at least derive some comfort from the knowledge that son, husband or brother was lying in a named and tended grave in a cemetery in Stuttgart or Hanover, and not just somewhere between Munich or Berlin and the North European coast.

Later on the remains of all RAF aircrew were taken from umpteen resting-places all over Germany and reinterred in British military cemeteries which are looked after by the Commonwealth Graves Commission; these are situated in Berlin, Reichswald, Rheinberg, Durnbach and Bad Tolz, and there are smaller ones at Soltau and Oldenburg. The great majority of the British airmen (nearly 3000) who lie in the Berlin War Cemetery were victims of the Battle of Berlin; the Reichswald Cemetery, near Kleve, contains more RAF fliers than any other in Germany (almost 4000); the cemetery at Rheinberg, a few miles north-west of Gelsenkirchen, is the burial-place of close on 3000 aircrew, almost all of whom died in raids on the Ruhr - and somewhat meaningfully one might say, not a great distance from the area where huge decoy fires were lit to confuse the bombers; the Durnbach War Cemetery is located in beautiful hilly countryside in Bavaria and is the last resting-place of those who operated against targets such as Munich and Augsburg and Nuremberg or were killed while on their way to Italian targets or returning from them.

Candlish realised that the experience would be a grisly one, and testing too, especially if he had to gaze upon and search the broken and putrefying remains of someone he knew, (improbable on account of the huge numbers involved, but still well within the realms of possibility) because that was exactly what the job entailed; yet at the same time he felt his participation would be an appropriate farewell to all those who had been less fortunate than he and whose trials and tribulations he himself had shared. Moreover his German would benefit enormously. In the prison camp he had had sporadic exchanges of words with some of the guards, who had been rather illiterate fellows on the whole, and what he

The Great Ingratitude

needed was conversation and discussions at a much higher level so that he could brush up the vocabulary and idiom which he was fast forgetting. A further spell in Germany would stand him in good stead for his - he hoped - fairly imminent return to his studies at St Andrews.

He was summoned to Gatwick and there he, who could drive a Lancaster, was taught how to drive a car. Even so he was given a corporal driver and a Humber 4x4 (a type of military estate car) and some items of specialised equipment. The unit, comprising about a dozen vehicles, travelled in convoy to Harwich and embarked for the German port of Cuxhaven.

The corporals took the cars from there to Hamburg and the officers went by train. As they entered the southern outskirts they saw for themselves what had happened to the city. Candlish's thoughts, like those of some of the others in the group, went back to a certain July night in 1943 when they had been about four miles above where they were now, and the utter desolation gave them a good idea of what it must have been like for the citizens of Hamburg during those fateful hours.

After spending a few days in an ex-Luftwaffe camp in an Elbeside suburb (Blankenese) from which could be seen overturned blocks of concrete, as big as houses, which had sheltered U-boat pens until Wallis's mighty bombs had uprooted them less than a year before, Candlish and half a dozen fellow Research Officers set off down the autobahn with their drivers and a cook to the headquarters of No 4 Missing Research and Enquiry Unit, and their home for some time to come. This was a former Nazi mansion standing just outside the town of Iserlohn and about 12 miles from Dortmund. They knew enough about 'Happy Valley' to suspect, rightly, that they could not have been allocated a more difficult area in the whole of Europe in which to carry out their duties; they knew only too well that the Ruhr had been attacked from the earliest days of the war right to its very end, that it had endured God knows how many 700-900 bomber raids and claimed a high proportion of the total number of aircrew lost. Whitleys and Hampdens, Wellingtons and Manchesters, Halifaxes and Lancasters had fallen into its towns and outlying areas so frequently that its surviving policemen and officials, unable to produce many of the records because they had been consumed by fire, would be incapable of remembering any particular aircraft out of many which had come down on any particular night. It was a much lighter task for units covering countries like Norway or Switzerland or Italy, where a crashed RAF bomber was not a common occurrence and could therefore be recalled with a fair amount of accuracy even if not documented. Like all Research Officers, Candlish was offered the services of an English-speaking fräulein as an interpreter, but rejected this on the grounds already mentioned; you arrive at oral mastery of a language only by speaking it, not by listening to others doing so.

Each missing bomber was dealt with individually by the Air Ministry on a sheet which gave all the essential and pertinent information: its type and number, the target, the date of the raid, time of take-off, the names and rank and service numbers of each member of its crew and, in some cases, its last known position. It was always easier to learn where the aircraft had crashed if it had come down in open country - in the case of No 4 MREU between the Ruhr and the Dutch border - whereas it was often an exacting and even insuperable exercise trying to trace the occupants of a bomber which had ploughed into a large town such as Cologne or Essen on a night when a score of others had done the same thing. One can imagine that on the morning following a large-scale bombardment the German authorities were more concerned with a whole multitude of tasks they considered more pressing than the burial of the remains of the 'terror fliers' who had caused the havoc and the carnage which surrounded them. In such cases dead aircrew were disposed of unceremoniously after much more vital work had been done and were often thrown into convenient holes - Benny's unwitting remark in the pub was unfortunately true - and it frequently happened that hungry town-dwellers were somewhat peeved when told by a Research Officer that their well-tended vegetable patch was to be dug up because there were probably RAF bodies beneath it. To an urban population long hardened to all the horrors of big raids the loss of their potatoes or their cabbages was a matter of far greater concern than the fact that the bodies of human beings lay nurturing their soil.

Candlish spent the night before his first exhumation all alone in a hut on a derelict airfield near Krefeld, his driver having been offered a bed by a small British Army detachment nearby, but where, unfortunately, there was no accommodation for an officer. Sharing with them would not have bothered him in the slightest, but then the Army had always insisted on a rigid distinction between men of commissioned and non-commissioned rank, even when they were asleep. His fitful dozing was punctuated by weird and frightful dreams which were not so far from becoming nightmares, and he was glad to rise early and take a stroll across the grass in the crisp morning air, reflecting that the air might not be crisp

The Great Ingratitude

for very long. His driver, Corporal Ritchie, reported as arranged to drive him back to the army unit, where he ate a not very hearty breakfast all on his own before they set out for the Bürgermeister's office, partly demolished but with a room or two still serviceable.

Candlish asked to see the mayor and explained to him the purpose of his visit. Lancaster B1 NR 532 LT-S had not returned from a big raid on Krefeld on the night of June 21/22, 1943, and the Air Ministry knew that one of its crew, Flying-Officer John Desmond, had been identified and buried in the cemetery of the small town of Kempen about 10 kilometres to the north-west. Candlish told him that his aim was to find and identify the others and hoped Herr Vogler would have some useful information. The mayor said he remembered the raid well as it was a particularly heavy one, with a large area of the city on fire for several hours and nearly 6000 houses destroyed; nevertheless he would see what he could do, asked to be excused for a few minutes, and soon returned with a large file, remarking that they were indeed fortunate as many records had been consumed in the flames, which had engulfed the entire city centre. He flipped through the pages and found the bomber in question. Four of its crew were interred in unidentified graves in Kempen alongside Flying-Officer Desmond. Of the two others there had been no trace whatsoever.

Candlish ordered him to recruit a squad of diggers right away and to tell them to have the graves open, but not the coffins, by 11 am.

On arriving at the cemetery he caught sight of the small working party standing around in a group. He walked up to them, bade them "Guten Morgen", and took a good deep breath before looking down into the first hole of the four that had been dug. The coffin was a simple, rough wooden box. Having already changed into gum boots he donned mask and rubber gloves, and told them to remove the lid.

It was prized off with iron bars and Candlish found himself confronted with what appeared to be a pile of multi-coloured rags which exuded the most awful stench he had ever known and bore little resemblance to the form of a human being. Gingerly he lowered himself into the hole and removed as much of the rotten clothing as he could. But it yielded nothing. He scraped around in the coffin with a tool but the result was the same. Not a promising start.

"Close it up. Fill it in again."

The cross remained unaltered.

Bomber Command in World War II

In the second grave he came upon a sergeant's stripes and, after much probing around, a ring. The crew had consisted of four officers and three sergeants, so he felt he might be getting somewhere this time. The ring went into a small pouch, which he labelled.

The third man, like John Desmond, was a Flying-Officer, as revealed by the insignia on a battle-dress épaulette. As there had been only two men of this rank in the crew, he could be no other than Flying-Officer Alan Sutton.

All he could find on the next body - in a top tunic pocket - was an unopened and apparently unharmed packet of Durex. Not much help. But the man was definitely a sergeant.

He had seen no sign of the identity discs which all aircrew wore round their necks. This was because, for some strange reason, they were normally removed by the Germans, yet not used to identify the bodies. He asked several officials why this was so, but never received a satisfactory answer. Even if the discs had not been tampered with they were too easily hidden in the decaying flesh.

He ordered Vogler to see that Flying Officer Sutton received a new cross suitably inscribed as soon as possible, and returned to Iserlohn. There he wrote out a report on his findings and despatched it to the Air Ministry along with the ring. The latter was examined in turn by the next of kin of the three sergeants in the crew and was identified as having belonged to Sergeant Ronnie Thompson. Of the other two sergeants it could not be established who was Sergeant Robert Smith and who was Sergeant Michael Senior. The process of identification was invariably a process of elimination - if you were dealing with a pair of similar rank and you got one of them it meant you knew who the other was as well. Apart from rings and watches (if these had not been appropriated before burial) items such as letters, unusual mascots, and even tickets could prove to be invaluable.

A few weeks after the exhumation Candlish again contacted Bürgermeister Vogler and Sergeant Thomson's grave too was provided with a new cross bearing his name, rank and date of death. He felt reasonably satisfied with the results of his first case, having been warned to expect only a modest rate of success. He carried out many other investigations where he achieved much less than he would have liked in performing a task which was difficult in its execution and emotionally distressing. He was thwarted by a variety of factors, including the non-existence of German records amongst people who were the most record-

The Great Ingratitude

minded on earth or, as he at times suspected, the unwillingness of German officials to produce them, it being so easy to say that they knew nothing of the aircraft in question or that the records must have been destroyed. He was also aware that in some cases the missing men might have been murdered. There were other problems such as water-filled graves (in Mönchen-Gladbach for instance) which would have turned a rat's stomach and had to be hastily abandoned, or cemeteries which had been hit by high explosive bombs so that British and German dead were intermingled to such an extent that the authorities had no idea who was who and the only answer had been a large communal grave. There were profitless digs in open ground where airmen were said to have been buried, but time and circumstances had often dulled the minds of those who had participated in the disposal of the bodies. Candlish even encountered cases of half a dozen or more fliers buried together in coffinless holes and, once, with horses.

In the course of his investigations he had ample opportunity to study the attitude of Germans to RAF men like himself, who, in the area in which he was operating, had made their lives a terror and a misery for years. They were obedient, polite, apparently pleased to co-operate; he also traced a mixture of fear and respect - and, occasionally, ill-concealed hate.

Thankfully he was assigned to the occasional more intriguing case like that of the Norwegian officer pilot of a rocket-firing Typhoon who, it was stated on the Air Ministry form, had definitely been seen alive and well by his former ground staff when a prison camp was liberated. Yet the Germans had reported him as killed very late in the war and buried in a village cemetery near Osnabrück. Candlish was ordered to investigate and, while interviewing the local Bürgermeister, noticed that the latter became slightly taken aback when told the grave was to be exhumed. Accordingly he pumped him with a barrage of questions and the hesitant and unconvincing replies he received only served to confirm his initial impression.

In order to prevent any further hanky-panky - Candlish was fairly certain that all was not right - he said he would go to the cemetery without delay and await the arrival of the diggers, whom he expected within the next half-hour.

They duly appeared and he stood to one side as they got down to work. When the coffin, almost intact thanks to its relatively short spell underground, was opened, Candlish could not subdue a gasp of astonishment as he gazed down upon a perfect human skeleton, absolutely devoid of all flesh - quite improbable considering the short time lapse - and apparently wearing only an unzipped RAF Irving flying-jacket. He got down into the grave and found, clearly printed in indelible ink on a tag at the back of the collar, the Norwegian's name, rank and number, exactly the same as was inscribed on his cross and in the Air Ministry particulars; not a single item of underwear, no trousers, no socks, nothing else; and, as far as he could tell, not a single bone had been broken anywhere in his entire body - making it blatantly obvious that this man had not met his end thundering into the ground in a Typhoon.

Candlish made his report, emphasising his strong suspicions about the surreptitious nature of the whole matter, and was informed in due course that a Home Office pathologist would be sent out to investigate. If the latter did eventually arrive it must have been after Candlish was demobilised. Several times he meant to write to the Air Ministry to ask about the final outcome, but was too wrapped up in his new life and, when he finally did so, was told that nothing could be done without the name of the pilot in question. Unfortunately he just couldn't recall it.

He wondered if the Norwegian pilot had been working for enemy Intelligence and reported by the grateful Germans as killed so that he might escape punishment. If the ground staff had been right in their identification - and they were adamant that they had had no doubts whatsoever - the man could easily have lost himself in the waves of wandering humanity which were part and parcel of the immediate post-war scene all over Europe. But on the other hand why should the Germans, who throughout the war had never shown much concern for other nationalities, have bothered to go to such pains in the spring of 1945 when everything was collapsing around them? Then again he found it difficult to accept that any of them, notorious as they were for lack of subtlety in their thinking, would have resorted to a ploy so unbelievably amateurish that it wouldn't have duped a five-year old. And, finally, was it likely that a young Norwegian pilot, who had escaped from his country in a small boat to reach the UK, had in fact gone there to work for the enemy? Yet stranger things had happened.

Such case examples, however, were extremely rare, and the one just described quite exceptional. Usually the work entailed the same old slog day after day, moving about amidst the rubble and the decay and the pitiable inhabitants of what had been one of the greatest industrial complexes on earth. As Candlish operated in cemetery after cemetery, month after month in this forbidding environment, he grew more and more

The Great Ingratitude

depressed. It was not only the ghoulish nature of his task, combined with the odds against achieving satisfying results, which affected him, but the soul-destroying experience of continually being reminded of this slaughter of the cream of British and Commonwealth youth, of the seed corn for the future. He fervently wished that up and coming politicians had been given to do what he was doing then.

So there came a day when he decided he had had enough and applied for a 'Class B' release to enable him to go back to university.

This was granted.

He returned, after an absence of more than six years, and certainly much wiser, to 'the old grey city by the Northern Sea', to resume his studies of, ironically, the language and the literature and the history of a people who had been instrumental in creating for him experiences which would be on his mind for ever; and on the minds of tens of millions of others.

Bomber Command had done the job it had been asked to do. He too, as he had been part of it. But he had had his fill of death and destruction; no doubt he himself had killed and he had certainly destroyed; now it was time to concern himself with life and the living, time to be active in some worthwhile field and try to make up the leeway.

He decided he would be a teacher ... and felt he would have a lot more to offer his charges than merely a knowledge of the German language.

APPENDIX   1

SIN OF OMISSION - DESECRATION AND DERELICTION - AND SOME RECTIFICATION

When the war ended the flat shires of the East of England from Yorkshire down to Cambridge, formed an unending patchwork - labyrinth might be a more accurate term - of great bomber stations, so numerous that the circuits of two or more often overlapped. This was the region of the UK which launched the massed air fleets, both of Bomber Command and the United States Army Air Force, against *Fortress Europa,* and was the home of thousands of aircrew, if a very temporary one in many cases, and of tens of thousands of ground staff. The hectic round-the-clock activity of a single bomber base and its endless demands on all its personnel from the Commanding Officer down to the squads of 'erks', has already been described in Chapter 7; multiply this some scores of times and you had in fact what was a vast proliferation of self-sufficient units which had to effect with each other, on most nights of the week for at least three years of the war, a degree of co-operation, emanating first of all from Harris at High Wycombe and then from all Group Headquarters, which was so detailed and delicate as to render it seemingly impossible to achieve. The intercommunicating roads between airfields, interminably used by vehicles ranging from the elongated aircraft transporters and huge petrol tankers to the ubiquitous little jeep, contributed to the turning of this vast area into a type of conurbation created almost solely for the deployment of the four-engined bomber. For a number of years this was Britain's front line in the truest possible sense of the term, because it was from this part of the country, and almost exclusively from this part alone, that the Germans were attacked where it hurt them most - on their native soil; it was from this rural area of England that Bomber Command alone set off with nearly a million tons of bombs in its prodigious effort, first of all to halt, and then to destroy, the Nazi menace, and from which more than 50,000 aircrew who operated from its airfields did not return; and add to that the magnificent role played by the Americans who, far from their native land, took off regularly in daylight from many of the bases to fly into all corners of the Reich and also suffered grievous losses.

By 1945 Bomber Command was much more than the largest body within the Royal Air Force; by then it had become an institution, a great and unique British institution which symbolised the spirit, the courage and the devotion of the aircrews who had achieved so much and in so doing had paid so dearly; which symbolised no less the unremitting dedication of the scores of thousands of groundstaff from mechanics to clerks, from armourers to medicos and telephonists, who did so much to make the Command the professionally competent force it eventually became. Therefore the failure to maintain at least one large Bomber Command airfield on its authentic wartime footing was a rare opportunity lost on the part of authority to allow succeeding generations a better understanding of the amount of organisation and endeavour that had been required day after day, night after night, to prosecute the long and bloody battle that was fought from these green acres of the British countryside. What do we have instead? Runways either overgrown or torn up for motorway construction, crumbling buildings with rusted window-frames and doors swaying and creaking eerily in the wind, buildings which are now tenanted by foxes and owls and, some say, with ghosts of the past; a general air of dilapidation and decay as if the existence of the stations was simply a passing phase of as little consequence as a line of empty, run-down shops in the seediest quarter of some run-down town.

It is true, of course, that by 1945 Great Britain had taken quite a battering herself and the new Labour Government was beset with a host of urgent industrial, economic and social problems; it was therefore hardly surprising that little thought was given to all the paraphernalia of war which lay piled up everywhere, except to clear it out of the way or destroy it if it constituted a danger to the public; but even taking account of these factors it is still difficult to accept that there were not one or two individuals with sufficient clout and historical foresight to insist on the retention of a typical heavy bomber station, housing examples of the aircraft which had been the mainstay of Bomber Command, together with briefing-rooms, control tower, hangars, workshops, crews' quarters, bomb trolleys, petrol bowsers, Grand Slams and Tallboys and a thousand-and-one other exhibits. Such an exposition, in the days of mass tourism which were just round the corner, would have regularly attracted large numbers of visitors from all over the country and from abroad as well, and would have kept on doing so. In this respect it is pleasant to report that the Yorkshire Air Museum at Knaresborough is pressing ahead with its plans to establish a genuine wartime airfield at Elvington, which was an RAF bomber base (Halifaxes) until 1945 and a USAAF station from 1954 till 1958. But how infinitely better it would have been, and so much easier, if an operational field had simply been retained lock stock and barrel when the war ended and enhanced with the addition of the types of Bomber Command aircraft it did not itself possess. The cost of maintaining and running such a project would no doubt have been recouped from entry charges, and any profits could have been channelled into the RAF Benevolent Fund to help all those airmen who still suffer because of the part they played in their country's wars.

But at least we can be thankful that, as the years rolled by, there appeared a number of individuals who regretted this great omission and banded themselves into bodies and, with infinite difficulty and often at considerable expense to themselves, set about retrieving what could still be retrieved. The result was the founding, by the early nineties, of more than 100 Air Museums throughout the UK. There are also a large number of small collections, mostly of memorabilia. World War Two aircraft, or parts of them, have been traced all over the world and dug out of fields and raised from lakes and waterways and painstakingly restored to their former war condition. It must have been both an exciting and a vexing experience for the enthusiastic souls who undertook this difficult work: one can imagine their jubilation when they heard confirmed reports of the battered and rusted wreck of a Wellington or Lancaster which lay at the bottom of some Swedish or German lake; at the same time they must have thought bitterly of the thousands that had been airworthy only a decade or two before, only to be hastily destroyed as so many pieces of useless junk; and they must have felt like a philatelist who, the victim of some inexplicable aberration, had thrown away what he had considered to be a worthless collection and later discovered the opposite to be the case - and had to start all over again, knowing full well that what he ended up with would be but a poor substitute for the treasures he had unwittingly possessed and so rashly discarded. It is both galling and exasperating to think - and quite incomprehensible to understand - that many of the most historical and famous types were hastily disposed of by setting them on fire with apparently no thought for the survival of even a single example! It would appear that there is not a solitary Whitley or Stirling or Manchester to be seen anywhere, and that of others no more than the occasional nose, cockpit or tail sections are still in existence and on display. But all, happily, has not been lost, and we must be thankful that one or two of the foremost machines - for example the Lancaster, Mosquito, Spitfire and Hurricane - have survived in a complete state and that some of them can still take to the air.

Obviously we cannot list here all the places where

The Great Ingratitude

aircraft and the various items pertaining to Bomber Command can be viewed by the public, but these are detailed in two useful publications - *British Aviation Museums* (Key Publishing Ltd, 1 Worthorpe Road, Stamford, Lincolnshire, PE9 2JR), and in *Wrecks and Relics* by Ken Ellis (Midland Counties Publications, 24 The Hollow, Earl Shilton, Leicester, LE9 7NA). We shall therefore restrict ourselves to dealing with some of the largest museums (which provide comprehensive brochures on request) whose displays are particularly relevant.

The Royal Air Force Museum and Bomber Command Museum at Hendon on the north-west outskirts of London (Grahame Park Way, NW9 5LL) is open practically every day and is one of those well worth a visit. (The fact that the Hendon Museum was not opened until 1972, 27 years after the war had ended, and the Bomber Command Museum not until 1983, reflects both the uncaring attitude on the part of the authorities towards the preservation of important wartime memorabilia and the desire by independent bodies to bring about a belated rectification of the situation). Apart from a wealth of other exhibits such as a Tornado simulator (which visitors are allowed to 'fly'), there are film shows, an Audio Tour, a museum shop, and more than 60 aircraft can be viewed under cover. The Bomber Command Museum has a Lancaster which completed 137 operations, during which it clocked 800 hours flying time. Originally it had stood at the gate at RAF Scampton (home of 617 Squadron) before arriving at Hendon in 1972. Halifaxes, unfortunately, are conspicuous by their total absence in museums everywhere, with only nose or cockpits being left, but it is hoped that one day a completely restored example rebuilt from pieces retrieved from the Isle of Lewis in the Hebrides, will be on display at the Yorkshire Air Museum at Knaresborough (mentioned above). However Hendon does have the substantial remains of an aircraft which made a forced landing on frozen Lake Hoklingen in Norway during one of the attempts to sink the *Tirpitz* on April 27, 1942 (see Chapter 20, Big Bangs). The Halifax, of course, went to the bottom when the ice melted, and was retrieved in 1973 after a delicate and costly operation. The Wellington on display was a non-operational crew trainer aircraft but has had turrets added and is now restored to full wartime specifications. The Mosquito, too was a training aircraft. The Museum is also the proud owner of two bombers from the USAAF - a B-17 Flying Fortress and a Mitchell B-25, and apart from Bomber Command aircraft there is a Tiger Moth, Beaufighter, Spitfires, a Hudson, a Typhoon, a Tempest, a Meteor, and many early and more recent machines (World War One aircraft, flying-

Bomber Command in World War II

boats and jets); not to mention a Messerschmitt Me 109E, a Heinkel He 162, a Junkers Ju 88 and a Focke-Wulf Fw 190F.

The Aerospace Museum at RAF Cosford, West Midlands, a few miles north-west of Wolverhampton, opened in 1979 and is a magnificent establishment with more than 70 aircraft, missiles, engines and uniforms - and various other memorabilia. The types of bomber include a Mosquito, a Liberator which arrived from India (and the only example in Europe) and a restored Lincoln. There is also a Spitfire, an Anson, a Catalina, a Dakota, a Junkers Ju 52, a Messerschmitt Me 262, and a Messerschmitt Me 163 Komet. Nor are Japanese Second World War aircraft absent - on display are a Kawasaki Ki-100 (believed to be the only example in existence) and a Yokosuka Okha (specially designed for the suicide rôle). Also on display are a V-1 and a V-2 and other German rockets and missiles such as the Rheinbote, the Rheintochter, the Enzian flak rocket and the Hagelkorn glide bomb. The Lincoln should be interesting to lovers of the Lancaster because it was the latter's successor and big brother, and the last piston-engined bomber in the RAF. The one on display at Cosford (RF 398) saw service at RAF Stations Wroughton, Kemble, Aldergrove and Watton and flew sorties from Malta, Gibraltar and Tripoli. As a type the Lincoln arrived too late to see action in World War Two although the prototype had made its maiden flight in June, 1944. Lincolns were assigned to the 'Tiger Force' for the bombing of Japan, but that country surrendered before the force became operational. Otherwise the Japanese might have come to fear it as much as the Germans did its predecessor. Also on view to the public at Cosford is a Shackleton, a further development of the Lancaster and famous for its long service as a 'flying radar station' during the Cold War (it was eventually replaced by the Nimrod). It could remain airborne for 18 hours and one of its unique features was the provision of two sets of propellers driving in opposite directions on each of its four piston engines. Something of an anachronism in an age of jets, the noisy and uncomfortable 'Shackle' was once described as 'a million loose rivets flying in close formation'. Even so it was thoroughly reliable (like its war-proven ancestor) and much loved by its 9-man crews - partly due to its famous lineage. The last four Shackletons were withdrawn from service in 1991 but, fortunately, three of them were conserved and found homes at Winthorpe (Nottinghamshire), Charlwood (Surrey) and at Long Marston in Warwickshire. There is a further example in the Greater Manchester Museum of Science and Industry.

The Duxford Aviation Society has its home at Duxford

The Great Ingratitude

Airfield about 10 miles south of Cambridge. One of its most interesting projects is the restoration to air worthiness of a very rare Blenheim. A Royal Canadian Air Force Lancaster too, is under restoration here, also a Mosquito and a Lysander. It was Duxford which, in 1989, accommodated five Flying Fortresses for the filming of 'Memphis Belle'. On show are examples of First World War biplanes right through to modern jets, and include five machines which are airworthy - a Spitfire, a Tiger Moth, a Mustang, a Catalina and a Kittyhawk. There are also two Ansons and a further two Spitfires, a Hurricane, an Oxford, a Swordfish, three Meteors, and in addition a Sea Hawk and a Shackleton which are being restored. The cockpit section of a Typhoon is also on display.

The Mosquito Aircraft Museum, the only establishment which concentrates on a specific machine, is located at Salisbury Hall, near St Albans, Hertfordshire. It is operated by the de Havilland Aircraft Museum Trust and possesses a prototype DG98 Mosquito. It was here that *DH* the aircraft was built and then taken over to Hatfield in Hertfordshire for its maiden flight on November 25, 1940. Three more prototypes were constructed at Salisbury Hall and flew from an adjoining field. It is almost beyond belief, but true nevertheless, that the Company had given orders for the first prototype to be burned, but thanks to the efforts of a PR man, a Mr W Baird, it was secretly taken apart and stored away at Hatfield and Panshanger. The Company were persuaded to allow the machine to return to the place of its birth in 1959. Another Mosquito which arrived in 1971 has been completely restored, and a third example is envisaged - a fuselage has already come from Holland and a wing from Israel.

Even in 1954, only nine years after the war, it was only with great difficulty that five Lancasters were found, converted to the correct configurations and made airworthy for the Dambusters film (they were manned by Lincoln crews). Now, in the early nineties, only one airworthy Lancaster exists in Gt. Britain, and is based at RAF Coningsby. This is PA 474, the 'City of Lincoln', built in 1945 to become part of the 'Tiger Force' and now lovingly looked after by the city of Lincoln, which adopted her in view of the long and close rapport that existed between the town, its cathedral (a welcome sight on umpteen occasions for weary crews as they staggered home after a particularly nasty trip over the Reich), and Bomber Command in general. This is the aircraft which took part in films such as " The Guns of Navarone" and Operation *Crossbow*, and since 1973 has joined the Spitfires and the Hurricanes each year in The Battle of Britain Memorial Flight. The people of Britain can see simultaneously and in proud formation in the September sky the two fighter types which were allotted the crucial task of successfully defending their country in 1940, and the heavy bomber which did more than any other to wear out the enemy by remorselessly mauling him in his own backyard, and being itself mauled in the process.

We cannot help but ponder on the riches lost and on what might have been, and to say that one should be grateful for small mercies would seem a banal statement to make when there could so easily have been so much more. Yet we are deeply indebted to all those who, saddened but not undaunted by the unpardonable remissness of many who should have known better, have shown themselves resourceful enough to place at the nation's disposal whatever it has been possible for them to salvage and renovate. Their mission is to reach a target of whose limits even they are ignorant, but it is likely that relics will keep turning up and that museums will grow in size and perhaps even in number.

Some consolation at least!

The Great Ingratitude

APPENDIX 2

THAT STATUE

As soon as the Bomber Command Association announced its plans, in September 1991, to erect a statue of its wartime leader (emphasising that this was intended to serve equally as a memorial to airmen of Bomber Command alive or dead) the half-century old controversy, for some time more or less latent, immediately exploded afresh - and with a blast which, thanks to the media, was more powerful and far-reaching than ever. The mayor of Pforzheim was the first to send the arrows flying on the German side and was soon joined in his crusade by his counterparts in Cologne, Hamburg, Dresden, and other badly bombed cities, all of whom made official objections to the British Ambassador in Bonn and also wrote to the City Council of Coventry (with which city Dresden, amongst others, is twinned) asking for their support in having the statue banned, a request which, it would appear, was not unfavourably received. The German media went to town and one newspaper carried the headline: 'The Butcher of Dresden is being commemorated', while others considered they were making a very valid point by reminding their countrymen - and the British as well - that even the latter had often referred to the Bomber Chief as 'Butcher' Harris, in addition to the less defamatory 'Bomber' Harris, and that his crews had always used the abbreviated form 'Butch'. The Germans, I'm afraid, interpreted such sobriquets with their usual literalness (had Luftwaffe personnel used a similar, and apparently derogatory term when alluding to Goering, they would probably have been court-martialled). Even allowing for this lack of understanding on the part of the Germans there were many in the UK who, remembering the infamous 'Butcher of Belsen' (Josef Krämer) and others of his kind, bitterly resented the equation of the Chief of Bomber Command with barbarous liquidators such as they.

It was hardly surprising that the great majority of ex-aircrew and of their compatriots reacted angrily to the German protests which, after all, had they been successful, would have been more or less tantamount to having Harris branded as a war criminal; and their indignation was intensified because this latest hullabaloo arose at a time when much publicity, both in the British press and on TV, was being accorded noisily active and ever-growing neo-Nazi groups in Germany (a

Bomber Command in World War II

court in Münster refused to permit a police ban on an anti-statue demonstration in Bonn by the far-right 'Free Workers' Party'); and it did little to assuage their feelings when it was learned that General Inspector Klaus Naumann had said in a confidential report that more and more professional soldiers in the German army were joining the neo-Nazi movement and were chanting Nazi slogans when off duty. Members of the Bomber Command Association and of Aircrew Associations nationwide wrote to the mayors of the German towns in question, explaining the reasons for erecting the statue; others saw no need for such diplomacy, were less polite, and gave them to understand that it was, in any case, 'none of their business'. They further expressed their amazement that they, of all people, should complain about the death of innocent human beings by incineration.

And those in Great Britain who were vehemently opposed to the statue could not be silenced either. Countless letters appeared in both the national and local press, reiterating the same old accusations - Harris had been a mass murderer, a psychopath, a paranoiac, a man who had delighted so much in mass slaughter that he fell into the same category as the worst of the Nazi exterminators because he had fashioned Bomber Command into what was virtually a vast airborne incineration plant; he had prolonged the war by anything up to two years and in so doing had also sent thousands of his young airmen to untimely deaths; so the proposed statue would be no less than a glorification of his own sadistic and callous acts in particular and of war in general; it would, if allowed to materialise, open old wounds and jeopardise our now friendly relations with the new Germany and everyone's dreams of a firmly united and harmonious Europe; and so on and so forth - the degree of vituperation and the hyperbolic terms employed to express it were boundless and in most cases attempts to offer sensible and logical arguments against the Air Offensive were plainly lacking and substituted with outbursts in which emotion played the dominant rôle. These inspired pro-Harris replies and the battle raged on throughout the spring of 1992 and gathered momentum in the week before the statue was due to be unveiled by the Queen Mother on May 31, an ill-chosen date in the eyes of many who seized on the opportunity to point out that it was on that very night 50 years before that the first 1000-bomber raid was launched against Cologne. Moreover, her acceptance of the invitation to perform the ceremony was interpreted by the antis as condonation on her part, even her personal approval, of Bomber Command's strategy of the destruction of vast human habitations and their inhabitants.

The Great Ingratitude

It has to be said that a large number of the country's citizens were of the opinion that the invitation placed her in rather a delicate and embarrassing situation, but reports from royal sources cleared the air somewhat by stating that it would certainly have been declined had the Queen Mother herself considered the statue to be in bad taste. She, of course, had herself lived through the entire London Blitz.

Harris's opponents also made great play of the fact that at the very moment (midday) Her Majesty was scheduled to pull the cord to reveal the statue to the world, Herbert Wagner, the mayor of Dresden, would be standing in silence, together with survivors of the fire storm, in front of the ruins of the famous church, the Frauenkirche, left as it was in memory of Dresden as it had been and of all the victims of the Second World War.

The German mayors wrote to her personally, asking her to think again, and one of them, Norbert Burger of Cologne (who as a schoolboy experienced the 1000-bomber raid on the city) appeared on BBC Television's Newsnight and explained why, in his opinion, no such monument should ever have materialised.

But those who protested by writing letters to the newspapers and in appearing on TV served the Bomber Command Association well by increasing both its membership and the donations it received towards the cost of the statue; they also found they had doughty adversaries and one eminent peer, Lord Mackie, declared: 'It ill becomes a nation who deliberately killed millions of innocent people to object to commemorating a man who did much to free them from the Nazi régime'. It was noticeable that the great majority of the anti-statue lobby had had no direct experience of war; and that the more responsible sections of the British media supported the Harris cause.

In the edition of the Sunday Times published on the day of the unveiling ceremony, Robert Harris (no relation to Sir Arthur!) wrote a penetrating article in which he made what is surely a very valid point:

'But, to me, the most disturbing feature of the campaign against the statue has been the rise of moral equivalence: that the British terror bombing campaign puts us on the same level as the Nazis ... Well, there is a moral distinction, and the day the rest of us lose sight of it we are in trouble. In October 1941, the Nazis began the systematic extermination of a race; no act of surrender, no amount of collaboration, no retreat, nothing could save you if you were born a Jew. The following year, the British began the destruction of German cities with the aim of forcing to

Bomber Command in World War II

a halt the Nazi war machine that had conquered half Europe. It was a ruthless policy. It may have been misguided. But to have been as wicked as the Nazis, Harris would have had to have gone on bombing until every single German was dead. There is the distinction. It is huge.

So let the men of Bomber Command have their statue. It will be, if nothing else, a unique war memorial: a reminder that war corrupts even the most honourable of causes; that it generally becomes a choice between evils; but that in 1945, thank God, by far the lesser evil won.'

I would like to add one further point: perhaps, in World War Two, too great a distinction is now drawn between civilians and soldiers. Most of the latter, after all, were merely civilians rapidly put into uniform; moreover, there were few 'civilians' whose work did not contribute in large measure to the waging of war, of the 'total war' which Hitler had invited. In such circumstances is one not as justified in killing workers in overalls who make guns in factories as soldiers in uniform who fire them on the field of battle? The former are every bit as important as the latter and when you forget about the 'legality of uniform' and get down to brass tacks there is surely no fundamental difference.

***

The bronze 9-foot high statue, the work of sculptress Faith Winter, cost £100,000, all of which was donated privately, the bulk of it from ex-aircrew or personnel now serving with the RAF, but including sums such as £10,000 from Rolls Royce and the McRobert Trust. It depicts Harris in the characteristic posture remembered so well by all who came in contact with him - the resolute stance and purposeful expression - which some find 'heroic', others 'aggressive'. It stands in the forecourt of the RAF church, St Clement Danes, in the Strand, next to that of Lord Dowding, Chief of Fighter Command and the architect of its victory in the Battle of Britain, a happy or incongruous juxtaposition - depending on whose side you are on in the great Harris debate - with the man who saved Gt. Britain and possibly the world in 1940 standing alongside the man who took the war to Germany and, again irrespective of one's approval or disapproval of the methods employed, achieved so much towards final victory in 1945, a victory which had appeared so improbable a few years before.

At the unveiling ceremony on May 31 anti-Harris

The Great Ingratitude

demonstrators were predictably present in considerable numbers, but in spite of interruptions to her speech Her Majesty retained her usual calm and dignity and performed splendidly. Millions watched the event later that day on TV and also saw the lone Lancaster, the bomber which symbolised the Air Offensive more than any other, fly sedately overhead in what was probably a final salute to Harris and his crews. Just a few hours earlier many of those present in the Strand had glared, with contempt in their eyes, first at the machine and then at the statue; while those who had served Harris, with Group Captain Lord Cheshire among them, looked from the   (#) Lanc to the man ... they reminisced, swallowed hard, and quietly departed the scene.

***

The statue came back into the news at the end of September, 1992, when it was learned that Germany planned to celebrate, at Peenemünde, the 50th anniversary of the first launch of the V-2. German sources justified the ceremony on the grounds that it was the supersonic V-2 which inspired, and made possible, the exploration of space.

Leading figures in British public life immediately drew attention to the terror and high death rate caused by the weapon in London and to the 20,000 slave-labourers killed in its manufacture. They also expressed surprise that such an event should take place in the wake of the strong German objections to the Harris statue. There were Germans too, who disapproved, and the proposed ceremony on October 3rd was palpably toned down - only a few elderly people were present 'to mark the invention of the rocket as the first step into space'. Yet TV pictures taken and beamed to many countries showed that a model of the V-1 (in addition to one of the V-2) was also on display at the entrance to the site.

If the statue should never have been erected for the reasons specified by those so much agin it, then it could be argued, by the same yardstick, that there are other memorials up and down the country which would have had to be pulled down. But Harris stands there in Central London for all to see, if to see him differently. I hope that now, at the end of this book, the reader has acquired enough of the facts to enable him to decide for himself.

(#) At the ceremony Group Captain Cheshire looked a very sick man, and was to die a few weeks later.

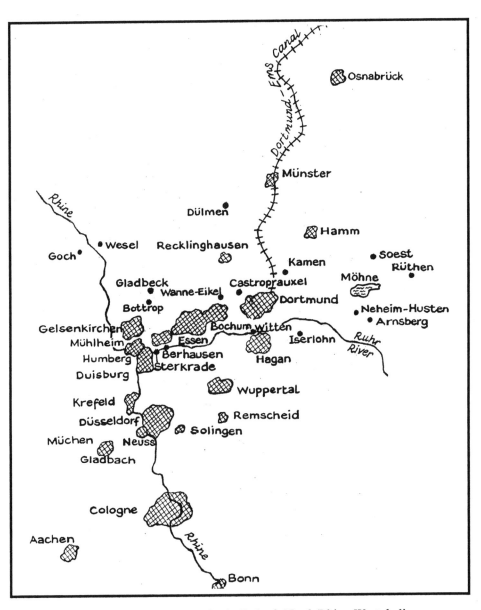

Bomber Command Targets in the Ruhr & North Rhine-Westphalia

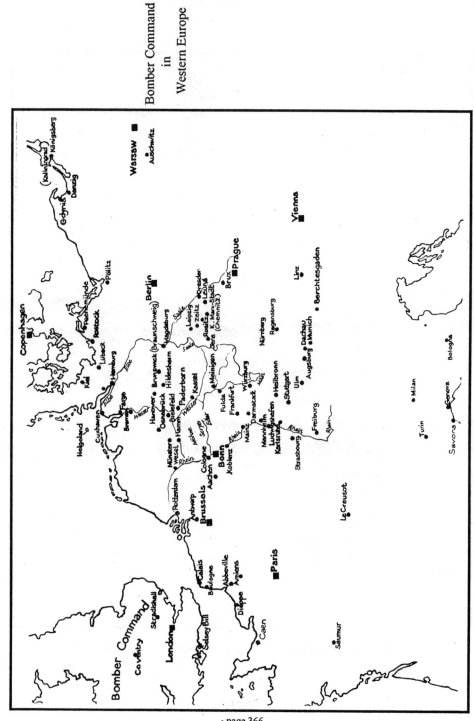

Bomber Command
in
Western Europe

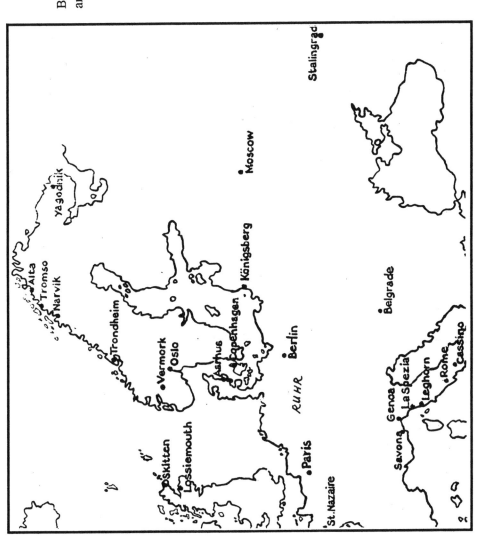

INDEX

BIBLIOGRAPHY

AUTHOR	TITLE	PUBLISHER
Barker, Ralph	The Thousand Plan	Chatto & Windus 1965
Bekker, C	The Luftwaffe Diaries	Macdonald & Jane's 1967
Bennett, Donald C.T.	Pathfinder	Goodall Publications 1983
Bowyer, Chas	Mosquito at War	Ian Allan 1973
.. ..	Guns in the Sky:	
	The Air Gunners of World War II	Dent 1979
Bowyer, Michael	The Stirling Bomber	Faber & Faber 1980
.. ..	Mosquito	Faber & Faber 1984
Brickhill, Paul	Reach for the Sky	Collins 1957
.. ..	The Dam Busters	Evans Bros 1977
.. ..	The Great Escape	New Portway 1951
Cooper, Alan	Bombers over Berlin	Kimber 1980
.. ..	Beyond the Dams to tirpitz	Kimber 1983
Ellis, Ken	Wrecks & Relics	Midland Counties Pubs 1990
Ethel, Jeffrey & Price, Alfred	The German Jets in Combat	Jane's 1979
Falconer, Jonathan	Stirling at War	Ian Allan 1991
Frankland, Noble	Bomber Offensive: the Devastation	
	of Europe	Purnell 1970
Frischauer, Willy	The Rise & Fall of Herman Goering	Boston 1952
Gallant, Adolf	The First & The Last	Fontana 1970
Garbett, M & Goulding, B	Lancaster at War (Vols 1,2,3,&4)	Ian Allan 1971-86
Gibson, Guy	Enemy Coast Ahead	Michael Joseph 1946
Girbig, J	Six Months to Oblivion: The Eclipse	
	of the Luftwaffe Fighter Force	Ian Allan 1975
Harris. Sir Arthur	Bomber Offensive	Collins 1947
Hastings, Max	Bomber Command	Michael Joseph 1979
Held, W & Nauroth, H	The Defence of the Reich - Hitler's	
	Night-Fighter Planes & Pilots	Arms & Armour 1971
Irving, David	The Rise & Fall of the Luftwaffe	Weidenfeld & Nicholson 1973
.. ..	The Destruction of Dresden	Kimber 1963
Jackson, A S	Pathfinder Bennett	Terrence Dalton 1991

BIBLIOGRAPHY (cont)

AUTHOR	TITLE	PUBLISHER
Jackson, R	Storm From the Skies: The Strategic Bombing Offensive, 1943-1945	Arthur Barker 1974
Jackson, W. G. F.	Overlord: Normady 1944	Davis Poynter 1978
Jary, Christopher	Portrait of a Bomber Pilot	Sydney Nary 1990
Jones R.V.	Most Secret War - British Scientific Intelligence, 1939 - 1945	Coronet Books 1979
Kurzman, Dan	Day of the Bomb - Hiroshima 1945	Weidenfeld & Nicholson 1986
Longmate, Norman	The Doodlebugs - The Story of the Flying Bombs	Hutchison 1981
Maitland, Andrew	Through the Bombsight	Kimber 1986
Mason, Herbert Malloy	The Rise of the Luftwaffe, 1918-1940	Cassell 1973
Middlebrook, Martin	The Nuremberg Raid	Allen Lane 1979
Middlebrook, Martin & Everitt, Chris	The Bomber Command War Diaries	Penguin 1990
Musgrove, G.	Pathfinder Force - A History of 8 Group	Macdonald & Jane's 1976
Ogden, Bob	British Aviation Museums	Key Publishing 1986
Parry, Simon	Intruders over Britain	Kristall 1987
Prince, Alfred	The Luftwaffe, 1933-45 (Vols 1,2,3,&4)	Arms & Armour
.. ..	Battle over the Reich	Arthur Barker 1982
Rapier, Brian	Halifax at War	Ian Allan 1990
Revie, Alastair	The Lost Command	Corgi 1972
Robertson, Bruce	Lancasters: The Story of a Famous Bomber	Harleyford 1964
Rumpf, Hans	The Bombing of Germany (English Edition)	Muller 1963
Saundby, Sir Robert	Air Bombardment: The Story of its Development	Chatto & Windus 1961
Sweetman, John	Operation Chastise-The Dams Raid: Epic or Myth	Jane's 1982
Taylor, Eric	Operation Millennium	Hale 1987
Terraine, John	The Right of the Line	Hodder & Stoughton 1985
Verner, A	The Bomber Offensive	Batsford 1968
Webster, Sir Charles & Frankland, Noble	The Strategic Air Offensive against Germany, 1939-45	HMSO 1961

•*Valiant Endeavours*•

An anthology of personal experiences recalled by members of the Dumfries & Galloway Branch of the Air Crew Association ranging from the Northwest Frontier to the Gulf War.

Over 200 pages, full colour hardback, with illustrations and photographs.

"In reading these remarkable stories I cannot avoid being impressed by the universal enthusiasm shown for one of the most dangerous occupations in war, that of aircrew. Taking into account that environmental belief amongst these splendid young men that "It couldn't happen to me" it is nevertheless well known, and was known at that time, that the losses in aircrew were very heavy. In the war all young men were compelled to join one or the other of the armed forces, but there was never any compulsion to become aircrew. All were volunteers and this remained so throughout the War. That there were never any shortage of applicants is a tribute to the British character.

In these stories time and again is recorded tales of courage, inginuety, devotion to duty and unselfishness and above all comradeship of young men never knowing what might be their last moment. I congratulate the Dumfries and Galloway Branch of the Aircrew Association on their enterprise."

Kenneth Cross,
Air Chief Marshal RAF (Retired)

PRICE: £15.00 publication date October 1993.
please add £1.50 post & packing

Available from: Dumfries & Galloway Air crew Association,
The Branch Secretary, Ken Anderson DFC
West View, Springholm, Scotland DG7 3LP
Tel: 055 665 309

If in difficulty contact the publishers:
GC Books Ltd, Wigtown, Scotland, DG8 9HL
Tel/Fax: 098 84 2499

All profits from this book are being donated to the RAF Benevolent Association

ISBN 1 872350 80 1

•The Mulberry Harbour Project in Wigtownshire 1942-1944•

This book details the development of the Mulberry Harbour in South West Scotland, and its impact on the outcome of the Second World War.

Tom Murchie, the author, (whose book entitled "The RAF in Galloway" achieved a high position in the list of best selling Scottish books) carried out much of his research in the Public Records Office at Kew.

Many local people still remember the activity and secrecy surrounding the development. Many others were employed on its construction. They, however, at the time were not privy to the ultimate use for which the project was intended. To this end the booklet explains many things that was peviously heresay. Also included are black and white photos of the construction and development in Rigg Bay, Cairnhead and Loch Ryan.

Limp Cover 40pp   **Price £4.00 plus 75p p&p**

Available from the publishers:
GC BOOKS LTD
WIGTOWN
SCOTLAND   DG8 9HL

ISBN 1 872350 70 4

•The RAF in Galloway•

A record of the activities of the Royal Air Force in South West Scotland. Detailed descriptions of the various bases, airfields, training units and aircraft in use throughout the period 1913 up to the present day.

Contains many photos. Foreword by Flight Lieutenant Bill Reid VC, who actually started his RAF career at Wigtown along with many other thousands of navigators, gunners and pilots.

Over 100pp, hardback laminated with full colour illustration.
Price £12.95 plus £1.00 post & packing
Available from:

> GC BOOKS LTD
> WIGTOWN
> SCOTLAND   DG8 9HL
> Tel/Fax: 098 84 2499

ISBN 1 872350 40 2